JOHN WILLIS'

SCREEN WORLD

1976

Volume 27

CROWN PUBLISHERS, INC.
ONE PARK AVENUE
NEW YORK, N.Y. 10016

Library of Congress Catalog Card No. 50-3023

Sincerely
Mary Pickford

1915

1923

1924

1926

TO

MARY PICKFORD

... a film pioneer to whom the industry owes eternal gratitude; and the first great international film star, aptly crowned by her millions of fans with the accolade "America's Sweetheart"

1928
full page left: 1933

1930

1934

1950 with her husband,
Charles "Buddy" Rogers

LOUISE FLETCHER AND JACK NICHOLSON
in "One Flew Over The Cuckoo's Nest"
Winners of 1975 Academy Awards for Best Actress, Best Actor and Best Picture

CONTENTS

EDITOR: JOHN WILLIS

Assistant Editor: Stanley Reeves

STAFF: Joe Baltake, Alberto Cabrera, Mark Cohen, Frances
Crampon, Miles Kreuger, Don Nute, Evan Romero, Robert Stolinsky

ACKNOWLEDGMENTS: This volume would not be possible without the generous
cooperation of Ted Albert, Ray Axelrod, Cheryl Bakerman, Mike Berman, Susan
Bloch, Barry Brown, Philip Castanza, Judy Cohn, Walter Durell, Helen Eisenman,
Caryl Feldman, Billy Fine, Stuart Fink, Barry Fishel, Lawrence Fredericks, Dore
Freeman, Marvin Friedlander, Bernice Glaser, Sergei Goncharoff, Joseph Green, Ross
Hagen, Howard Haines, Glenn Hasselrooth, Claude Hill, Roger Karnbad, Seymour
Krawitz, Don Krim, Andrew Lamy, Ruth Pologe Levinson, Bryan Lindquist, Arlene
Ludwig, Sam Madell, Howard Mahler, Leonard Maltin, Tom Miller, Charles Moses,
Adam Moos, Anne Murton, Richard Nash, Eric Naumann, George Nice, John O'-
Rourke, Kent Paul, Ronald Perkins, Karen Raiman, Arthur Rubine, Joseph Saitta,
Suzanne Salter, Charles Sellier, Allan Shackleton, Deborah Shaffer, Irvin Shapiro,
Hortense Shorr, Eve Siegel, David Simon, Solters & Roskin, Helene Spinner, John
Springer, John Sutherland, John Tilley, Bill Werneth, John Wiencko, Sandra Wixon,
Betty Zipf

1. Robert Redford

2. Barbra Streisand

3. Al Pacino

4. Charles Bronson

5. Paul Newman

6. Clint Eastwood

7. Burt Reynolds

8. Woody Allen

9. Steve McQueen

10. Gene Hackman

11. Jack Nicholson

12. James Caan

13. Dustin Hoffman

14. Faye Dunaway

15. John Wayne

16. Liza Minnelli

TOP 25 BOX OFFICE STARS OF 1975

17. Warren Beatty

18. Tom Laughlin

19. Peter Sellers

20. Raquel Welch

1975 RELEASES

January 1 through December 31, 1975

21. Candice Bergen

22. Sean Connery

23. Marlon Brando

24. Peter Fonda

25. Diana Ross

Gena Rowlands

Roger Moore

Diahann Carroll

ALICE DOESN'T LIVE HERE ANYMORE

(WARNER BROS.) Producers, David Susskind, Audrey Maas; Director, Martin Scorsese; Associate Producer, Sandra Weintraub; Screenplay, Robert Getchell; Photography, Kent L. Wakeford; Designer, Toby Carr Rafelson; Editor, Marcia Lucas; Assistant Directors, Mike Moder, Mike Kusley; In Technicolor; Rated PG; 113 minutes; January release.

CAST

Alice Hyatt	Ellen Burstyn
David	Kris Kristofferson
Donald	Billy Green Bush
Flo	Diane Ladd
Bea	Lelia Goldoni
Rita	Lane Bradbury
Mel	Vic Tayback
Audrey	Jodie Foster
Ben	Harvey Keitell
Vera	Valerie Curtin
Jacobs	Murray Moston
Bartender	Harry Northup
Tommy	Alfred Lutter
Alice age 8	Mia Bendixsen
Old Woman	Ola Moore
Lenny	Martin Brinton
Chicken	Dean Casper

Left: Ellen Burstyn, and below with
Billy Green Bush

Alfred Lutter, Ellen Burstyn

Ellen Burstyn, Harvey Keitel
Above: Diane Ladd, Ellen Burstyn

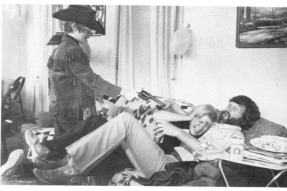

Ellen Burstyn, Harvey Keitel
Above: Kris Kristofferson, Ellen Burstyn

Alfred Lutter, Ellen Burstyn, Kris Kristofferson

REPORT TO THE COMMISSIONER

(UNITED ARTISTS) Producer, M. J. Frankovich; Director, Milton Katselas; Screenplay, Abby Mann, Ernest Tidyman; Based on novel by James Mills; Photography, Mario Tosi; Designer, Robert Clatworthy; Editor, David Blewitt; Music, Elmer Bernstein; Songs sung by Vernon Burch; Words and Music, Vernon Burch, Spencer Proffer, Jeffrey Marmelzat; Costumes, Anna Hill Johnstone; Assistant Director, Richard Moder; In color; Rated PG; 112 minutes; January release.

CAST

Beauregard "Bo" Lockley	Michael Moriarty
Richard "Crunch" Blackstone	Yaphet Kotto
Patty Butler	Susan Blakely
Captain d'Angelo	Hector Elizondo
Thomas "Stock" Henderson	Tony King
Lt. Hanson	Michael McGuire
Capt. Strichter	Edward Grover
Chief Perna	Dana Elcar
Joey Egan	Robert Balaban
Asst. D. A. Jackson	William Devane
Police Commissioner	Stephen Elliott
Billy	Richard Gere
Lt. Seidensticker	Vic Tayback
Det. Schulman	Albert Seedman
Samantha	Noelle North
Dorothy	Bebe Drake Hooks
Detectives	Sonny Grosso, Lee Delano, Vincent Van Lynn, Bob Golden

Right: Robert Balaban, Yaphet Kotto, Michael Moriarty Top: Michael Moriarty, Susan Blakely

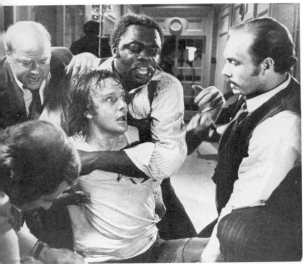

Susan Blakely Above: Sonny Grosso, Dana Elcar, Yaphet Kotto, Michael Moriarty, Hector Elizondo

Tony King, Susan Blakely

10

SHEILA LEVINE IS DEAD AND LIVING IN NEW YORK

(PARAMOUNT) Producer, Harry Korshak; Director, Sidney J. Furie; Screenplay, Kenny Solms, Gail Parent; Based on novel by Gail Parent; Music, Michel Legrand; Photography, Donald M. Morgan; Editor, Argyle Nelson; Designer, Fernando Carrere; Assistant Directors, Gene Marum, Barry R. Steinberg; Costumes, Ronald Talsky; In Panavision and Technicolor; Songs by Leo Robin and Ralph Rainger, Hal David and Leon Carr; Rated PG; 113 minutes; February release.

CAST

Sheila Levine	Jeannie Berlin
Sam Stoneman	Roy Scheider
Kate	Rebecca Dianna Smith
Bernice	Janet Brandt
Manny	Sid Melton
Wally	Charles Woolf
Agatha	Leda Rogers
Uncle Herm	Jack Bernardi
Rabbi	Allen Secher
Rochelle	Talley Parker
Norman	Jon Miller
Principal	Noble Willingham
Attendant	Richard Rasof
Miss Burke	Evelyn Russell
Harold	Don Carrara
Melissa	Sharon Martin Goldman
Aunt Min	Karen Anders
Steve	Craig Littler
Artist	Sandy Helberg
Conductor	John Morgan Evans
Engineer	Charles Walker
Clerk	Charles Arthur
Typists	Cecilia McBride, Susan Waugh
Girl	Erin Fleming
Pianist	Lyle Moraine
Performers	Sandra Golden, Victor Raphael

Right: Jeannie Berlin, Roy Scheider, Rebecca Dianna Smith Top: Janet Brandt, Jeannie Berlin

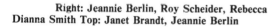

Jeannie Berlin

Jeannie Berlin, Roy Scheider

SHAMPOO

(COLUMBIA) Producer, Warren Beatty; Director, Hal Ashby; Screenplay, Robert Towne, Warren Beatty; Photography, Laszlo Kovacs; Editor, Robert C. Jones; Music, Paul Simon; Designer, Richard Sylbert; Art Direction, Stu Campbell; Assistant Director, Art Levinson; In Technicolor; Rated R; 109 minutes; February release.

CAST

George	Warren Beatty
Jackie	Julie Christie
Jill	Goldie Hawn
Felicia	Lee Grant
Lester	Jack Warden
Johnny Pope	Tony Bill
Lorna	Carrie Fisher
Norman	Jay Robinson
Bank Officer	George Furth
Senator	Brad Dexter
Producer	William Castle

Left: Warren Beatty

*Lee Grant received a 1975 Academy Award
for Best Supporting Actress*

**Jack Warden, Lee Grant
Above: Julie Christie,
Warren Beatty**

**Warren Beatty, Carrie Fisher
Above: Julie Christie, Warren Beatty,
Goldie Hawn, Tony Bill**

Jack Warden, Warren Beatty Above: Goldie
Hawn, Lee Grant Top: Goldie Hawn, Tony Bill

Julie Christie, Goldie Hawn, Tony Bill, Warren
Beatty Above: Christie, Beatty Top: Jack
Warden, Christie

THE STEPFORD WIVES

(COLUMBIA) Producer, Edgar J. Scherick; Executive Producer, Gustave M. Berne; Director, Bryan Forbes; Screenplay, William Goldman; From novel by Ira Levin; Photography, Owen Roizman; Editor, Timothy Gee; Music, Michael Small; Designer, Gene Callahan; Assistant Director, Peter Scoppa; A Palomar Pictures International Production; In TVC Color; Rated PG; 114 minutes; February release.

CAST

Joanna	Katharine Ross
Bobby	Paula Prentiss
Walter	Peter Masterson
Carol	Nanette Newman
Dale Coba	Patrick O'Neal
Charmaine	Tina Louise
Dr. Fancher	Carol Rosson
Artist	William Prince
Welcome Wagon Lady	Paula Trueman
Atkinson	Remak Ramsay
Policeman	John Aprea

Right: Tina Louise

Patrick O'Neal, Nanette Newman

Katharine Ross, Peter Masterson

MR. RICCO

(UNITED ARTISTS) Producer, Douglas Netter; Director, Paul Bogart; Screenplay, Robert Hoban; Story, Ed Harvey, Francis Kiernan; Photography, Frank Stanley; Editor, Michael McLean; Music, Chico Hamilton; Art Director, Herman A. Blumenthal; Assistant Director, Daniel J. McCauley; A Metro-Goldwyn-Mayer Production; In Metrocolor; Rated PG; 98 minutes; February release.

CAST

Joe Ricco	Dean Martin
Detective Cronyn	Eugene Roche
Frankie Steele	Thalmus Rasulala
Irene Mapes	Denise Nicholas
Jamison	Cindy Williams
Katherine Fremont	Geraldine Brooks
Purvis Mapes	Philip Thomas
Detective Barrett	George Tyne
Justin	Robert Sampson
Detective Tanner	Michael Gregory
Markham	Joseph Hacker
Detective Jackson	Jay Fletcher
Calvin Mapes	Oliver Givins
Uncle Enzo	Frank Puglia
Sally	Ella Edwards
Luther	H. B. Barnum III

Right: Thalmus Rasulala

Dean Martin, Denise Nicholas, Philip Thomas
Above: Cindy Williams, Dean Martin

Jay Fletcher, Eugene Roche, H. B. Barnum III,
Ella Edwards Above: Cindy Williams,
Joseph Hacker

15

W. W. AND THE DIXIE DANCEKINGS

(20th €ENTURY-FOX) Executive Producer, Steve Shagan; Producer, Stanley S. Canter; Director, John G. Avildsen; Screenplay, Thomas Rickman; Music, Dave Gruskin; Photography, Jim Crabe; Assistant Director, Ric Rondell; Designer, Larry Paull; Color by TVC; Prints by DeLuxe; Rated PG; 91 minutes; February rlease.

CAST

W. W.	Burt Reynolds
Deacon	Art Carney
Dixie	Conny Van Dyke
Wayne	Jerry Reed
Junior	James Hampton
Butterball	Richard Hurst
Leroy	Don Williams
Mel Tillis	Mel Tillis
Elton Bird	Sherman Lloyd
Gas Station Attendant	Bill McCutcheon
June Ann	Sherry Mathis
Patrolman	Hal Needham
Rosie	Nancy Andrews
Della	Peg Murray

Left: Burt Reynolds

Conny Van Dyke, Burt Reynolds

Fred Stuthman, Burt Reynolds Above: Jerry Reed, Don Williams, Reynolds, Conny Van Dyke, Richard Hurst

Burt Reynolds, Furry Lewis Above: Art Carney,
Reynolds Top: Reynolds, Ned Beatty

Conny Van Dyke, Burt Reynolds Top: Don
Williams, Conny Van Dyke, Jerry Reed

THE GREAT WALDO PEPPER

(UNIVERSAL) Producer-Director, George Roy Hill; Screenplay, William Goldman; Story, George Roy Hill; Associate Producer, Robert L. Crawford; Photography, Robert Surtees; Art Director, Henry Bumstead; Editor, William Reynolds; Costumes, Edith Head; Assistant Directors, Ray Gosnell, Jerry Ballew; A Jennings Lang Presentation; In Technicolor and Todd-AO 35; Rated PG; 107 minutes; March release.

CAST

Waldo Pepper	Robert Redford
Axel Olsson	Bo Svenson
Ernst Kessler	Bo Brundin
Mary Beth	Susan Sarandon
Newt	Geoffrey Lewis
Ezra Stiles	Edward Herrmann
Dillhoefer	Philip Bruns
Werfel	Roderick Cook
Patsy	Kelly Jean Peters
Maude	Margot Kidder
Duke	Scott Newman
Ace	James S. Appleby
Scooter	Patrick W. Henderson, Jr.
Farmer	James Harrell
Farmer's Wife	Elma Aicklen
Farmer's Daughter	Deborah Knapp
Director Western Set	John A. Zee
Western Star	John Reilly
Director Spanish Set	Jack Manning
Policeman	Joe Billings
Theatre Manager	Robert W. Winn
German Star	Lawrence Casey
Assistant Director	Greg Martin

Right: Robert Redford

Robert Redford

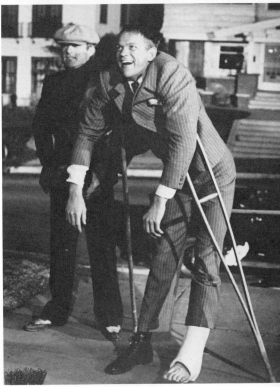

Robert Redford, Bo Svenson

18

ESCAPE TO WITCH MOUNTAIN

(BUENA VISTA) Executive Producer, Ron Miller; Producer, Jerome Courtland; Director, John Hough; Screenplay, Robert Malcolm Young; Based on book by Alexander Key; Photography, Frank Phillips; Music, Johnny Mandel; Art Directors, John B. Mansbridge, Al Roelofs; Editor, Robert Stafford; Assistant Directors, Fred Brost, Jerry Ballew; Costumes, Chuck Keehne, Emily Sundby; A Walt Disney Production; In Technicolor; Rated G; 97 minutes; March release.

CAST

Jason	Eddie Albert
Aristotle Bolt	Ray Milland
Deranian	Donald Pleasence
Tia	Kim Richards
Tony	Ike Eisenmann
Sheriff Purdy	Walter Barnes
Mrs. Grindley	Reta Shaw
Uncle Bene	Denver Pyle
Astrologer	Alfred Ryder
Ubermann	Lawrence Montaigne
Biff Jenkins	Terry Wilson
Grocer	George Chandler
Truck	Dermott Downs
Guru	Shepherd Sanders
Gasoline Attendant	Don Brodie
Sergeant Foss	Paul Sorenson
Policeman #3	Alfred Rossi
Lorko	Tiger Joe Marsh
Captain Malone	Harry Holcombe
Mate	Sam Edwards
Psychic	Dan Seymour
Cort	Eugene Daniels
Deputy	Al Dunlap
Hunters	Rex Holman, Tony Giorgio

Ike Eisenmann, Eddie Albert, Kim Richards

Top: Ike Eisenmann, Donald Pleasence, Kim Richards, Ray Milland

THE PRISONER OF SECOND AVENUE

(WARNER BROS.) Producer-Director, Melvin Frank; Screenplay, Neil Simon; Based on his play of the same name; Photography, Philip Lathrop; Art Director, Preston Ames; Editor, Bob Wyman; Music, Marvin Hamlisch; Costumes, Joel Schumacher; Assistant Directors, Bruce Satterlee, Howard Roessel; In Panavision and Technicolor; Rated PG; 105 minutes; March release.

CAST

Mel	Jack Lemmon
Edna	Anne Bancroft
Harry	Gene Saks
Pauline	Elizabeth Wilson
Pearl	Florence Stanley
Belle	Maxine Stuart
Man Upstairs	Ed Peck
Charlie	Gene Blakely
Psychiatrist	Ivor Francis
Detective	Stack Pierce

Left: Anne Bancroft, Jack Lemmon

Jack Lemmon, Elizabeth Wilson, Florence Stanley, Gene Saks

Jack Lemmon, Anne Bancroft Top: (L) Anne Bancroft
(R) Jack Lemmon, Anne Bancroft

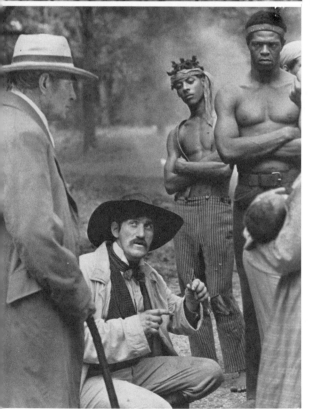

MANDINGO

(PARAMOUNT) Executive Producer, Ralph Serpe; Producer, Dino De Laurentiis; Director, Richard Fleischer; Screenplay, Norman Wexler; Based on novel by Kyle Onstott and play therefrom by Jack Kirkland; Photography, Richard H. Kline; Music, Maurice Jarre; Song sung by Muddy Waters; Designer, Boris Leven; Costumes, Ann Roth; Assistant Directors, Fred Brost, Gary D. Daigler, Albert Shepard; Editor, Frank Bracht; In Technicolor; Rated R; 127 minutes; March release.

CAST

Maxwell	James Mason
Blanche	Susan George
Hammond	Perry King
Agamemnon	Richard Ward
Ellen	Brenda Sykes
Mede	Ken Norton
Lucrezia Borgia	Lillian Hayman
Doc Redfield	Roy Poole
Cicero	Ji-Tu Cumbuka
Brownlee	Paul Benedict
Charles	Ben Masters
Wallace	Ray Spruell
De Veve	Louis Turenne
Topaz	Duane Allen
Babouin	Earl Maynard
Lucy	Beatrice Winde
Dite	Debbie Morgan
Mrs. Redfield	Irene Tedrow
Big Pearl	Reda Wyatt
Madame Caroline	Simon McQueen
Beatrix	Evelyn Hendrickson
Major Woodford	Stanley Reyes
Le Toscan	John Barber
Meg	Durwyn Robinson
Alph	Kerwin Robinson
Tense	Deborah Ann Young
Blonde Girl	Debra Blackwell
Black Mother	Kuumba
Wilson	Stocker Fontelieu

James Mason, Paul Benedict, Ken Norton
Top: Perry King, Susan George

Top: Perry King, Brenda Sykes
Below: Ken Norton, Susan George

Ji-Tu Cumbuka, Perry King, Ken Norton
Above: Brenda Sykes, King, Norton
Top: Ken Norton, Susan George

Brenda Sykes, Susan George
Top: James Mason

RANCHO DELUXE

(UNITED ARTISTS) Producer, Elliott Kastner; Director, Frank Perry; Screenplay, Thomas McGuane; Photography, William A. Fraker; Music, Jimmy Buffett; Assistant Directors, Charles Okun, David S. Hamburger; Art Director, Michael Haller; Editor, Sid Katz; In color; Rated R; 93 minutes; March release.

CAST

Jack McKee	Jeff Bridges
Cecil Colson	Sam Waterston
Cora Brown	Elizabeth Ashley
Laura Beige	Charlene Dallas
John Brown	Clifton James
Henry Beige	Slim Pickens
Curt	Harry Dean Stanton
Burt	Richard Bright
Betty Fargo	Patti D'Arbanville
Mary Fargo	Maggie Wellman
Wilbur Fargo	Bert Conway
Karl	Anthony Palmer
Dizzy	Joseph Sullivan
Mrs. Castle	Helen Craig
Dee	Ronda Copland
Circular Face	John Quade
Skinny Face	Sandy Kenyon
Colson	Joseph Spinell
Mrs. Colson	Wilma Riley
McKee	Richard McMurray
Mrs. McKee	Danna Hansen

and Doria Cooke (Anna), John Rodgers (Clerk), Paula Jermunson (Lady Foreman), Patti Jerome (Madame), Pat Noteboom (Prostitute), Bob Wetzel (Truck Driver), Ben Mar, Jr. (Cook), Arnold Huppert (Policeman), Richard Cavanaugh (Judge), Angela Cramer (Ranch Lady), Esther Black (Grandma) Oneida Broderick (Another Lady)

Right: Elizabeth Ashley, Clifton James
Top: Jeff Bridges, Sam Waterston

Sam Waterston, Maggie Wellman, Jeff Bridges,
Patti D'Urbanville

Patti D'Urbanville, Maggie Wellman

ROSEBUD

(UNITED ARTISTS) Producer-Director, Otto Preminger; Screenplay, Eric Lee Preminger; Additional Dialogue, Marjorie Kellogg; Based on novel by Joan Jemingway, Paul Bonnecarrere; Music, Laurent Petitgirard; Photography, Denys Coop; Editors, Peter Thornton, Thom Noble; In color; Rated PG; 126 minutes; March release

CAST

Larry Martin	Peter O'Toole
Sloat	Richard Attenborough
Hamlekh	Cliff Gorman
Fargeau	Claude Dauphin
Senator Donovan	John V. Lindsay
Lord Carter	Peter Lawford
Kirkbane	Amidou
George Nikolaos	Raf Vallone
Lady Carter	Adrienne Corri
Hacam	Josef Shiloa
Sabine	Brigitte Ariel
Helene	Isabelle Huppert
Margaret	Lalla Ward
Joyce	Kim Cattrall
Gertrude	Debra Berger
Patrice	Georges Beller
Melina Nikolaos	Francoise Brion
Julian Pettifer	Himself
Edward Behr	Himself

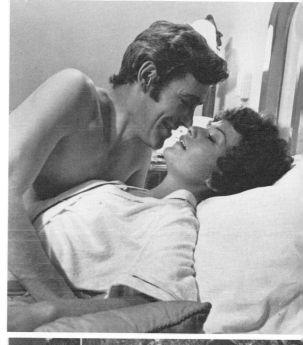

Right: Peter O'Toole, Isabelle Huppert

Adrienne Corri, Lola Ward Above: Peter O'Toole, Richard Attenborough

Peter O'Toole, John V. Lindsay
Above: Cliff Gorman, Kim Cattrall,
Peter O'Toole

25

FUNNY LADY

(COLUMBIA) Producer, Ray Stark; Director, Herbert Ross; Screenplay, Jay Presson Allen, Arnold Schulman; Story, Arnold Schulman; Photography, James Wong Howe; Songs, John Kander, Fred Ebb; Designer, George Jenkins; Editor, Marion Rothman; A Rastar Production; In Technicolor; Rated PG; 136 minutes; March release.

CAST

Fanny Brice	Barbra Streisand
Billy Rose	James Caan
Nick Arnstein	Omar Sharif
Bobby	Roddy McDowall
Bert Robbins	Ben Vereen
Norma Butler	Carole Wells
Bernard Baruch	Larry Gates
Eleanor Holm	Heidi O'Rourke
Fran	Samantha Huffaker
Buck Bolten	Matt Emery
Painter	Joshua Shelley
Conductor	Corey Fischer
Production Singer	Garrett Lewis
Man at wedding	Don Torres
Buffalo Handler	Raymond Guth
Ned	Gene Troobnick
Adele	Royce Wallace

Barbra Streisand
(also top)

Barbra Streisand, Ben Vereen
Above: Barbra Streisand, Omar Sharif

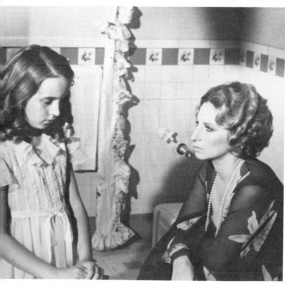

Samantha Huffaker, Barbra Streisand Above: Larry
Gates, Streisand, Roddy McDowall Top: Carole
Wells

Barbra Streisand, also above, and top
with James Caan

27

THE EIGER SANCTION

(UNIVERSAL) Executive Producers, Richard D. Zanuck, David Brown; Producer, Robert Daley; Director, Clint Eastwood; Screenplay, Hal Dresner, Warren B. Murphy, Rod Whitaker; Based on novel by Trevanian; Photography, Frank Stanley; Editor, Ferris Webster; Music, John Williams; Art Directors, George Webb, Aurelio Crugnola; Assistant Directors, Jim Fargo, Craig Huston, Victor Tourjansky; Costumes, Charles Waldo; A Jennings Lang Presentation; In color; Rated R; 128 minutes; March release.

CAST

Jonathan Hemlock	Clint Eastwood
Ben Bowman	George Kennedy
Jemima Brown	Vonetta McGee
Miles Mellough	Jack Cassidy
Mrs. Montaigne	Heidi Bruhl
Dragon	Thayer David
Freytag	Reiner Schoene
Meyer	Michael Grimm
Montaigne	Jean-Pierre Bernard
George	Brenda Venus
Pope	Gregory Walcott
Art Student	Candice Rialson
Miss Cerberus	Elaine Shore
Dewayne	Dan Howard
Reporter	Jack Kosslyn
Kruger	Walter Kraus
Wormwood	Frank Redmond
Hotel Manager	Siegfried Wallach
Buns	Susan Morgan
Cab Driver	Jack Frey

Top: Clint Eastwood

Candice Rialson, Clint Eastwood
Above: Clint Eastwood, George Kennedy

THE WILD PARTY

(AMERICAN INTERNATIONAL) Executive Producers, Edgar Lansbury, Joseph Beruh; Producer, Ismail Merchant; Director, James Ivory; Screenplay, Walter Marks; Based on poem by Joseph Moncure March; Original Songs, Walter Marks; Photography, Walter Lassally; Art Director, David Nichols; Editor, Kent McKinney; Music Score, Larry Rosenthal; Musical Sequences staged by Patricia Birch; Associate Producer, George Manasse; Dance Music, Louis St. Louis; Costumes, Ron Talsky, Ralph Lauren, Ronald Kolodgie; Assistant Director, Edward Folger; Presented by Samuel Z. Arkoff; In Movielab color; rated R; 100 minutes; March release.

CAST

Jolly Grimm	James Coco
Queenie	Raquel Welch
Dale Sword	Perry King
Kate	Tiffany Bolling
Tex	Royal Dano
James Morrison	David Dukes
Mrs. Murchison	Dena Dietrich
Mr. Murchison	Regis Cordic
Madeline True	Jennifer Lee
Bertha	Marya Small
Wilma	Bobo Lewis
Nadine	Annette Ferra
Kreutzer	Eddie Laurence
Sergeant	Tony Paxton
Policeman	Waldo K. Berns
Nurse	Nina Faso
Tailor	Baruch Lumet
Editor	Martin Kove
Fruit Dealer	Ralph Manza
Rose	Lark Geib
Sam	Fredrick Franklyn
Morris	J. S. Johnson
Phil D'Armano	Skipper
Jackie the Dancer	Don De Natale

Right: Perry King, Raquel Welch
Top: Raquel Welch, James Coco

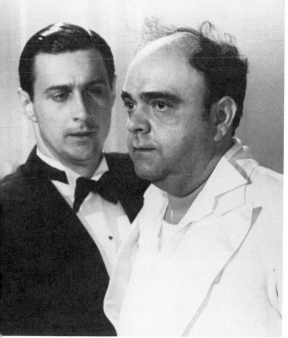

David Dukes, James Coco

Raquel Welch

THE OTHER SIDE OF THE MOUNTAIN

(UNIVERSAL) Producer, Edward S. Feldman; Director, Larry Peerce; Screenplay, David Seltzer; Based on "A Long Way Up" by E. G. Valens; Photography, David M. Walsh; Editor, Eve Newman; Music, Charles Fox; Song sung by Olivia Newton-John; Assistant Directors, Ken Swor, Henry Lange; Costumes, Grady Hunt; In Technicolor; Rated PG; 103 minutes; March release.

CAST

Jill Kinmont	Marilyn Hassett
Dick Buek	Beau Bridges
Audra-Jo	Belinda J. Montgomery
June Kinmont	Nan Martin
Bill Kinmont	William Bryant
Dave McCoy	Dabney Coleman
Buddy Werner	Bill Vint
Lee Zadroga	Hampton Fancher
Dr. Pittman	William Roerick
Cookie	Dori Brenner
Dean	Walter Brooke
Linda Meyers	Jocelyn Jones
Bob Kinmont	Greg Mabrey
Jerry Kinmont	Tony Becker
Herbie Johnson	Griffin Dunne
Dr. Enders	Warren Miller
Skeeter Werner	Robin Pepper
Boy in wheelchair	Brad Savage
Ambulance Driver	John Perell
Ambulance Attendant	Terry Hall
Head of ski patrol	Bruce Dennis Cosbey
Nurse	Sharri Zak
Man in car	Dick Winslow
Andrea Mead Lawrence	Candy McCoy

Left: Beau Bridges, Marilyn Hassett

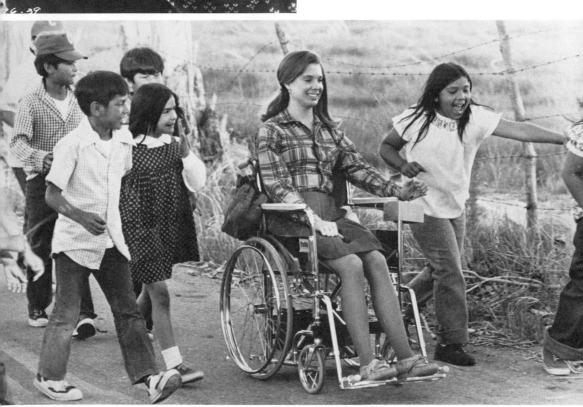

Marilyn Hassett

Bill Vint
Top: Beau Bridges, Marilyn Hassett

Belinda J. Montgomery

THE YAKUZA

(WARNER BROS.) Producer-Director, Sydney Pollack; Executive Producer, Shundo Koji; Co-Producer, Michael Hamilburg; Screenplay, Paul Schrader, Robert Towne; Story, Leonard Schrader; Music, Dave Grusin; Photography, Okazaki Kozo, Duke Callaghan; Editors, Fredric Steinkamp, Thomas Stanford, Don Guidice; Designer, Stephen Grimes; Assistant Directors, D. Michael Moore, Mike Abe; Costumes, Dorothy Jeakins; In Panavision and Technicolor; Rated R; 112 minutes; March release.

CAST

Harry Kilmer	Robert Mitchum
Tanaka Ken	Takakura Ken
George Tanner	Brian Keith
Wheat	Herb Edelman
Dusty	Richard Jordan
Eiko	Kishi Keiko
Tono	Okada Eiji
Goro	James Shigeta
Kato	Kyosuke Mashida
Hanako	Christine Kokubo
Spider	Go Eiji
Louise	Lee Chirillo
Boyfriend	M. Hisaka
Tanner's Guard	William Ross
Tono's Guard	Akiyama
Goro's Doorman	Harada

Robert Mitchum, Brian Keith Above:
Takakura Ken, Robert Mitchum (also top)

Top: Robert Mitchum, Takakura Ken
Below: Robert Mitchum, Kishi Keiko

AT LONG LAST LOVE

(20th CENTURY-FOX) Produced, Directed, and Written by Peter Bogdanovich; Music and Lyrics, Cole Porter; Associate Producer, Frank Marshall; Photography, Laszlo Kovacs; Design, Gene Allen; Art Director, John Lloyd; Costumes, Bobbie Mannix; Dance Coordinators, Albert Lantieri, Rita Abrams; Assistant Directors, Mickey McArdle, Jerry Ballew; Editor, Douglas Robertson; In Technicolor; Rated G; 118 minutes; March release.

CAST

Michael Oliver Pritchard III	Burt Reynolds
Brooke Carter	Cybill Shepherd
Kitty O'Kelly	Madeline Kahn
Johnny Spanish	Duilio Del Prete
Elizabeth	Eileen Brennan
Rodney James	John Hillerman
Mabel Pritchard	Mildred Natwick
Phillip	Quinn Redeker

and J. Edward McKinley, John Stephenson, Peter Dane, William Paterson, Lester Dorr, Liam Dunn, Elvin Moon, M. Emmet Walsh, Burton Gilliam, Albert Lantieri, Len Lookabaugh, Tanis Van Kirk, Merlena Joy, Roy Goldman, Fran Lee, Jim Mohlman, Tony Barberio, John Houy, David Pannieff, William Bartlett, Jack Konzal, Tucker Smith, Ian Bruce, Sam Kwasman, Bill Taliaferro, Ross Divito, Bert May, Roy Wilson, Bill Couch, Roberta Lynn Haines, Stephanie Haines, Maria Cokkinos, Elizabeth Edwards, Mary K. Peters, Sheila Condit, Ned Wertimer, Arthur Peterson, Barbara Ann Walters, Violet Cane, Roger Price, Loutz Gage, Diana Wyatt, Clive Morgan, Nelson Welch, Patricia O'Neal, Morgan Farley, Robert Terry, Artie Butler, Gene Lebelle, Basil Hoffman, Donald Journeaux, Jeffrey Byron, Loyd Catlett, Kevin O'Neal, Anna Bogdanovich, Rita Loewen, Joan Zajac, Rita Abrams, Antonia Bogdanovich, Alexandra Bogdanovich, Maurice Price, Christa Lang, William Shepherd, Manny Harmon

Right: Cybill Shepherd, Madeline Kahn, Eileen Brennan, Rodney Hillerman, Mildred Natwick, Duilio Del Prete, Burt Reynolds Top: Shepherd, Reynolds, Kahn, Del Prete

Eileen Brennan, Cybill Shepherd, Madeline Kahn Above: Burt Reynolds, Cybill Shepherd

Duilio Del Prete, Madeline Kahn Above: John Hillerman, Eileen Brennan

THE HIDING PLACE

(WORLD WIDE) Executive Producer, William F. Brown; Producer, Frank R. Jacobson; Director, James F. Collier; Photography, Michael Reed; Editor, Ann Chegwiden; Screenplay, Allan Sloane, Lawrence Holben; Based on book by Corrie ten Boom and John and Elizabeth Sherrill; Assistant Director, Robert Howard; Designer, John Blezard; Costumes, Klara Kerpin; In Metrocolor; Rated PG; 150 minutes; May release.

CAST

Betsie	Julie Harris
Katje	Eileen Heckart
Papa	Arthur O'Connell
Corrie	Jeannette Clift
Willem	Robert Rietty
Tine	Pamela Sholto
Peter	Paul Henley
Kik	Richard Wren
Dutch Policeman	Broes Hartman
Young German Officer	Lex Van Delden
Dr. Heemstra	Tom Van Beek
Pastor De Ruiter	Nigel Hawthorne
Professor Ziener	John Gabriel
Eusie	David De Keyser
The Snake (Camp Matron)	Carol Gillies
Chief Nurse	Lillias Walker
Wrochek	Irene Prador
Erika (pregnant girl)	Janette Legge

Left: Arthur O'Connell

Julie Harris, Paul Henley

Julie Harris

Jeannette Clift

FRENCH CONNECTION II

(20th CENTURY-FOX) Producer, Robert L. Rosen; Director, John Frankenheimer; Screenplay, Alexander Jacobs, Robert Dillon, Lauri Dillon; Story, Robert Dillon, Lauri Dillon; Assistant Directors, Bernard Stora, Thierry Chabert; Photography, Claude Renior; Music, Don Ellis; Designer, Jacques Saulnier; Art Directors, Gerard Viard, Georges Glon; Costumes, Jacques Fonteray; Editor, Tom Rolf; In DeLuxe Color; Rated R; 119 minutes; May release.

CAST

Popeye Doyle	Gene Hackman
Charnier	Fernando Rey
Barthelemy	Bernard Fresson
Raoul Diron	Jean-Pierre Castaldi
Miletto	Charles Millot
Old Lady	Cathleen Nesbitt
Old Pro	Pierre Collet
Young Tail	Alexandre Fabre
Jacques	Philippe Leotard
Inspector Genevoix	Jacques Dynam
Dutch Captain	Raoul Delfosse
Manfredi	Patrick Floersheim

Fernando Rey
Top: Gene Hackman, Bernard Fresson

36

Bernard Fresson, Gene Hackman, Jean-Pierre Castaldi
Top: Samantha Lottard, Fernando Rey

Gene Hackman, also top

SMILE

(UNITED ARTISTS) Producer-Director, Michael Ritchie; Executive Producers, David Picker, Marion Dougherty; Screenplay, Jerry Belson; Associate Producer, Tim Zinnemann; Photography, Conrad Hall; Costumes, Patricia Norris; Editor, Richard Harris; In color; Rated PG; 113 minutes; May release

CAST

"Big Bob" Freelander	Bruce Dern
Brenda DiCarlo	Barbara Feldon
Tommy French	Michael Kidd
Wilson Shears	Geoffrey Lewis
Andy DiCarlo	Nicholas Pryor
Connie Thompson/Miss Imperial County	Colleen Camp
Robin Gibson/Miss Angelope Valley	Joan Prather
Shirley Tolstoy/Miss San Diego	Denise Nickerson
Doria Houston/Miss Anaheim	Annette O'Toole
Maria Gonzales	Maria O'Brien
Emile Eidleman	Tito Vandis
Little Bob Freelander	Eric Shea

Contestants for Young American Miss Above: (L) Michael Kidd, (R) Barbara McCutchan, Marie Curry

38

Bruce Dern, and above with Barbara Feldon
Top: Jim Busche, Barbara Feldon, Geoffrey Lewis

Maria O'Brien Above: Eric Shea,
Brad Thompson

THE WIND AND THE LION

(UNITED ARTISTS) Producer, Herb Jaffe; Direction and Screenplay, John Milius; Music, Jerry Goldsmith; Photography, Billy Williams; Editor, Robert L. Wolfe; Art Director, R. Antonio Paton; Costumes, Richard E. LaMotte; Designer, Gil Parrando; Associate Producer, Phil Rawlins; Assistant Directors, Miguel A. Gil, Roberto Cirla, Roberta Parra, Miguel A. Barbero; In Panavision and Metrocolor; Rated PG; 119 minutes; May release.

CAST

Raisuli	Sean Connery
Eden Pedecaris	Candice Bergen
Theodore Roosevelt	Brian Keith
John Hay	John Huston
Cummere	Geoffrey Lewis
Capt. Jerome	Steve Kanaly
The Bashaw	Vladek Sheybal
Sherif of Wazan	Nadim Sawalha
Admiral Chadwick	Roy Jenson
Alice Roosevelt	Deborah Baxter
Quentin Roosevelt	Jack Cooley
Kermit Roosevelt	Chris Aller
William Pedecaris	Simon Harrison
Jennifer Pedecaris	Polly Gottesman
Von Roerkel	Antoine St. John
Ugly Arab	Aldo Sambrell
Gayaan the Terrible	Luis Barboo
Dreighton	Darrell Fetty
The Sultan	Marc Zuber
Sir Joseph	Billy Williams
Edith Roosevelt	Shirley Rothman
Marine Sergeant	Rusty Cox
Henry Cabot Lodge	Larry Cross
Elihu Root	Alex Weldon
Japanese General	Akio Mitamura
President's Aide	Frank Gassman
Miss Hitchcock	Audrey San Felix
Sketch Artist	Ben Tatar
President's Secretary	Michael Damian

Candice Bergen, and top with Sean Connery

Top: Brian Keith, John Huston Below: Candice Bergen, Sean Connery

Deborah Baxter, Brian Keith Above: Billy
Williams, Candice Bergen Top: Candice
Bergen, Steve Kanaly

Sean Connery, Candice Bergen, also above
Top: Steve Kanaly, Bladek Sheybal

41

THE DAY OF THE LOCUST

(PARAMOUNT) Producer, Jerome Hellman; Director, John Schlesigner; Screenplay, Waldo Salt; Based on novel by Nathanael West; Photography, Conrad Hall; Associate Producer, Sheldon Schrager; Music, John Barry; Editor, Jim Clark; Art Director, John Lloyd; Designer, Richard MacDonald; Costumes, Ann Roth; Assistant Directors, Tim Zinnemann, Charles Ziarcho, Barry Stern, Arnie Schmidt; In Panavision and Technicolor; Rated R; 144 minutes; May release.

CAST

Homer	Donald Sutherland
Faye	Karen Black
Harry	Burgess Meredith
Tod	William Atherton
Big Sister	Geraldine Page
Claude Estee	Richard A. Dysart
Earle Shoop	Bo Hopkins
Miguel	Pepe Serna
Mary Dove	Lelia Goldoni
Abe	Billy Barty
Adore	Jackie Haley
Mrs. Loomis	Gloria LeRoy
Mrs. Odlesh	Jane Hoffman
Mr. Odlesh	Norm Leavitt
Mrs. Johnson	Madge Kennedy
Lee Sisters	Ina Gould, Florence Lake
The Gingos	Margaret Willey, John War Eagle
Audrey Jennings	Natalie Schafer
Alice Estee	Gloria Stroock
Joan	Nita Talbot
Projectionist	Nicholas Cortland
Butler	Alvin Childress
Girls	Ann Coleman, Gyl Roland
Guests at Audrey Jennings	Byron Paul, Virginia Baker, Roger Price, Angela Greene, Robert Oliver Ragland, Abbey Geshler
Helverston	Paul Stewart
Ned Grote	John Hillerman
Director	William C. Castle
First Assistant Director	Fred Scheiwiller
Second Assistant Director	Wally Rose
French Lieutenant	Grainger Hines
Shoe Shine Boy	DeForest Covan
Major Domo	Michael Quinn
Apprentices	Robert Pine, Jerry Fogel, Dennis Dugan, David Ladd
Tour Guide	Bob Holt
Nightclub Entertainer	Paul Jabara
Palsied Lady	Queenie Smith
Choral Director	Margaret Jenkins
Undertaker	Jonathan Kidd
Boy in chapel	Kenny Solms
Theatre Manager	Wally Berns
Dick Powell	Dick Powell, Jr.
Announcer at premiere	Bill Baldwin

Left: Burgess Meredith, Karen Black Above: William Castle Top: Karen Black

Bo Hopkins, Karen Black

Jackie Haley, William Atherton

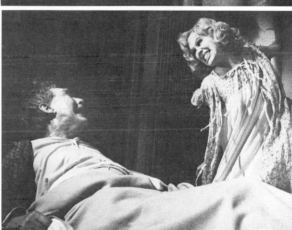

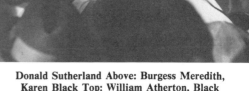

Karen Black, William Atherton, also above with
Paul Jabara, Donald Sutherland Top: Burgess
Meredith, Geraldine Page

Donald Sutherland Above: Burgess Meredith,
Karen Black Top: William Atherton, Black

43

THE MAN IN THE GLASS BOOTH

(AMERICAN FILM THEATRE) Producer, Ely Landau; Director, Arthur Hiller; Screenplay, Edward Anhalt; Executive Producer, Mort Abrahams; Designer, Joel Schiller; Photography, Sam Leavitt; Editor, David Bretherton; Costumes, John A. Anderson; In color; Rated PG; 117 minutes; May release.

CAST

Arthur Goldman	Maximilian Schell
Miriam Rosen	Lois Nettleton
Presiding Judge	Luther Adler
Charlie Cohn	Lawrence Pressman
Jack Arnold	Henry Brown
Moshe	Richard Rasof
Rami	David Nash
Uri	Martin Berman
Rudin	Sy Kramer
Dr. Weisberg	Robert H. Harris
Samuel	Leonidas Ossetynski
Churchill	Lloyd Bochner
Schmidt	Norbert Schiller

Right: Maximilian Schell, also below with Lawrence Pressman, Richard Rasof, David Nash

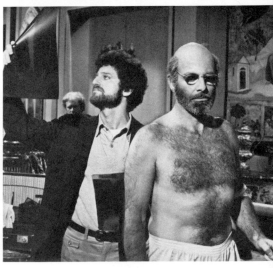

**Maximilian Schell, Lois Nettleton
Above: Maximilian Schell, Luther Adler (R)**

Richard Rasof, Maximilian Schell

RETURN TO MACON COUNTY

(AMERICAN INTERNATIONAL) Executive Producer, Samuel Z. Arkoff; Producer, Elliot Schick; Direction and Screenplay, Richard Compton; Photography, Jacques Marquette; Editor, Corky Ehlers; Music, Robert O. Ragland; Assistant Director, Robert Dijoux; In Movielab Color; Rated PG; 90 minutes; June release.

CAST

Bo Hollinger	Nick Nolte
Harley McKay	Don Johnson
Junell	Robin Mattson
Sgt. Whittaker	Robert Viharo
Tom	Eugene Daniels
Peter	Matt Greene
Betty	Devon Ericson
Steve	Ron Prather
Larry	Philip Crews
Libby	Laura Sayer
Big man in coffee shop	Walt Guthrie
Pat	Mary Ann Hearn
Cook	Sam Kilman
Sheriff Jackson	Bill Moses
Officer Harris	Pat O'Connor
Motel Owner	Maurice Hunt
Girl in car	Kim Graham
Boy in car	Don Higdon

Right: Don Johnson, Nick Nolte, also below

Nick Nolte, Robin Mattson, and above with
Robert Viharo

Don Johnson, Devon Ericson

ROLLERBALL

(UNITED ARTISTS) Producer-Director, Norman Jewison; Screenplay, William Harrison; Associate Producer, Patrick Palmer; Assistant Directors, Kip Gowans, Chris Kenny; Photography, Douglas Slocombe; Designer, John Box; Art Director, Robert Laing; Editor, Anthony Gibbs; Costumes, Julie Harris; In color; Rated R; 129 minutes; June release.

CAST

Jonathan E.	James Caan
Bartholomew	John Houseman
Ella	Maud Adams
Moonpie	John Beck
Cletus	Moses Gunn
Mackie	Pamela Hensley
Daphne	Barbara Trentham
Librarian	Ralph Richardson
Team Executive	Shane Rimmer
Team Trainer	Alfred Thomas
Jonathan's Captain of Guard	Burnell Tucker
Jonathan's Guard #1	Angus MacInnes
Batholomew's Aide	Rick Le Parmentier
Oriental Doctor	Burt Kwouk
Oriental Instructor	Robert Ito
Girl in library	Nancy Blair
Black Reporters	Loftus Burton, Abi Gouhad

John Beck, also above with James Caan

James Caan, Ralph Richardson
Above: Barbara Trentham, James Caan

John Beck, James Caan Above: Caan, Pamela
Hensley Top: John Houseman, Caan

John Houseman Above: James Caan, Moses Gunn
Top: Maud Adams, James Caan

BITE THE BULLET

(COLUMBIA) Produced, Directed and Written by Richard Brooks; Photography, Harry Stradling, Jr.; Editor, George Granville; Music, Alex North; Art Director, Robert Boyle; Assistant Director, Tom Shaw; In Metrocolor; Rated PG; 131 minutes; June release.

CAST

Sam Clayton	Gene Hackman
Miss Jones	Candice Bergen
Luke Matthews	James Coburn
"Mister"	Ben Johnson
Norfolk	Ian Bannen
Carbo	Jan-Michael Vincent
Mexican	Mario Arteaga
Reporter	Robert Donner
Lee Christie	Robert Hoy
J. B. Parker	Paul Stewart
Rosie	Jean Willes
Gebhardt	John McLiam
Jack Parker	Dabney Coleman
Woodchopper	Jerry Gatlin
Honey	Sally Kirkland
Steve	Walter Scott, Jr.

Gene Hackman, James Coburn
Top Left: Jan-Michael Vincent

Gene Hackman (R), and above with James Coburn
Top: Candice Bergen (L)

Candice Bergen, James Coburn
Top: Jan-Michael Vincent, Bergen

LOVE AND DEATH

(UNITED ARTISTS) Producer, Charles H. Joffe; Direction and Screenplay, Woody Allen; Executive Producer, Martin Poll; Associate Producer, Fred T. Gallo; Music, S. Prokofiev; Photography, Ghislain Cloquet; Art Director, Willy Holt; Editor, Ralph Rosenblum; Costumes, Gladys De Segonzac; Editor, Ron Kalish; Assistant Directors, Paul Feyder, Bernard Cohn; In Panavision and DeLuxe Color; Rated PG; 82 minutes; June release.

CAST

Boris	Woody Allen
Sonja	Diane Keaton

Georges Adet (Old Nehamkin), Frank Adu (Drill Sgt.), Edmond Ardisson (Priest), Feodor Atkine (Mikhail), Albert Augier (Waiter), Yves Barsacq (Rimsky), Lloyd Battista (Don Francisco), Jack Berard (Gen. Lecoq), Eva Bertrand (Woman Hygiene Class), George Birt (Doctor), Yves Brainville (Andre), Gerard Buhr (Servant), Brian Coburn (Dimitri), Henry Coutet (Minskov), Patricia Crown (Cheerleader), Henry Czarniak (Ivan), Despo Diamantidou (Mother), Sandor Eles (Soldier 2), Luce Fabiole (Grandmother), Florian (Uncle Nikolai), Jacqueline Fogt (Ludmilla), Sol L. Frieder (Voskovec), Olga Georges-Picot (Countess), Harold Gould (Anton), Harry Hankin (Uncle Sasha), Jessica Harper (Natasha), Tony Jay (Vladimir Maximovitch), Tutte Lemkow (Pierre), Jack Lenior (Krapotkin), Leib Lensky (Father Andre), Ann Lonn Berg (Olga), Roger Lumont (Baker), Alfred Lutter III (Young Boris), Ed Marcus (Raskov), Jacques Maury (Second), Narcissa McKinley (Cheerleader), Aubrey Morris (Soldier 4), Denise Peron (Spanish Countess), Beth Porter (Anna), Alan Rossett (Guard), Shimen Ruskin (Borslov), Persival Russel (Berdykov), Chris Sanders (Joseph), Zvee Scooler (Father), C. A. R. Smith (Father Nikolai), Fred Smith (Soldier), Bernard Taylor (Soldier 3), Clement-Thierry (Jacques), Alan Tilvern (Sgt.), James Tolkan (Napoleon), Helene Vallier (Madame Wolfe), Howard Vernon (Gen. Leveque), Glenn Williams (Soldier 1), Jacob Witkin (Suskin).

**Left: Diane Keaton, Woody Allen
Top: Woody Allen**

Olga Georges-Picot, Woody Allen

Woody Allen, Norman Rose

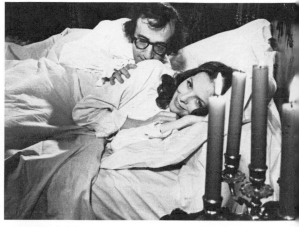

James Tolkan, Diane Keaton, Woody Allen
Above, Diane Keaton, Woody Allen

Woody Allen, Harold Gould Above: Despo Diamantidou,
Allen, Zvee Cooler Top: Allen, Diane Keaton

51

NASHVILLE

(PARAMOUNT) Producer-Director, Robert Altman; Screenplay, Joan Tewkesbury; Executive Producers, Martin Starger, Jerry Weintraub; Photography, Paul Lohmann; Music, Richard Baskin; Editors, Sidney Levin, Dennis Hill; Associate Producers, Robert Eggenweiler, Scott Bushnell; Assistant Directors, Tommy Thompson, Alan Rudolph; Wardrobe, Jules Melillo; In Panavision and MGM Color; Rated R; 159 minutes; June release.

CAST

Norman	David Arkin
Lady Pearl	Barbara Baxley
Delbert Reese	Ned Beatty
Connie White	Karen Black
Barbara Jean	Ronee Blakley
Tommy Brown	Timothy Brown
Tom Frank	Keith Carradine
Opal	Geraldine Chaplin
Wade	Robert Doqui
L. A. Joan	Shelley Duvall
Barnett	Allen Garfield
Haven Hamilton	Henry Gibson
Pfc. Glenn Kelly	Scott Glenn
Tricycle Man	Jeff Goldblum
Albuquerque	Barbara Harris
Kenny Fraiser	David Hayward
John Triplette	Michael Murphy
Bill	Alan Nicholls
Bud Hamilton	Dave Peel
Mary	Cristina Raines
Star	Bert Remsen
Linnea Reese	Lily Tomlin
Sueleen Gay	Gwen Welles
Mr. Green	Keenan Wynn
Jimmy Reese	James Dan Calvert
Donna Reese	Donna Denton
Trout	Merle Kilgore
Jewel	Carol McGinnis
Frog	Richard Baskin
Smokey Mountain Laurel	Sheila Bailey, Patti Bryant
Themselves	Jonnie Barnett, Vassar Clements, Misty Mountain Boys, Sue Barton, Elliott Gould, Julie Christie

**Left: Keith Carradine, Geraldine Chaplin
Above: David Hayward, Cristina Raines, Allan
Nicholls Top: Henry Gibson**

Ronee Blakley, Henry Gibson, Barbara Baxley

Lily Tomlin, Robert Doqui

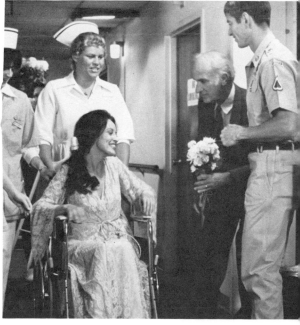

Allen Garfield, Ronee Blakley Above:
Barbara Harris Top: Harris, Karen Black

Ronee Blakley, Keenan Wynn, Scott Glenn
Above: Michael Murphy, Ned Beatty, Gwen Welles
Top: Lily Tomlin

RACE WITH THE DEVIL

(20th CENTURY-FOX) Executive Producer, Paul Maslansky; Producer, Wes Bishop; Director, Jack Starrett; Screenplay, Lee Frost, Wes Bishop; Photography, Robert Jessup; Music, Leonard Rosenman; Editor, Allan Jacobs; Assistant Directors, Fred Brost, Steve Lim; In DeLuxe Color; Rated PG; 88 minutes; June release.

CAST

Roger	Peter Fonda
Frank	Warren Oates
Alice	Loretta Swit
Kelly	Lara Parker
Sheriff	R. G. Armstrong
Delbert	Clay Tanner
Ethel	Carol Blodgett
Ricci Ware	Ricci Ware
Gun Shop Owner	James N. Harrell
Cal Mathers	Paul A. Partain
Kay	Karen Miller
Arkey Blue	Arkey Blue
Gas Station Attendant	Jack Starrett
Mechanic	Phil Hoover
Deputy Dave	Wes Bishop

Top Right: Warren Oates, Loretta Swit, Lara Parker, Peter Fonda

Peter Fonda (C) and above

Loretta Swit, Lara Parker
Above: Warren Oates, Peter Fonda

THE FORTUNE

(COLUMBIA) Producers, Mike Nichols, Don Devlin; Executive Producer, Hank Moonjean; Director, Mike Nichols; Screenplay, Adrien Joyce (Carol Eastman); Photography, Joan A. Alonzo; Editor, Stu Linder; Music, David Shire; Designer, Richard Sylbert; Art Director, W. Stewart Campbell; Assistant Director, Peter Bogart; In Technicolor; Rated PG; 88 minutes; June release.

CAST

Oscar	Jack Nicholson
Nicky	Warren Beatty
Freddie	Stockard Channing
Landlady	Florence Stanley
Chief Detective	Richard B. Shull
John the Barber	Tom Newman
Photographer	John Fiedler

Top Right: Stockard Channing, Warren Beatty, Jack Nicholson

Jack Nicholson, Warren Beatty

Jack Nicholson, and above with Warren Beatty

NIGHT MOVES

(WARNER BROS.) Producer, Robert M. Sherman; Director, Arthur Penn; Screenplay, Alan Sharp; Editor, Dede Allen; Photography, Bruce Surtees; Associate Producer, Gene Lasko; Music, Michael Small; Designer, George Jenkins; Assistant Directors, Jack Roe, Patrick H. Kehoe; In Technicolor; Rated R; 100 minutes; June release.

CAST

Harry Moseby	Gene Hackman
Paula	Jennifer Warren
Ziegler	Edward Binns
Marty Heller	Harris Yulin
Nick	Kenneth Mars
Arlene Iverson	Janet Ward
Quentin	James Woods
Marv Ellman	Anthony Costello
Tom Iverson	John Crawford
Delly Grastner	Melanie Griffith
Charles	Ben Archibeck
Boy	Dennis Dugan
Girl	C. J. Hincks
Stud	Maxwell Gail, Jr.
Ticket Clerks	Susan Barrister, Larry Mitchell
Ellen	Susan Clark

Left: Gene Hackman, Susan Clark

Jennifer Warren, Gene Hackman

Melanie Griffith Above: Gene Hackman,
Susan Clark Top: Hackman, Griffith,
Jennifer Warren

Gene Hackman

JAWS

(UNIVERSAL) Producers, Richard D. Zanuck, David Brown; Director, Steven Spielberg; Screenplay, Peter Benchley, Carl Gottlieb; Based on novel by Peter Benchley; Photography, Bill Butler; Designer, Joseph Alves, Jr.; Editor, Verna Fields; Music, John Williams; Underwater Photography, Rexford Metz; Assistant Directors, Tom Joyner, Barbara Bass; In Panavision and Technicolor; Rated PG; 124 minutes; June release.

CAST

Brody	Roy Scheider
Quint	Robert Shaw
Hooper	Richard Dreyfuss
Ellen Brody	Lorraine Gary
Vaughn	Murray Hamilton
Meadows	Carl Gottlieb
Hendricks	Jeffrey C. Kramer
Chrissie	Susan Backlinie
Cassidy	Jonathan Filley
Estuary Victim	Ted Grossman
Michael Brody	Chris Rebello
Sean Brody	Jay Mello
Mrs. Kintner	Lee Fierro
Alex Kintner	Jeffrey Voorhees
Ben Gardner	Craig Kingsbury
Medical Examiner	Dr. Robert Nevin
Interviewer	Peter Benchley

Roy Scheider, Lorraine Gary, Chris Rebello
Top: Ted Grossman

Roy Scheider, Robert Shaw

Roy Scheider, Richard Dreyfuss, also
top with Robert Shaw

Robert Shaw, also above
with Richard Dreyfuss

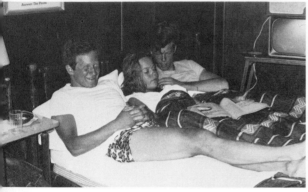

CRAZY MAMA

(NEW WORLD) Producer, Julie Corman; Director, Jonathan Demme; Screenplay, Robert Thom; Story, Francis Doel; Photography, Bruce Logan; Associate Producer, Peter Cornberg; Editors, Allan Holzman, Lewis Teague; Art Director, Peter Jamison; Costumes, Jac McAnelly; Assistant Director, Lamar Card; In Metrocolor; Rated PG; 80 minutes; June release.

CAST

Melba	Cloris Leachman
Jim Bob	Stuart Whitman
Sheba	Ann Sothern
Albertson	Jim Backus
Shawn	Donn Most
Cheryl	Linda Purl
Snake	Bryan Englund
Bertha	Merie Earle
Ella Mae	Sally Kirkland
Daniel	Clint Kimbrough
Wilbur Janeway	Dick Miller
Supermarket Manager	Carmen Argenziano
FBI Man	Harry Northup
Sheriff (1932)	Ralph James
Melba (1932)	Dinah Englund
Mover	Robert Reece
Mrs. Morgan	Mickey Fox
Marvin	John Aprea
Lucinda	Cynthia Songey
Bartender	Hal Marshall
Desk Clerk	Beach Dickerson
Lady Teller	Barbara Ann Walters
Bank Manager	Bill McLean
Newsman	William Luckey
Justice of the Peace	Warren Miller
Colonel Snodgrass	Saul Krugman
Homer	Vince Barnett
Sheba (1932)	Trish Sterling

Top: Cloris Leachman, Stuart Whitman, Donny Most, Linda Purl Below: Most, Purl, Bryan Englund

Cloris Leachman Above: Linda Purl, Bryan Englund
Top: Ann Sothern, Leachman, Englund

POSSE

(PARAMOUNT)Producer-Director, Kirk Douglas; Screenplay, William Roberts, Christopher Knopf; Story, Christopher Knopf; Executive Producer, Phil Feldman; Photography, Fred J. Koenekamp; Music, Maurice Jarre; Editor, John W. Wheeler; Designer, Lyle Wheeler; Assistant Directors, Jack Roe, Pat Kehoe; In Panavision and Technicolor; Rated PG; 94 minutes; June release.

CAST

Howard Nightingale	Kirk Douglas
Jack Strawhorn	Bruce Dern
Wesley	Bo Hopkins
Hellman	James Stacy
Krag	Luke Askew
Pensteman	David Canary
Pepe	Alfonso Arau
Mrs. Cooper	Katharine Woodville
Mr. Cooper	Mark Roberts
Mrs. Ross	Beth Brickell
Wiley	Dick O'Neill
McCanless	Bill Burton
Rains	Louie Elias
Reyno	Gus Greymountain
Telegrapher	Allan Warnick
Buwalda	Roger Behrstock
Hunsinger	Jess Riggle
Amie	Stephanie Steele
Laurie	Melody Thomas
Shanty Principals	Dick Armstrong, Larry Finley, Pat Tobin

Right: James Stacy, Kirk Douglas

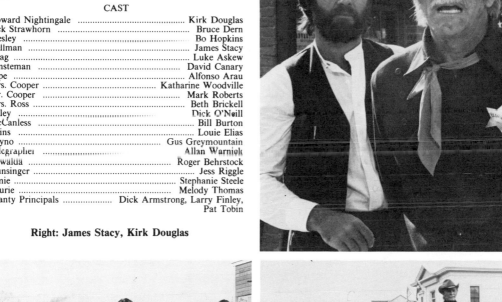

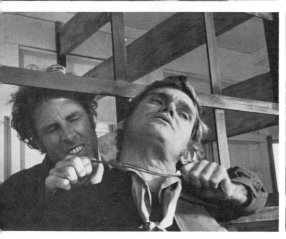

Bruce Dern, Bo Hopkins Above: Bill Burton, Louie Elias, Hopkins, Gus Greymountain, Luke Askew

Bruce Dern, Kirk Douglas (also above)

61

JACQUELINE SUSANN'S ONCE IS NOT ENOUGH

(PARAMOUNT) Producer, Howard W. Koch; Director, Guy Green; Screenplay, Julius J. Epstein; Based on novel by Jacqueline Susann; Executive Producer, Irving Mansfield; Photography, John A. Alonzo; Music, Henry Mancini; Editor, Rita Roland; Costumes, Moss Mabry; Designer, John DeCuir; Assistant Director, Howard W. Koch, Jr.; In Panavision and Movielab Color; Rated R; 121 minutes; June release.

CAST

Mike Wayne	Kirk Douglas
Deidre Milford Granger	Alexis Smith
Tom Colt	David Janssen
David Milford	George Hamilton
Karla	Melina Mercouri
Hugh	Gary Conway
Linda	Brenda Vaccaro
January	Deborah Raffin
Mabel	Lillian Randolph
Maria	Renata Vanni
Rheingold	Mark Roberts
Franco	John Roper
Dr. Peterson	Leonard Sachs
Scotty	Jim Boles
Girl at El Morocco	Ann Marie Moelders
Myrna	Trudi Marshall
Maitre D' Polo Lounge	Eddie Garrett
Waiter	Sid Frohlich
Weather Lady	Kelly Lange
Four Beautiful People	Maureen McCluskey, Harley Farber, Michael Millius, Tony Ferrara

Left: Kirk Douglas, Deborah Raffin

Kirk Douglas, Brenda Vaccaro

Deborah Raffin, Gary Conway
Above: Kirk Douglas, Alexis Smith

George Hamilton, Deborah Raffin Above: Alexis
Smith, Melina Mercouri Top: Raffin, Smith

Deborah Raffin, Kirk Douglas
Top: Raffin, David Janssen

THE DROWNING POOL

(WARNER BROS.) Producers, Lawrence Turman, David Foster; Director, Stuart Rosenberg; Screenplay, Tracy Keenan Wynn, Lorenzo Semple, Jr., Walter Hill; Based on novel by Ross MacDonald; Photography, Gordon Willis; Editor, John Howard; Music, Michael Small; Designer, Paul Sylbert; Assistant Director, Lee Rafner; Associate Producer-Assistant Director, Howard W. Koch, Jr.; Wardrobe, Donald Brooks; Art Director, Ed O'-Donovan; A First Artists Production; In Panavision and Technicolor; Rated PG; 108 minutes; July release.

CAST

Harper	Paul Newman
Iris	Joanne Woodward
Broussard	Tony Franciosa
Kilbourne	Murray Hamilton
Mavis	Gail Strickland
Schuyler	Melanie Griffith
Gretchen	Linda Haynes
Franks	Richard Jaeckel
Candy	Paul Koslo
Pat Reaves	Andy Robinson
Olivia	Coral Browne
James	Richard Derr
Elaine Reaves	Helena Kallianiotes
Red Head	Leigh French
Motel Switchboard Operator	Cecil Elliott

Right: Paul Newman, Linda Haynes

Richard Jaeckel, Paul Newman
Above: Joanne Woodward, Paul Newman

Paul Newman, Gail Strickland
Above: Paul Newman, Tony Franciosa

THE DEVIL'S RAIN

(BRYANSTON) Executive Producer, Sandy Howard; Producers, James V. Cullen, Michael S. Glick; Screenplay, Gabe Essoe, James Ashton, Gerald Hopman; Director, Robert Fuest; Associate Producer, Gerald Hopman; Editor, Michael Kahn; Photography, Alex Phillips, Jr.; Designer, Nikita Knatz; In color and Todd-AO 35; Rated PG; 85 minutes; July release.

CAST

Corbis	Ernest Borgnine
Dr. Richards	Eddie Albert
Mrs. Preston	Ida Lupino
Mark Preston	William Shatner
Sheriff Owens	Keenan Wynn
Tom Preston	Tom Skerritt
Julie Preston	Joan Prather
John	Woodrow Chambliss
Danny	John Travolta
Preacher	Claudio Brooks
Lilith	Lisa Todd
Steve Preston	George Sawaya
Aaronessa Fyffe	Erika Carlson

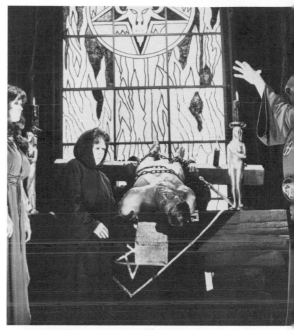

Right: Lisa Todd, Ida Lupino, William Shatner, Ernest Borgnine Below: Eddie Albert, Tom Skerritt

William Shatner, Ida Lupino Above: William Shatner

Joan Prather

THE APPLE DUMPLING GANG

(BUENA VISTA) Producer, Bill Anderson; Director, Norman Tokar; Screenplay, Don Tait; Based on book by Jack M. Bickham; Photography, Frank Phillips, Music, Buddy Baker; Title Song, Shane Tatum; Sung by Randy Sparks and The Back Porch Majority; Art Directors, John B. Mansbridge, Walter Tyler; Editor, Ray de Leuw; Costumes, Shelby Anderson; Assistant Directors, Ronald R. Grow, Pat Kehoe; In Technicolor; A Walt Disney Production; Rated G; 100 minutes; July release.

CAST

Russel Donavan	Bill Bixby
Magnolia Dusty Clydesdale	Susan Clark
Theodore Ogelvie	Don Knotts
Amos	Tim Conway
Col. T. T. Clydesdale	David Wayne
Frank Stillwell	Slim Pickens
Homer McCoy	Harry Morgan
Leonard Sharpe	John McGiver
John Wintle	Don Knight
Bobby Bradley	Clay O'Brien
Clovis Bradley	Brad Savage
Celia Bradley	Stacy Manning
Rudy Hooks	Dennis Fimple
Clemons	Pepe Callahan
Poker Polly	Iris Adrian
Mrs. Stockley	Fran Ryan
Herm Dally	Bing Russell
The Mouthpiece	James E. Brodhead
Easy Archie	Jim Boles
Rube Cluck	Olan Soule
Rowdy Joe Dover	Tom Waters
Big Foot	Dawn Little Sky
Broadway Phil	Joshua Shelley
Oh So	Richard Lee-Sung
No So	Arthur Wong
Slippery Sid	Dick Winslow
Fast Eddie	Bill Dunbar
Cheating Charley	Wally Berns

Left: John McGiver, David Wayne, Susan Clark, Bill Bixby Top: Tim Conway, Don Knotts, Harry Morgan

Stacy Manning, Clay O'Brien, Brad Savage

Iris Adrian, Harry Morgan, Bill Bixby, Stacy Manning (also top left)

Top Right: Bill Bixby, Susan Clark

WHITE LINE FEVER

(COLUMBIA) Producer, John Kemeny; Executive Producers, Gerald Schneider, Mort Litwack; Director, Jonathan Kaplan; Screenplay, Ken Friedman, Jonathan Kaplan; Photography, Fred Koenekamp; Editor, O. Nicholas Brown; Music, David Nichtern; Art Director, Sydney Litwack; Assistant Director, Don Heitzer; In Metrocolor; Rated PG; 89 minutes; August release.

CAST

Carrol Jo Hummer	Jan-Michael Vincent
Jerri Hummer	Kay Lenz
Duana Haller	Slim Pickens
Buck Wessle	L. Q. Jones
Josh Cutler	Don Porter
Pops	Sam Laws
Carnell	Johnny Ray McGhee
Lucy	Leigh French
Prosecutor	R. G. Armstrong
Clem	Martin Kove
Jamie	Jamie Anderson
Deputy	Ron Nix
Birdie	Dick Miller
Reporter	Arnold Jeffers
Defense Lawyer	Curgie Pratt
Witness Miller	John David Garfield

Jan-Michael Vincent, and above with Kay Lenz
Top Left: Jan-Michael Vincent

SIDECAR RACERS

(UNIVERSAL) Producer, Richard Irving; Director, Earl Bellamy; Screenplay, Jon Cleary; Photography, Paul Onorato; Editor, Robert L. Kimble; Music, Tom Scott; Assistant Directors, Jim Hogan, Les White, Michael Midlam; Rated PG; 100 minutes; August release.

CAST

Jeff Rayburn	Ben Murphy
Lynn Carson	Wendy Hughes
Dave Ferguson	John Clayton
Carson	Peter Graves
Ocker Harvey	John Meillon
Pete McAllister	John Derum
Rick Horton	Peter Gwynne
Bluey Wilson	Serge Lazareff
Bob Horton	Paul Bertram
Tex Wilson	Patrick Ward
Marlene	Arna Maria Winchester
Virginia	Vicki Raymond
Store Manager	Kevin Healy
Store Detective	Brian Anderson
Mrs. Horton	Brenda Senders
Cashier	Liddy Clark
Ambulance Man	Bryan Niland
Girl Singer	Loretta Saul

Top: Serge Lazareff, Patrick Ward

Top: Ben Murphy, Vicki Raymond

FAREWELL, MY LOVELY

(AVCO EMBASSY) Executive Producers, Elliott Kastner, Jerry Bick; Producers, George Pappas, Jerry Bruckheimer; Screenplay, David Zelag Goodman; Based on novel by Raymond Chandler; Music, David Shire; Assistant Directors, Henry Lange, David Sonsa; Photography, John Alonzo; Designer, Dean Tavoularis; Art Director, Angelo Graham; Editors, Walter Thompson, Joel Cox; An EK/ITC Production; In Fujicolor; Rated R; 97 minutes; August release.

CAST

Marlowe	Robert Mitchum
Mrs. Velma Grayle	Charlotte Rampling
Nulty	John Ireland
Mrs. Florian	Sylvia Miles
Moose Malloy	Jack O'Halloran
Brunette	Anthony Zerbe
Billy Rolfe	Harry Dean Stanton
Mr. Grayle	Jim Thompson
Marriott	John O'Leary
Amthor	Kate Murtagh
Tommy Ray	Walter McGinn
Georgie	Jimmy Archer
Nick	Joe Spinell
Kelly/Jonnie	Sylvester Stallone
Cowboy	Burt Gilliam

Left: Robert Mitchum

Charlotte Rampling, Robert Mitchum

Kate Murtagh, Robert Mitchum, Burt Gilliam,
Joe Spinell Top: Mitchum, Jack O'Halloran
(R) Mitchum, Charlotte Rampling

THE LAND THAT TIME FORGOT

(AMERICAN INTERNATIONAL) Executive Producer, Robert E. Greenberg; Producer, John Dark; Director, Kevin Connor; Screenplay, James Cawthorn, Michael Moorcock; Music, Douglas Gamley; Photography, Alan Hume; Art Director, Bert Davey; Editor, John Ireland; Designer, Maurice Carter; Associate Producer, John Peverall; Assistant Director, Allan James; Based on novel by Edgar Rice Burroughs; A Max J. Rosenberg and Milton Subotsky Production; Presented by Samuel Z. Arkoff; In Movielab Color; Rated PG; 90 minutes; August release.

CAST

Bowen Tyler	Doug McClure
Capt. Von Schoenvorts	John McEnery
Lisa Clayton	Susan Penhaligon
Bradley	Keith Barron
Dietz	Anthony Ainley
Borg	Godfrey James
Ahm	Bobby Farr
Olson	Declan Mulholland
Whiteley	Colin Farrell
Benson	Ben Howard
Plesser	Roy Holder
Sinclair	Andrew McCulloch
Jones	Ron Pember
Deusett	Graheme Mallard
Reuther	Andrew Lodge
Schwartz	Brian Hall
Hiller	Stanley McGeagh
Hindle	Peter Sproule
First Sto-Lu	Steve James

Doug McClure, Susan Penhaligon Above: John McEnery, Bobby Parr, Penhaligon Top: Penhaligon, McClure

Top: Declan Mulholland, Doug McClure
Below: Steve James, Susan Penhaligon

RUSSIAN ROULETTE

(AVCO EMBASSY) Executive Producer, Elliott Kastner; Producer, Jerry Bick; Director, Lou Lombardo; Screenplay, Tom Ardies, Stanley Mann, Arnold Margolin; Based on novel "Kosygin Is Coming" by Tom Ardies; Music, Michael J. Lewis; Associate Producers, Denis Holt, Marion Segal; Photography, Brian West; Editor, Richard Marden; Assistant Director, David Tringham,; Art Director, Roy Walker; In color; Rated PG; 93 minutes; August release.

CAST

Shaver	George Segal
Bogna	Cristina Raines
Vostik	Bo Brundin
Petapiece	Denholm Elliott
Hardison	Gordon Jackson
McDermott	Peter Donat
Ragulia	Richard Romanus
Ferguson	Nigel Stock
Henke	Val Avery
Midge	Louise Fletcher
Gorki	Jacques Sandulescu
Benson	Graham Jarvis
Samuel	Constantin de Goguel
Taggart	Wally Marsh
Kavinsky	Hagan Beggs
Lars	Douglas McGrath

Right: Louise Fletcher, George Segal

George Segal, Gordon Johnson
Above: Denholm Elliott, Cristina Raines

George Segal, and above
with Cristina Raines

73

DOG DAY AFTERNOON

(WARNER BROS.) Producers, Martin Bregman, Martin Elfand; Director, Sidney Lumet; Screenplay, Frank Pierson; Associate Producer, Robert Greenhut; Editor, Dede Allen; Photography, Victor J. Kemper; Assistant Directors, Burtt Harris, Alan Hopkins; Based on magazine article by P. F. Kluge, Thomas Moore; Designer, Charles Bailey; Costumes, Anna Hill Johnstone; Art Director, Doug Higgins; In Technicolor; Rated R; 130 minutes; September release.

CAST

The Bank:
Sylvia	Penny Allen
Mulvaney	Sully Boyar
Sal	John Cazale
Margaret	Beulah Garrick
Jenny	Carol Kane
Deborah	Sandra Kazan
Miriam	Marcia Jean Kurtz
Maria	Amy Levitt
Howard	John Marriott
Edna	Estelle Omens
Sonny	Al Pacino
Bobby	Gary Springer

The Law:
Sheldon	James Broderick
Moretti	Charles Durning
Carmine	Carmine Foresta
Murphy	Lance Henriksen
Phone Cop	Floyd Levine
Policeman with Angie	Thomas Murphy

The Family:
Vi's Husband	Dominic Chianese
Vi's Friend	Marcia Haufrecht
Vi	Judith Malina
Angie	Susan Peretz
Leon	Chris Sarandon

The Street:
TV Studio Anchorman	William Bogert
TV Reporter	Ron Cummins
Sam	Jay Gerber
Doctor	Philip Charles Mackenzie
Maria's Boyfriend	Chu Chu Malave
Pizza Boy	Lionel Pina
Limo Driver	Dick Williams

Left: John Cazale, Al Pacino

Sandra Kazan, Carol Kane, Penny Allen, Marcia Jean Kurtz, John Marriott, Al Pacino

Sully Boyar, Al Pacino, Lance Henrikson Top Left: Charles Durning Below: Al Pacino
Penny Allen Top Right: Al Pacino, below James Broderick, Chris Sarandon

THREE DAYS OF THE CONDOR

(PARAMOUNT) Producer, Stanley Schneider; Director, Sydney Pollack; Screenplay, Lorenzo Semple, Jr., David Rayfiel; Based on novel of same name by James Grady; Photography, Owen Roizman; Music, Dave Grusin; Designer, Stephen Grimes; Miss Dunaway's Clothes, Theoni V. Aldredge; Assistant Directors, Pete Scoppa, Mike Haley, Ralph Singleton, Kim Kurumada; Editor, Don Guidice; Costumes, Joseph C. Aulisi; A Milkwood Enterprises Co-Production; In Panavision and Technicolor; Rated R; 117 minutes; September release.

CAST

Turner	Robert Redford
Kathy	Faye Dunaway
Higgins	Cliff Robertson
Joubert	Max von Sydow
Mr. Wabash	John Houseman
Atwood	Addison Powell
Barber	Walter McGinn
Janice	Tina Chen
Wicks	Michael Kane
Dr. Lappe	Don McHenry
Fowler	Michael Miller
Mitchell	Jess Osuna
Thomas	Dino Narizzano
Mrs. Russell	Helen Stenborg
Martin	Patrick Gorman
Jennings	Hansford Rowe, Jr.
Mae Barber	Carlin Glynn
Mailman	Hank Garrett
Messenger	Arthur French
Tall Thin Man	Jay Devlin
Jimmy	Frank Savino
Newberry	Robert Phalen
Beefy Man	John Randolph Jones
Hutton	Garrison Phillips
Heidegger	Lee Steele
Ordinance Man	Ed Crowley
TV Reporter	John Connell
Alice Lieutenant	Norman Bush
Store Clerk	James Keane
Customer	Ed Setrakian
Civilians	Myron Natwick, Michael Prince
Landlady	Carol Gustafson
Locksmith	Sal Schillizi
CIA Agent	Harmon Williams
Telephone Worker	David Bowman
CIA Receptionist	Eileen Gordon
Santa Claus	Robert Dahdah
Kids	Steve Bonino, Jennifer Rose, David Allen, Glenn Ferguson, Paul Dwyer
Nurses	Marian Swan, Dorothi Fox
Teenager	Ernest Harden, Jr.

Left: Robert Redford, Tina Chen
Top: Robert Redford

Faye Dunaway, Cliff Robertson, Robert Redford

Jay Devlin, Max von Sydow, Hank Garrett

76

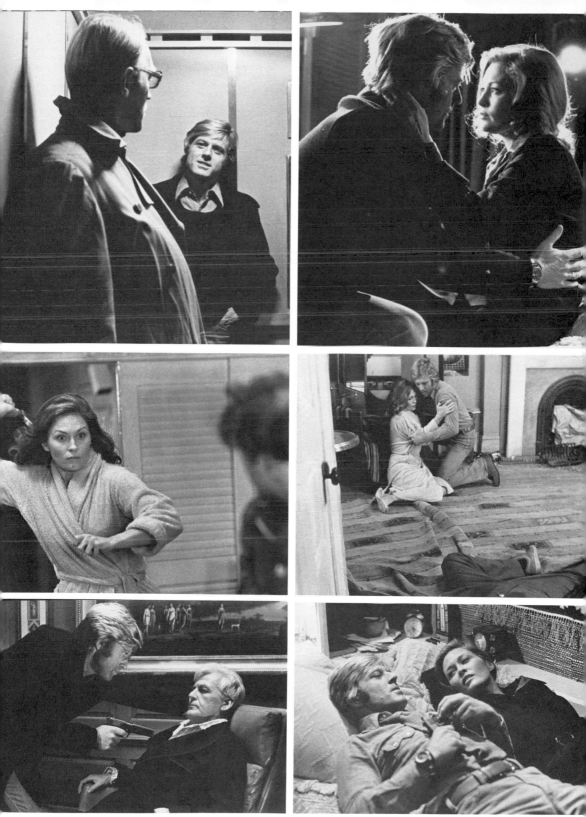

Robert Redford, Addison Powell Above: Hank
Garrett, Faye Dunaway Top: Max von Sydow,
Robert Redford

Robert Redford, Faye Dunaway
(also above and top)

HEARTS OF THE WEST

(UNITED ARTISTS) Producer, Tony Bill; Director, Howard Zieff; Screenplay, Bob Thompson; Photography, Mario Tosi; Editor, Edward Warschilka; Art Director, Robert Luthardt; Music, Ken Lauber; In Metrocolor; Rated PG; 102 minutes; October release.

CAST

Lewis Tater	Jeff Bridges
Howard Pike	Andy Griffith
A. J. Nietz	Donald Pleasence
Miss Trout	Blythe Danner
Kessler	Alan Arkin
Fat Man	Richard B. Shull
Polo	Herbert Edelman
Earl	Alex Rocco
Pa Tater	Frank Cady
Lean Man	Anthony James
Lester	Burton Gilliam
Jackson	Matt Clark
Waitress	Candy Azzara
Bank Manager	Thayer David
Lyle	Wayne Storm
Woman in Nevada	Marie Windsor

Left: Jeff Bridges

Alan Arkin, Jeff Bridges

Blythe Danner, Jeff Bridges Above: Alan Arkin (R)
Top: Danner, Andy Griffith

Blythe Danner, Alan Arkin Above: Tucker Smith
Top: Blythe Danner, Jeff Bridges

LET'S DO IT AGAIN

(WARNER BROS.) Producer, Melville Tucker; Director, Sidney Poitier; Screenplay, Richard Wesley; Story, Timothy March; Photography, Donald M. Morgan; Music, Curtis Mayfield; Associate Producer-Editor, Pembroke J. Herring; Designer, Alfred Sweeney; All songs performed by The Staple Singers; Assistant Directors, Reuben L. Watt, Richard A. Wells; In Technicolor; Rated PG; 112 minutes; October release.

CAST

Clyde Williams	Sidney Poitier
Billy Foster	Bill Cosby
Biggie Smalls	Calvin Lockhart
Kansas City Mack	John Amos
Beth Foster	Denise Nicholas
Dee Dee Williams	Lee Chamberlin
Ellison	Mel Stewart
Bubbletop Woodson	Julius Harris
Jody Tipps	Paul E. Harris
Lt. Bottomley	Val Avery
Bootney Farnsworth	Jimmie Walker
Elder Johnson	Ossie Davis

Right: Bill Cosby, Sidney Poitier Below: Val Avery, Poitier, Denise Nicholas, Lee Chamberlain

Julius Harris, John Amos, Paul Harris
Above: Talya Ferro, Denise Nicholas, Calvin Lockhart

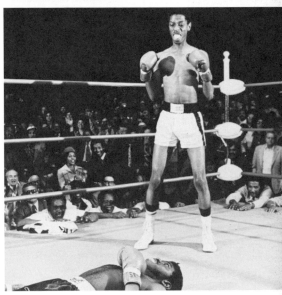

Rudolphus Lee Hayden, Jimmie Walker

ROOSTER COGBURN

(UNIVERSAL) Producer, Hal B. Wallis; Director, Stuart Millar; Screenplay, Martin Julien; Suggested by character in novel "True Grit" by Charles Portis; Photography, Harry Stradling, Jr.; Editor, Robert Swink; Art Director, Preston Ames; Music, Laurence Rosenthal; Miss Hepburn's Wardrobe, Edith Head; Assistant Directors, Pepi Lenzi, Richard Hashimoto; In Panavision and Technicolor; Rated PG; 107 minutes; October release.

CAST

Rooster Cogburn	John Wayne
Eula	Katharine Hepburn
Breed	Anthony Zerbe
McCoy	Strother Martin
Hawk,	Richard Jordan
Judge Parker	John McIntire
Luke	Paul Koslo
Red	Jack Colvin
Rev. Goodnight	Jon Lormer
Wolf	Richard Romancito
Leroy	Lane Smith
Babgy	Warren Vanders
Nose	Jerry Gatlin

Right: John Wayne, Katharine Hepburn

Katharine Hepburn, Jon Lormer Above: Richard Romancito, Hepburn, John Wayne, Strother Martin

Katharine Hepburn, John Wayne Above: John Wayne, John McIntire

MAHOGANY

(PARAMOUNT) Producers, Rob Cohen, Jack Ballard; Director, Berry Gordy; Screenplay, John Byrum; Based on story by Toni Amber; Photography, David Watkin; Editor, Peter Zinner; Costumes, Diana Ross; Art Directors, Leon Erickson, Aurelio Crugnola; Music, Michael Masser; Assistant Directors, Andrew Grieve, Robert Dahlin, Piero Amati; In Panavision and color; Rated PG; 109 minutes; October release.

CAST

Tracy (Mahogany)	Diana Ross
Brian	Billy Dee Williams
Sean	Anthony Perkins
Christian Rosetti	Jean-Pierre Aumont
Florence	Beah Richards
Miss Evans	Nina Foch
Carlotta Gavin	Marisa Mell
Wil	Lenard Norris
Stalker	Ira Rogers
Instructress	Kristine Cameron
Sweatshop Foreman	Ted Liss
Cab Driver	Marvin Corman
Radio Announcer	E. Rodney Jones
Giuseppe	Daniel Daniele
Princess Galitzine	Herself
Auctioneer	Jacques Stany
Designers	Bruce Vilanch, Don Howard, Albert Rosenberg

Right: Diana Ross, Billy Dee Williams
Below: Diana Ross, Jean-Pierre Aumont

Diana Ross

Anthony Perkins, Diana Ross

82

Billy Dee Williams, Anthony Perkins Left: Jean-Pierre
Aumont, Marisa Mell, Diana Ross Top: Ross, Williams,
Perkins

THE MASTER GUNFIGHTER

(TAYLOR-LAUGHLIN) Producer, Philip P. Parslow, Director,
Frank Laughlin; Photography, Jack A. Marta; Editors, William
Reynolds, Danford Greene; Music, Lalo Schifrin; In color; Rated
PG; 121 minutes; October release.

CAST

Finley	Tom Laughlin
Paulo	Ron O'Neal
Chorika	Geo Anne Sosa
Eula	Barbara Carrera

Tom Laughlin, Barbara Carrera

HESTER STREET

(MIDWEST) Producer, Raphael D. Silver; Written and Directed by Joan Micklin Silver; Adapted from "Yekl" by Abraham Cahan; Photography, Kenneth Van Sickle; Editor, Katherine Wenning; Music, William Bolcom; In black and white; Rated PG; 92 minutes; October release.

CAST

Jake	Steven Keats
Gitl	Carol Kane
Bernstein	Mel Howard
Mamie	Dorrie Kavanaugh
Mrs. Kavarsky	Doris Roberts
Joe Peltner	Stephen Strimpell
Fanny	Lauren Frost
Joey	Paul Freedman
Rabbi	Zvee Scooler
Rabbi's Wife	Eda Reiss Merin

Left: Carol Kane, Mel Howard

Steven Keats, Carol Kane, Paul Freedman

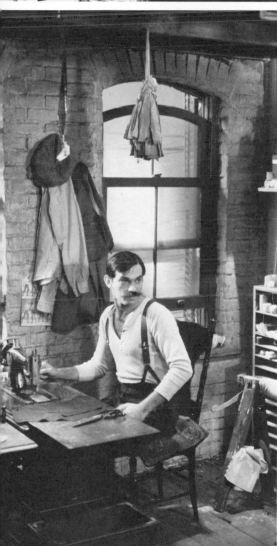

**Steven Keats, and above with Zvee Cooler,
Carol Kane**

Carol Kane
Above: Mel Howard, Paul Freedman

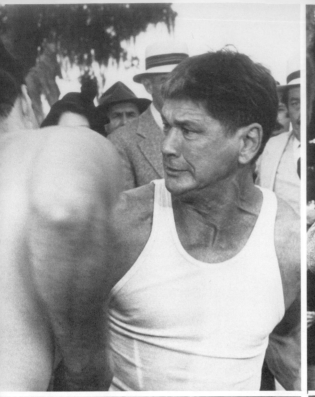

HARD TIMES

(COLUMBIA) Producer, Lawrence Gordon; Executive Producer, Paul Maslansky; Director, Walter Hill; Screenplay, Walter Hill, Bryan Gindorff, Bruce Henstell; Story, Bryan Gindorff, Bruce Henstell; Photography, Philip Lathrop; Editor, Roger Spottiswoode; Music, Barry DeVorzon; Art Director, Trevor Williams; Assistant Director, Michael Daves; In Metrocolor; Rated PG; 92 minutes; October release.

CAST

Chaney	Charles Bronson
Speed	James Coburn
Lucy	Jill Ireland
Poe	Strother Martin
Gayleen	Maggie Blye
Gandil	Michael McGuire
Jim Henry	Robert Tessier
Street	Nick Dimitri
Le Beau	Felice Orlandi
Doty	Bruce Glover
Pettibon	Edward Walsh

Charles Bronson, and above with James Coburn, Felice Orlandi

Top: James Coburn, Charles Bronson
Below: Nick Dimitri, Charles Bronson

THE HUMAN FACTOR

(BRYANSTON) Producer, Frank Avianca; Executive Producer, Terry Lens; Director, Edward Dmytryk; Screenplay, Tom Hunter, Peter Powell; Music, Enrico Moriconi, Associate Producer, Peter Inwards; Assistant Directors, Ray Frift, Peter Bennett, Andy Armstrong; Photography, Qusama Rawi; Editor, Alan Strachen; Assistant Director, Ferinando Monaco; In color; Rated R; 96 minutes; October release.

CAST

John Kinsdale	George Kennedy
Mike McAllister	John Mills
Dr. Lupo	Raf Vallone
General Fuller	Arthur Franz
Janice	Rita Tushingham
Kamal	Frank Avianca
Pidgeon	Haydee Politoff
Taylor	Tom Hunter
Edmonds	Barry Sullivan
Ann Kinsdale	Fiamma Verges
Mark Kinsdale	Danny Houston
Phillips	Michael Mandeville
Jeffrey Kinsdale	Ricky Harrison
Linda Kinsdale	Hillary Lief
Eddy Fonseca	Robert Lowell
Agnes Fonseca	Mrs. Robert Lowell
Carter (CIA)	Shane Rimmer
Mrs. Simpson	Anne Ferguson
Mr. Gerardi	Lewis Charles
Mrs. Gerardi	Corinne Dunne
Alice Garardi	Sharon Kellogg
Rodney Gerardi	Eugene Wade
Aldo	West Buchanan
Sandra Pallavicini	Conchita Airoldi
CIA Man	Joe Jenkins
Lupo's Driver	Vincenzo Crocitti

Right: John Mills, George Kennedy, and below with Raf Vallone

John Mills, Arthur Franz
Above: George Kennedy

Frank Avianca

ONE FLEW OVER THE CUCKOO'S NEST

(UNITED ARTISTS) Producers, Saul Zaentz, Michael Douglas; Director, Milos Forman; Screenplay, Lawrence Hauben, Bo Goldman; Based on novel of same title by Ken Kesey; Photography, Haskell Wexler, William Fraker, Bill Butler; Music, Jack Nitzsche; Editors, Richard Chew, Lynzee Klingman, Sheldon Kahn; Associate Producer, Martin Fink; Designer, Paul Sylbert; Art Director, Edwin O'Donovan; Assistant Directors, Irby Smith, William St. John; In color; Rated R; 129 minutes; November release.

CAST

R. P. McMurphy	Jack Nicholson
Nurse Ratched	Louise Fletcher
Harding	William Redfield
Ellis	Michael Berryman
Billy Bibbit	Brad Dourif
Col. Matterson	Peter Brocco
Dr. Spivey	Dean R. Brooks
Miller	Alonzo Brown
Turkle	Sherman "Scatman" Crothers
Warren	Mwako Cumbuka
Martini	Danny De Vito
Sefelt	William Duell
Bancini	Josip Elic
Nurse Itsu	Lan Fendors
Washington	Nathan George
Beans Garfield	Ken Kenny
Harbor Master	Mel Lambert
Cheswick	Sydney Lassick
Night Supervisor	Kay Lee
Taber	Christopher Lloyd
Ellsworth	Dwight Marfield
Hap Arlich	Ted Markland
Rose	Louisa Moritz
Woolsey	Phil Roth
Chief Bromden	Will Sampson
Nurse Pilbow	Mimi Sarkisian
Fredrickson	Vincent Schiavelli
Candy	Marya Small
Scanlon	Delos V. Smith, Jr.
Ruckley	Tin Welch

Left: Jack Nicholson, also above
with Bob Milan
*1975 Academy Awards for Best Picture,
Best Screenplay, Best Actor (Nicholson)
Best Actress (Fletcher), Best Director*

Danny DeVito, Jack Nicholson,
Christopher Lloyd

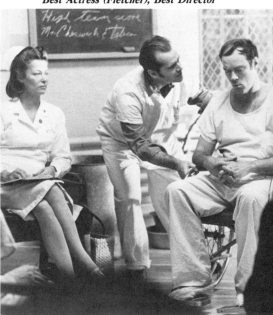

Louise Fletcher, Jack Nicholson,
Ted Markland

Jack Nicholson, Marya Small Above: William Duell,
Vincent Schiavelli, Delos V. Smith, Jr., Nicholson,
Brad Dourif, William Redfield Top: Louise Fletcher,
Jack Nicholson

Louise Fletcher, Brad Dourif, Nathan George
Top: Josip Elic, Jack Nicholson, Will Sampson

THE SUNSHINE BOYS

(UNITED ARTISTS) Producer, Ray Stark; Director, Herbert Ross; Screenplay, Neil Simon from his play of the same title; Associate Producer, Roger M. Rothstein; Photography, David M. Walsh; Designer, Albert Brenner; Editors, Margaret Booth, John F. Burnett; A Rastar Production; In Panavision and Metrocolor; Rated PG; 111 minutes; November release.

CAST

Willy Clark	Walter Matthau
Al Lewis	George Burns
Ben Clark	Richard Benjamin
Nurse in sketch	Lee Meredith
Doris	Carol Arthur
Nurse	Rosetta LeNoire
Mechanic	F. Murray Abraham
Commercial Director	Howard Hesseman
TV Director	Jim Cranna
TV Floor Manager	Ron Rifkin
Helen	Jennifer Lee
Men at audition	Fritz Feld, Jack Bernardi
Stage Manager	Garn Stephens
Desk Clerk	Santos Morales
Assistant at audition	Archie Hahn
Patient	Sid Gould
Card Player	Tom Spratley
Woman in hotel	Rashel Novikoff
Man on street	Sammy Smith
Mr. Ferranti	Dan Resin
Doctor	Milt Kogan
Waiter	Bob Goldstein

Richard Benjamin, Walter Matthau
Top: George Burns, Walter Matthau

George Burns received a 1975 Academy Award for Best Supporting Actor

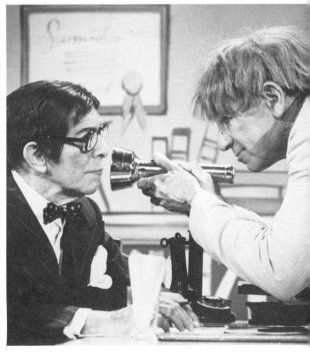

George Burns, Lee Meredith, Walter Matthau
Above: Richard Benjamin, Jennifer Lee
Top: George Burns, Walter Matthau

George Burns, Walter Matthau
also above

THE KILLER ELITE

(UNITED ARTISTS) Co-Producers, Martin Baum, Arthur Lewis; Executive Producer, Helmut Dantine; Director, Sam Peckinpah; Music, Jerry Fielding; Screenplay, Stirling Silliphant; Photography, Phil Lathrop; Associate Producer, Joel Freeman; Assistant Directors, Newton Arnold, Ron Wright, Jim Bloom, Cliff Coleman; An Exeter/Persky-Bright Feature; In color; Rated PG; 130 minutes; December release.

CAST

Mike Locken	James Caan
George Hansen	Robert Duvall
Cap Collis	Arthur Hill
Laurence Weyburn	Gig Young
Yuen Chung	Mako
Miller	Bo Hopkins
Mac	Burt Young
O'Leary	Tom Clancy
Tommie Chung	Tiana
Amy	Katy Heflin
Tao Yi	James Wing Woo
Bruce	George Kee Cheung
Jimmy Fung	Simon Tam
Ben Otake	Rick Alemany
Hank	Hank Hamilton
Walter	´Walter Kelley
Eddie	Billy J. Scott
Donnie	Johnnie Burrell
Kid	Matthew Peckinpah

Left: James Caan

Robert Duvall, James Caan, Helmut Dantine

James Caan Above: Bo Hopkins Top: Bo
Hopkins, James Caan

Tiana Above: Johnnie
Burrell, James Caan

93

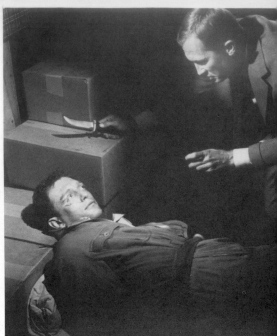

THE HINDENBURG

(UNIVERSAL) Director, Robert Wise; Screenplay, Nelson Gidding; Story, Richard Levinson, William Link; Based on book by Michael M. Mooney; Photography, Robert Surtees; Designer, Edward Carfagno; Editor, Donn Cambern; Music, David Shire; Costumes, Dorothy Jeakins; Assistant Directors, Howard Kazanjian, Wayne Farlow; A Filmakers Group Production; In Technicolor-black and white; Rated PG; 125 minutes; December release.

CAST

Ritter	George C. Scott
The Countess	Anne Bancroft
Boerth	William Atherton
Martin Vogel	Roy Thinnes
Edward Douglas	Gig Young
Emilio Pajetta	Burgess Meredith
Captain Pruss	Charles Durning
Lehmann	Richard A. Dysart
Joe Spah	Robert Clary
Major Napier	Rene Auberjonois
Reed Channing	Peter Donat
Albert Breslau	Alan Oppenheimer
Mrs. Mildred Breslau	Katherine Helmond
Mrs. Channing	Joanna Moore
Capt. Fellows	Stephen Elliott
Eleanore Ritter	Joyce Davis
Valerie Breslau	Jean Rasey
Knorr	Ted Gehring
Freda Halle	Lisa Pera
Schulz	Joe di Reda
Ludecke	Peter Canon
Kirsch	Charles Macaulay
Dimmler	Rex Holman
Speck	Jan Merlin

Betsy Jones-Moreland (Stewardess Imhoff), Colby Chester (Eliot Howell III), Teno Pollick (Frankel), Curt Lowens (Elevator Man), Kip Niven (Lt. Truscott), Michael Richardson (Rigger), Herbert Nelson (Dr. Eckener), Scott Walker (Gestapo Major), Ruth Kobart (Hattie), Greg Mullavey (Morrison), Val Bisoglio (Lt. Lombardi), Simon Scott (Luftwaffe General), William Sylvester (Luftwaffe Colonel), David Mauro (Goebbels), Joseph Turkel (Det. Moore), Sandy Ward (Det. Grunberger), Johnny Lee (Paul Breslau), Stephen Manley (Peter Breslau)

Burgess Meredith, Anne Bancroft Above: George C. Scott, Rene Auberjonois, Roy Thinnes, Meredith, Bancroft

**Top: William Atherton, Roy Thinnes
Left: William Sylvester, George C. Scott**

LUCKY LADY

(20th CENTURY-FOX) Producer, Michael Grushkoff; Director, Stanley Donen; Screenplay, Willard Huyck, Gloria Katz; Music, Ralph Burns; Songs, Fred Ebb, John Kander; Photography, Geoffrey Unsworth; Editors, Peter Boita, George Hively; In color; Rated PG; 118 minutes; December release.

CAST

Kibby	Gene Hackman
Claire	Liza Minnelli
Walker	Burt Reynolds
Capt. Aaron Mosley	Geoffrey Lewis
Christy McTcague	John Hillerman
Billy Webber	Robby Benson
Capt. Rockwell	Michael Hordern
Mr. Tully	Anthony Holland
Rass Huggins	John McLiam
Dolph	Val Avery
Bernie	Louis Guss
Charley	William H. Bassett
"Ybarra"	Emilio Fernandez

Right: Burt Reynolds, Liza Minnelli, and below with Gene Hackman

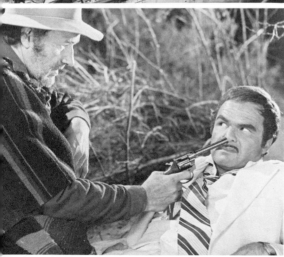

Gene Hackman, Burt Reynolds, and above with Robby Benson, Liza Minnelli

Liza Minnelli

HUSTLE

(PARAMOUNT) Producer-Director, Robert Aldrich; Screenplay, Steve Shagan; Photography, Joseph Biroc; Associate Producer, William Aldrich; Music, Frank DeVol; Art Director, Hilyard Brown; Editor, Michael Luciano; Assistant Directors, Malcolm Harding, Phil Ball,/Song "Yesterday When I Was Young" by Charles Aznavour; English lyrics, Herbert Kretzmer; Sung by Charles Aznavour; Choreography, Alex Romero; In color; Rated R; 120 minutes; December release.

CAST

Lt. Phil Gaines	Burt Reynolds
Nicole Britton	Catherine Deneuve
Marty Hollinger	Ben Johnson
Sgt. Louis Belgrave	Paul Winfield
Paula Hollinger	Eileen Brennan
Leo Sellers	Eddie Albert
Santoro	Ernest Borgnine
Peggy Summers	Catherine Bach
Herbie Dalitz	Jack Carter
Bus Driver	James Hampton
Gloria Hollinger	Sharon Kelly
Morgue Attendant	Chuck Hayward
Albino	David Estridge
Minister	Peter Brandon
Jerry Bellamy	David Spielberg
Woman Hostage	Naomi Stevens
Albino Beating Cop	Med Flory
Cops in elevator	Steve Shaw, Dino Washington
Laugher	Anthony Eldridge

and John Duke Russo, Don Billett, Hal Baylor, Nancy Bonniwell, Don "Red" Barry, Karl Lukas, Gene Chronopoulos, Patrice Rohmer, Alvin Hammer, Dave Willock, Queenie Smith, Marilyn Moe, Robert Englund, George Memoli, Fred Willard, Thad Geer, Kelly Wilder, Ben Young, Tasso Bravos, Jimmy R. Hampton, Nathan Hardin, John Furlong, Jason Wingreen, Ron Nyman, Victoria Carroll

Left: Burt Reynolds, Catherine Deneuve

Ben Johnson, Eileen Brennan

Burt Reynolds, Eddie Albert Above: Reynolds, Paul Winfield, Ernest Borgnine

Eddie Albert, Catherine Deneuve Above: Ben Johnson, Eileen Brennan, Paul Winfield, Burt Reynolds Top: Reynolds, Deneuve

Catherine Deneuve, Paul Winfield Above: Robert Englund, Burt Reynolds Top: Reynolds, Jack Carter

THE BLACK BIRD

(COLUMBIA) Producers, Michael Levee, Lou Lombardo; Executive Producer, George Segal; Direction and Screenplay, David Giler; Story, Don M. Mankiewicz, Gordon Cotler; Photography, Phil Lathrop; Editors, Margaret Booth, Walter Thompson, Lou Lombardo; Music, Jerry Fielding; Designer, Harry Horner; Assistant Director, Art Levinson; In Metrocolor; Rated PG; 98 minutes; December release.

CAST

Sam Spade, Jr	George Segal
Anna Kemidon	Stephane Audran
Immelman	Lionel Stander
Effie	Lee Patrick
Wilmer	Elisha Cook, Jr.
Litvak	Felix Silla
Dr. Crippen	Signe Hasso
DuQuai	John Abbott
Decoy Girl	Connie Kreski
Hawaiian Thugs	Titus Napoleon, Harry Kenoi
Kerkorian	Howard Jeffrey
Prizer	Richard B. Shull
McGregor	Ken Swafford

Left: Stephane Audran, George Segal Top: George Segal, Lionel Stander, Stephane Audran, Lee Patrick

Signe Hasso, George Segal

Stephane Audran, George Segal Above: Lee Patrick, Lionel Stander, George Segal

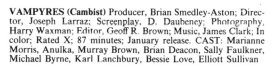

"Vampyres"   "Refinements in Love"

VAMPYRES (Cambist) Producer, Brian Smedley-Aston; Director, Joseph Larraz; Screenplay, D. Daubeney; Photography, Harry Waxman; Editor, Geoff R. Brown; Music, James Clark; In color; Rated X; 87 minutes; January release. CAST: Marianne Morris, Anulka, Murray Brown, Brian Deacon, Sally Faulkner, Michael Byrne, Karl Lanchbury, Bessie Love, Elliott Sullivan

HOW COME NOBODY'S ON OUR SIDE? (American Films Ltd.) Producer, Maurice Smith; Director, Richard Michaels; Screenplay, Leigh Chapman; Editor, Rick Beckmeyer; Photography, Jack Beckett; Music, Lamont Johnson, Sun Moon & Stars, B.M.I.; All vocals by Arthur Johnson; Assistant Directors, John Anderson, Charles Norton; Associate Producer, Jean Blake; In Movielab Color; Rated PG; 84 minutes; January release. CAST: Adam Roarke (Person), Larry Bishop (Brandy), Alexandra Hay (Brigitte), Rob Reiner (Miguelito), Penny Marshall (Theresa), John Garwood (Border Guard), Eldon Quick (Hal), Richard Yniguez (Juan), Robert Rothwell (Lawyer), Betty Hanna (Receptionist), Gil Barreta (Farmer), Bert Madrid (Store Owner), Eddie Lo Russo (Truck Driver), Priscilla Garcia (Pisces Girl), Roger La Joie (Theatre Manager), Margaret Garcia (Juan's Mother), Woody Lee (Bartender), George Banks (Second Guard), Bill Barney, Bob Tessier (Bike Riders)

THE NAUGHTY STEWARDESSES (Independent International) Director, Al Adamson; In Movielab Color; Rated R; 102 minutes; January release. CAST: Robert Livingston, Connie Hoffman, Donna Desmond, Tracy King, Richard Smedley, Sydney Jordan, Addison Randall, Jerry Mills

TEENAGE MILKMAID (Monarch) Produced, Directed and Written by Roberta Findlay; Presented by Allan Shackleton; In color; Rated X; 82 minutes; January release. CAST: Cathy Correl, Tony Day

THE WHISTLE BLOWERS (Dielst) Director, Milton Vickers; In color; Rated X; January release. CAST: Tanya Tickler, Gail Sunshine, Tina Russell, Sam Reilly, Bigelow Small

UP YOUR ALLEY (Group I) Director, Art Lieberman; In color; Rated R; January release. CAST: Frank Corsentino, Haji, Gordon McGill

REFINEMENTS IN LOVE (Hollywood International) Produced, Directed and Photographed by Carlos Tobalina; In color; Rated X; 90 minutes; January release. CAST: Liz Renay, George Bernard Sands, Ron Darby, Anita de Moulin, Susan Harbor, Rose Monroe

BROKEN TREATY AT BATTLE MOUNTAIN (Soho Cinema) Producer-Director, Joel L. Freeman; Narrated by Robert Redford; A documentary in color; 60 minutes; January release.

BIRTH OF A LEGEND (American National Enterprises) Producer, CVD Studios; Director, Dick Robinson; In color; Rated G; January release. A wildlife documentary.

ECSTASY OF THE MACUMBA (Hollywood International) A Carlos Tobalina Production; In color; Rated X; January release. CAST: Nina Fause, John Fox, Heather Leight

I'M A STRANGER HERE MYSELF (October) Producer, James Gutman; Director, David Helpern, Jr.; Written by Myron Meisel, James Gutman, David Helpern, Jr.; Narrated by Howard Da Silva; Photography, Austin de Besche; Editors, Richard Bock, Frank Galvin; In color; 61 minutes; January release. A documentary on film director Nicholas Ray.

BROTHER OF THE WIND (Sun International) Producers, Dick Robinson, John Mahon; Director, Dick Robinson; Screenplay, John Mahon; Executive Producer, G. M. Ridges; Narration written by John Champion; Narrated by Leon Ames; Photography, Rod Lackey; Editors, John Joyce, John W. Levins; In color; Rated G; 87 minutes; January release. CAST: Dick Robinson (Sam Monroe)

NOTHING BY CHANCE (R. C. Riddle) Producer-Director, William H. Barnett; Narration written by Richard Bach based on his book of the same title; Narrated by Hugh Downs; Photography, Flemming Olsen, Mogens Gander; Music, Lee Holdridge; Executive Producer, Hugh Downs; Associate Producer, Molly McGreevy; A Raylin Productions and Creature Enterprises presentation; In color; Rated G; 93 minutes; January release. CAST: Richard Bach, Jack Brown, Chris Cagle, Stu MacPherson, Spence Nelson, Glenn Norman, Steve Young

Larry Bishop, Alexandra Hay, Adam Roarke in "How Come Nobody's on Our Side?"

"Broken Treaty at Battle Mountain"

"Nana, Mom and Me"

Keenan Wynn
in "The Legend of Earl Durand"

NANA, MOM AND ME (New Day) Producer-Director, Amalie R. Rothschild; Editors, Browen Sennish, Amalie R. Rothschild; Photography, Danie Drasin, Amalie R. Rothschild; Music, Randolph S. Rothschild; In color; 47 minutes; January release. CAST: Amalie Randolph Rothschild, Amalie Rosenfeld Rothschild, Addye Goldsmith Rosenfeld.

PACIFIC CHALLENGE (Concord) Producer, Manuel Arango; Direction and Screenplay, Robert Amram; Narrated by Robert Webber; Photography, Gaston Collin, Greg Holden, Tom Ward, Robert Hillman, Armando Carillo, John Carnemolla, Alvin Lawson, Bob Collins; Editors, Henry Berman, Frank C. Decot, Dick Weber; Music, Bill Conti; In CFI Color; Rated G; 83 minutes; January release. CAST: Vital Alsar, Marc Modena, Jorge Ramirez, Gabriel Salas, Gaston Collin, Fernand Robichaud, Tom McCormick, Mike Fitzgibbons, Tom Ward, Anibal Guevara, Hugo Becerra, Greg Holden

ONE BY ONE (Leavell-Brunswick) Producer, Peter Leavell; Director, Claude DuBoc; Narrator, Stacy Keach; In color; 100 minutes; January release. A documentary about car racing featuring Francois Cevert, Peter Revson, Jackie Stewart, Mile Hailwood

BLACK STARLETT (Omni) Executive Producer, Ken Rogers; Producer, Daniel B. Cady; Director, Chris Munger; Screenplay, Howard Ostroff; Story, Daniel B. Cady; Music, Joe Hinton, Dee Ervin; Assistant Director, Duane Hartzell, Damu King; Editors, Warren Hamilton, Jr., Don Walters; In color; Rated R; 90 minutes; January release. CAST: Juanita Brown (Clara/Carla), Eric Mason (Briscoe), Damu King (Scully), Rockne Tarkington (Ben), Diane Holden (Joyce), Noah Keen (Phil), Peter Dane (Les), Al Lewis (Sam), Crane Jackson, Nicholas Worth, Rai Tasco, Jack Donner, Kip King, James Broadhead, Joe Billings, Marlene Selsman, Gary Battaglia, James Paul Vitale, Emanuel Thomas, Marland Proctor

THE LEGEND OF EARL DURAND (Howco International) Producer-Director, John D. Patterson; Screenplay, J. Frank James; Music, Jack Elliott, Allyn Ferguson; In color; Rated PG; 110 minutes; January release. CAST· Peter Haskell, Slim Pickens, Keenan Wynn, Martin Sheen, Anthony Caruso, Albert Salmi

SEXUAL ECSTASY OF THE MACUMBA (Hollywood International) Director, Jeremiah Schlotter; Screenplay, Mike Merino, Susane Foughtz; Editors, Lawrence Dolph, Susan Wang; Photography, Shang Fu K; Rated X; January release. CAST: Nina Fause, John Fox, Stacy Holmes, Jeff DuClois, Bob Ricardi, Susi Wenien, Rose Dolores, Linda Rabin

STREET GIRLS (New World) Producers, Paul Ponpian, Jeff Begun; Director, Michael Miller; Screenplay, Barry Levinson, Michael Miller; Songs, Muddy Waters, Terry Smith; In Metrocolor; Rated R; 84 minutes; January release. CAST: Carol Case (Sally), Christine Souder (Angel), Paul Pompian (Irv), Art Burke (Sven), Jimmy Smith (Jimmy), Michael Albert Weber (Michael), Jay Deringer (Mario), Linda Reynolds (Adele), Fred Garra (Roy), B. J. Harris

THE SENSUOUS THREE (Group I) Director, Steve Amberg; In color; Rated R; 95 minutes; January release. CAST: Jennifer Ames, Althea Grant, Anthony Harms, Marie Anders, Carol Flynn

DEAR DEAD DELILAH (Southern Star) Producer, Jack Clement; Direction and Screenplay, John Farris; In Eastmancolor; Rated R; 95 minutes; January release. CAST: Agnes Moorehead (Delilah), Will Geer (Ray), Michael Ansara (Morgan), Patricia Carmichael (Luddy), Dennis Patrick (Alonzo), Anne Meacham (Grace), Robert Gentry (Richard), Elizabeth Eis (Ellen), Ruth Baker (Buffy), Ann Giggs (Young Luddy), John Marriott (Marshall)

THE NIGHT GOD SCREAMED (Cinemation) Producers, Gil Lasky, Ed Carlin; Director, Lee Madden; Screenplay, Gil Lasky; In color; Rated R; 85 minutes; January release. CAST: Jeanne Crain, Alex Nichol, Daniel Spelling, Michael Sugich, Barbara Hancock, Dawn Cleary, Gary Morgan

Michael Ansara
in "Dear Dead Delilah"

Joe Flynn, Eve Arden
in "The Strongest Man in the World"

**Mackenzie Phillips, Sally Kellerman, Alan Arkin
in "Rafferty and the Gold Dust Twins"**

**Divine
in "Female Trouble"**

DEFIANCE (Stu Segall Associates) Producer, Jason Russel; Direction and Screenplay, Armand Weston; Photography, Steve Todd; Set and Costumes, Tyrone Brown; Editor, James Cutwelle; Music, Alex Allan; In color; Rated x; 78 minutes; January release. CAST: Jean Jennings (Cathy), Fred Lincoln (Dr. Gabriel), Day Jason (Susan), Holly Landis (Cathy's Mother), Roderick Usher (Cathy's Father), Ellen Hill (Miss Caine), David Harrison (Krausse), Kevin Andre (Hirsch), Turk Turpin (Male Nurse), Dulce Mann (Nurse), Frank Baker (Orderly), Tony Marcus, Marc Stevens, Barry Clarke, Sandy Foxx, Michael Johns, Tyrone Lowe, Doug Johns, Faith Jones, Mickie Oats, Sal Sanderone, Jaime Gillis, Pam Sanders, Sonny Landham, Alexander Life, Jack Conner

RAFFERTY AND THE GOLD DUST TWINS (Warner Bros.) Producers, Michael Gruskoff, Art Linson; Director, Dick Richards; Screenplay, John Kaye; Photography, Ralph Woosley; Editor, Walter Thompson; Music, Artie Butler; Associate Producer, Jerry Bruckheimer; Art Director, Joel Schiller; Assistant Director, Charles Myers; A Gruskoff/Venture/Linson Production; In Panavision and Technicolor; Rated R; 92 minutes; February release. CAST: Alan Arkin (Rafferty), Sally Kellerman (Mac), MacKenzie Phillips (Frisbee), Alex Rocco (Vinnie), Charlie Martin Smith (Alan), Harry Dean Stanton (Billy), John McLiam (John), Richard Hale (Jesus Freak), Louis Prima (Himself), Sam Butera (Himself)

THE STRONGEST MAN IN THE WORLD (Buena Vista) Producer, Bill Anderson; Director, Vincent McEveety; Screenplay, Joseph L. McEveety, Herman Groves; Photography, Andrew Jackson; Music, Robert F. Brunner; Art Directors, John B. Mansbridge, Jack Senter; Editor, Cotton Warburton; Assistant Directors, Dick Caffey, Pat Kehoe; Costumes, Chuck Keehne, Emily Sundby; A Walt Disney Production in Technicolor; Rated G; 92 minutes; February release. CAST: Kurt Russell (Dexter), Joe Flynn (Dean Higgins), Eve Arden (Harriet), Cesar Romero (A. J.), Phil Silvers (Krinkle), Dick Van Patten (Harry), Harold Gould (Dietz), Michael McGreevey (Schuyler), Dick Bakalyan (Cookie), William Schallert (Quigley), Benson Fong (Ah Fong), James Gregory (Chief Blair)

FEMALE TROUBLE (New Line Cinema) Written, Directed, Filmed by John Waters, Editor, Charles Roggero; Art Director, Vincent Peranio; Costumes, Van Smith; A Dreamland Production in color; Rated X; 95 minutes; February release. CAST: Divine (Dawn/Earl), David Lochary (Donald), Mary Vivian Pearce (Donna), Mink Stole (Taffy), Edith Massey (Ida), Cookie Mueller (Concetta), Susan Walsh (Chiclett), Michael Potter (Gater), Ed Peranio (Wink), Paul Swift (Butterfly), George Figgs (Dribbles), Susan Lowe (Vikki), George Hulse (Teacher), Roland Hertz (Dawn's Father), Betty Woods (Mother), Hilary Taylor (Taffy as a child), Channing Wilroy (Prosecutor), Seymour Avigdor (Defense Lawyer), Elizabeth Coffey (Ernestine)

ARTHUR RUBINSTEIN LOVE OF LIFE (New Yorker) Producers, Francois Reichenbach, Bernard Gavoty; Directors, Francois Reichenbach, S. G. Patris; In color; February release. A documentary with Arthur Rubinstein, Mrs. Rubinstein, Israeli Philarmonic, and Paris Orchestras.

ALL THE YOUNG WIVES (International Cinefilm) Producer-Director, Mike Ripps; In color; Rated R; 92 minutes; January release. CAST: Gerald Richards, Linda Cook, Edmond Genest, Johnny Popwell, April Johnson, Philip Pleasants

ASYLUM OF SATAN (Studio I) Producer, J. Patrick Kelly III; Direction, Music and Screenplay, William Girdler; Photography, William Asman; Editor, Gene Ruggiero; In Color; Rated PG; February release. CAST: Charles Kissinger, Carla Borelli, Nick Jolly

NYMPH (Jack H. Harris) Producer, Tom Blanchard; Director, William Dear; In color; Rated R; February release. CAST: Peggy Kramer, Burton Dunning, Jack Donachie

SASSY SUE (Boxoffice International) Direction and Screenplay, Buckalew; In Movielab Color; February release. CAST: John Tully, Sharon Kelly, Talie Cochrane, Rachel Wols

HYPNOROTICA (Savage Enterprises) Produced, Directed and Written by Armond Peters; In color; Rated X; February release. CAST: Tina Russell, Andrea True

**Kurt Russell
in "The Strongest Man in the World"**

"Arthur Rubinstein Love of Life"

"Panorama Blue"

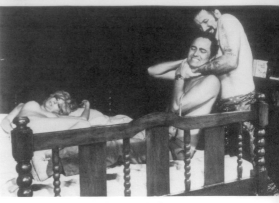

"Dragon Lady"

PANORAMA BLUE (Ellman Film Enterprises) Producer-Director, Alan Roberts; Screenplay, Steve Michaels; Costumes, Leigh Mitchell; Associate Producers, Donald Alvin, Thomas Shelton, Bernard Ellman, Stephen B. Ginsberg; Photography, Bob Brownell; Editor, James Walters; Music, Steve Michaels; Executive Producer; In Super Widescreen Panoramascope and color; 85 minutes; February release. CAST: Richard S. Ellman (Host), Carona Faoro, Stephen Nave, Sue Moses, Dennis Zlamal, Rene Bond, Sandy Dempsey, John Paul Jones, Ric Loots, Linda York, John Holmes, Rene Bond, Rick Cassidy, Sandy Dempsey, Uschi Digard, Bob Silvani, John Holmes, Dristi Fletcher, Charlotte Ruse, Bob Taylor, Reg Bartram, Melody Dillberg, Jenni Such, Lizzy Koske, Ruth Robinson, Sidney Jollivette, John Cole, Randolph Hardesty, Ron Lawrence, Kristin Schwarzer, Duane Paulsen, Rick West, Mary Ann Whitney, William Margold, Con Covert, Johna Lee, Liz Wolfe, Robert De Chatelenne, Cyndee Summers, Rick Cassidy, Roberto Rogisini

THE GOOD THE BAD AND THE BEAUTIFUL (Orrin) In color; Rated R; 82 minutes; February release. CAST: Allan Garfield, Janis Young, Jennifer Welles, Harold Herbsman

WIN, PLACE OR STEAL (Cinema National) formerly "Three for the Money"; Producer, Thomas D. Cooney; Director, Richard Bailey; Screenplay, Anthony Monaco, Richard Bailey; Music, Tim McIntire; A Syn-Frank Enterprises Presentation in Eastmancolor; Rated PG; 81 minutes; February release. CAST: Dean Stockwell, Russ Tamblyn, Alex Karras, McLean Stevenson, Alan Oppenheimer, Kristina Holland, Harry Dean Stanton, Liv Von Linden

I AM CURIOUS TAHITI (Hollywood International) Produced, Directed and Photographed by Carlos Tobalina; In color; Rated X; February release. CAST: Maria Pia, William Larra Bure, Leticia Young, Susane Parker, Jay Colonna

THE PRIVATE AFTERNOONS OF PAMELA MANN (Hudson Valley) Director, Henry Paris; In Eastmancolor; Rated X; 88 minutes; February release. CAST: Barbara Bourbon, Marc Stevens, Georgina Spelvin, Eric Edwards, Kevin Andre, Naomi Jason, Darby Lloyd Rains, Jamie Gillis, Sonny Landhan, John Ashton, Lola LaGrace, Alan Marlow

DRAGON LADY (Joseph Green) Producer, Marvin Farkas; Associate Producers, Water Hoffman, S. M. Churn; Director, Joel M. Reed; In color; Rated R; February release. CAST: Tom Keena, Anna Ling, Vicki Racimo, Angelique Pettyjohn

BOGARD (L-T Films) Producers, Peter S. Traynor, William D. Sklar; Director, Timothy Galfas; Screenplay, Tim Kelly, Melvyn Frohman; Music, Ed Townsend; A Centaur Film; In color; Rated X; 87 minutes; February release. CAST: Richard Lawson (Leroy), Dabney Coleman (Cop), Robert Burr, Anazette Chase, Joseph Ruskin, Sherry Boucher

L'CHAIM—TO LIFE (American Women's Organization for Rehabilitation) Producer-Director, Harold Mayer; Written by Lynne Rhodes Mayer; Narrated by Eli Wallach; Editor, Alan Pesetsky; Not rated; 84 minutes; February release. A documentary covering the struggles of Russian Jewry from the 17th century.

BOSS NIGGER (Dimension) Producers, Fred Williamson, Jack Arnold; Director, Jack Arnold; Screenplay, Fred Williamson; Rated PG; 87 minutes; February release. CAST: Fred Williamson (Boss Nigger), D'Urville Martin (Amos), H. H. Armstrong (Mayor), William Smith (Jed), Carmen Hayworth (Clara Mae), Barbara Lee (Miss Pruitt)

CHINA GIRL (Variety) Producer, Summer Brown; Director, Paolo Uccello; Screenplay, Edwin Brown; Music, Hadley Calliman; In Eastmancolor; Rated X; February release. CAST: Anette Haven

THE OUTER SPACE CONNECTION (Sun Classic) Producer, Alan Landsburg; Executive Producer, Lawrence D. Savadove; Directed and Written by Fred Warshofsky; Based on book of same title by Alan Landsburg; Narrated by Rod Serling; Music, Roger Wagner; Editors, Thea Bentler, Jeffery Weston; Photography, Jeri Sopanen, Paul Desatoff, Barry Herron, Andrew Reichline; Rated G; 94 minutes; February release. A film dealing with the belief that Earth was visited and perhaps colonized by "ancient astronauts," as related in Alan Landsburg's book.

Russ Tamblyn, Alex Karras, Dean Stockwell in "Win, Place or Steal"

"The Outer Space Connection"

"No Place to Hide"

"Swiss Bank Account"

NO PLACE TO HIDE (American Films Ltd) Producer-Director-Editor, Robert Allen Schnitzer; Screenplay, Robert Allen Schnitzer, Larry Beinhart; Music, Michael Smith Combination; Associate Director, Ted Mornel; Photography, Marty Knoph; A Galaxy Film Production; In Technicolor; Rated R; 84 minutes; February release. CAST: Antony Page (Tommy), Sylvester E. Stallone (Jerry), Vickey Lancaster (Estelle), Dennis Tate (Ray), Barbara Lee Govan (Marlena)

SWISS BANK ACCOUNT (American Films Ltd.) Producer-Director, Robert Anderson; Executive Producer, Terence Anderson; Associate Producer, Joseph Dimmitt; Story and Screenplay, Kevin Davis; Photography, John Toll; Music, Ray Martin; Editor, Frank Urioste; Assistant Director, Michael Messinger; A Tempo Enterprises Production; In DeLuxe Color; Rated PG; 87 minutes; February release. CAST: Bill Ewing (Cy), Frank Bonner (Clete), Jacques Aubushon (Chief Belkins), Sharon DeBord (Gracie), Don Dubbins (Sgt. O'Roherty), Harriett Gibson (Mrs. Petrucci), James Drum (Drunk), Ann Morrison (Mrs. Dempsey), John Lawrence (Kreuzlinger), Larry Burrill (Newscaster)

THE GREAT LESTER BOGGS (Starmaster) Producer, John Braden; Director, Harry Thomason; Screenplay, Don McLemore; In DeLuxe Color; Rated PG; 94 minutes; February release. CAST: Bob Ridgely, Alex Karras, Scott McKenzie, Willie Jones, Susan Denbo, Dean Jagger

TRUCKIN' (Dimensions) Producers, Jack Wright III, Richard Pollak, Director, Ken Handler; Screenplay, Michael Thomas; In Metrocolor; Rated PG; February release. CAST: Nicholas Wahler, Dorothy Tristan, Craig Horrall, Albert Salmi

BLACK LOLITA (Parliament) Producer-Director, Stephen Gibson; Screenplay, Stephen Gibson, Mike Brown; In 3-D and color; Rated R; February release. CAST: Yolanda Love, Ed Cheatwood, Joey Ginza, Susan Ayres

IF YOU DON'T STOP IT YOU'LL GO BLIND (Topar) A Callie-Levy Film; A Tom Parker Presentation; Written by Mike Callie and Bob Levy; Rated R; February Release. No other details available.

THE SECOND GUN (American Films Ltd) Producers, Theodore Charach, Gerard Alcan; Directed and Adapted by Gerard Alcan, Based on probe by Theodore Charach; Music composed and performed by Travis E. Pike; Prologue Voice, T. Miratti; Narrator, Dean Randall; Photographed and Edited by Gerard Alcan; Assistant Director, Ellen Hibler; In Technicolor; Rated PG; 98 minutes; March release. A documentary on the assassination of Robert F. Kennedy.

THE DEVIL AND MR. JONES (Stolen Moments) Producer, Sidney Falco; Director, David Davidson; Screenplay, Kiki Young; Photography, David Measles; In color; Rated X; 71 minutes; March release. CAST: Tom Newman (Buck), Erica Eaton (Ms. Tyme), Colter Duncan (Teacher), Yuba (Masseur), Charles Blue, Don Allen, Stuart Helm, Rod Halvorsin, C. J. Bretton

A MAN, A WOMAN AND A KILLER (Schmidt) Created by Richard A. Richardson, Richard R. Schmidt, Wayne Wang; Directors, Richard R. Schmidt, Wayne Wang; Filmed, Edited and Produced by Richard R. Schmidt; Executive Producer, Lura S. Janda; 78 minutes; March release. CAST: Richard A. Richardson (Dick), Edward Nylund (Ed), Caroline Zaremba (Z)

LENNY BRUCE WITHOUT TEARS (Fred Baker) Produced, Directed, Narrated and Written by Fred Baker; Continuity and Narration, John Parson; Editor, Edward Deitch; 78 minutes; March release. A documentary on the late Lenny Bruce.

FOREPLAY (Cinema National) Producers, Benni Korzen, David G. Witter; Executive Producer, Carl Gurevich; Screenplay, Dan Greenberg, Jack Richardson, David Odell; Photography, Jeff Lion Weinstock, Adam Giffard, Ralf Bode; Directors, Robert J. McCarty, Bruce Malmuth, John G. Avildsen; A Syn-Frank Enterprises Production in color; Rated R; 84 minutes; March release. CAST: Zero Mostel (President/Don Pasquale), Estelle Parsons (First Lady/Bar Maid), Pat Paulsen (Norman), Jerry Orbach (Lorsey), George S. Irving (Reverend/Muse), Michael Clarke-Lawrence (BBC Announcer), Deborah Loomis (Doll), Laurie Heineman (Trixie), Andrew Duncan (Hurdlemeyer), Joe Palmiere (Alfredo), Kevin Sanders (TV Announcer)

"If You Don't Stop It You'll Go Blind"

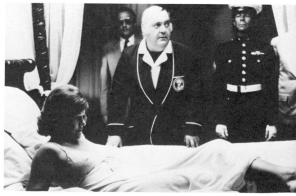

Estelle Parsons, Zero Mostel
in "Foreplay"

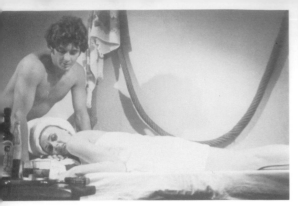

Arell Blanton, Jaqueline Hyde
in "Five at the Funeral"

Rod Perry, Angela Milton
in "Black Gestapo"

DELINQUENT SCHOOLGIRLS (Rainbow) Producer, Maurice Smith; Executive Producer, John Lamb; Director, Gregory Corarito; Theme Music, Randy Johnson, Fred Selden; In Eastmancolor; Rated R; March release. CAST: Michael Pataki, Bob Minor, Stephen Stucker, Sharon Kelley, Brenda Miller, Roberta Pedon

THE FIVE AT THE FUNERAL (Gamalex) Formerly "House of Terror"; Producer-Director, Sergei Goncharoff; Executive Producer, George A. Gade; Screenplay, Tony Crechales, E. A. Charles; Art Director, Phedon Papamichael; Assistant Director, Frank Bolger; Photography, Robert Maxwell; A Rancho La Paz Production; In Eastmancolor; Rated PG; 90 minutes; March release. CAST: Jenifer Bishop (Jenifer), Arell Blanton (Mark), Mitchell Gregg (Emmett), Irenee Byatt (Norma), Ernie Charles (Lawyer), Jacquelyn Hyde (Marsha/Dolores)

SHEBA, BABY (American International) Producer, David Sheldon; Written and Directed by William Girdler; Story, William Girdler, David Sheldon; Photography, William Asman; Editors, Henry Asman, Jack Davies; Designer, J. Patrick Kelly 3rd; Music, Monk Higgins, Alex Brown; Songs, Cleveland & Ranifere; Sung by Barbara Mason; In Movielab Color; Rated PG; 90 minutes; March release. CAST: Pam Grier (Sheba), Austin Stoker (Brick), D'Urville Martin (Pilot), Rudy Challenger (Andy), Dick Merrifield (Shark), Christopher Joy (Walker), Charles Kissinger (Phil), Charles Broaddus (Hammerhead), Maurice Downs (Killer), Ernest Cooley (Whale), Edward Reece, Jr. (Racker), William Foster, Jr. (Waldo), Bobby Cooley (Tank), Paul Greyber (Fin), Sylvia Jacobson (Tail), Leroy Clark, Jr. (Customer), Mike Clifford (Cop), Rose Ann Deel (Policewoman)

TNT JACKSON (New World) Producer-Director, Cirio Santiago; Screenplay, Dick Miller, Ken Metcalf; Photography, Philip Sacdalan; Editors, Gervasio Santos, Barbara Pokras; In Metrocolor; Rated R; 75 minutes; March release. CAST: Jeanne Bell (TNT), Stan Shaw (Charlie), Pat Anderson (Elaine), Ken Metcalf (Sid), and Leo Martin, Chiquito, Chris Cruz, Percy Gordon, June Gamble

THE BLACK GESTAPO (Bryanston) Executive Producer, Ronald K. Goldman; Producer, Wes Bishop; Director, Lee Frost; Assistant Director, Marland Proctor; Screenplay, Lee Frost, Wes Bishop; Story, Ronald K. Goldman, Lee Frost, Wes Bishop; Photography, Derek Scott; Art Director, Richard Schuyler; In color; Rated R; 88 minutes; March release. CAST: Rod Perry (Gen. Ahmed), Charles P. Robinson (Col. Kojah), Phil Hoover (Vito), Ed Cross (Delmay), Angela Brent (Marsha), Wes Bishop (Ernest), Lee Frost (Vincent), Dona Desmond (White Whore), Charles Howerton (Joe), Rai Tasco (Dr. Lisk), David Bryant (Pusher)

THE PASSIONS OF CAROL (Ambar) Direction and Screenplay, Amanda Barton; Based on Charles Dickens' "A Christmas Carol"; Photography, David Measles; Editor, Amanda Barton; Assistant Director, Brenda Morganstern; Design, Graig Esposito; In color; Rated X; 76 minutes; March release. CAST: Mary Stuart (Carol), Marc Stevens (Marley), Jamie Gillis (Hatchet), Kim Pope (Mrs. Hatchet), Arturo Millhouse, Kevin Andre, Helmuth Richler, Rose Cranston, Daniela Di Orici, Angela Dermer, Sonny Landham, Alan Barow, Stuart Dickerson, Alan Grodin

THE OTHER HALF OF THE SKY: A CHINA MEMOIR (MacLaine) Produced and Written by Shirley MacLaine; Directors, Claudia Weill, Shirley MacLaine; Editors, Aviva Slesin, Claudia Weill; In color; 74 minutes; March release. A documentary on mainland Chinese life.

LORD SHANGO (Bryanston) Producers, Steve Bono, Ronald Hobbs; Director, Raymond Marsh; Screenplay, Paul Carter Harrison; Music, Howard Roberts; Photography, Edward Brown; Assistant Directors, Mel Howard, Burtt Harris; Art Director, Hank Aldrich; Assistant Producer, Vincent DeStefano; Associate Producer, Ann Kindberg; Editor, George Norris; In color; Rated R; 91 minutes; March release. CAST: Lawrence Cook (Jabo), Marlene Clark (Jenny), Wally Taylor (Memphis), Bill Overton (Femi), Avis McCarthur (Billie), John Russell (Rev. Slater), Stanley Greene (Tibbles), B. A. Ward (Davis), Maurice Woods (Clut Leader), Dwayne Oliver (Assistant Leader), Sandi Franklin (Bebe), Ella Mitchell (Lead Singer), Ethel Ayler (Lady in bar)

**Stan Shaw, Jeanne Bell
in "TNT Jackson"**

"Lord Shango"

WHERE THE RED FERN GROWS (Doty-Dayton) Producer, Lyman Dayton; Director, Norman Tokar; Screenplay, Douglas Stewart, Eleanor Lamb; Executive Producer, G. Ellis Doty; Music, Lex De Azevedo; Songs written by The Osmonds; Sung by Andy Williams; In DeLuxe Color; Rated G; March release. CAST: James Whitmore (Grandpa), Beverly Garland (Mother), Jack Ging (Father), Lonny Chapman (Sheriff), Stewart Petersen (Billy), Jill Clark (Alice), Jeanna Wilson (Sara), Bill Thurman (Sam), Bill Dunbar (Ben), Rex Corley (Rubin), John Lindsey (Rainie), Gardland McKinney (Pritchard), Robert Telford (Station Master), Charles Seat (Carl), Roger Pancake (Shopkeeper), Marshall Edwards (Preacher)

TEENAGE CHEERLEADER (Mature) In color; Rated X; No other credits; March release. CAST: Harry Reems, Susie Mitchell, Marc Stevens, Jamie Gillis

CARNAL MADNESS (Rainbow) Producer, Maurice Smith; Director, Gregory Corarito; In Eastmancolor; Rated R; March release; No other credits available. CAST: Michael Pataki, Bob Minor, Sharon Kelly, Stephen Stucker, Brenda Miller, Roberta Pedon

THE NO MERCY MAN (Cannon) Director, Daniel Vance; Executive Producer, Paul Rubey Johnson; Screenplay, Daniel Vance, Mike Nolin; In color; Rated R; 91 minutes; March release. CAST: Steven Sandor, Rockne Turkington, Richard X. Slattery, Heidi Vaughn, Michael Layne

TRIP WITH THE TEACHER (Crown International) Produced, Directed and Written by Earl Barton; A Barton/United Film Organization Production; In DeLuxe Color; Rated R; 91 minutes; March release. CAST: Zalman King, Brenda Fogarty, Robert Porter, Robert Gribbin, Jill Voigt, Dina Ousley, Cathy Worthington

SEXTOOL (Halsted/Brown) Producer and Second Unit Director, Taylor Brown; Direction and Photography, Fred Halsted; Music, Donald Geoffreys, Eric Satie; In color; 60 minutes; March release. No other credits.

THE WOMAN HUNT (New World) Producers, Eddie Romero, John Ashley; Director, Eddie Romero; A Four Associates production; In Metrocolor; Rated R; 80 minutes; March release. CAST: John Ashley, Pat Woodell, Laurie Rose, Charlene Jones, Lisa Todd, Sid Haig, Eddie Garcia, Ken Metcalfe

HOT OVEN (Smith & Jones) Producer-Director, Carter Stevens; In color; Rated X; 68 minutes; March release. CAST: Eric Edwards, Ginger Snaps, Jamie Gillis, Rita Davis, Leo Lovelace, Max Packs, Suzette Jones

COUNTRY BLUE (General Films) Producers, Emmett Alston, Jack Conrad; Director, Jack Conrad; Co-producer, John Mansfield; Music, Kelly Gordon, Larry Muhoberac; Vocals, Abby Marable; In color; Rated R; 95 minutes; March release. CAST: Dub Taylor, Jack Conrad, Rita George, David Huddleston, Mildred Brown

TEENAGE LOVERS No credits available. Rated X; In color; March release. CAST: John C. Holmes, Rene Bond

SPECIALTY HOUSE (Pyramid II) Producer, William Dancer; Director, C. E. Munger; Screenplay, Joseph Dreury; In color; Rated X; 78 minutes; March release. CAST: Shannon Korbel, Michele Simon, Deadalus Psyche, Sally Stephens, Paula Timbel, Michael Van Scott

THE THIRSTY DEAD (International Amusements) Producer, Wesley E. DePue; Director, Terry Becker; In Movielab Color; Rated PG; 90 minutes; March release. CAST: John Considine, Jennifer Billingsley, Judith McConnell, Fredricka Meyers, Tani Guthrie

WILLIE AND SCRATCH (Libert Films International) Produced, Directed and Written by Robert J. Emery; Rated R; In color; 88 minutes; March release. CAST: Paul Vincent, Claudia Jennings, Mike Hatfield

DEAFULA (Signscope) Producer, Gary Holstrom; Directed and Written by Peter Wechsberg; March release. The first commercial film to use sign language to communicate with deaf audiences

THE CLAMDIGGER'S DAUGHTER (Monarch) Produced, Directed and Written by Roberta Findlay; Photography, Steve Colwell; Presented by Allan Shackleton; In color; Rated X; 84 minutes; March release. CAST: Chris Jordan, Eric Edwards, Kim Pope, Trudee Able, David Kirk, Dennis Nichols, Arlana Blue, Olivia DeVito

MUDDY MAMA (North American Films) Producer-Director, Bob Favorite; In color; Rated X. March release. CAST: Morgana (Maude), Art Schill (Mack), Sheree Mon (Cloe)

**Shari Eubank
in "Supervixens"**

SUPERVIXENS (RM Films International) Executive Producer, A. James Ryan; Produced, Directed, Written, Photographed, Edited by Russ Meyer; Music, William Loose; Designer, Michael Levesque; In DeLuxe Color; Rated X; 106 minutes; March release. CAST: Shari Eubank (Superangel/Supervixen), Charles Napier (Harry), Uschi Digard (Supersoul), Charles Pitts (Clint), Henry Rowland (Martin), Christy Hartburg (Superlorna), Sharon Kelly (Supercherry), John LaZar (Cal), Stuart Lancaster (Lute), Deborah McGuire (Supereula), Glenn Dixon (Luther), Haji (Superhaji), Big Jack Orovan (Sheriff), Garth Pillsbury (Fisherman), Ron Sheridan (Policeman), John Lawrence (Dr. Scholl), F. Rufus Owens (Rufus), Paul Fox (Tire Thief), E. E. Meyer (Motel Manager), John Furlong (Narrator)

ORGY AMERICAN STYLE (Hollywood International) A Carlos Tobalina Production; In color; Rated X; 94 minutes; March release. CAST: Sharon Kelly, Rick Lootz, Sandy Dempsey, Buck LaFleur, Becky Sharpe, Rene Bond, Keith Erickson, Angela Carnon, Fred Hoedel, Sandy Carey, Gary Grifan

JUST THE TWO OF US (Boxoffice International) Producer, David Novik; Director, Barbara Peeters; Photography, Jaque Beerson; In color; Rated X; 82 minutes; April release. CAST: Elizabeth Plumb, Alicia Courtney, John Aprea, Marland Proctor, Wayne Want, Luann Roberts

THE SEDUCTION OF LYNN CARTER No credits available; Rated X; In color; April release. CAST: Andrea True, Jamie Gillis

THE REINCARNATION OF PETER PROUD (American International) Producer, Frank P. Rosenberg; Director, J. Lee Thompson; Executive Producer, Charles A. Pratt; Screenplay, Max Ehrlich; Photography, Victor J. Kemper; Editor, Michael Anderson; Music, Jerry Goldsmith; Art Director, Jack Martin Smith; Assistant Director, David (Buck) Hall; A BCP presentation; In Technicolor; Rated R; 104 minutes; April release. CAST: Michael Sarrazin (Peter), Jennifer O'Neill (Ann), Margot Kidder (Marcia), Cornelia Sharpe (Nora), Paul Hecht (Dr. Goodman), Tony Stephano (Jeff), Normann Burton (Dr. Spear), Anne Ives (Ellen), Debralee Scott (Suzy)

**Michael Sarrazin
in "The Reincarnation of Peter Proud"**

Gabriel Dell, Barbara Harris
in "The Manchu Eagle Murder Caper Mystery"

"Kiss Me Monster"

THE MANCHU EAGLE MURDER CAPER MYSTERY (United Artists) Producer, Edward K. Dodds; Director, Dean Hargrove; Screenplay, Dean Hargrove, Gabriel Dell; Music, Dick De Benedictus; Associate Producer, Gary Neibuhr; Photography, Bill Butler; Assistant Director, Carter DeHaven; Art Director, Arch Bacon; A Strathmore Production; In color; Rated PG; 80 minutes; April release. CAST: Gabriel Dell (Malcolm), Will Geer (Dr. Simpson), Joyce Van Patten (Ida Mae), Anjanette Comer (Arlevia), Vincent Gardenia (Big Daddy), Barbara Harris (Miss Fredericks), Jackie Coogan (Chief), Huntz Hall (Roy), Howard Storm (Freddie), Sorrel Booke (Dr. Melon), Nita Talbot (Jasmine), Dick Gautier (Oscar), Nick Colasanto (Bert)

KISS ME MONSTER (Joseph Green) Producer, Adrian Hoven; Director, Jesus Franco; Screenplay, Luis Revenga, Jesus Franco; Music, Jerry Van Rooyen; Photography, Jorge Herrero, Franz Hofer; In color; Rated R; 80 minutes; April release. CAST: Janine Reynault, Rossana Yanni, Adrian Hoven, Michel Lemoine, Chris Howland, Manolo Velasco, Ana Cesares, Manuel Otero

KEEP OFF! KEEP OFF! (Gamalex) Producers, Albert J. Salzer, Austin and Irma Kalish; Director, Shelley Berman; Executive Producer, Allan D. Yasnyi; Screenplay, Austin and Irma Kalish; Photography and Edited by Robert A. Weaver; Art Director, Lesley B. Yasnyi; Assistant Directors, Susan S. Grapes, Paul Ehrmann; Music, Norma Green, Jim Helms, Gary LeMel; A New Millennium Film; In Eastmancolor; Rated PG; 90 minutes; April release. CAST: Micky Dolenz (You Know), Marcus J. Grapes (Wolfman), Gary Wood (Jerry), Everette Addington (Twila), Louis Quinn (Maury), Ed Kearney (Cal), Gerald McRaney (David), Christine Nelson (Rose), Herb Nelson (Horace), Richard Hurst (Grady), Christina Hart (Rita), Denise DeFelice (Sandy), Arthur Giron (Bingo), Nita Wilson (Jessica), Michael Anthony (Eddie), Linda Yasnyi (Fire Fly), Susan Gebhardt (Suze)

WILD HONEY (Shermart) Producer, Rick Rogers; Direction and Screenplay, Don Edmonds; In color; Rated X; 95 minutes; April release. CAST: Donna Young, Kipp Whitman, Carol Hill, Alan Warnick, Jeffrey Sands, Lynn Harris, Donna Stanley

LIVE A LITTLE, STEAL A LOT (American International) formerly "Murph the Surf"; Producers, J. Skeet Wilson, Chuck Courtney; Director, Marvin Chomsky; Executive Producer, Caruth C. Byrd; Screenplay, E. Arthur Kean; Based on story by Allan Dale Kuhn; Music, Phillip Lambro; Designer, James Vance; In CFI Color; Rated PG; 101 minutes; April release. CAST: Robert Conrad (Allan), Don Stroud (Jack), Donna Mills (Ginny), Robyn Millan (Sharon), Luther Adler (Max), Paul Stewart (Avery), Morgan Paull (Arnie), Ben Frank (Hopper), Burt Young (Bernasconi), Pepper Martin (Terwilliger), Don Matheson (Hauser), Lindsay Crosby (Thomas)

BROTHER, CAN YOU SPARE A DIME? (Dimension) Producers, Sandy Lieberson, David Puttnam; Director, Philippe Mora; Editor, Jeremy Thomas; A Goodtimes Enterprises Production; In black and white and color; Rated PG; 106 minutes; April release. A documentary of depression America with film clips from newsreels and movies.

STUD BROWN (Cinemation Industries) Producers, Jim Rein, Marvin Logonoff; Executive Producer, Samuel M. Sherman; Director, Al Adamson; Music, Charles Earland; Photography, R. Michael Stringer; Editor, John Winfield; An ASAM Presentation; A Larien Management—Producers Commercial Production; In color; 94 minutes; April release. CAST: Alan Tang, Timothy Brown, James Hong, Aldo Ray, Carolyn Ann Speed, Don Oliver

ALOHA, BOBBY AND ROSE (Columbia) Producer, Fouad Said; Executive Producer, Edward J. Rosen; Direction and Screenplay, Floyd Mutrux; Photography, William A. Fraker; Editor, Danford B. Greene; Assistant Director, Mike Moder; In Metrocolor; A Cine Artists International Production; Rated PG; 88 minutes; April release. CAST: Paul LeMat (Bobby), Dianne Hull (Rose), Tim McIntire (Buford), Leigh French (Donna Sue), Noble Willingham (Uncle Charlie), Martine Bartlett (Rose's Mother), Robert Carradine (Moxey), Erick Hines, Mario Gallo, Tony Gardenas, Eddie Olmos, Tip Fredell, William Dooley, Cliff Emmich, David Bond, Dorothy Love

Mickey Dolenz (L)
in "Keep Off! Keep Off!"

Dianne Hull, Paul LeMat
in "Aloha, Bobby and Rose"

Marianna Hill
in "Messiah of Evil"

"Last Tango in Acapulco"

MESSIAH OF EVIL (International Cinefilm) Produced, Directed and Written by Gloria Katz, Williard Huyck; Executive Producer, Alan Riche; Photography, Stephen Katz; Assistant Director, Alan Howard; Art Director, Jack Fiske; Editor, Morgan Fisher; In Technicolor and Techniscope; Rated R; 90 minutes; April release. CAST: Michael Greer (Thom), Marianna Hill (Arletty), Joy Bang (Toni), Anitra Ford (Laura), Royal Dano (Joseph Lang), Elisha Cook (Charley)

THE LAST TANGO IN ACAPULCO (Hollywood International) Produced, Directed and Written by Carlos Tobalina; Music, Alberto Soria; In Eastmancolor; Rated X; 120 minutes; April release. CAST: Rebecca Sharpe (Susan), Bill Cable (Miguel), Keith Erickson (Father), Maria Pia (Silvia), Linda Tobalina (Young Susy), Jake Monroy (Bum), Brian Sheriff (Cop), Enrique Fefer (Stone), Andrea Yakamoto (Sister), Carlos Tobalina (Impresario), Rudolfo Cuesta (Waiter)

SHARKS' TREASURE (United Artists) Produced, Directed and Written by Cornel Wilde; Assistant Director, John Stoneman; Photography, Jack Atcheler, Al Giddings; Editor, Byron "Buzz" Brandt; Music, Robert O. Ragland; Theme Song, Jefferson Paschal, Sung by Ken Darrie; In color; Rated PG; April release. CAST: Cornel Wilde (Jim), Yaphet Kotto (Ben), John Neilson (Ron), Cliff Osmond (Lobo), David Canary (Larry), David Gilliam (Juanito), Caesar Cordova (Pablo), Gene Borkan (Kook), Dale Ishimoto (Ishy), Carmen Argenziano (Lt.), Roxanna Bonilla (Girl), Marv Fisher (Convict)

SMOKE IN THE WIND (Gamalex) Executive Producer. Jack Horton; Story and Screenplay, Eric Allen; Producer, Robert "Whitey" Hughes, Bill Hughes; Director, Joseph Kane; Photography, Mario Tosi; Presented by Frontier Productions; April release. CAST: John Ashley (Whipple), John Russel (Cagle), Myron Healy (Mort), Walter Brennan (H. B. Kingman), Susan Houston (Laries) Linda Weld (Sarah), Henry Kingi (Smoky), Adair Jameson (Hannah), Daniel White (Col. Cullen), Lorna Thayer (Ma Mondier), Billy Hughes, Jr. (Till), Bill Foster (Stapp), Jack Horton (Jebb), Bill McKenzie (Bartender)

A DIRTY WESTERN (Cricket) Producer, Michael Darrin; Direction and Screenplay, David Fleetwood; Photography, Robert Rubin; Editor, Jay Reilly; Music, Steve Jason, Lee O'Donnell; Sung by Steve Jason; In Eastmancolor; Rated X; 72 minutes; April release. CAST: Barbara Bourbon (Sarah), Richard O'Neal (Luke), Dick Payne (Ned), Levi Richards (Barney), Vern Rossi (Sheriff), Geoffrey Parker (Nate), Simone, Louis Grant, Gloria Hope, L. Q. O'Donnell, Sonny Frazese

FORCE FOUR (Howard Mahler) Producers, Michael Fink, Joel Schild, Marvin Schild; Director, Michael Fink; Executive Producer, Franz Schneider; Original score performed by Life U. S. A.; A Landfall Systems Production; In color; Rated R; April release. CAST: Malachi Lee (Eric), Warhawk Tanzania (Adam), Owen Watson (Jason), Judy Soriano (Billie), Sydney Filson, Sam Schwartz

KITTY CAN'T HELP IT (Mammoth) Producer, Jim Buckley; Director, Peter Locke; In color; Rated R; 88 minutes; April release. CAST: Kitty Carl, Fay DeWitt, Pamela Miller, Lisa Farringer, Walter Wonderman

TO HEX WITH SEX (RAF Industries) Producer-Director, Simon Nuchtern; An August Films Production; In Eastmancolor; April release. CAST: Stefan Peters, Paula Shaw, Diana Goble, Larry Hunter, Jack Taylor, Linda Boyce, Lynn Milgrim

SUNBURST (Cinema Financial of America) Producer-Director, James Polakof; Executive Producer, Ronald Peck; In Metrocolor; Rated R; April release. CAST: Peter Hooten, Kathrine Baumann, James Keach, Peter Brown, Rudy Vallee

INSIDE AMY (Adpix) A Dart Production; Producer-Director, Ron Garcia; Executive Producer, Dave Arthur; Screenplay, Helene Arthur; Photography, Don Jones; Editor, R. Victor Garcia; Art Director, Ron Foreman; Music, Jack Preisner; In Eastmancolor; Rated R; 100 minutes; April release. CAST: Jan Mitchell (Amy), Eastman Price (Charlie), Gary Kent (Jim), Marsha Jordan (Irene), Phillip Luther (Jerry), Ann Perry (Donna), Ron Darby (Bill), Rene Bond (Diane), Paul Oberon (Rod), Mickey Nadar (Marge), Ushi Digart (Lois)

John Ashley
in "Smoke in the Wind"

Cornel Wilde, Yaphet Kotto
in "Shark's Treasure"

**Susan Blakely, Ben Gazzara
in "Capone"**

CAPONE (20th Century-Fox) Producer, Roger Corman; Director, Steve Carver; Screenplay, Howard Browne; Music, David Grisman; Photography, Vilis Lapenieks; Editor, Richard Meyer; In DeLuxe Color; Rated R; 101 minutes; April release. CAST: Tony Curtis (Capone), Susan Blakely (Iris), Harry Guardino (Torrio), John Cassavetes (Frankie Yale), Sylvester Stallone (Frank Natti), Peter Maloney (Jake), Frank Campanella (Big Jim), Royal Dano (Cermak), John Orchard (O'Banion), John D. Chandler (Hymie)

NOT NOW DARLING (Dimension) Producers, Peter J. Thompson, Martin C. Shute; Directors, David Croft, Ray Cooney; Screenplay, John Chapman; An LMG-Sedgemoor Production; Rated R; 93 minutes; April release. CAST: Leslie Phillips, Julie Ege, Ray Cooney

DEATH RACE 2000 (New World) Producer, Roger Corman; Director, Paul Bartel; Screenplay, Charles B. Griffith, Robert Thom; Photography, Tak Fullmoto; Music, Paul Chihara; Editor, Tina Hirsch; In color; Rated R; 78 minutes; April release. CAST: David Carradine (Frankenstein), Simone Griffith (Annie), Sylvester Stallone (Joe), Louisa Moritz (Myra), Mary Woronov (Jane)

THE BRASS RING (E. O. Productions) Producer, Earl Owensby; Director, Martin Beck; Screenplay, Grey Lynelle; In color; Rated PG; April release. CAST: Earl Owensby, Johnny Popwell, Elizabeth Upton, Doug Hale, Fred Covington, Maurice Hunt, Sandra Beck, Skip Lundby, Bob Hawkins, Jeff MacKay, Kathleen Devine, Dennis Owensby

THE ANGEL ABOVE AND THE DEVIL BELOW (Martoni Enterprises) Producer, Mary Turner; Screenplay, Jon Cutaia, Katherine Merlin; In color; Rated X; 83 minutes; April release. CAST: Brittany Laine, Starlyn Simone, Robert Bedford, Mindy Brandt

IDAHO TRANSFER (Cinemation Industries) Producer, William Hayward; Director, Peter Fonda; Screenplay, Thomas Matthiesen; Photography, Bruce Logan; Editor, Chuck McClelland; Music, Bruce Langehorne; Assistant Director, Rick Marcus; In CFI Color; 87 minutes; April release. CAST: Kelley Bohanan (Karen), Kevin Hearst (Ronald), Caroline Hildebrand, Keith Carradine (Arthur)

Simone Griffith, David Carradine in "Death Race 2000"

FUGITIVE KILLER (Boxoffice International) Producer-Director, Emile A. Harvard; A Poinciana Film; In Eastmancolor; Rated R; 90 minutes; April release. CAST: Neil Patrick, Karen Hansen, John-Scott Schroeder, Cheryl Patton

THE INNOCENCE OF VALERIE (Brown) Produced, Directed and Written by Steve Brown; In color; Rated X; 70 minutes; April release. CAST: Katrina Rexford (Valerie)

BLOOD WATERS OF DR. Z (Capital) Producer-Director, Don Barton; Story, Lee Larew, Ron Kivett; A Sol Fried presentation; In Eastmancolor; Rated PG; 92 minutes; April release. CAST: Marshall Grauer, Wade Popwell, Sanna Ringhaver, Paul Galloway, Dave Dickerson, Gerald Cruse

PICTURES AT AN EXHIBITION (April Fools) No credits available; Rated G; In color; 95 minutes; April release. A concert starring the rock group Emerson, Lake & Palmer

LINDA LOVELACE FOR PRESIDENT (General Film) Producers, Charles Stroud, David Winters; Director, Claudio Guzman; Screenplay, Jack S. Margolis; Executive Producers, Arthur Marks, William Silberkleit; Photography, Robert Birchall; In color; Rated R; 109 minutes; April release. CAST: Linda Lovelace, Fuddle Bagley, Skip Burton, Val Bisoglio, Jack DeLeon, Mickey Dolenz, Joey Forman, Gary Goodrow, Morgan Upton

SAVAGE ABDUCTION (Cinemation) Produced, Directed and Written by John Lawrence; In color; Rated R; 82 minutes; April release. CAST: Tom Drake, Stephen Oliver, Joseph Turkel

INTENSIVE CARE No credits available; Rated X; In color; April release. CAST: Harry Reems, Cindy West, Darby Lloyd Rains, Marc Stevens

THE MANHANDLERS (Premiere) A Lasky/Carlin/Polsky Production; Director, Lee Madden; Screenplay, Gil Lasky; In Technicolor; Rated R; 85 minutes; April release. CAST: Cara Burgess, Judy Brown, Rosalind Miles, Vince Cannon, Henry Brandon

LADY ON THE COUCH (Beattie) No credits available; In color; Rated X; May release. CAST: Andrea True, Lynn Stevens, Don Allen, Darby Lloyd Rains, Marc Stevens

THE LEGENDARY CURSE OF LEMORA (Media Cinema) Producer, Robert Fern; Director, Richard Blackburn; Music, Daniel Neufield; Costumes, Rosanna Norton; Rated PG; In color; 90 minutes; May release. CAST: Lesley Gilb (Lemora), Cheryl Smith (Lila), William Whitton (Alvin), Steve Johnson (Ticket Man), Monte Pyke (Bus Driver), Maxine Ballantyne (Old Lady), Parker West (Young Man), Richard Blackburn (Reverend)

SEVEN ALONE (Doty-Dayton) Producer, Lyman D. Dayton; Director, Earl Bellamy; Associate Producer, Hubie Kerns, Sr.; Music, Robert O. Ragland; Sung by Pat Boone; Screenplay, Douglas Stewart, Eleanor Lamb; Based on book "On to Oregon" by Honore Morrow; Narrator, Ann Seymour; Assistant Director, Russell Llewelyn; Photography, Robert Stumm; Editor, Dan Greer; Designer, Ray Markham; Assistant Director, William H. White; In color; Rated G; 96 minutes; May release. CAST: Dewey Martin (Henry), Aldo Ray (Dr. Dutch), Anne Collings (Naome), Dean Smith (Kit), James Griffith (Billy), Stewart Petersen (John), Dehl Berti (White Elk), Bea Morris (Sally), Scott Petersen, Debbie Van Orden, Diane Petersen, Suzanne Petersen, Julie Petersen, Christy Clark, Kilss Sparks, Pat Wilde, Craig Larson, Roger Pancake, Ann David, Riley Morgan

LOOSE ENDS (American Eagle/Fat Chance) Producer, Victoria Woxniak; Director, David Burton Morris; Executive Producer, Allan Fingerhut; Screenplay, Victoria Wozniak, David Burton Morris; Photography, Gregory Cummins; Art Director, Ann Morris; Associate Producer, A. L. Milgrom; Music, John Paul Hammond; In black and white; 103 minutes; May release. CAST: Chris Mulkey (Billy), John Jenkins (Eddie), Linda Jenkins (Jenny), Bobby Jenkins (Jason), Irv Fink (Farrell), Karlos Ozols (Drunk), Gerald Drake (Grocery Clerk), Judith Poplinski (Waitress), Christian Mulkey, Sr. (Foreman), Pamela LaVarre, Faye Gallos, Darlette Engelmeier, Ruby Tuesday, S. R. Griffis, Bill Tilton, Bret Larson, Bucky Jandrich

THE SPECIALIST (Crown International) Producer-Director, Hikmet Avedis; Executive Producer, Marlene Schmidt; Screenplay, Ralph B. Potts, Marlene Schmidt, Hikmet Avedis; Based on "Come Now the Lawyers" by Ralph B. Potts; Photography, Masoud Joseph; Theme Song, Sammy Fain, Paul Francis Webster; Sung by Lou Rawls; A Renaissance Production; In DeLuxe Color; Rated R; 93 minutes; May release. CAST: Adam West (Jerry), John Anderson (Pike), Ahna Capri (Londa), Alvy Moore (Bailiff), Marlene Schmidt (Elizabeth), Harvey Jason (Hardin), Russell Schmidt (Sharkey), Charles Knapp (Judge)

**Robert Duvall, Charles Bronson
in "Breakout"**

"Switchblade Sisters"

MARY, MARY, BLOODY MARY (Translor) Producers, Robert Yamin, Henri Bollinger; Executive Producer, Jaime Jimenez Pons; Director, Juan Lopez Moctezuma; Screenplay, Malcolm Marmorstein; Story, Don Rico, Don Henderson; Editor, Federico Landeras; Photography, Miguel Garzon; Music, Tom Bahler; In color; Rated R; 101 minutes; May release. CAST: Cristina Ferrare (Mary), David Young (Ben), Helena Rojo (Greta), John Carradine (Mary's Father)

BREAKOUT (Columbia) Producers, Robert Chartoff, Irwin Winkler; Executive Producer, Ron Buck; Director, Tom Gries; Screenplay, Howard B. Kreitsek, Marc Norman, Elliott Baker; Based on novel by Warren Hinckle, William Turner, Eliot Asinof; Photography, Lucien Ballard; Editor, Bud Isaacs; Music, Jerry Goldsmith; Art Director, Ira Bates; Assistant Director, Ronald L. Schwary; In Eastmancolor; Rated PG; 96 minutes; May release. CAST: Charles Bronson (Nick), Robert Duvall (Jay), Jill Ireland (Ann), John Huston (Harris), Randy Quaid (Hawk), Sheree North (Myrna), Alejandro Rey (Sanchez), Paul Mantee (Cable), Roy Jenson (Spencer), Alan Vint (Pilot), Jorge Moreno (Soza)

FRANKIE AND JOHNNY WERE LOVERS (LCB) Direction and Screenplay, Alan C. Colberg; In color; Rated X; May release. CAST: Rene Bond (Frankie), Rick Lutz (Johnny), Cindy Summers (Alice)

TRUCKIN' MAN (Preacherman) Producer, W. Henry Smith; Director, Will Zens; Rated R; In Technicolor; May release. CAST: Michael Hawkins, Mary Cannon, Doodles Weaver, Sid Rancer, Larry Drake, Lynne Bradley, Peggy Linville, Larry Lambeth, Philip Rubinstein

FAREWELL SCARLET (Command) Producer, Howard Winters; Director, Chuck Vincent; Screenplay, J. Vidos, Howard Winters, Chuck Vincent; Photography, Stephen Todd; Costumes, Eddie Heath; Art Director, F. Maltese; Editor, Marc Ubell; In color; Rated X; May release. CAST: J. P. Paradine, National Velvet, Kim Pope, Doug Wood, Darby Lloyd Rains, Al Levitsky, Jennifer Jordan, Eric Edwards, Bob Stevens, Marlow Ferguson, Katia Mara, Dulce Mann, Chris Jordan

RIPPED-OFF (Cinema Shares International) Director, Franco Prosperi; A White Mountain Properties Presentation; In Eastmancolor; Rated R; May release. CAST: Robert Blake, Ernest Borgnine, Catherine Spaak

SWITCHBLADE SISTERS (Centaur) Formerly "The Jezebelles"; Executive Producers, Frank Moreno, Jeff Begun; Producer, John Prizer; Director, Jack Hill; Screenplay, F. X. Maier; In CFI Color; Rated R; May release. CAST: Robbie Lee, Joanne Nail, Monica Gayle, Kitty Bruce, Janice Karman, Marlene Clark

SUPERCOCK (Hagen-Wayne) Producer, Ross Hagen, Executive Producers, Gail Wayne, Lettie B. Soriano; Associate Producer, Miguel Lorza; Director, Gus Trikonis; Assistant Director, Fred Galang; Photography, Fred Soriano, Jr.; Screenplay, Michael Laton; Editor, Gervasio I. Santos; Music, Tito Sotto; In CFI Color; Rated PG; 90 minutes; May release. CAST: Ross Hagen (Seth), Nancy Kwan (Yuki), Tony Lorea (G. I. Joe), Subas Herrero (Seeno), Eric Lidberg (Swede), Joonee Gamboa (Speeno), Louie Florentino (Heeno), Charlie Davao (Spaniard), Joe Garcia (Yaso), Logan Clark (Thief), Frank Zarrate, Cricket Lorza (Goons), Friendly

THE INTIMATE TEENAGERS (William Mishkin) Director, Walter Boos; In Eastmancolor; Rated X; 87 minutes; May release. CAST: Darby Lloyd Rains, Marc Stevens, Kim Pope, Jaques Killy, Big Sally Stroke, Cherry Pye

CORNBREAD, EARL AND ME (American International) Producer-Director, Joe Manduke; Executive Producer-Writer, Leonard Lamensdorf; Associate Producer, Martin Fink; Photography, Jules Brenner; Editor, Aaron Stell; Costumes, Ann McCarthy; Art Director, Dave Haber; Presented by Samuel Z. Arkoff; In Movielab Color; Rated PG; 95 minutes; May release. CAST: Moses Gunn (Blackwell), Rosalind Cash (Sarah), Bernie Casey (Atkins), Madge Sinclair (Leona), Keith Wilkes (Cornbread), Tierre Turner (Earl), Antonio Fargas (One Eye), Vincent Martorano (Golich), Charles Lampkin (Jenkins), Stack Pierce (Sam), Logan Ramsey (Deputy Coroner), Thalmus Rasulala (Charlie), Bill Henderson (Watkins), Sarina C. Grant (Mrs. Parsons), Stefan Gierasch (Sgt. Danaher), Larry Fishburne III (Wilford)

**Nancy Kwan, Ross Hagen
in "Supercock"**

**Madge Sinclair, Keith Wilkes
in "Cornbread, Earl and Me"**

**Max Baer, Forrest Tucker, Janice Heiden
in "The Wild McCullochs"**

**Glynn Turman, Cynthia Davis
in "Cooley High"**

THE WILD McCULLOCHS (American International) Executive Producer, Roger Camras; Produced, Directed and Written by Max Baer; Music, Ernest Gold; Photography, Fred Koenekamp; Editor, David Berlatsk; Associate Producer, Mark Sussman; A Samuel Z. Arkoff Presentation; Color by Consolidated; Rated PG; 93 minutes; May release. CAST: Forrest Tucker (J.J.), Max Baer (Culver), Julie Adams (Hannah), Janice Heiden (Ali), Dennis Redfield (Steven), Don Grady (R.J.), William Demarest (Farther), Harold J. Stone (George), Vito Scotti (Tony), Sandy Kevin (Rad), Chip Hand (Gary), Lillian Randolph (Missy), Doodles Weaver (Pop), James Gammon (Detective), Candice Smith (Marsha), Mike Mazurki (Cliff)

S. O. S. (Mammoth) Producer, David Buckley; Direction and Screenplay, Jim Buckley; Photography, Ralf Bode; Music, Ron Frangipane; Designer, Jack Cardinale; Assistant Directors, Clint Jakeman, Michael Maurer; In color; Rated X; 84 minutes; May release. CAST: Honeysuckle Divine, Jody Maxwell, Spider Webb, Jim Buckley, Al Goldstein, Melissa Evers, Ronnie Love, Erica Eaton, David Savage, Helen Ready, Eric Edwards, Steven Kraus, Heidi High, Don Allen, A. C. "Boner" Jones, Darby Lloyd Rains, Sandi Foxx, Tony Steiner, Marc Stevens

THE HARDY GIRLS (Gold) Director, Allen Ruskin; Producer, Robert Simon; In color; Rated X; May release. CAST: Tina Russell, Peaches Hardin

THE CANDY TANGERINE MAN (Moonstone) Director, Matt Cimber; Screenplay, George Theakos; Music, Smoke; In color; Rated R; 95 minutes; May release. CAST: Tom Hankerson, John Daniels, Eli Haynes, Marva Farmer, Buck Flower, Richard Kennedy, Tracy King, George Pelster, Mik Angel

YOUNG AND WILD (Boxoffice International) Director, Dwayne Avery; In color; Rated R; 90 minutes; May release. CAST: Carl Monson, Angela Carnon, Maybe Smith, Sharon Masters, Christopher Culhane, Pepe Russo

FIVE LOOSE WOMEN (S.C.A.) Producer-Director, A. C. Stephen; In Eastmancolor; Rated R; May release. CAST: Jabie Abercrombie, Rene Bond, Talie Cochrane, Dona Desmond, Margie Lanier

THE WRONG DAMN FILM (Davidson) Produced, Directed, Written and Edited by Carson Davidson; Music, Arnold Eidus; Photography, Richard Francis; 84 minutes; May release. CAST: Barry Bostwick (Alex Rounder), Barbara Dana (Donna Compare/Agent Bradford), Keene Curtis (Wilton/Hughes/Gen. Hatfield)

HEAVY LOAD (AIC) Producer, Ward Summers; Director, Mark Ubell; In Eastmancolor; Rated X; 70 minutes; May release. CAST: Jeffrey Hurst, Andrea True, Darby Lloyd Rains, Kim Pope, Samantha McLaren, Jamie Gillis

COOLEY HIGH (American International) Executive Producer, Samuel Z. Arkoff; Producer, Steve Krantz; Director, Michael Schultz; Screenplay, Eric Monte; Photography, Paul Vom Brack; Editor, Christopher Holmes; Assistant Director, Frank Beetson; Music, Freddie Perren; In Movielab Color; Rated PG; 107 minutes; May release. CAST: Glynn Turman (Preach), Lawrence-Hilton Jacobs (Cochise), Garrett Morris (Mason), Cynthia Davis (Brenda), Corin Rogers (Pooter), Maurice Leon Havis (Willie), Joseph Carter Wilson (Tyrone), Sherman Smith (Stone), Norman Gibson (Robert); Maurice Marshall (Damon), Steven Williams (Jimmy), Jackie Taylor (Johnny Mae), Christine Jones (Sandra), Lynn Caridine (Dorothy)

THE YOUNG PASSIONS (Hollywood International) Executive Producers, Rick Clark, Doug Stoker; Direction and Screenplay, Bobby Davis; In Eastmancolor; Rated X; 90 minutes; May release. CAST: Diana Hardy, Jim Cody, Eddie Sands, Sim Williams, Kathy Hilton, Vanita Dickson, Stuart Andrews, Maria Arnold, Susan Bergdahl, Russ Dvorak, Lynn Meins, Frank Boyd, Bobby Tripp

NAKED CAME THE STRANGER (Catalyst) Producer, L. Sultana; Director, Henry Paris (Radley Metzger); Screenplay, Jake Barnes; Based on novel of same title by Penelope Ashe; Photography, Robert Rochester; Editor, Doris Barrow; Music, George Craig; Art Director, Michael Springer; In color; Rated X; 89 minutes; May release. CAST: Darby Lloyd Rains, Levi Richards, Mary Stuart, Alan Marlow, Christina Hutton, Kevin Andre, Helen Madigan, Jerry Grant

**Jim Buckley, Al Goldstein
in "S. O. S."**

**Julie Adams, Forrest Tucker
in "The Wild McCullochs"**

**Nina Fause, William Margold
in "Marilyn and the Senator"**

"The Man Who Would Not Die"

MARILYN AND THE SENATOR (Hollywood International) Produced, Directed, Written, Edited by Carlos Tobalina; Assistant Director, William Margold; Music, Linda and Carlos Tobalina; In color; Rated X; 125 minutes; May release. CAST: Nina Fause (Marilyn), William Margold (Senator), Bill Kaye (Euriah), Heather Leight (Mrs. Wolfe), Sharon Thorpe (Nancy), Liz Renay (Madame Mercy), Eroff Lynn (Doctor), Zarina Guillian, Glem St. George, Sally Loren, Trevor Rick, Jess Alban, Renee Loudon, Dick Hill, Susan Niven, Rose Anderson, Clem St. George.

THE HAPPY HOOKER (Cannon) Executive Producers, Dennis Friedland, Marlene Hess; Producer, Fred Caruso; Director, Nicholas Sgarro; Screenplay, William Richert; Based on Book by Xaviera Hollander, Robin Moore and Yvonne Dunleavy; Music, Don Elliott; Photography, Dick Kratina; Assistant Director, Ted Zachary; Designer, Gene Callahan; Costumes, Ann Roth; Editor, Jerry Greenberg; Choreography, Donald Saddler; In color; 96 minutes; May release. CAST: Lynn Redgrave (Xaviera), Jean Pierre Aumont (Yves), Lovelady Powell (Madelaine), Nicholas Pryor (Carl), Elizabeth Wilson (Mrs. Gordon), Tom Poston (Conrad), Conrad Janis (Fred), Richard Lynch (Cop), Owen Hollander (Lt. Taggert), Inga Bunsch (Finch), Stefan Schnabel (Elderly Gentleman), Lee Wallace (Knowlton), Gwyda DonHowe (Mrs. Knowlton), George Dzunda (Chet), Kenneth Tigar (Steve), Dorothy Fox (Rosita), Barton Heyman (Dirty Harry), Mathew Cowles (Albert), Murray Moston (Customs Officer), Allan Rich (Desk Sgt.), William Duell (Meek Man), Vincent Schiavelli (Geru), Florence Tarlow (Petulia), Dan Resin (Under-secretary), Guillermo Irizarry (Carlos), Pat Henry (Aurora), Sharon Laughlin (Nadine), Anita Morris (Linda Jo or May), Darlene Parks (April), Trish Hawkins (Chris), Donna Mitchell (Lucille), Denise Galik (Cynthia), Rochelle Oliver (Norma), Mary Olga (Rosie).

AFFAIRE IN RIO DE JANEIRO (Hollywood International) Produced, Directed, Written, Photographed, Edited by Carlos Tobalina; Theme Music, Carlos Tobalina; In Color; Rated X; 90 minutes; June release. CAST: Phyllis Claire (Sonia), Carlos Tobaline (Claude), Maria Pia (Silvia), Luigi Fellini (Medical Student), Gerry Gordon (Madame Lulu), Monique La Ferre (Tania), Gale Ammer (Rose)

THE MAN WHO WOULD NOT DIE (Centaur) Producers, Lawrence M. Dick, Robert Arkless; Director, Robert Arkless; Executive Producer, Rick Lede; Screenplay, George Chesbro, Stephen Taylor, Robert Arkless; Story based on novel "The Sailcloth Shroud" by Charles Williams; Photography, Lowell McFarland; Music, Art Harris; Editor, Arline Garson; In color by Movielab; Rated PG; 83 minutes; June release. CAST: Dorothy Malone (Paula), Keenan Wynn (Victor), Aldo Ray (Frank), Alex Sheafe (Marc), Joyce Ingalls (Pat), Fred Scollay (Lt. Willetts), James Monks (Reagan), Jesse Osuna (Soames), Dennis McMullen (Harry), Hal Lasky (Reporter), Kathy Triffon (Jackie), Valerie Shorr (Girlfriend), Rick Lede (Ramirez), Barry Simco (C.P.O. Murthy), John Peters (Yardman)

BUCKTOWN (American International) Executive Producer, Ric R. Roman; Producer, Bernard Schwartz; Director, Arthur Marks; Screenplay, Bob Ellison; Photography, Robert Birchall; Editor, George Fosley, Jr.; Music, Johnny Pate; Associate Producer, Phillip Hazelton; Art Directors, George Costello, John Carter; "Bucktown" sung by Luther Rabb; In Movielab Color; Rated R; 94 minutes; June release. CAST: Fred Williamson (Duke), Pam Grier (Aretha), Thalmus Rasulala (Roy), Tony King (T.J.), Bernie Hamilton (Harley), Art Lund (Chief Patterson), Tierre Turner (Steve), Morgan Upton (Sam), Carl Weathers (Hambone), Jim Bohan (Clete), Robert Burton (Merle), Gene Simms (Josh), Bruce Watson (Bagman)

SATURDAY NIGHT AT THE BATHS (Buckley Bros.) Producers, David Buckley, Steve Ostrow; Director, David Buckley; Screenplay, Franklin Khedouri, David Buckley; Photography, Ralf Bode; Editors, Jackie Raynal, Suzanne Fenn; Rated R; 102 minutes; June release. CAST: Ellen Sheppard (Tracy), Robert Aberdeen (Michael), Don Scotti (Himself), Caleb Stonn (Judy Garland), J. C. Gaynor (Shirley Bassey), Pedro Valentino (Carmen Miranda), Toyia (Diana Ross), Janie Olivor, Phillip Owens, Steve Ostrow, R. Douglas Brautigham, Paul J. Ott, Paul Vanase, Lawrence Smith

**Thalmus Rasulala, Fred Williamson
in "Bucktown"**

**Philip Owens
in "Saturday Night at the Baths"**

**Joe Don Baker, Linda Evans
in "Mitchell"**

**Jesse Vint, Richard Gilliland, Bradford Dillman
in "Bug"**

MITCHELL (Allied Artists) Executive Producer, Benjamin Melniker; Producer, R. Ben Efraim; Director, Andrew V. McLaglen; Screenplay, Ian Kennedy Martin; Photography, Harry Stradling; Associate Producer, H. T. Morrison, Jr.; Assistant Director, Jerry Ziesmer; Wardrobe, Glen Wright; Music, Larry Brown, Jerry Styner; Editor, Fred A. Chulack; title song sung by Hoyt Axton; An Essex Enterprises Ltd. Production; Presented by Emmanuel L. Wolf; In Technicolor; Rated R; 97 minutes; June release. CAST: Joe Don Baker (Mitchell), Martin Balsam (James Arthur Cummins), John Saxon (Walter Deaney), Linda Evans (Greta), Merlin Olsen (Benton), Morgan Paull (Salvatore), Harold J. Stone (Tony), Robert Phillips (Chief Pallin), Buck Young (Det. Aldridge), Rayford Barnes (Det. Tyzack), Todd Bass (Child), Jerry Hardin (Desk Sgt.), Lilyan MacBride (Rich Lady), Robin Narke (Customs Officer), Sidney Clute (rudy Moran), Duffy Hambleton (Edmondo), Carole Estes (Prudence), Vicky Peters (Helena), John Ashby (Burglar), Bill Sullivan (Don), Jim B. Smith (Sgt. O'Hagen), Charles Glover (Danziger), Charles Tamburro (Pilot), Gary M. Combs (Officer), Stan Stone (Sgt.), Tom Lawrence (Patrolman), Alan Gibbs (Mustang Hood), Dick Ziker, Phil Altman (Alley Hoods), Bob Orrison, Gary McLarty, Paul Nuckles (Mistretta Hoods)

DOC SAVAGE THE MAN OF BRONZE (Warner Bros.) Producer, George Pal; Director, Michael Anderson; Screenplay, George Pal, Joe Morhaim; Based on novel by Kenneth Robeson; Photography, Fred Koenekamp; Music, John Philip Sousa; Adapted by Frank De Vol; Editor, Thomas McCarthy; Assistant Directors, Jack W. Aldworth, Bruce Satterlee, Albert Shepard; Art Director, Fred Harpman; Costumes, Patrick Cummings; In Technicolor; Rated G; 111 minutes; June release. CAST: Ron Ely (Doc), Paul Gleason (Long Tom), Bill Lucking (Renny), Michael Miller (Monk), Eldon Quick (Johnny), Darrell Zwerling (Ham), Paul Wexler (Capt. Seas), Janice Heiden (Andriana), Robyn Hilton (Karen), Pamela Hensley (Mona), Bob Corso (Don Rubio Gorro), Carlos Rivas (Kulkan), Chuy Granco (Cheelok), Alberto Morin (Jose), Victor Millan (Chief Chaac), Jorge Cervera, Jr. (Col. Ramirez), Frederico Roberto (El Presidente), Michael Berryman (Coroner), Robert Tessier (Dutchman), Grace Stafford (Little Lady), Scott Walker (Borden)

BUG (Paramount) Producer, William Castle; Director, Jeannot Szwarc; Screenplay, William Castle, Thomas Page; Based on "The Hephaestus Plague" by Thomas Page; Photography, Michel Hugo; Music, Charles Fox; Wardrobe, Guy Verhille; Assistant Director, Jack Roe; Editor, Alan Jacobs; Art Director, Jack Martin Smith; In Panavision and Movielab Color; Rated PG; 99 minutes; June release. CAST: Bradford Dillman (James), Joanna Miles (Carrie), Richard Gilliland (Gerald), Jamie Smith Jackson (Norma), Alan Fudge (Mark), Jesse Vint (Tom), Patty McCormack (Sylvia), Brendan Dillon (Charlie), Fred Downs (Henry), James Greene (Rev. Kern), Jim Poyner (Kenny), Sam Jarvis (Taxi Driver), Bard Stevens (Guard)

SATAN'S CHILDREN (Sterling International) Producer-Director, Joe Wiezycki; Screenplay, Gary Garrett; In Eastmancolor; Rated R; 87 minutes; June release. CAST: Kathy Archer, Stephen White, Joyce Molloy, Bob Ray, Rosemary Orlando, Eldon Mecham, Bob Barbour

POT! PARENTS! POLICE! (Hampton International) Producers, Clark Johnson, Phillip Pine; Direction and Screenplay, Phillip Pine; In Eastmancolor; Rated PG; 89 minutes; June release. CAST: Phillip Pine, Robert Mantell, Madelyn Keen, Martin Margules, Arthur Batanides, Dawn Frame

PURSUIT (Key International) Producer, Vern Piehl; Director, Thomas Quillen; In color; Rated R; 86 minutes; June Release. CAST: Ray Danton, DeWitt Lee, Troy Nabers, Diane Taylor, Eva Kovacs, Jason Clark

LEPKE (Warner Bros.) Producer-Director, Menahem Golan; Executive Producer, Yoram Globus; Story, Wesley Lau; Screenplay, Wesley Lau, Tamar Hoffs; Photography, Andrew Davis; Editor, Dov Hoenig; Music, Ken Wannberg; Designer, Jack Degovia; Costumes, Jodie Tillen; Assistant Director, Fred Miller; In Panavision and Technicolor; Rated R; 110 minutes; June release. CAST: Tony Curtis (Lepke), Anjanette Comer (Bernice), Michael Callan (Kane), Warren Berlinger (Gurrah), Gianni Russo (Anastasia), Vic Tayback (Luciano), Mary Wilcox (Marion), Jack Ackerman (Little Augie), Louis Guss (Max), Vaughn Meader (Walter Winchell), Milton Berle (Meyer)

**Robyn Hilton, Ron Ely
in "Doc Savage. . . ."**

**Tony Curtis, Warren Berlinger, Milton Berle
in "Lepke"**

**Hetty Galen (c)
in "The Night They Robbed Big Bertha's"**

**Earth, Wind and Fire
in "That's the Way of the World"**

THE NIGHT THEY ROBBED BIG BERTHA'S (Scotia American) Producer-Director, Peter Kares; Executive Producer, Sidney Ginsberg; Based on story by Albert T. Viola and Robert Vervoordt; From an idea by Robert N. Langworthy; In Movielab Color; Rated R; 87 minutes; June release. CAST: Robert Nichols (Professor), Hetty Galen (Big Bertha), Doug Hale (Corncob), Gary Allen (Wilbur), Josie Johnson (Sara Sue), Bill Moses (Rufus), Walter Guthrie (Sheriff), Frank Nastasi (Chief White Eagle), Laura Sayer (Priscilla), Terrell Bennett (Preacherman), Kathleen Devine (Savannah), Mary Mendum (Veronica), Mike Tucci (Lou), Harrison Ressler (Manny), Chuck Ransdell (Robbie), Bob Wier (George), Christa Kale (Urchin), Glenda Pierce (Flora Mae), George Ellis (Henry), Don Higdon (Barnibus), Jay Mann (Newscaster), Emily Bell (Faith), Joan Jaffe (Mrs. Oxhammer), Joyce Lee (Mrs. Hornsby), Paige Connor (Orphan), Maurice Hunt (Dean), Larry Robinson (Narrator)

THE $50,000 CLIMAX SHOW (Artimes) Produced and Directed by Anonymous; Screenplay, J. P. Paradine; In color; Rated X; 71 minutes; June release. CAST: J. P. Paradine, Marc Stevens, Kevin Andre, Darby Lloyd Rains

LOVE, LUST & VIOLENCE (M & R) Producer-Director, Norbert Meisel; Executive Producer, Gunter Rittmuller; Screenplay, Stan Kamber; Photography, Bob Maxwell; Art Director, Jack Naylor; Assistant Director, Mark Grossan; In color; Rated X; 98 minutes; June release. CAST: Anthony Fortunado (Joe), Sara Bloom (Louise), Mike Perry (Tony), Arem Fisher (Gen. Amsford), Francisco Garcia (Spike), Alan Fox, Frank Gentile, Nick DeAngelo, Rafael Peralta, Roger Ferrari, Norbert Meisel, Don Jolly, Steve Alexander, Jenn Gillian, Alena Nordin, Bridget Huttercr, Heather Leigh

WHEN A WOMAN CALLS (Tania) Producer, Roberta Prentiss; Associate Producer, Ron Hall; Director, William Haddington, Jr.; Screenplay, Luigi di Gaspany; Editor, Craig Harrison; Photography, Valentine Mu Rana; In color; 87 minutes; June release. CAST: Jamie Gillis, Brie Anthony, Rita Davis, Cheryl Whita, Helen Madigan, Polly Wilson, John Ashton, Merie Prince, Peonies

FIVE SEXY KITTENS (Lurco) Producer, Jean-Francois Davy; Director, Roger Fellous; In Eastman Color, Rated R; 80 minutes; June release. CAST: Marie-Claire Davy, Elizabeth Drancourt, Pauline Larrieu, Anne Libert, Marie-Georges Pascal, Philippe Gaste

THAT'S THE WAY OF THE WORLD (United Artists) Producer-Director, Sig Shore; Story and Screenplay, Robert Lipsyte; Photography, Alan Metzger; Editor, Bruce Wittkin; Score and title theme composed and performed by Maurice White and Earth, Wind and Fire; Associate Producers, Ron Gorton, Philip Fenty; Assistant Director, Steve Shore; Rated PG; 100 minutes; June release. CAST: Harvey Keitel (Buckmaster), Ed Nelson (Carlton), Cynthia Bostick (Velour), Bert Parks (Franklyn), Jimmy Boyd (Gary), Michael Dante (Mike), Maurice White (Early), Ron Gorton (Warren), Valerie Shepherd (Ellen), Herb Towner (Player), Francesca Di Sapio (Amanda), Charles MacGregor (Mantan), Fred Versacci (Ferrara), Murray Moston (Buck's Father), Mike Richards (Norman), Chuck Stepney (Johnny), Linda Fields (Annabel), Nick La Padula (Al), Steve Shore (The Kid), Murray the "K" (Big John), Vi Higgenson (Wonder Woman), Frankie Crocker (Himself), Dick Stewart (Mel), Ramon Feliciano (Busboy), Aubrey De Souza (Chauffeur), Jerry Rush (TV Interviewer), John Powers (The Greek), Leonard Smith (Bouncer), John Haney (Engineer), Doris Troy (Pianist), Barbara Engel (Secretary), Andrew Blau (TV Director), and Earth, Wind and Fire

DOCTOR FEELGOOD (Monarch) Presented by Allan Shackleton; In color; Rated X; 80 minutes; June release. CAST: Harry Reems, Inger Kissin

THE SILENT STRANGER (MGM) Producer, Tony Anthony, Director, Vance Lewis; Screenplay, Vincenzo Cerami, Giancarlo Ferrando; Story, Tony Anthony; Photography, Mario Capriotti; Music, Stelvio Cipriani; Editor, Renzo Lucidi; An Allen Klein-ABKCO Industries Production; Presented by United Artists; Rated PG; June release. CAST: Tony Anthony (The Stranger), Lloyd Barrista (The American), Kin Omac, Kenji Ohara, Kita Mura, Sato, Yoshio Nukano

**Harvey Keitel, Cynthia Bostick, Jimmy Boyd, Bert Parks
in "That's the Way of the World"**

**Tony Anthony
in "Silent Stranger"**

"High School Fantasies"

SLIPUP (Slip-Art) Direction and Screenplay, Harold Hindgrind; Music, S. Ziplow, Slim Pickens; In Eastmancolor; Rated X; 80 minutes; June release. CAST: Darby Lloyd Rains, Jamie Gillis, Eric Edwards, Marc Stevens

YOU AND ME (Filmmakers International) Producer, Bill Record; Director; David Carradine; Story and Screenplay, Robert Henderson; Photography, Bob Collins; Presented by Skip Sherwood; In color; 96 minutes, June release. CAST: David Carradine (Zeto), Richard Chadbourne II (Jimmy), Bobbi Shaw (Wynona), Barbara Seagull (Waitress), Dennis Fimple, Keith Carradine, Bob Carradine, Gary Busey

POOR PRETTY EDDIE (Westamerican Films) Producer-Director, Richard Robinson; Screenplay, B. W. Sandefur; A Michael Thevis Enterprise; In Technicolor; Rated R; 86 minutes; June release. CAST: Leslie Uggams (Liz), Shelley Winters (Bertha), Michael Christian (Eddie), Ted Cassidy (Keno), Dub Taylor (Floyd), Slim Pickens (Sheriff)

NIGHT OF THE STRANGLER (Howco) Producer, Albert J. Salzer; Director, Joy N. Houck, Jr.; In color; Rated R; June release. CAST: Mickey Dolenz (Vance), Chuck Patterson (Priest), James Ralston (Dan), Michael Anthony, Susan McCullough, Katie Tilley, Ann Barrett

THE SISTER-IN-LAW (Crown International) Producers, Jonathan Krivine, Joseph Ruben; Direction and Screenplay, Joseph Ruben; Photography, Bruce G. Sparks; In DeLuxe Color; Rated R; 85 minutes; June release. CAST: Anne Saxon, John Savage, W. G. McMillan, Meridith Baer, Frank Scioscia, Jon Oppenheim, Tom Mahoney

LOVE GIRLS REPORT (New Line) Producer-Director, Stanley Long; Screenplay, Suzanne Mercer, Stanley Long; In color; Rated X; June release. CAST: Lee Donald, Brenda Peters, Nena Francis

A TOUCH OF GENIE (808 Pictures) Producer, Jason Russell; In color; Rated X; June release. CAST: Douglas Stone, Karen Craig, Tina Russell, Harry Reems, Marc Stevens, Eric Edwards, Lynn Stevens, John Ashton, Ultra Max, Sandy Foxx

"Prisoners"

SEXTEEN (Mad Dog) Director, Peter Locke; In color; Rated X; June release. CAST: Gwen Starr, Sue Rowan, Jamie Gillis, Grover Griffith, Candy Love, Angel Barrett

ISLAND OF LOST GIRLS (Hampton International) Producers, Theodore Werner, Ralph Zucker; In Eastmancolor; Rated R; 85 minutes; June release. CAST: Brad Harris, Tony Kendall, Monica Pardo

TEENAGE HITCHHIKERS (NMD) Producer, Jerome S. Kaufman; Director, Gerri Sedley; Screenplay, Rod Whipple; In color; Rated R; 74 minutes; June release. CAST: Kathie Christopher, Sandra Peabody, Nikki Lynn, Claire Wilbur, Ric Mancini, Peter Carew

BLACK SOCKS (Cineprobe) Director, Ronald Sullivan; Screenplay, Joel Gross; A Fieldston Film Production; In color; Rated X; 83 minutes; June release. CAST: Buck Flower, Norman Field, Harrison Phillips, Jamie Gillis, Sandy Dempsey, Linda York

HIGH SCHOOL FANTASIES (Freeway) Producer, Damon Christian; Directed and Written by Morris Deal; Assistant Director, Keith Houze; Photography, Bill Foster; Designer, Pete Lautrec; Editor, Keith Houze; Music, Gene Struman, Bill Spater; Music performed by Damon & The Mysterions; In color; Rated X; 70 minutes; July release. CAST: Larry Barnhouse (Freddie), Rene Bond (Mary), Ric Loots (Buddy), Tony Mazziotti (Moose), Nicole Riddell (Candy), Leo Lyons (Perwin), Cindy Taylor (Polly), April Grant (Weird), Lucille Bragg (Fred's Mother), Maggie Best (Girl in shower), Fred Lorenzo, Steve Harrod (Toughs)

PRISONERS (American Films Ltd.) Producers, W. John Seig, Lewis M. Horwitz; Director, William H. Bushnell, Jr.; Screenplay, William H. Bushnell, Jr., John Marley; Based on the novel "The Prisoners of Quai Dong" by Victor Kolpacoff; Photography, Stephen Katz; Designer, Jackson DeGovia; Editor, Stephen Michael; Music, Ronald Stein; Associate Producer, Joel Michaels; Assistant Director, David Rodgers; A Williams Production; In color; Rated R; 88 minutes; July release. CAST: Jesse Dizon (The Boy), Robert Reece (Sgt. Thompson), Peter Hooten (Lt. Buckley), Howard Hesseman (Maj. Milliams), Mark Bramwell (Kreuger), David Moody (Cowley), Ron McIlwain (Cpl. Russell), Mako (Sgt. Nguyen), Daniel Spelling (Cpl. Finley), Paul Camen (Dr. Mason), Carla LaBrizzi (Nurse Roberts), Linda Wolfe (Stripper), Karen McCormick (Stripper's Manager), Richard Schuyler (Capt. Walters), Ann Carandang, Marsha Nardo, Francisco Paredes, John Estrella, Honorato Estravez, Ivan Moody, Stephen Albert, Joel Polus, Lanny Broyles, Henry Johnson, Albert Robertson, Tony Campisi, Rhoden Styles, James Dillard, Caroline Dukes, Ann Nadel, Drew Pfifer, Michael Grievin, John Robinson, Kurt Woodler, J. D. Del-Juri, Jerry Darwin, Douglas Widmark, Leland Olson, Neal Speir, J. Douglas Cox, M. Spitz

A NEW GIRL IN TOWN (Stone) Direction and Screenplay, Veronica Stone; Music, Paul West; In Eastmancolor; Rated X; July release. CAST: Lola Valentine, Marcus Wayne, Julie Hayes

THE SWINGING BARMAIDS (Premiere) Producer, Ed Carlin; Director, Gus Trikonis; Screenplay, Charles B. Griffith; In color; Rated R; 88 minutes; July release. CAST: Bruce Watson, Laura Hippe, Katie Saylor, Renie Radich, William Smith, Zitto Kazann, Dyanne Thorne, James Travis, Ray Glavin, John Alderman, Judith Roberts, Andre Tayir, Dick Yarmy, Milt Kogan, M. J. Kane

FLIP CHICKS No credits available; Rated X; In color; July release. CAST: Georgina Spelvin, Harry Reems, Marc Stevens, Jeffrey Hurst

SUPER BUG (Allied Artists) A Scorpio Film; In Technicolor; Rated G; 83 minutes; July release. CAST: Robert Mark, Sal Bogese

SALTY (Saltwater) Producer, Kobi Jaeger; Director, Ricou Browning; Screenplay, Ricou Browning, Jack Cowden; In color; Rated G; 90 minutes; July release. CAST: Clint Howard (Tim), Mark Slade (Taylor), Nina Foch (Mrs. Penninger), Julius W. Harris (Clancy), Linda Scruggs (Girl)

DELIVER US FROM EVIL (Dimension) Produced, Directed and Written by Robert McCahon; Executive Producer, Ted Tetrick; In color; Rated G; 104 minutes; July release. CAST: Lloyd Bridges, Dina Merrill, Pat Hingle, Morgan Woodward, Gilbert Roland, R. G. Armstrong, Lonnie Chapman

GOD'S BLOODY ACRE (Omni) Producers, Andrew Lane, Wayne Crawford; Director, Harry E. Kerwin; Screenplay, Robert Woodburn, Wayne Crawford; Music, Michael Shaw; in color; 87 minutes; Rated R; July release. CAST: Scott Lawrence, Jennifer Gregory, Sam Moree, Daniel Schweitzer, Thomas Wood, Robert Rosano

"The Great Massage Parlor Bust"

"Cover Girl Models"

THE GREAT MASSAGE PARLOR BUST (Hollywood International) Producer, John Harris; Director, Eddy Karek-Las; Associate Producers, Marvin Rothman, John Lewis; Photography, Louie Hortwath, Sony, John Harris, Marvin Rothman; A United American Production; 90 minutes; July release. CAST: Paul Glawion, Sam Dana, Deena Kartiz, Bunny Ashcraft, John Lewis, Fred Petersen, Troy Cory, Bobbi Davis, Barbie Foster, Tom Carter, Peter Modler, Alan Ogle, Jennifer Stewart, Sherry Thurman, Rachel English, Trudie Levin, Erica Williams, Irving Wasserman, Evelyn Cortez, Flower Buck

CLEOPATRA JONES AND THE CASINO OF GOLD (Warner Bros.) Produced and Written by William Tennant; Director, Chuck Bail; Based on characters created by Max Julien; Photography, Alan Hume; Art Director, Johnson Tsao; Editor, Willy Kemplen; Music, Dominic Frontiere; Assistant Directors, Bobby Canavarro, William Cheung Kin; In Panavision and Technicolor; Rated R; 96 minutes; July release. CAST: Tamara Dobson (Cleopatra Jones), Stella Stevens (Dragon Lady), Tanny (Mi Ling), Norman FEll (Stanley), Albert Popwell (Matthew), Caro Kenyatta (Melvin), Chan Sen (Soo), Christopher Hunt (Mendez), Lin Chen Chi (Madalyna), Liu Loke Hua (Tony), Eddy Donno (Morgan), Bobby Canavarro (Lin Ma Chen), Mui Kwok Sing (Benny), John Cheng (David)

FRIGHTMARE (Ellman) Producer-Director, Peter Walker; Executive Producer, Tony Tenser; Screenplay, David McGillivray; Story, Peter Walker; Photography, Peter Jessop; Music, Stanley Myers; Art Director, Chris Burke; Editor, Robert Dearburg; Assistant Directors, Brian Lawrence, James Hamilton; Presented by Maureice Smith; In Eastmancolor; Rated R, 86 minutes; July release. CAST: Rupert Davies (Edmund), Sheila Keith (Dorothy), Deborah Fairfax (Jackie), Paul Greenwood (Graham), Kim Butcher (Debbie), Fiona Curzon (Merle), Jon Yule (Robin), Tricia Mortimer (Lilian), Pamela Farbrother (Delia), Edward Kalinski (Alec), Victor Winding (Detective Inspector), Anthony Hennessy (Sgt.), Noel Johnson (Judge), Michael Sharvell-Martin (Barman), Tommy Wright (Nightclub Manager), Andrew Sachs (Barry), Nicholas John (Pete), Jack Dagmar (Old Man), Leo Genn (Dr. Lytell), Gerald Flood (Matthew)

COVER GIRL MODELS (New World) Producer-Director, Cirio Santiago; Screenplay, Howard R. Cohen; Photography, Philip Sacadalon; Music, D'Amarillo; Associate Producer, Robert Waters; Assistant Director, Loe Mari Avellana; Gowns, Jose Moreno; Editors, Gervacio Santos, Richard Anderson; A Filmgroup International Presentation; In Metrocolor; Rated R; 82 minutes; July release. CAST: Pat Anderson (Barbara), Lindsay Bloom (Claire), Tara Strohmeier (Mandy), John Kramer (Mark), Rhonda Leigh Hopkins (Pamela), Mary Woronov (Diane), Vic Diaz (Julik), Tony Ferrer (Ray) A. C. Castro (Rebel), Nory Wright (Tracy), Mark Lebeuse (Sam), Ken Metcalf (Tom), Joe Zucchero (Embassy Man), Zeneida Amador (Juanita), Jordan Rosengarten (Sailor), Joonie Gamboa (Chen), Leo Martin (Wong), Bernard Beam (Ric), Howard Shaw (Publisher), Barbara Perez (Model)

DOLEMITE (Dimension) In color; Rated R; 89 minutes; July release; No other credits available. CAST: Rudy Ray Moore, D'Urville Martin

THE WRESTLING QUEEN (Harnell) Producer, Wayne Wellons; Photography, John Sammons; Music, Michael Baldwin; in Color; Rated PG; July release. CAST: Vivian Vachon, "Cowboy" Dill Watts, "Mad Dog" Vachon, "Grizzly" Smith, Marie "Fifi" Laverne, Danny Hodge, Jean "The Giant" Ferre, "Butcher" Vachon

THE MOUNT OF VENUS (Classic) Producer-Director, Carter Stevens (Malcolm Worob); Screenplay, Merry Seaman; Photography, Prudence Prevails; Editor, Philip Beans; In color; Rated X; 72 minutes; July release. CAST: Jamie Gillis, Georgina Spelvin, Kim Pope, Kevin Andre, Eric Edwards, Rita Davis, Leo Lovelace, Max Packs, Claire Lumere, Nova Kane, Tom D. Bird

SEX DEMON (J.D.G.) Direction and Screenplay, J. C. Cricket; Editor, Craig Harrison; In color; Rated X; July release. CAST: Steve Spahn, Jeff Fuller, Max Scott, David Rivers, Bo Kent, Panama Johnson, Kevin Lowell, Juan Damone, K. Bottler, W. Dukes, David Krystel

"Frightmare"

Tamara Dobson (L), Stella Stevens (R)
in "Cleopatra Jones and the Casino of Gold"

"Beach Blanket Bango"

Candice Rialson, Pat Anderson, Thonda Leigh Hopkins in "Summer School Teachers"

THE SINS OF RACHEL (R. A. Enterprises) Producer-Director, Richard Fontaine; Screenplay, Ann Noble; Music, Robert Bassett: In Eastmancolor; Rated R; 94 minutes; July release. CAST: Ann Noble, Jerome Scott, Brett Marriott, Chase Cordell, Patricia Rees, Bruce Campbell, Stephen Lester

WINTER HAWK (Howco International) Produced, Directed and Written by Charles B. Pierce; Music, Lee Holdridge; Photography, Jim Roberson; Narrator, Dawn Wells; In Technicolor and Techniscope; Rated PG; July release. CAST: Michael Dante (Winter Hawk), Leif Erickson (Gunthrie), Dawn Wells (Clayanna), Woody Strode (Big Rude), Denver Pyle (Arkansas), Elisha Cook, Jr. (Finley), L. Q. Jones (Gates), Dennis Fimple (Scoby), Arthur Hunnicutt (McClusky), Chuck Pierce, Jr. (Cotton), Sacheen Littlefeather (Pale Flower), Jimmy Clem (Little Smith), Ace Powell (Old Indian), Seamon Glass (Big Smith)

THE COLLEGIATES (MSW) Direction, Carter Stevens, Robert Josephs; In color; Rated X; July release. CAST: Harry Reems, Tanya T. Tickler, Mark Andrews, Gloria Von Stuben

PLEASURE MASTERS (Good Time) Produced, Directed and Written by Alex DeRenzy; In color; Rated X; August release. CAST: Kikko, Crystal Lil

FRAMED (Paramount) Producers, Mort and Joel Briskin; Director, Phil Karlson; Screenplay, Mort Briskin; From the novel by Art Powers and Mike Misenheimer; Photography, Jack A. Marta; Music, Pat Williams; Editor, Harry Gerstad; Designer, Stan Jolley; Assistant Director, Robin Clark; Costumes, Eric Seelig; In Metrocolor; Rated R; 106 minutes; August release. CAST: Joe Don Baker (Ron), Conny Van Dyke (Susan), Gabriel Dell (Vince), John Marley (Sal), Brock Peters (Sam), John Larch (Bundy), Warren Kemmerling (Morello), Paul Mantee (Frank), Walter Brooke (Senator), Joshua Bryant (Andrew), Hunter Von Leer (Dewey), Les Lannom (Gary), H. B. Haggerty (Bickford), Hoke Howell (Decker), Lawrence Montaigne (Deputy Allison), Red West (Mallory), Brenton Banks (Jeremiah), Al Hager (Emmett), Ken Lester (Big Jim), Henry O. Arnold (Lenny), Gary Gober (Kenny), Lloyd Tatum (Deputy Wilson), Roy Jenson (Haskins)

SUMMER SCHOOL TEACHERS (New World) Producer, Julie Corman; Direction and Screenplay, Barbara Peeters; Photography, Eric Saarinen; Editor, Barbara Pokras; Music, J. J. Jackson; Associate Producer, Nicole Scott; Assistant Director, Teri Schwartz; Art Director, Marty Bercaw; In Metrocolor; Rated R; 86 minutes; August release. CAST: Candice Rialson (Conklin T), Pat Anderson (Sally), Rhonda Leigh Hopkins (Denise), Will Carney (Jeremy), Grainger Hines (Bob), Christopher Barrett (Jeff), Dick Miller (Sam), Vince Barnett (Principal), Norman Bartold (Agwin), Michael Greer (John John), Barbara Peil (Janice), Ka-Ron Sowell Brown (Jessie), Merie Earle (Ethel), Cecil Elliott (Freida), John Kerry (Hiram), C. D. Smith (Cy), Brian Enright (Slick), Walter O. Miles (Carter), Beach Dickerson (Apartment Manager), Gary Morgan (Roger), Ken Smedberg (James), Bill Thornbury (Arthur), Mike McHenry (Hal), Michael Miller (Neighbor)

BEACH BLANKET BANGO (Freeway) Producer, Damon Christian; Director, Morris Deal; Screenplay, Pete Turner; Photography, Keith House; Art Director, Pete Lautrec; An Amerikon Interpersonal Production; In color; Rated X; 97 minutes; August release. CAST: Rene Bond (Veronica), Tony Mazziotti (Tommy), Cindy Taylor (Candy), Ric Lutz (Lance), Nicole Riddell (Nicky), Sebastian Figg (McWhirter), Larry Barnhouse (Buford), Fred Lorenzo (Zippo), Paul Stiffleren (Bumsteader), Frank Michaels (Ellis), Tim Eastman, Titus Moody (Policemen), Bert Littlebeau (Larry), Lazaro Valdez (Conga Player), April Grant (Girl)

THE HARD HEADS (K-Tel) formerly "The Great Lester Boggs": In DeLuxe Color; Rated PG; August release. Starring Alex Karras.

COONSKIN (Bryanston) Producer, Albert S. Ruddy; Direction and Screenplay, Ralph Bakshi; Photography, William A. Fraker; Design, Don Morgan, John Sparey, Charlie Downs; Editor, Donald W. Ernst; Assistant Director, James Roden; Music composed and performed by Chico Hamilton; In Technicolor; Rated R; 83 minutes; August release. CAST: Barry White (Samson/Brother Bear), Charles Gordone (Preacher/Brother Fox), Scat Man Crothers (Pappy/Old Man Bone), Philip Thomas (Randy/-Brother Rabbit)

Joe Don Baker, Conny Van Dyke in "Framed"

"Coonskin"

92 IN THE SHADE (United Artists) Executive Producer, Elliott Kastner; Producer, George Pappas; Direction and Screenplay, Thomas McGuane; Music, Michael J. Lewis; Photography, Michael C. Butler; Editor, Ed Rothkowitz; Associate Producers, Denis Holt, Marion Rosenberg; Assistant Director, Louis A. Stroller; In color; Rated R; 88 minutes; August release. CAST: Peter Fonda (Tom), Warren Oates (Nichol), Margot Kidder (Miranda), Elizabeth Ashley (Jeannic Carter), Burgess Meredith (Goldsboro), Harry Dean Stanton (Carter), Sylvia Miles (Bella), William Hickey (Skelton), Louise Latham (Mrs. Skelton), Joe Spinell (Ollie), William Roerick (Rudleigh), Evelyn Russell (Mrs. Rudleigh), John Quade (Roy), John Heffernan (Myron), Warren Kemmerling (Powell), Robert Kruse (Waiter), Scott Palmer (Michael)

TONITE ... I LOVE YOU (Hollywood International) Producer-Director, Carlos Tobalina; Photography, William Larrabure; Editor, Alberto Soria; Music, Soria-Tobi; In Technicolor; Rated X; 90 minutes; August release. CAST: Liz Renay (Christy), Luane Roberts (Lou Ann), Barbara Mills (Barby), Carlos Tobalina (Marco), Marsha Jordan (Marsha), Brenda Renay (Call Girl), Morgan Lane (Perkins), J. L. Heart (Barber)

HARDCORE WOMAN (Dog Eat Dog Films) Producer, Carmen Rodriguez; Director, Abe Snake (Peter Locke); Screenplay, Abe Snake, Hort Badorties; Photography, Hort Badorties; Music, Jacques Urbont; In color; Rated X; 78 minutes; Augusts release. CAST: Carah Nicholson, Eric Edwards, Helen Madigan, Erica Eaton, Lefty Cooper, Ellis Deigh

A WOMAN FOR ALL MEN (General Film Corp.) Producer, Robert Blees; Director, Arthur Marks; In color; Rated R, 95 minutes; August release. CAST: Keenan Wynn, Judith Brown, Andy Robinson, Alex Rocco, Don Porter, Peter Hooten, Lois Hall, Skip Ward

THE TAKERS (Boxoffice International) Director, Carlos Monsoya; In Eastmancolor; Rated X; 81 minutes; August release. CAST: Susan Apple, Fred Bush, Coe Bart, Louise Douglas

SIX CARD STUD (Zodiac) Director, Mike Taylor; Photography, Robert Shaw; In color; 65 minutes; August release. CAST: Clay Russel, Paul Strand, Dave Daniels

JOHNNY FIRECLOUD (Entertainment Ventures) Producers, David F. Friedman, William Allen Castleman, Peter B. Good, Anton Wickremasinghe; Director, William Allen Castleman; Story and Screenplay, Wilston Denmark; In Panavision and Technicolor; Rated R; 90 minutes; August release. CAST: Victor Molica, Ralph Meeker, David Canary, Frank DeKova, Christina Hart, Sacheen Littlefeather, Jason Ledger

IN SARAH'S EYES (MSW) Director, Carter Stevens; Screenplay, Katya Kiss; In color; Rated X; August release. CAST: Lorraine Alraune, Anna Livia Plurabella, Eric Edwards, Tony Richards, Bill Morgan, Lynn Harris, Peony Jones, Marc Stevens, Star Bright, Crystal Fontaine, Leo Lovelace, Dick Long, Peter Pudd, William Willing

DISCIPLES OF DEATH (Artists International) Producer, Michael F. Cusack; Director, Frank Q. Bobbs; In color; Rated PG; August release. CAST: Joshua Bryant, Irene Kelly, Dave Cass

WHO? (Allied Artists) Director, Jack Gold; Screenplay, John Gould; In color; Rated PG; 91 minutes; August release. CAST: Elliott Gould, Trevor Howard, Joseph Bova, Ed Grover, John Lehne, James Noble

COUNTRY HOOKER (Boxoffice International) Director, Lou Gwinn; Executive Producer, Harry Novak; In Movielab Color; Rated X; 75 minutes; August release. CAST: Rene Bond, Sandy Dempsey, Rick Loots, Marie Arnold, John Paul Jones, Louis Geno

GLADYS AND HER ALL GIRL BAND No credits available; Rated X; In color; August release. CAST: Paula Roberts, Dotti Sissler, Jimmy Harris, Max Andrews

THE BITE (808 Pictures) Director, Jerry Denby; Music, Tom Charles, Michael Face; In color; Rated X; 80 minutes; August release. CAST: Jennifer Fordan (Kate), Eric Edwards (Toledo Kid), Alan Marlo (John), Hardy Harrison (Francis), Sonny Landham (Tex), Kevin Andre (Governor), Felicity Browning (Madam), Jamie Gillis (Customer), Ginger Snaps, Rita Davis

THE HANGING WOMAN (International Artists) In color; Rated R; 90 minutes; September release. CAST: Vicki Nesbitt, Stanley Cooper

Margot Kidder, Peter Fonda
in "92 in the Shade"

THRESHOLD: THE BLUE ANGELS EXPERIENCE (Ambassador) Producer-Director, Paul Marlow; Associate Producer-Photography, Dave Gardner; Narrative, Frank Herbert; Narrated by Leslie Nielsen; in color; Rated G; 93 minutes; September release.

THE GODSON (Boxoffice International) Produced, Directed and Written by William Rotsler; In color; 92 minutes; September release. CAST: Jason Yukon, Orita DeChadwick, Damon Kebroya, Don Garcia, Lois Mitchell

THE KOWLOON CONNECTION No credits available; In color; Rated X; September release. CAST: John C. Holmes, Suzy Chung

PICK-UP (Crown International) Producers, Jack Winter, Bernie Hirschenson; Director, Bernie Hirschenson; Music, Patrick Adams, Michael Rod; A Winter/Gregoravich Production; In color; Rated R; 80 minutes; September release. CAST: Jill Senter, Alan Long, Gini Eastwood, Tom Quinn, Bess Douglass, Don Penny, John Winter, Elizabeth Sinn, Nate Clark, and voices of Grayson Hall, Jim Bouton, Evelyn Paige

MIRAGE d'AMOUR (Command Cinema) alternate title "Illusion of Love"; Presented by Chuck Vincent and Howard Winters, In color; Rated X; September release. CAST: Iris Flouret, Jamie Gillis

ANYONE BUT MY HUSBAND (Anonymous) Director, Robert Norman; In color; Rated X; September release. CAST: C. J. Laing, Tony Perez; Jennifer Jordan, Eric Edwards, Bree Anthony, Robert Kerr, Dianna Darby, Robert Combs

SOUP DU JOUR (ART) Executive Producer, Beula Brown; Producer, Jim Holiday; Director, Beau Buchanan; Editor, Jim Holiday; Art Director, Chuck Lawrence; Music, Kenny Armstrong, Joseph Gallelo; In color, Rated X; September release. CAST: Toni Roam, Shelly Dinah Myte, Peony Jones, Jennifer Jordan, Susan Barret, Kevin Andre, Jackie Beardsley, Bert Blake, Chad Davis, Wirlyn Dervich, Dean Edwards, John Fraser, Jamie Gillis, Grover Griffith, Jake Hudson, Micky Humm, Chris Walton, Harry Watson

Carlos Tobalina, Liz Renay
in "Tonite ... I Love You"

**Muhammad Ali
in "Ali the Man"**

GEMINI AFFAIR (Moonstone) Director, Matt Cimber; Music, Herschel Burke Gilbert; In Movielab Color; Rated X; 92 minutes; September release. CAST: Marta Kristen, Kathy Kersh, Anne Seymour, Victoria Carroll, Herb Eden, Rudy Durand, John Hart, Buck Flower, Tom Pittman

GONE WITH THE WEST (International Cinefilm) Producer, William Collins; Director, Bernard Girard; A Laurel Associates Presentation; In color; Rated R; September release. CAST: James Caan, Stefanie Powers, Aldo Ray, Robert Walker, Jr., Barbara Werle, Sammy Davis, Jr.

BLAZING STEWARDESSES (Independent International) Producer, Samuel M. Sherman; Director, Al Adamson; In Metrocolor; Rated R; 89 minutes; September release. CAST: Yvonne DeCarlo, Bob Livingston, Connie Hoffman, Regina Carrol, T. A. King, Don "Red" Barry, Geoffrey Land, Harry Ritz, Jimmy Ritz, Sheldon Lee, Carol Bilger, Nicole Riddell

PART 2 WALKING TALL (American International) Producer, Charles A. Pratt; Director, Earl Bellamy; Screenplay, Howard B. Kreitsek; Photography, Keith Smith; Editor, Art Seid; Music, Walter Scharf; Art Director, Phil Jeffries; Assistant Director, David (Buck) Hall; In DeLuxe Color; Rated PG; 109 minutes; September release. CAST: Bo Svenson (Buford), Luke Askew (Pinky), Noah Beery (Carl), John Chandler (Ray), Robert Doqui (Obra), Bruce Glover (Grady), Richard Jaeckel (Stud), Brooke Mills (Ruby), Logan Ramsey (John), Angel Tompkins (Marganne), Lurene Tuttle (Grandma), William Bryant (FBI Agent), Leif Garrett, Dawn Lyn (Pusser Children)

GIVE 'EM HELL, HARRY! (Theatre Television) Producers, Al Ham, Joseph E. Bluth; Executive Producers, Bill Sargent, John J. Tennant; Directed and Edited by Steve Binder; Screenplay, Samuel Gallu; Photography, Ken Palius; Designer, James Hamilton; Assistant Director, James Stahr; In Technicolor; 104 minutes; September release. CAST: James Whitmore as Harry S. Truman

**James Whitmore
in "Give 'Em Hell Harry!"**

ALI THE MAN: ALI THE FIGHTER (CinAmerica) Producers, Shintaro Katsu, William Greaves; Directors, Rick Baxter, William Greaves; Music, Simon Stokes; Performed by Richie Havens; In color; Rated G; 142 minutes; September release. A documentary in two parts spanning the career of Muhammad Ali.

EVERY INCH A LADY (Mature) Produced, Directed and Written by John and Len Amero; Photography, Roberta Findlay; Editor, Len Amero; Music, Firth DeMule; In Eastmancolor; Rated X; September release. CAST: Darby Lloyd Rains, Harry Reems, Andrea True, Kim Pope, Jamie Gillis, Marc Stevens, Erica Eaton, Kurt Mann, David Savage; Tiv Davenport, Fabian Stuart, Tony Vito, Loyd Bacon, Richard Weigle, Dr. Infinity

DRIFTER (Eurpean Film Exchange) Produced, Directed, Photographed and Edited by Pat Rocco; Screenplay, Edward Middleton; In Technicolor; Rated R; September release. CAST: Joe Adair (Drifter), David Russell (Steve), Joe Caruso (Geno), Dean Shah-Kee (Wagner), Bambi Allen (Klamath), Inga-Marie Pinson, (Karen), Ann Collins (Maxine), Gerald Strickland (Dana)

HURRY TOMORROW (Hound Dog Films) Producers, Richard Cohen, Kevin Rafferty; Director, Richard Cohen; Photography, Kevin Rafferty; In color; 80 minutes; September release. A documentary about a men's psychiatric ward in a state hospital.

SEXUAL SENSORY PERCEPTION (Hollywood International) Produced, Directed and Written by Jack Mattis, Martin Margulies; Additional Material, Larry Hilbrand; Photography, Tom Denove, Jim Schandler; Art Director, Linelle Dali; Editor, Tom Denove; Associate Producer, Peter Cicero; In color; Rated X; 78 minutes; September release. CAST: Kathy Norris, Sandy Dempsey, Jim Cassidy, Nina Beauscia, Jason Yukon, Terry Johnson, Sandy Carey, Ray Sebastian, Annette Funiviola, Becky Pearlman, Susan Dreger, Al Ward, Maria Arnold, Allen Marcus, Wayne Chapman, Philip Ready, Joanne Cloreaux, Diane Castillo, Ginger Kelly, Jake Fissure, Larry Hilbrand, Jay Phyllson, Louise Karloff, Jack Harper, Martin Margulies, Jon Mattisse, Vic Tannoy, Mickey Casa

PANHANDLE CALIBER 38 (Scotia American) Producer, F. T. Gay; Director, Tony Secchi; In Color; September release. CAST: Keenan Wynn, Scott Holden (No other details available)

ABIGAIL LESLIE IS BACK IN TOWN (Monarch) Direction and Screenplay, Joe Sarno; Presented by Allan Shackleton; Rated X; In color; 96 minutes; September release. CAST: Rebecca Brooke, Sarah Nicholson, Jamie Gillis, Jennifer Welles

SODOM AND GOMORRAH—THE LAST SEVEN DAYS (Mitchell Brothers) Producers and Directors, Jim Mitchell, Artie Mitchell; Screenplay, Billy Boyer; Rated X; In color; September release. CAST: Sean Prancato, Gina Fornelli, George McDonald, Johnnie Keyes, Jacquie Brody, Deborah Brast, Thom Blardon, Tyler Reynolds, Ken Turner, Sharon Thorpe

AN EYE FOR AN EYE (Brentwood) Director, Larry Brown; Screenplay, Walter C. Dallenbach; Associate Producer, Barbara Kieserman; Executive Producers, Thomas P. Richardson, Jackson Bostwick; Photography, Jack Beckett; In color; Rated PG; 86 minutes; September release. CAST: Tom Basham, Gene Carlson, Gretchen Kanne, Dave Carlile, Barbara Grover, Lance Larson

THE GARDENER (United Marketing/KKI) Direction and Screenplay, James H. Kay III; Associate Producer, Chalmer G. Kirkbridge, Jr.; In color; Rated R; 97 minutes; October release. CAST: Katharine Houghton, Rita Gam, Joe Dallesandro, James Congdon, Teodorina Bello, Anne Meacham

RETURN TO CAMPUS (Cinepix) Produced, Directed and Written by Harold Cornsweet; Photography, Steve Shuttack, Pierre Janet; Music, Gordon Zahler, Harry Fields, OSU Band; Director, Robert Hare; In color; 100 minutes; October release. CAST: Earl Keyes (Hal), Ray Troha (Bruce), Al Raymond (Rupp), Robert Gutin (Pighead), Paul Jacobs (Esco), Helen Killinger (Joyce), Norma Joseph (Barbara), Arnold Palmer (Spike), John Barner (Dean), Connie O'Connell (Singer), Tom Harmon, Jesse White (Sports Announcers)

ABDUCTION (Venture) Producer, Kent E. Carroll; Director, Joseph Zito; Screenplay, Kent E. Carroll; Based on "Black Abductor" by Harrison James; Photography, Joao Hernandez; Editor, James Macreading; Music, Ron Frangipane, Robbie Farrow; A Blackpool Partnership Production; In Technicolor; Rated R; 100 minutes; October release. CAST: Judith-Marie Bergan (Patricia), David Pendleton (Dory), Gregory Rozakis (Frank), Leif Erickson (Prescott), Dorothy Malone (Mrs. Prescott), Lawrence Tierney (FBI Agent), Presley Caton (Angie), Catherine Lacy (Carol), Andrew Rohrer (Michael), Andrew Bloch (Jake), David Carroll (Cop), Pat Hernon, Dan Daniel, John Bartholomew Tucker (Newscasters)

**"The Best of Walt Disney's
True-Life Adventures"**

**Roger E. Mosley, Trina Parks
in "Darktown Strutters"**

SEXUAL KUNG FU IN HONG KONG (Hollywood International) Produced, Directed, Adapted, and Photographed by Carlos Tobalina; Written by Lawrence Samuelson; In Eastmancolor, Rated X; 90 minutes; October release. CAST: Maria Pia (Russian Spy), Nina Fause (Susie), Nancy Young (Kathy), Burt Raymond (Kokus), Jeff Goodman (Sy), Simone Rosen (Flor), Terry Capone (Chinese Maid), William Larrabure (Russian General), Paul Taylor (5 O'clock Jim)

THE BEST OF WALT DISNEY'S TRUE-LIFE ADVENTURES (Buena Vista) Producers, Ben Sharpsteen, James Algar; Director, James Algar; Narration, James Algar, Winston Hibler, Ted Sears; Narrated by Winston Hibler; Photography, Alfred G. Milotte, Elma Milotte, N. Paul Kenworthy, Jr., Robert H. Crandall, Hugh A. Wilmar, James R. Simon, Herb and Lois Crisler, Tom McHugh, Jack C. Couffer; Music, Paul Smith, Oliver Wallace, Buddy Baker; Editors, Norman Palmer, Anthony Gerard, Lloyd L. Richardson, Gregg McLaughlin, Gordon Brenner; In Technicolor; Rated G; 89 minutes; October release.

DARKTOWN STRUTTERS (New World) Director, William Witney; Screenplay, George Armitage; Photography, Joao Fernandes; Editor, Morton Tubor; Assistant Director, Frank Beetson; Designer, Jack Fisk; Art Director, Peter Jamison; Costumes, Michael Nicola; In Metrocolor; Rated PG; 90 minutes; October release. CAST: Trina Parks (Syreena), Edna Richardson (Carmen), Bettye Sweet (Miranda), Shirley Washington (Theda), Roger E. Mosley (Mellow), Christopher Joy (Wired), Stan Shaw (Raunchy), Dewayne Jesse (V. D.), Charles Knapp (Tubbins), Edward Marshall (Emmo), Dick Miller (Hugo), Milt Kogan (Babel), Norman Bartold (Cross), Gene Simms (Flash), Sam Laws (Philo), Frankie Crocker (Stuff), Della Thomas (Lixie), Ed Bakey (Rev. Tilly), Fuddle Bagley (Casabah), Frances Nealy (Cinderella), Barbara Morrison (Mrs. Parasol), Raymond Allen (Six Bits), Charles Woolf (Fallow), Alvin Childress (Bo), Zara Cully (Lorelai), The Dramatics, John Gary Williams and The Newcomers, Oaky Miller and Company, The Minstrels

JOYCE CHOPRA (Phoenix) Three short films by Joyce Chopra: "Girls at 12," "Clorae and Albie," "Matina Horner, Portrait of a Person"; 82 minutes; October release.

YESSONGS (Ellman) Presented by Richard Ellman; In color; Rated G; 75 minutes; October release. A filmed concert of the Yes: Rick Wakeman, Steve Howe, John Anderson, Alan White, Chris Squire

MILESTONES (Stone) Producers, Barbara Stone, David C. Stone; Directed, Written and Photographed by Robert Kramer, John Douglas; In black and white, and color; 195 minutes; October release. CAST: Grace Paley (Helen), David C. Stone (Joe), John Douglas (John), Laurel Berger (Laurel), Mary Chapelle (Mama), Bobby Buechler (Jamie), Liz Dear (Liz), Jay Foley (Terry), Suey Hagadorn (Suey), Harvey Quintal (Harvey), Kalaho (Erika), Lou Ho (Lou), Tina Shepherd (Elizabeth), Paul Zimet (Peter)

THE MEAL (Ambassador) Produced, Directed and Written by R. John Hugh; Music, Stu Phillips; In color; Rated R; October release. CAST: Dina Merrill, Carl Betz, Leon Ames, Susan Logan, Vicki Powers, Steve Potter, Corinne Bustad, Mike Rasmussen, Bill Dunnagan

THE PIGKEEPER'S DAUGHTER (Boxoffice International) Producer-Director, Bethel G. Buckalew; In Movielab Color; 93 minutes; October release. CAST: Terry Gibson, Patty Smith, Gina Paluzzi, John Keith, Peter James, Buck Wayner, Paul Stanley, Nick Armans

TAKE A HARD RIDE (20th Century-Fox) Producer, Harry Bernsen; Director, Anthony M. Dawson; Screenplay, Eric Bercovici, Jerry Ludwig; Music, Jerry Goldsmith; Photography, Riccardo Pallotini; Co-Produced by Cine Y Television; In color; Rated PG; 103 minutes; October release. CAST: Jim Brown (Pike), Lee Van Cleef (Kiefer), Dana Andrews (Morgan), Barry Sullivan (Kane), Harry Carey, Jr. (Dumper), Robert Donner (Skave), Fred Williamson (Tyree), Charles McGregor, Ronald Howard, Leonard Smith, Ricardo Palacios, Robin Levitt

**Lee Van Cleef, Barry Sullivan
in "Take a Hard Ride"**

**Fred Williamson, Catherine Spaak, Jim Brown
in "Take a Hard Ride"**

Anthony Andrews, Timothy Bottoms, Nicola Pagett in "Operation Daybreak"

STEVIE, SAMSON AND DELILAH (Libert Films International) Producer-Director, Steve Hawkes; Narrated by William Windom; Photography, Jack McGowan; in color; Rated G; 86 minutes; October release. CAST: Steven Hawkes, Jr. (Stevie), Steve Hawkes, Chuck Hall

SPIKEY'S MAGIC WAND (Different Strokes) Producer, Vance Farlowe; Music, Moog Synthecisor; In color; Rated X; October release. CAST: Harry Reems, Georgina Spelvin, Elethia Lewis, Mary Madigan, Amy Mathieu, Inger Kissin

BORN TO RAISE HELL (Marathon) A Psycho Films Production; Conceived and Directed by Roger Earl; Photography, Ray Tamarago; Editor, Robert Shaw, Music, Rod Riker; Assistant Director, Lucas Johns; In Eastmancolor; Rated X; 90 minutes; October release. CAST: Val Martin (Sadist), Quave Dalton (Assistant), John Detour, Steve Richards, Eric Lansing, Tiger John, David Andrews (Masochists), Paul Joseph, Craig Roberts (Policemen)

IMPULSE (Camelot Entertainment) Producer, Socrates Ballis; Director, Willliam Grefe; Screenplay, Tony Crechales; Associate Producer, Doug Hobart; Executive Producer, Rick Diaz; In Technicolor; Rated PG; 89 minutes; October release. CAST: William Shatner, Ruth Roman, Harold Sakata, Kim Nicholas, Jennifer Bishop, James Dobbs, Marcie Knight

THE GIANT SPIDER INVASION (Group I) Producers, Richard L. Huff, Bill Rebane; Director, Bill Rebane; Executive Producer, William W. Gillette, Jr.; A Transcentury Picture; In color; Rated PG; October release. CAST: Steve Brodie (Dr. Vance) Barbara Hale (Jenny), Leslie Parrish (Ev), Robert Easton (Kester), Alan Hale (Sheriff), Dianne Lee Hart (Terri), Bill Williams (Dutch), Christiane Schmidtmer (Helga)

SO SAD ABOUT GLORIA (Libert Films International) Director, Harry Thomason; A Centronics International Production; In color; Rated PG; 90 minutes; October release. CAST: Lori Saunders, Dean Jagger, Bob Ginnaven, Seymour Treitman

Jennifer O'Neill, Elliott Gould in "Whiffs"

THE BOOB TUBE (Independent International) A V/M Production; Presented by Dan Q. Kennis; In Eastmancolor; Rated X; 82 minutes; October release. CAST: John Alderman, Sharon Kelly, Lyllah Torena, Lois Laine, Paxton Quigley

THE DIRTY MIND OF YOUNG SALLY (Boxoffice International) Producer-Director, Bethel G. Buckalew; In Movielab Color; 94 minutes; October release. CAST: Sharon Kelly, C. D. LaFleure, Robyn Whitting, Cliff Bradley, James Mathers, Angela Carnon, Jay Pe Jones

WET ROCK (Variety Films) A Cambridge Film Production; In color; Rated X; October release. CAST: Dawn O'Neal, Jamie Gillis, Vaughn Parks

BOTH WAYS (Douglas) Director, Jerry Douglas; In Cinemascope and color; Rated X; October release. CAST: Andrea True, Gerald Grant, Dean Tait

THE JOURNEY OF O (Inner Films) A Hunt Conning Production; In color; Rated X; October release. CAST: Vanessa Jorson, Marilyn Berg, Susan Hurley, Georgina Spelvin

TRAIN RIDE TO HOLLYWOOD (Taylor-Laughlin) A Billy Jack Enterprises production; Executive Prodcers, George G. Braunstein, Ronald N. Hamady; Producer, Gordon A. Webb; Director, Charles Rondeau; Screenplay, Dan Gordon; Photography, Al Francis; Editor, Jim Heckert; Art Director, Phil Jefferies; Music, Pip Williams; Songs, Bloodstone; In color; Rated G; 85 minutes; October release. CAST: Bloodstone (The Sinceres), Michael Payne (Producer), Pete Gonneau (Assistant Producer), Michael Payne (Eric), Don Dandridge (Porter), Guy Marks, Jay Lawrence, Phyllis E. Davis, Jay Robinson, Roberta Collins, John Nyhers, Elliot Robins, Ann Willis, Peter Ratray, Bill Oberlin, Tracy Reed, Gerri Reddick, Jessamine Milner, Burt Mustin, Jack DeLeon, Whitey Hughes, Jimmy Lennon

NOT MY DAUGHTER (Carvel) Producer-Director, Jerry Schafer; Screenplay and Story, Lawrence Holden; In Techniscope and Technicolor; Rated R; October release. CAST: James J. Griffith, Karen Arthur, Belinda Palmer, Jimmy Cavaretta, Joe Hooker, Judy Strangis

SEXUAL COMMUNICATION (Hollywood International) Executive Producer, Lester Craig; Producer, Justin Boyd; Direction and Screenplay, Albert Irving; Editor, Zemai; Photography, Bob Miller; Music, M. Hooper; In Eastmancolor; Rated X; November release. CAST: Sheila I. Rossi (Dr. Young), Donald Williams (Dr. Meyers), John Franks (Dr. Warner), Rosemary Morgan (Cynthia), George Martin (Peter), Linda Curtis (Maude), Tracy Shaw (Harry), Donna Snow (Secretary)

OPERATION DAYBREAK (Warner Bros.) Producer, Carter De Haven; Director, Lewis Gilbert; Screenplay, Ronald Harwood; From novel "Seven Men at Daybreak" by Alan Burgess; Associate Producer, Stanley O'Toole; Photography, Henry Decae; Editor, Thelma Connell; Music, David Hentschel; Art Directors, William McCrow, Bob Kulic; In Technicolor; November release. CAST: Timothy Bottoms (Jan), Martin Shaw (Karel), Joss Ackland (Janak), Nicola Pagett (Anna), Anthony Andrews (Josef), Anton Diffring (Reinhard), Diana Coupland (Aunt Marie), Ronald Radd (Her Husband), Kim Fortune (Ata), Pavla Matejovska (Jindriska), Carl Duering (Karl), Cyril Shaps (Father Petrek), Ray Smith (Hajek)

WHIFFS (20th Century-Fox) Producer, George Barrie; Director, Ted Post; Screenplay, Malcolm Marmorstein; Music, John Cameron; Associate Producer, Don Erickson; Photography, David Walsh; Editor, Robert Lawrence; Art Director, Fernando Carrere; Assistant Director, Daniel McCauley; A Brut Production; In color; Rated PG; 90 minutes; November release. CAST: Elliott Gould (Dudley Frapper), Eddie Albert (Col. Lockyer), Harry Guardino (Chops), Godfrey Cambridge (Dusty), Jennifer O'Neill (Scottie), Alan Manson (Sgt. Poultry), Donald Barry (Post), Richard Masur (Lockyer's Aide), Howard Hesseman (Gopian), Matt Greene (Sentry), James Brown (Trooper)

THE DEVIL'S CLEAVAGE (Kuchar) Directed, Written and Photographed by George Kuchar; Additional Photography, Larry Huston, Mike Kuchar; 115 minutes; November release. CAST: Curt McDowell, Kathleen Hohalek, Virginia Giritlian, Michele Gross, John Thomas, Mark Ellinger, Ilka Normile, Ann Knutson, Janey Sneed, Charlie Thomas, Barbara Linkevitch

THE ADVENTURES OF THE WILDERNESS FAMILY (Pacific International Enterprises) Producer, Arthur R. Dubbs; Direction and Screenplay; Music, Stewart Raffill; Music, Gene Kauer, Douglas Lackey; Color by CFI; Rated G; 94 minutes; November release. CAST: Robert F. Logan (Skip), Susan Damante Shaw (Pat), Hollye Holmes (Jenny), Ham Larsen (Toby)

THE NAUGHTY VICTORIANS (Hawthorne International) Producer, John Butterworth; Director, Robert S. Kinger; Screenplay, Robert S. Kinger; From Grove Press edition of "A Man with a Maid"; Photography, Joe Mann; Editor, Leonard Hirsch; Music, Arthur Sullivan; Art Director, Francis Pezza; Costumes, Susan Buck; In color; Rated X; November release. CAST: Beerbohm Tree (Jack), Susan Sloane (Alice), Angel Barrett (Molly), Jennifer Jordan (Lady Bunt), Heather Brown (Cicely)

CRUISIN' 57 (Toby Ross) Producer-Director, Toby Ross; In color; Rated S; 65 minutes; No other credits available; November release. CAST: Terry Winter, Mike Muni, David Larson, Gary Nelson, Peanuts, Mike Tennis

THE STORY OF JOANNA (Blueberry Hill) Produced, Directed and Written by Gerard Damiano; Photography, Harry Flecks; Art Director, Tydis Brown; Music, Edward Earle; In color; Rated X; November release. CAST: Jamie Gillis (Jason), Terri Hall (Joanna), Zebedy Colt (Griffin), Juliet Graham (Gena), Steven Lark (Dancer), John Busche, John Koven, Roy Carlton

A BOY AND HIS DOG (LGJaf) Producer, Alvy Moore; Direction and Screenplay, L. Q. Jones; Based on novella by Harlan Ellison; Photography, John Arthur Morrill; Editor, Scott Conrad; Music, Tim McIntire; Designer, Ray Boyle; 87 minutes; November release. CAST: Don Johnson (Vic), Susanne Benton (Quilla June), Tiger (Blood), Tim McIntire (Voice of Blood), Charles McGraw (Preacher), Jason Robards (Craddock), Alvy Moore, Helene Winston (Committee Members)

ORIENTAL BLUE (A & B) Producer, Lin Cho Chiang; Director, Philip T. Drexler, Jr.; Screenplay, V. Merania; Based on "Lady Fang" stories by Chio-Len Huk; Photography, Valentine Mu Rana; Editor, B. Art Ditmar; In color; Rated X; November release. CAST: Peonies Jong, Bree Anthony, Bobby Astyr, Jamie Gillis, Steven Lark, National Velvet, Juliet Graham, Alan Marlo, Tony Rich, Kim Pope, Maureen Anderson, Fred Ainsley, C. J. Laing, Cedar Houston

BANJOMAN (Blue Pacific) Producers, Richard G. Abramson, Robert French, Michael C. Varhol; Directors, Richard G. Abramson, Michael C. Varhol; In DeLuxe Color; 105 minutes; November release. CAST: Earl Scruggs, Ramblin' Jack Elliott, Joan Baez, Tracy Nelson, Mother Earth, David Bromberg, Nitty Gritty Dirt Band, The Byrds, Doc & Merle Watson

TIMBER TRAMPS (Howco International) Produced and Written by Chuck Keen; In color; Rated PG; November release. CAST: Claude Akins, Tab Hunter, Cesar Romero, Eve Brent, Leon Ames, Rosie Grier, Joseph Cotten

THE CHAPERONE (Mirage) Produced, Directed and Photographed by Jaacov Jaacovi; Music, John Jones; Rated X; In color; 87 minutes; November release. CAST: Sandy Dempsey, Walter Roland Moore, Paula Lane, John Tull, Sandy Carey, Doug Senior, Jonne Shepler

DR. MINX (Dimension) Produced, Directed and Written by Hikmet Avedis; Executive Producer, Marlene Schmidt; Music, Shorty Rogers; Editor, Norman Wallerstein; Photography, Masoud Joseph; In color; 94 minutes; Rated R; November release. CAST: Edy Williams, Randy Boone, Harvey Jason, Marlene Schmidt, Alvy Moore, William Smith

THE YOUNG DIVORCEES (Monarch) Producer-Director, Laurance E. Mascott; Co-Producer, William Lipper; Screenplay, Holly Mascott; In color; Rated X; 90 minutes; November release. CAST: Tom Fielding, Holly Mascott, George Takei

WELCOME HOME, BROTHER CHARLES (Crown International) Produced, Directed and Written by Jamaa Fanaka; Photography, James Babij; Theme Music, Jamaa Fanaka; In Metrocolor; A Bea-Bob production; Rated R; November release. CAST: Marlo Monte, Reatha Grey, Stan Kamber, Tiffany Peters, Ven Bigelow, Jake Carter, Ed Sandor, Jackie Ziegler

ENCOUNTER WITH THE UNKNOWN (Libert) Producer, Joe Glass; Director, Harry Thomason; Narrated by Rod Serling; A Centronics International Production; In color; Rated PG; 87 minutes; November release. CAST: Rosie Holotick, Gary Brockette, Gene Ross, Annabelle Weenick, Bob Ginnaven, August Sehven, Kevin Kieberly

AROUND THE WORLD WITH JOHNNY WADD (Cunard) Presented by Donald C. Cunard; In color; Rated X; November release. CAST: John C. Holmes

COME AND JUDGE (D.D.J.) Producer, David P. Buckley; Director, D. Lawrence Thomas; Music, Ronald Frangipane; In color; Rated X; November release. A documentary on the 1973 Supreme Court decision on pornography.

**Jim Hutton
in "Psychic Killer"**

SEX CLINIC GIRLS Producer-Director, Alex Robbins; In color; Rated X; November Release. CAST: Veronica Claire, Erika Ingers, Dora Darling

CARNAL HAVEN (Troy Benny) Produced, Directed, Written, Photographed, and Edited by Troy Benny; Assistant Producer, Sharon Thorp; Music, Lyrics, Carl Esser; In color; Rated X; December release. CAST: Sharon Thorpe, Leslie Bovee, John L. Dupre, Annette Haven, Miguel Jones, Pat Lee, Bonnie Holiday, Bob Migliano

PSYCHIC KILLER (AVCO Embassy) Executive Producer, Mohammed Rustam; Producer, Mardi Rustam; Director, Raymond Danton; Screenplay, Greydon Clark, Mike Angel, Raymond Danton; Music, William Kraft; Assistant Producer, Greydon Clark; Assistant Directors, Ron Smith, Bob Hargrove; Art Director, Joel Leonard; In color; Rated PG; 90 minutes; December release. CAST: Jim hutton (Arnold), Julie Adams (Laura), Paul Burke (Det. Morgan), Nehemiah Persoff (Dr. Gubner), Aldo Ray (Anderson), Neville Brand (Lemonowski), Della Reese (Mrs. Gibson), Rod Cameron (Dr. Commanger), Joe Della Sorte (Sanders), Harry Holcomb (Judge), Robyn Raymond (Jury Foreman), Jerry James (Dead Doctor), Diane Deininger (Arnold's Mother), John Dennis (Frank), Judith Brown (Anne), Mary Wilcox (Martha), Bill Quinn (Coroner), Marland Proctor (Motorcycle Cop), Bill Bonner (Ambulance Driver), Walter Miles (Coroner), Whit Bissell (Dr. Taylor), Stack Pierce (Emilio), Ed Cross (Old Man), Mello Alexandria (Cop), Sheldon Lee (Inmate), Greydon Clark (Sowash)

FRIDAY FOSTER (American International) Producer-Director, Arthur Marks; Executive Producer, Charles Stroud; Screenplay, Orville Hapton; From story by Arthur Marks; Based on comic strip "Friday Foster"; Photography, Harry May; Editor, Stanley Frazen; Music, Luchi De Jesus; Song "Friday," Bodie Chandler; Assistant Director, Gene De Ruelle; In Movielab Color; Rated R; 89 minutes; December release. CAST: Pam Grier (Friday Foster), Yaphet Kotto (Colt), Godfrey Cambridge (Ford), Thalmus Rasulala (Blake), Eartha Kitt (Madam Rena), Jim Backus (Enos), Scatman Crothers (Rev. Franklin), Ted Lange (Fancy), Tierre Turner (Cleve), Paul Benjamin (Sen. Hart)

**Yaphet Kotto, Pam Grier, Stan Stratton
in "Friday Foster"**

Kevin Hooks, Irene Cara, Wanda Velez, Leon Pinkney in "Aaron Loves Angela"

DISTANCE (Cine Bright) Directed, Edited and Photographed by Anthony Lover; Screenplay, Jay Castle; Producer, George Coe; In color 93 minutes; December release. CAST: Paul Benjamin (Elwood), Eiia Pokkinen (Greta), James Woods (Larry), Bibi Bosch (Joanne), Hal Miller (Jesse), Polly Holliday (Mrs. Herman)

BUGS BUNNY SUPERSTAR (Hare Raising Films) Producer-Director, Larry Jackson; Narrated by Orson Welles; Featuring Bob Clampett, Tex Avery, Fritz Freleng; 90 minutes; December release.

KEEP IT UP, JACK! (Topar) Producer-Director, Tom Parker; Rated R; December release; No other credits available. CAST: Mark Jones, Sue Longhurst, Maggi Burton (Penthouse Pet), Steve Viedor (Muscles)

THE AMAZING LOVE SECRET (TOPAR) Producer-Director, Tom Parker; Rated R; December release; No other credits available. CAST: John Holmes, Sandy Dempsey, Kathy Rowland, Maria Arnold, George Carey, Starr Lynn Comb

BEST FRIENDS (Crown International) Producer-Director, Noel Nosseck; Screenplay, Arnold Somkin; Photography, Stephen M. Katz; Editor, Robert Gordon; Music, Rick Cunha; Art Director, Jodie Tillen; In Movielab Color; Rated R; 83 minutes; December release. CAST: Richard Hatch (Jesse), Susanne Benton (Kathy), Doug Chapin (Pat), Ann Noland (Jo Ella), Renee Paul, Ralph Montgomery, Roger Bear, John McKee, Bonnie Erkel

AGAINST A CROOKED SKY (Doty-Dayton) Producer, Lyman D. Dayton; Associate Producer, Dan Greer; Director, Earl Bellamy; Assistant Directors, Morris Abrams, Ed Ledding; Art Director, Carl Anderson; Music, Lex DeAzevedo; Photography, Joe Jackman; Editor, Marsh Hendry; Screenplay, Douglas C. Stewart, Eleanor Lamb; In color; Rated G; 89 minutes; December release. CAST: Richard Boone (Russian), Stewart Petersen (Sam), Geoffrey Land (Temkai), Clint Ritchie (John), Shannon Farnon (Molly), Margaret Willey (Old Hag), Brenda Venus (Askhea), Henry Wilcoxon (Cut Tongue), Vincent St. Cyr (Shokabob), Jewel Blanch (Charlotte), Gordon Hanson (Shumeki)

Ernestine Jackson, Robert Hooks in "Aaron Loves Angela"

LADY COCOA (Dimension) Producer-Director, Matt Cimber; Screenplay, George Theokos; Photography, Ken Gibb; Editor, Bud Warner; Music, Luchi de Jesus; In color; Rated R; December release. CAST: Lola Falana, Gene Washington, Alex Dreier, "Mean" Joe Green, James R. Watson, Millie Perkins, Gary Harper

AARON LOVES ANGELA (Columbia) Producer, Robert J. Anderson; Co-Producer, Diana Young; Executive Producer, Morton J. Mitosky; Director, Gordon Parks, Jr.; Screenplay, Gerald Sanford; Photography, Richard Kratina; Editor, William E. Anderson; Music and Songs, Jose Feliciano, Janna Merlyn Feliciano; Assistant Director, Kurt Baker; In Metrocolor; Rated R; 99 minutes; December release. CAST: Kevin Hooks (Aaron), Irene Cara (Angela), Moses Gunn (Ike), Robert Hooks (Beau), Ernestine Jackson (Cleo), Leon Pinkney (Willie), Wanda Velez, Lou Quinones, Charles McGregor, Norman Evans, Alex Stevens, William Graeff, Jr., Frank Aldrich, Jose Feliciano, Walt Frazier

THE ASTROLOGER (Republic Arts) Producer, John William; Executive Producer, Ernest J. Helm; Director, Craig Denney; Screenplay, Dorothy June Pidgeon; Photography, Alan Gornick, Jr.; Editor, Owen Gladden; Designer, Kurt Grunert; Assistant Director, Mitch Tipton; In CFI Color; Rated R; 96 minutes; December release. CAST: Craig Denney, Rocky Barbanica, Darrien Earle, Arthyr Chadbourne, Harvey Hunter, Florence Marley, Jacqueline Day, Donald Davies

CYNTHIA'S SISTER (Boxoffice International) Director, Arnold Baxter; Screenplay, Michael Hardy; In Movielab Color; 86 minutes; December release. CAST: Flanagan (Cynthia), Paul Kirby (Edward), Susan Bowen (Tess), Emmett Hennessy (Philip), Preben Mahrt, June Fremont

FRENCH SHAMPOO A Philip T. Drexler production; In color; Rated X; December release. CAST: Darby Lloyd Rains, Bobby Astyr, Kim Pope, Annie Sprinkles, Marc Stevens

FANTASY IN BLUE (Manson) Direction and Screenplay, Roger Kramer; A Frederick Fox Production; Rated X; In color; December release. CAST: Sharon Thorpe, John Toland, Georgina Spelvin, Joan Devlon, Lance Hemming, Melva Peach, Britt Swanson, Dee Marshall, Claire Lemmiere, Turk Lion, Jerry Rome

NAKED EVIL (Hampton International) Producers, Richard Gordon, Gerald A. Fernback; Director, Stanley Goulder; Executive Producer, Steven Pallos; Based on play "The Obi" by Jon Manchip White; Rated PG; In color; 80 minutes; December release. CAST: Anthony Ainley, Suzanne Neve

MYSTERIES FROM BEYOND THE EARTH (CineVue Inc.) Producer-Director, George Gale; Screenplay, Ralph Blum, Judy Blum, Don Scioli; Music, Jaime Mendoza-Nava; In DeLuxe Color; Rated G; 105 minutes; December release. A documentary about UFO's and other bizarre phenomena.

MR. SYCAMORE (Film Venture) A Capricorn production; Producer-Director, Pancho Kohner; Executive Producer, Robert O. Kaplan; Screenplay, Ketti Frings, Pancho Kohner; From a story by Robert Ayre and a play by Ketti Frings; Photography, John Morrill; Editors, George Van Noy, Andrew Herbert; Music, Maurice Jarre; Song, Paul Francis Webster; Art Director, Charles French; In CFI Color; 87 minutes; December release. CAST: Jason Robards (John), Sandy Dennis (Jane), Jean Simmons (Estelle), Robert Easton (Fred), Mark Miller (Rev. Fletcher), Richard Bull (Dr. Fernfield), Brenda Smith, David Osterhout, Lou Picetti, Ian Wolfe, Jerome Thor, Richard Redd, Ron D'Ippolito, Curtis Taylor

MACKINTOSH & T. J. (Penland) Producer, Tim Penland; Director, Marvin J. Chomsky; Screenplay, Paul Savage; Photography, Terry Mead; Editor, Howard Smith; Music, Waylon Jennings; Art Director, Alan Smith; Assistant Director, Claude Binyon, Jr.; Rated PG; In Technicolor; 96 minutes; December release. CAST: Roy Rogers (Mackintosh), Clay O'Brien (T. J.), Billy Green Bush (Luke), Andrew Robinson (Coley), Joan Hackett (Maggie), James Hampton (Cotton), Dennis Fimple (Schuster), Luke Askew (Cal), Larry Mahan, Walter Barnes, Edith Atwater, Ted Gehring, Jim Harrell, Dean Smith, Ron Hay, Guich Koock, Autry Ward, Steve Ward, Troy Ward

THE GORILLA GANG (Hampton International) A Rialto Film Preben production; Director, Alfred Vohrer; Photography, Karl Lob; Music, Peter Thomas; Screenplay, Freddy Gregor; In color; Rated R; 96 minutes; December release. CAST: Horst Tappert, Uschi Glas, Uwe Friedrichsen, Herbert Fux, Albert Lieven, Hubert von Meyenrinck

PROMISING NEW ACTORS OF 1975

ISABELLE ADJANI

KEITH CARRADINE

BRAD DOURIF

SUSAN BLAKELY

RONEE BLAKLEY

NICK NOLTE

PERRY KING

STOCKARD CHANNING

MARILYN HASSETT

CHRIS SARANDON

BEN VEREEN

JENNIFER WARREN

125

Diane Keaton, Al Pacino
Above: Robert De Niro, Leopoldo Trieste

THE GODFATHER, PART II

(PARAMOUNT) Producer-Director, Francis Ford Coppola; Screenplay, Francis Ford Coppola, Mario Puzo; Based on novel "The Godfather" by Mario Puzo; Co-Producers; Gray Frederickson, Fred Roos; Photography, Gordon Willis; Designer, Dean Tavoularis; Editors, Peter Zinner, Richard Marks, Barry Malkin; Costumes, Theadora Van Runkle; Associate Producer, Mona Skager; Music, Nino Rota; Art Director, Angelo Graham; Assistant Directors, Newton Arnold, Henry J. Lange, Jr., Chuck Myers, Alan Hopkins, Burt Bluestein, Tony Brandt; Additional Music, Carmine Coppola; In Technicolor; Rated R; 200 minutes; December release.

CAST

Michael	Al Pacino
Tom Hagen	Robert Duvall
Kay	Diane Keaton
Vito Corleone	Robert De Niro
Fredo Corleone	John Cazale
Connie Corleone	Talia Shire
Hyman Roth	Lee Strasberg
Frankie Pentangeli	Michael V. Gazzo
Senator Pat Geary	G. D. Spradlin
Al Neri	Richard Bright
Fanucci	Gaston Moschin
Rocco Lampone	Tom Rosqui
Young Clemenza	B. Kirby, Jr.
Genco	Frank Sivero
Young Mama Corleone	Francesca De Sapio
Mama Corleone	Morgana King
Deanna Corleone	Mariana Hill
Signor Roberto	Leopoldo Trieste
Johnny Ola	Dominic Chianese
Michael's Bodyguard	Amerigo Tot
Merle Johnson	Troy Donahue
Young Tessio	John Aprea
Willi Cicci	Joe Spinell
Tessio	Abe Vigoda
Theresa Hagen	Tere Livrano
Carlo	Gianni Rosso
Vito's Mother	Maria Carta
Vito Andolini as a boy	Oreste Baldini
Don Francesco	Giuseppe Sillato
Don Tommasino	Mario Cotone
Anthony Corleone	James Gounaris
Mrs. Marcia Roth	Fay Spain
F.B.I. Man #1	Harry Dean Stanton
F.B.I. Man #2	David Baker
Carmine Rosato	Carmine Caridi
Tony Rosato	Danny Aiello
Policeman	Carmine Foresta
Bartender	Nick Discenza
Father Carmelo	Father Joseph Medeglia

and William Bowers (Senate Committee Chairman), Joe Della Sorte, Carmen Argenziano, Joe Lo Grippo (Michael's Buttonmen), Ezio Flagello (Impressario), Livio Giorgi (Tenor), Kathy Beller (Girl in "Senza Mamma"), Saveria Mazzola (Signora Colombo), Tito Alba (Cuban President), Johnny Naranjo (Translator), Elda Maida (Pentangeli's Wife), Salvatore Po (Pentangeli's Brother), Ignazio Pappalardo (Mosca), Andrea Maugeri (Strollo), Peter La Corte (Abandando), Vincent Coppola (Vendor), Peter Donat (Questadt), Tom Dahlgren (Corngold), Paul B. Brown (Senator Ream), Phil Feldman, Roger Corman (Senators), Yvonne Coll (Yolanda), J. D. Nichols (Attendant), Edward Van Sickle (Ellis Island Doctor), Gabria Belloni (Nurse), Richard Watson (Custom Official), Venancia Grangerard (Cuban Nurse), Erica Yohn (Governess), Theresa Tirelli (Midwife), and special participation by James Caan

1974 Academy Awards for Best Picture, Best Supporting Actor (Robert De Niro), Best Director, Best Screenplay, Best Art Direction, Best Set Direction, Best Musical Score

Top Left: The Corleone family
Below: (L) Al Pacino, Robert Duvall
(R) John Cazale, Al Pacino

ART CARNEY
in "Harry and Tonto"
1974 ACADEMY AWARD FOR BEST PERFORMANCE BY AN ACTOR

ELLEN BURSTYN
in "Alice Doesn't Live Here Anymore"

1974 ACADEMY AWARD FOR BEST PERFORMANCE BY AN ACTRESS

ROBERT DE NIRO
in "The Godfather Part II"

1974 ACADEMY AWARD FOR BEST SUPPORTING PERFORMANCE BY AN ACTOR

INGRID BERGMAN
in "Murder on the Orient Express"
1974 ACADEMY AWARD FOR BEST SUPPORTING PERFORMANCE BY AN ACTRESS

AMARCORD

(ROGER CORMAN/NEW WORLD) Producer, Franco Cristaldi; Director, Federico Fellini; Story and Screenplay, Federico Fellini, Tonino Guerra; Photography, Giuseppe Rotunno; Editor, Ruggero Mastroianni; Music, Nino Rota; Art Director-Costumes, Danilo Donati; Assistant Director, Maurizio Mein; An Italian-French Co-Production; In Panavision and Technicolor; Rated R; 127 minutes; September release.

CAST

Gradisca	Magali Noel
Titta	Bruno Zanin
Titta's Mother	Pupella Maggio
Titta's Father	Armando Brancia
Titta's Grandfather	Giuseppe Lanigro
Pataca	Nando Orfei
Uncle Teo	Ciccio Ingrassia
Lawyer	Luigi Rossi
Bisein	Gennaro Ombra
Volpina	Josiane Tanzilli
Tobacconist	Antonietta Beluzzi
Don Baravelli	Gianfilippo Carcano
Fascist Leader	Ferruccio Brembilla
Math Teacher	Dina Adorni

and Antonino Faa'DiBruno, Ferdinando Villella, Aristide Caporale, Domenico Pertica, Mauro Misul, Antonino Spaccatini, Genaro Ombra, Stefano Proietti, Bruno Scagnetti, Marcello Di Falco, Bruno Lenzi

Right: Bruno Zanin, Magali Noel

Magali Noel (C)

Bruno Zanin (C), Bruno Lenzi (R)

1974 ACADEMY AWARD FOR BEST FOREIGN LANGUAGE FILM

Ernest Borgnine   **Gloria Grahame**   **George Chakiris**   **Sophia Loren**   **Ray Milland**

PREVIOUS ACADEMY AWARD WINNERS

(1) Best Picture, (2) Actor, (3) Actress, (4) Supporting Actor, (5) Supporting Actress, (6) Director, (7) Special Award, (8) Best Foreign Language Film

1927–28: (1) "Wings" (2) Emil Jannings in "The Way of All Flesh", (3) Janet Gaynor in "Seventh Heaven", (6) Frank Borzage for "Seventh Heaven", (7) Charles Chaplin.

1928–29: (1) "Broadway Melody", (2) Warner Baxter in "Old Arizona", (3) Mary Pickford in "Coquette", (6) Frank Lloyd for "The Divine Lady".

1929–30: (1) "All Quiet on the Western Front", (2) George Arliss in "Disraeli", (3) Norma Shearer in "The Divorcee", (6) Lewis Milestone for "All Quiet on the Western Front".

1930–31: (1) "Cimarron", (2) Lionel Barrymore in "A Free Soul", (3) Marie Dressler in "Min and Bill", (6) Norman Taurog for "Skippy".

1931–32: (1) "Grand Hotel", (2) Fredric March in "Dr. Jekyll and Mr. Hyde", tied with Wallace Beery in "The Champ", (3) Helen Hayes in "The Sin of Madelon Claudet", (6) Frank Borzage for "Bad Girl".

1932–33: (1) "Cavalcade", (2) Charles Laughton in "The Private Life of Henry VIII", (3) Katharine Hepburn in "Morning Glory", (6) Frank Lloyd for "Cavalcade".

1934: (1) "It Happened One Night", (2) Clark Gable in "It Happened One Night", (3) Claudette Colbert in "It Happened One Night", (6) Frank Capra for "It Happened One Night", (7) Shirley Temple.

1935: (1) "Mutiny on the Bounty", (2) Victor McLaglen in "The Informer", (3) Bette Davis in "Dangerous", (6) John Ford for "The Informer", (7) D. W. Griffith.

1936: (1) "The Great Ziegfeld", (2) Paul Muni in "The Story of Louis Pasteur", (3) Luise Rainer in "The Great Ziegfeld", (4) Walter Brennan in "Come and Get It", (5) Gale Sondergaard in "Anthony Adverse", (6) Frank Capra for "Mr. Deeds Goes to Town".

1937: (1) "The Life of Emile Zola", (2) Spencer Tracy in "Captains Courageous", (3) Luise Rainer in "The Good Earth", (4) Joseph Schildkraut in "The Life of Emile Zola", (5) Alice Brady in "In Old Chicago", (6) Leo McCarey for "The Awful Truth", (7) Mack Sennett, Edgar Bergen.

1938: (1) "You Can't Take It with You", (2) Spencer Tracy in "Boys' Town", (3) Bette Davis in "Jezebel", (4) Walter Brennan in "Kentucky", (5) Fay Bainter in "Jezebel", (6) Frank Capra for "You Can't Take It with You", (7) Deanna Durbin, Mickey Rooney, Harry M. Warner, Walt Disney.

1939: (1) "Gone with the Wind", (2) Robert Donat in "Goodbye, Mr. Chips", (3) Vivien Leigh in "Gone with the Wind", (4) Thomas Mitchell in "Stagecoach", (5) Hattie McDaniel in "Gone with the Wind", (6) Victor Fleming for "Gone with the Wind", (7) Douglas Fairbanks, Judy Garland.

1940: (1) "Rebecca", (2) James Stewart in "The Philadelphia Story", (3) Ginger Rogers in "Kitty Foyle", (4) Walter Brennan in "The Westerner", (5) Jane Darwell in "The Grapes of Wrath", (6) John Ford for "The Grapes of Wrath", (7) Bob Hope.

1941: (1) "How Green Was My Valley", (2) Gary Cooper in "Sergeant York", (3) Joan Fontaine in "Suspicion", (4) Donald Crisp in "How Green Was My Valley", (5) Mary Astor in "The Great Lie", (6) John Ford for "How Green Was My Valley", (7) Leopold Stokowski, Walt Disney.

1942: (1) "Mrs. Miniver", (2) James Cagney in "Yankee Doodle Dandy", (3) Greer Garson in "Mrs. Miniver", (4) Van Heflin in "Johnny Eager", (5) Teresa Wright in "Mrs. Miniver", (6) William Wyler for "Mrs. Miniver", (7) Charles Boyer, Noel Coward.

1943: (1) "Casablanca", (2) Paul Lukas in "Watch on the Rhine", (3) Jennifer Jones in "The Song of Bernadette", (4) Charles Coburn in "The More the Merrier", (5) Katina Paxinou in "For Whom the Bell Tolls", (6) Michael Curtiz for "Casablanca".

1944: (1) "Going My Way", (2) Bing Crosby in "Going My Way", (3) Ingrid Bergman in "Gaslight", (4) Barry Fitzgerald in "Going My Way", (5) Ethel Barrymore in "None but the Lonely Heart", (6) Leo McCarey for "Going My Way", (7) Margaret O'Brien, Bob Hope.

1945: (1) "The Lost Weekend", (2) Ray Milland in "The Lost Weekend", (3) Joan Crawford in "Mildred Pierce", (4) James Dunn in "A Tree Grows in Brooklyn", (5) Anne Revere in "National Velvet", (6) Billy Wilder for "The Lost Weekend", (7) Walter Wanger, Peggy Ann Garner.

1946: (1) "The Best Years of Our Lives", (2) Fredric March in "The Best Years of Our Lives", (3) Olivia de Havilland in "To Each His Own", (4) Harold Russell in "The Best Years of Our Lives", (5) Anne Baxter in "The Razor's Edge", (7) Laurence Olivier, Harold Russell, Ernst Lubitsch, Claude Jarman, Jr.

1947: (1) "Gentleman's Agreement", (2) Ronald Colman in "A Double Life", (3) Loretta Young in "The Farmer's Daughter", (4) Edmund Gwenn in "Miracle On 34th Street", (5) Celeste Holm in "Gentleman's Agreement", (6) Elia Kazan for "Gentleman's Agreement", (7) James Baskette, (8) "Shoe Shine."

1948: (1) "Hamlet", (2) Laurence Olivier in "Hamlet", (3) Jane Wyman in "Johnny Belinda", (4) Walter Huston in "The Treasure of the Sierra Madre", (5) Claire Trevor in "Key Largo", (6) John Huston for "The Treasure of the Sierra Madre", (7) Ivan Jandl, Sid Grauman, Adolph Zukor, Walter Wanger, (8) "Monsieur Vincent".

1949: (1) "All the King's Men", (2) Broderick Crawford in "All the King's Men", (3) Olivia de Havilland in "The Heiress", (4) Dean Jagger in "Twelve O'Clock High", (5) Mercedes McCambridge in "All the King's Men", (6) Joseph L. Mankiewicz for "A Letter to Three Wives", (7) Bobby Driscoll, Fred Astaire, Cecil B. DeMille, Jean Hersholt, (8) "The Bicycle Thief."

1950: (1) "All about Eve", (2) Jose Ferrer in "Cyrano de Bergerac", (3) Judy Holliday in "Born Yesterday", (4) George Sanders in "All about Eve", (5) Josephine Hull in "Harvey", (6) Joseph L. Mankiewicz for "All about Eve", (7) George Murphy, Louis B. Mayer, (8) "The Walls of Malapaga".

1951: (1) "An American in Paris", (2) Humphrey Bogart in "The African Queen", (3) Vivien Leigh in "A Streetcar Named Desire", (4) Karl Malden in "A Streetcar Named Desire", (5) Kim Hunter in "A Streetcar Named Desire", (6) George Stevens for "A Place in the Sun", (7) Gene Kelly, (8) "Rashomon."

| **Dorothy Malone** | **Cliff Robertson** | **Patricia Neal** | **George C. Scott** | **Estelle Parsons** |

1952: (1) "The Greatest Show on Earth", (2) Gary Cooper in "High Noon", (3) Shirley Booth in "Come Back, Little Sheba", (4) Anthony Quinn in "Viva Zapata", (5) Gloria Grahame in "The Bad and the Beautiful", (6) John Ford for "The Quiet Man", (7) Joseph M. Schenck, Merian C. Cooper, Harold Lloyd, Bob Hope, George Alfred Mitchell, (8) "Forbidden Games."

1953: (1) "From Here to Eternity", (2) William Holden in "Stalag 17", (3) Audrey Hepburn in "Roman Holiday", (4) Frank Sinatra in "From Here to Eternity", (5) Donna Reed in "From Here to Eternity", (6) Fred Zinnemann for "From Here to Eternity", (7) Pete Smith, Joseph Breen.

1954: (1) "On the Waterfront", (2) Marlon Brando in "On the Waterfront", (3) Grace Kelly in "The Country Girl", (4) Edmond O'Brien in "The Barefoot Contessa", (5) Eva Marie Saint in "On the Waterfront", (6) Elia Kazan for "On the Waterfront", (7) Greta Garbo, Danny Kaye, Jon Whitely, Vincent Winter, (8) "Gate of Hell."

1955: (1) "Marty", (2) Ernest Borgnine in "Marty", (3) Anna Magnani in "The Rose Tattoo", (4) Jack Lemmon in "Mister Roberts", (5) Jo Van Fleet in "East of Eden", (6) Delbert Mann for "Marty", (8) "Samurai."

1956: (1) "Around the World in 80 Days", (2) Yul Brynner in "The King and I", (3) Ingrid Bergman in "Anastasia", (4) Anthony Quinn in "Lust for Life", (5) Dorothy Malone in "Written on the Wind", (6) George Stevens for "Giant", (7) Eddie Cantor, (8) "La Strada."

1957: (1) "The Bridge on the River Kwai", (2) Alec Guinness in "The Bridge on the River Kwai", (3) Joanne Woodward in "The Three Faces of Eve", (4) Red Buttons in "Sayonara", (5) Miyoshi Umeki in "Sayonara", (6) David Lean for "The Bridge on the River Kwai", (7) Charles Brackett, B. B. Kahane, Gilbert M. (Bronco Billy) Anderson, (8) "The Nights of Cabiria."

1958: (1) "Gigi", (2) David Niven in "Separate Tables", (3) Susan Hayward in "I Want to Live", (4) Burl Ives in "The Big Country", (5) Wendy Hiller in "Separate Tables", (6) Vincente Minnelli for "Gigi", (7) Maurice Chevalier, (8) "My Uncle."

1959: (1) "Ben-Hur", (2) Charlton Heston in "Ben-Hur", (3) Simone Signoret in "Room at the Top", (4) Hugh Griffith in "Ben-Hur", (5) Shelley Winters in "The Diary of Anne Frank", (6) William Wyler for "Ben-Hur", (7) Lee de Forest, Buster Keaton, (8) "Black Orpheus."

1960: (1) "The Apartment", (2) Burt Lancaster in "Elmer Gantry", (3) Elizabeth Taylor in "Butterfield 8", (4) Peter Ustinov in "Spartacus", (5) Shirley Jones in "Elmer Gantry", (6) Billy Wilder for "The Apartment", (7) Gary Cooper, Stan Laurel, Hayley Mills, (8) "The Virgin Spring."

1961: (1) "West Side Story", (2) Maximilian Schell in "Judgment at Nuremberg", (3) Sophia Loren in "Two Women", (4) George Chakiris in "West Side Story", (5) Rita Moreno in "West Side Story", (6) Robert Wise for "West Side Story", (7) Jerome Robbins, Fred L. Metzler, (8) "Through a Glass Darkly."

1962: (1) "Lawrence of Arabia", (2) Gregory Peck in "To Kill a Mockingbird", (3) Anne Bancroft in "The Miracle Worker", (4) Ed Begley in "Sweet Bird of Youth", (5) Patty Duke in "The Miracle Worker", (6) David Lean for "Lawrence of Arabia", (8) "Sundays and Cybele."

1963: (1) "Tom Jones", (2) Sidney Poitier in "Lilies of the Field", (3) Patricia Neal in "Hud", (4) Melvyn Douglas in "Hud", (5) Margaret Rutherford in "The V.I.P's", (6) Tony Richardson for "Tom Jones", (8) "8½".

1964: (1) "My Fair Lady", (2) Rex Harrison in "My Fair Lady", (3) Julie Andrews in "Mary Poppins", (4) Peter Ustinov in "Topkapi", (5) Lila Kedrova in "Zorba the Greek", (6) George Cukor for "My Fair Lady", (7) William Tuttle, (8) "Yesterday, Today and Tomorrow."

1965: (1) "The Sound of Music", (2) Lee Marvin in "Cat Ballou", (3) Julie Christie in "Darling", (4) Martin Balsam in "A Thousand Clowns", (5) Shelley Winters in "A Patch of Blue", (6) Robert Wise for "The Sound of Music", (7) Bob Hope, (8) "The Shop on Main Street".

1966: (1) "A Man for All Seasons", (2) Paul Scofield in "A Man for All Seasons", (3) Elizabeth Taylor in "Who's Afraid of Virginia Woolf?", (4) Walter Matthau in "The Fortune Cookie", (5) Sandy Dennis in "Who's Afraid of Virginia Woolf?", (6) Fred Zinnemann for "A Man for All Seasons", (8) "A Man and A Woman."

1967: (1) "In the Heat of the Night", (2) Rod Steiger in "In the Heat of the Night", (3) Katharine Hepburn in "Guess Who's Coming to Dinner", (4) George Kennedy in "Cool Hand Luke", (5) Estelle Parsons in "Bonnie and Clyde", (6) Mike Nichols for "The Graduate", (8) "Closely Watched Trains."

1968: (1) "Oliver!", (2) Cliff Robertson in "Charly", (3) Katharine Hepburn in "The Lion in Winter" tied with Barbra Streisand in "Funny Girl", (4) Jack Albertson in "The Subject Was Roses", (5) Ruth Gordon in "Rosemary's Baby", (6) Carol Reed for "Oliver!", (7) Onna White for "Oliver!" choreography, John Chambers for "Planet of the Apes" make-up, (8) "War and Peace."

1969: (1) "Midnight Cowboy", (2) John Wayne in "True Grit", (3) Maggie Smith in "The Prime of Miss Jean Brodie", (4) Gig Young in "They Shoot Horses, Don't They?", (5) Goldie Hawn in "Cactus Flower", (6) John Schlesinger for "Midnight Cowboy", (7) Gary Grant, (8) "Z."

1970: (1) "Patton", (2) George C. Scott in "Patton", (3) Glenda Jackson in "Women in Love," (4) John Mills in "Ryan's Daughter", (5) Helen Hayes in "Airport", (6) Franklin J. Schaffner for "Patton", (7) Lillian Gish, Orson Welles, (8) "Investigation of a Citizen above Suspicion."

1971: (1) "The French Connection," (2) Gene Hackman in "The French Connection," (3) Jane Fonda in "Klute," (4) Ben Johnson in "The Last Picture Show," (5) Cloris Leachman in "The Last Picture Show," (6) William Friedkin for "The French Connection," (7) Charles Chaplin, (8) "The Garden of the Finzi-Continis."

1972: (1) "The Godfather," (2) Marlon Brando in "The Godfather," (3) Liza Minnelli in "Cabaret," (4) Joel Grey in "Cabaret," (5) Eileen Heckart in "Butterflies Are Free," (6) Bob Fosse for "Cabaret," (7) Edward G. Robinson, (8) "The Discreet Charm of the Bourgeoisie."

1973: (1) "The Sting," (2) Jack Lemmon in "Save the Tiger," (3) Glenda Jackson in "A Touch of Class," (4) John Houseman in "The Paper Chase," (5) Tatum O'Neal in "Paper Moon," (6) George Roy Hill for "The Sting," (8) "Day for Night"

1974: (1) "The Godfather Part II," (2) Art Carney in "Harry and Tonto," (3) Ellen Burstyn in "Alice Doesn't Live Here Anymore," (4) Robert DeNiro in "The Godfather Part II," (5) Ingrid Bergman in "Murder on the Orient Express," (6) Francis Ford Coppola for "The Godfather Part II," (7) Howard Hawks, Jean Renoir, (8) "Amarcord"

FOREIGN FILMS
GALILEO

(AMERICAN FILM THEATRE) Producer, Ely Landau; Director, Joseph Losey; Screenplay, Barbara Bray, Joseph Losey; From Charles Laughton's English version of the German play by Bertolt Brecht; Executive Producer, Otto Plaschkes; Music, Hans Eisler, Richard Hartley; Photography, Michael Reed; Editor, Reginald Beck; In color; Rated PG; 145 minutes; January release.

CAST

Galileo Galilei	Topol
Cardinal Inquisitor	Edward Fox
Priuli	Colin Blakely
Ballad Singer's Wife	Georgia Brown
Ballad Singer	Clive Revill
Court Lady	Margaret Leighton
Old Cardinal	John Gielgud
Sagredo	Michael Gough
Cardinal Barberini/Pope	Michael Lonsdale
Fulganzio	Richard O'Callaghan
Ludovico	Tim Woodward
Angelica Sarti	Judy Parfitt
Federzoni	John McEnery
Cardinal Bellarmin	Patrick Magee
Virginia	Mary Larkin
Andrea (boy)	Ian Travers
Andrea (Man)	Tom Conti

Left: Topol, Iain Travers

Topol, Michael Gough

Topol, John Gielgud Above: Topol, Tom Conti, John McEnery, Richard O'Callaghan

Topol, Mary Larkin Above: Clive Revill, Georgia Brown

Topol Top: Michael Lonsdale, Vernon Dobtcheff, Patrick Magee, Topol

LA RUPTURE

(NEW LINE CINEMA) English title "The Breakup"; Producer, Andre Genoves; Direction and Screenplay, Claude Chabrol; Based on novel by Charlotte Armstrong; Photography, Jean Rablier; Editor, Jacques Gaillard; Music, Pierre Jansen; In color; French with English subtitles; 125 minutes; January release.

CAST

Helene	Stephane Audran
Paul Thomas	Jean-Pierre Cassel
M. Regnier	Michel Bouquet
Mme. Regnier	Marguerite Cassan
Charles Regnier	Jean-Claude Drouot
Mme. Pinelli	Annie Corey
M. Pinelli	Jean Carmel
Elise Pinelli	Katia Romanoff

Left: Stephane Audran

Jean-Claude Drouot

Stephane Audran, Jean-Pierre Cassel
Top: Jean-Claude Drouot, Stephane Audran

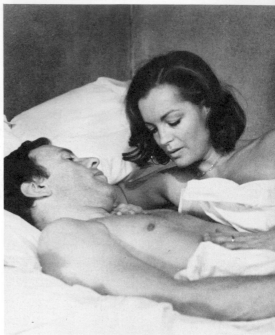

Romy Schneider, Jean-Louis Trintignant
Top: Jean-Louis Trintignant, Jean-Pierre Cassel

THE FRENCH WAY

(PEPPERCORN-WORMSER) title changed from: "Love at the Top"; Producer, Leo Fuchs; Director, Michel Deville; Screenplay, Christopher Frank; Based on novel by Roger Blondel; Photography, Claude Lecomte; French with English subtitles; Music, Saint-Saens; In Movelab Color;/Rated R; 105 minutes; January release.

CAST

Nicholas	Jean-Louis Trintignant
Roberta	Romy Schneider
Fabre	Jean-Pierre Cassel
Marie-Paule	Jane Birkin
Flora	Florinda Bolkan
Lourceuil	George Wilson
Berthoud	Henri Garcin

Jean-Louis Trintignant with Florinda Bolkan, and above with Romy Schneider, top with Jane Birkin

WHY ROCK THE BOAT?

COLUMBIA) Producer, William Weintraub; Executive Producer, James deB. Domville; Director, John Howe; Screenplay, William Weintraub from his novel; Photography, Savas Kalogeras; Music and Lyrics, John Howe; Designer, Earl Preston; Costumes, Philippa Wingfield; Associate Producer, Malca Gillson, Assistant/Directors, Ashley Murray, Robbie Malenfant; In color; 112 minutes; January release.

CAST

Harry Barnes	Stuart Gillard
Julia Martin	Tiiu Leek
Ronny Waldron	Ken James
Fred O'Neill	Budd Knapp
Philip L. Butcher	Henry Beckman
Herb Scannell	Sean Sullivan
Isobel Scannell	Patricia Gage
Senor Gomez	Ruben Morena
Carmichael	Cec Linder
Club President	Henry Ramer
Guest Speaker	Maurice Podbrey
Benson	Barrie Baldaro
Hilda	Patricia Hamilton
Smith	Ian deVoy
Ridley	Basil Fitzgibbon
Irene	Anna Reiser
Saint-Onge	Robert Rivard
Harrison	Don MacIntyre
Bartender	J. Leo Gagnon
Lapierre	Jean-Pierre Masson
Suzanne	Marie-France Beaulieu
Miss Stevens	Mary Morter
Peterson	Peter MacNeill
Pierre Beaulac	Thomas Donohue
Ski Instructor	Benoit Lepine
Policeman	Kirk McColl

Right: Stuart Gillard Above: Stuart Gillard, Tiiu Leek Top: Stuart Gillard (R)

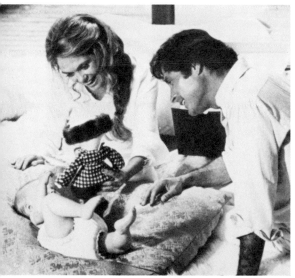

Dyan Cannon, Donald Pilon

CHILD UNDER A LEAF

(CINEMA NATIONAL) Producers, Murray Shostak, Robert Baylis;/Written, directed and Edited by George Bloomfield; Music, Francis Lai; Photography, Don Wilder; Art Director, Jocelyn Joly; Assistant Directors, Sunny Cullen, John Fretz, Maury Chaykin; A Potterson Production in association with Ethos Productions; Presented by Creative Equity Corp.; Rated R; 120 minutes; February release.

CAST

Domino	Dyan Cannon
Her Husband	Joseph Campanella
Joseph	Donald Pilon

and Albert S. Waxman, Micheline Lanctot, Bud Knapp, Bess Bloomfield, Julia Bullock

A BRIEF VACATION

(ALLIED ARTISTS) Producers, Marina Cicogna, Arthur Cohn; Director, Vittorio De Sica; Screenplay, Cesare Zavattini; Story, Rodolfo Sonego; Art Director, Luigi Scaccianoce; Costumes, Nadia Vitali; Assistant Director, Luisa Alessandri; Editor, Kim Arcalli; Music, Manuel De Sica; Title Song sung by Christian De Sica; Presented by Emanuel L. Wolf; In color; Rated PG; 106 minutes; February release.

CAST

Clara	Florinda Bolkan
Husband	Renato Salvatori
Luigi	Daniel Quenaud
Ciranni	Jose Maria Prada
Gina	Teresa Gimpera
Brother-in-law	Hugo Blanco
Edvige	Julia Pena
Orderly Guidotti	Miranda Campa
LaRossa	Angela Cardile
Mother-in-law	Anna Carena
Maria	Monica Guerritore
Orderly Garin	Maria Mizar
Son	Alessandro Romanazzi
La Scanziani	Adriana Asti

Left: Florinda Bolkan, also below

Renato Salvatori, Florinda Bolkan

Anna Carena, Hugo Blanco, Florinda Bolkan, Renato Salvatori Above: Bolkan, Salvatori

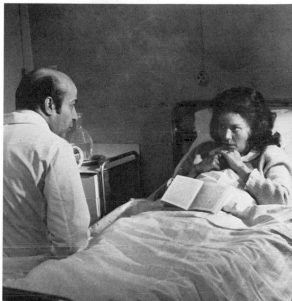

**Florinda Bolkan, Daniel Quenaud
(also top)**

**Florinda Bolkan, and above
with Daniel Quenaud**

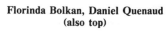

141

**Mort Shuman, Elly Stone, also top
with Joe Masiell**

JACQUES BREL IS ALIVE AND
WELL AND LIVING IN PARIS

(AMERICAN FILM THEATRE) Producers, Paul Marshall,
Cinevideo; Executive Producer, Claude Heroux; Director, Denis
Heroux; Screenplay, Eric Blau; Music, Jacques Brel; Movement,
Moni Yakim; Editor, Yves Langlois, Photography, Rene Verzier;
In color; Presented by Ely Landau; Rated G; 98 minutes plus
intermission; February release.

CAST

Elly Stone
Mort Shuman
Joe Masiell
Jacques Brel

**Top: Elly Stone Below: Mort Shuman,
Elly Stone, Joe Masiell**

DONKEY SKIN

(JANUS FILMS) Producer, Mag Bodard; Direction and Screenplay, Jacques Demy; Story, Charles Perrault; Photography, Ghislain Cloquet; Music, Michel Legrand; In color; 90 minutes; March release.

CAST

Peau d'Ane .... Catherine Deneuve
Prince .... Jacques Perrin
Blue King .... Jean Marais
Fairy Godmother .... Delphine Seyrig
Red King .... Fernand Ledoux
Red Queen .... Micheline Presle

Right: Delphine Seyrig, Catherine Deneuve

**Catherine Deneuve, Jacques Perrin
Above: Catherine Deneuve**

**Delphine Seyrig Above: Catherine
Deneuve, Jean Marais**

THE FOUR MUSKETEERS

(20th CENTURY-FOX) Producer, Alexander Salkind; Director, Richard Lester; Screenplay, George MacDonald Fraser; Based on Alexander Dumas' novel "The Three Musketeers"; Photography, David Watkins; Editor, John Victor Smith; Music, Lalo Schifrin; In DeLuxe Color; Rated PG; 108 minutes; March release.

CAST

Athos	Oliver Reed
Mme. Bonancioux	Raquel Welch
Aramis	Richard Chamberlain
D'Artanan	Michael York
Porthos	Frank Finlay
Rochefort	Christopher Lee
Louis XIII	Jean Pierre Cassel
Anne of Austria	Geraldine Chaplin
Duke of Buckingham	Simon Ward
Milady	Faye Dunaway
Cardinal Richelieu	Charlton Heston
Maid	Nicole Calfan

Left: Charlton Heston, Christopher Lee

Oliver Reed, Richard Chamberlain, Michael York, Frank Finlay

AND NOW MY LOVE

(AVCO EMBASSY) Director, Claude Lelouch; Screenplay, Claude Lelouch, Pierre Uytterhoeven; Photography, Jean Collomb; Designer, Francois De Lamothe; Editor, Georges Klotz; Music, Francis Lai; A Rizzoli and Les Films 13 production; In Technicolor; Presented by Joseph E. Levine; Rated PG; 121 minutes; March release.

CAST

Sarah/Her Mother/ Her Grandmother	Marthe Keller
Simon	Andre Dussollier
Sarah's Father/Operator/ Sarah's Grandfather	Charles Denner
Sarah's Italian Girlfriend	Carla Gravina
Simon's Friend	Charles Gerard
Gilbert Becaud	Himself
Understudy	Alain Basnier
14-18 year old hero	Daniel Boulanger
Amorous union man	Elie Choraqui
Wife of the lawyer	Nathalie Courval
Lawyer	Andre Falcon
A stud	Angelo Infanti
A Woman of Simon	Annie Kerani
Restaurant Owner	Sam Lethrone
Wife of the operator	Judith Magre
Director of L'Usine	Gerard Sire
Six-day husband	Gabriele Tinti
Very-Italian Italian man	Venantino Venantini
Lover among many	Harry Walter
General's Aide	Yvan Tanguy

BRANNIGAN

(**UNITED ARTISTS**) Executive Producer, Michael Wayne; Producers, Arthur Gardner, Jules Levy; Screenplay, Christopher Trumbo, Michael Butler, William P. McGivern, William Norton; Story, Christopher Trumbo, Michael Butler; Director, Douglas Hickox; Music, Dominic Frontiere; Art Director, Ted Marshall; Costumes, Emma Porteous; Editor, Malcolm Cooke; In Panavision and color; Rated PG; 111 minutes; March release.

CAST

Jim Brannigan	John Wayne
Commander Swann	Richard Attenborough
Jennifer Thatcher	Judy Geeson
Mel Fields	Mel Ferrer
Larkin	John Vernon
Gorman	Daniel Pilon
Traven	John Stride
Charlie	James Booth
Drexel	Del Henney
Luana	Lesley Ann Down
Julian	Barry Dennen
Freddy	Anthony Booth
Jimmy the Bet	Brian Glover
Captain Moretti	Ralph Meeker
Carter	Jack Watson
Angell	Arthur Batanides
Alex	Stewart Bevan
Miss Allen	Kathryn Leigh Scott
Geef	Don Henderson

Right: John Wayne, Judy Geeson
Below: Lesley Ann Down, Daniel Pilon

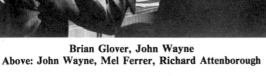

Brian Glover, John Wayne
Above: John Wayne, Mel Ferrer, Richard Attenborough

John Wayne, Richard Attenborough

IN CELEBRATION

(AMERICAN FILM THEATRE) Executive Producer, Otto Plaschkes; Producer, Ely Landau; Director, Lindsay Anderson; Screenplay, David Story; Editor, Russell Lloyd; Art Director, Alan Withy; Photography, Dick Bush; Assistant Director, Richard Jenkins; In color; Rated PG; 131 minutes; March release.

CAST

Andrew Shaw	Alan Bates
Colin Shaw	James Bolam
Steven Shaw	Brian Cox
Mrs. Shaw	Constance Chapman
Mrs. Burnett	Gabrielle Daye
Mr. Shaw	Bill Owen

Alan Bates, James Bolam, Gabrielle Daye, Constance Chapman, Bill Owen
Above Left: James Bolam, Alan Bates, Brian Cox

Alan Bates, James Bolam, Brian Cox

Bill Owen, Alan Bates

TOMMY

(COLUMBIA) Producers, Robert Stigwood, Ken Russell; Executive Producers, Beryl Vertue, Christopher Stamp; Direction and Screenplay, Ken Russell; Based on musical drama by Peter Townshend, Photography, Dick Bush, Ronnie Taylor, Robin Lehman; Editor, Stuart Baird; Music, Peter Townshend, John Entwistle, Keith Moon; Art Director, John Clark; Designer, Paul Dufficey; Assistant Director, Jonathan Benson; In Metrocolor; Rated PG; 111 minutes; March release.

CAST

Nora Walker	Ann-Margret
Frank Hobbs	Oliver Reed
Tommy	Roger Daltrey
Pinball Wizard	Elton John
Preacher	Eric Clapton
Uncle Ernie	Keith Moon
Specialist	Jack Nicholson
Capt. Walker	Robert Powell
Cousin Kevin	Paul Nicholas
Acid Queen	Tina Turner
Young Tommy	Barry Winch
Sally Simpson	Victoria Russell
The Who .. Peter Townshend, Roger Daltrey, John Entwistle, Keith Moon

Ann-Margret, Jack Nicholson Above: Oliver Reed, Barry Winch, Ann-Margret (also top c)

150

Top: Ann-Margret, Oliver Reed Below: Oliver Reed

Oliver Reed, Ann-Margret Above: Ann-Margret,
Roger Daltrey Top: Elton John

Ann-Margret Above: Ann-Margret, Roger Daltrey,
Eric Clapton Top: Oliver Reed, Keith Moon

THE MAIDS

(AMERICAN FILM THEATRE) Producer, Robert Enders; Director, Christopher Miles; Screenplay, Robert Enders, Christopher Miles; Based on play by Jean Genet; Translation, Minos Volanakis; Executive Producer, Bernard Weitzman; Associate Producer, Gordon L. T. Scott; Editor, Peter Tanner; Art Director, Robert Jones; Music, Laurie Johnson; Photography, Douglas Slocombe; In color; Rated PG; 95 minutes; April release.

CAST

Solange .... Glenda Jackson
Claire .... Susannah York
Madame .... Vivien Merchant

Right: Vivien Merchant, Susannah York

Susannah York Above: Vivien Merchant, Glenda Jackson, Susannah York

Susannah York, Glenda Jackson

THE INVITATION

(JANUS) Executive Producer, Yves Gasser; Director, Claude Goretta; Screenplay (French with English subtitles), Claude Goretta, Michel Viala; Photography, Jean Zeller; Editor, Joelle van Effenterre; Music, Patrick Moraz; 100 minutes; April release.

CAST

Maurice	Jean-Luc Bideau
Emile	Francois Simon
Alfred	Jean Champion
Simone	Corinne Coderey
Remy	Michel Robin
Aline	Cecile Vassort
Helene	Rosine Rochette
Rene	Jacques Rispal
Emma	Neige Dolsky
Pierre	Pierre Collet
Mme. Placet	Lucie Aveney
Thief	Roger Jendely

STORY OF A LOVE AFFAIR

(New Yorker) Producers, Gino Rossi, Franco Villani, Stefano Caretta; Director, Michelangelo Antonioni; Screenplay, Michelangelo Antonioni, Daniele d'Anza, Silvio Giovaninetti, Francesco Maselli, Piero Tellini; Assistant Director, Francesco Maselli; Photography, Enzo Serafin; Costumes, Ferdinando Sarmi; Music, Giovanni Fusco; 102 minutes; April release.

CAST

Paola	Lucia Bose
Guido	Massimo Girotti
Fontana	Ferdinando Sarmi

and Gino Rossi, Marika Rowsky, Rosa Mirafiore, Rubi d'Alma

Left: Paola-Lucia Bose, Guido-Massimo Girotti

Guido-Massimo Girotti, Paola-Lucia Bose

Paola-Lucia Bose, Fontana-Ferdinando Sarmi
Top: Paola-Lucia Bose, Guido-Massimo Girotti

THE PASSENGER

(UNITED ARTISTS) Producer, Carlo Ponti; Director, Michaelangelo Antonioni; Screenplay, Mark Peploe, Peter Wollen, Michelangelo Antonioni; Story, Mark Peploe; Executive Producer, Alessandro von Normann; Photography, Luciano Tovoli; Art Director, Piero Poletto; Editors, Franco Arcalli, Michelangelo Antonioni; Costumes, Louise Stjensward; Assistant Directors, Enrico Sannia, Claudio Taddei, Enrica Fico; In Metrocolor; Rated PG; 123 minutes; April release.

CAST

Locke	Jack Nicholson
Girl	Maria Schneider
Rachel	Jenny Runacre
Knight	Ian Hendry
Stephen	Stephen Berkoff
Achebe	Ambroise Bia
Hotel Keeper	Jose Maria Cafarel
Witch Doctor	James Campbell
German Stranger	Manfred Spies
Murderer	Jean Baptiste Tiemele
Police Inspector	Angel Del Pozo
Robertson	Chuck Mulvehill

Jenny Runacre, Jack Nicholson, Maria Schneider
Top Left: Maria Schneider, Jack Nicholson

Maria Schneider, Jenny Runacre Above: Jack
Nicholson, and top with Maria Schneider

Jack Nicholson, Maria Schneider
(also at top)

MONTY PYTHON AND THE HOLY GRAIL

(CINEMA 5) Executive Producer, John Goldstone; Producer, Mark Forstater; Directors, Terry Gilliam, Terry Jones; Screenplay, Graham Chapman, John Cleese, Terry Gilliam, Eric Idle, Terry Jones, Michael Palin; Editor, John Hackney; Photography, Terry Bedford; Songs, Neill Innes; Additional Music, De Wolfe; In color; Rated PG; 90 minutes; April release.

CAST

Graham Chapman
John Cleese
Terry Gilliam
Eric Idle
Terry Jones
Michael Palin
Connie Booth
Carol Cleveland
John Young

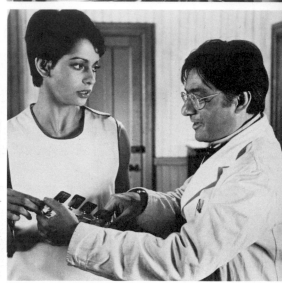

THE WILBY CONSPIRACY

(UNITED ARTISTS) Producer, Martin Baum; Director, Ralph Nelson; Screenplay, Rod Amateau, Harold Nebenzal; Executive Producer, Helmut Dantine; Based on a novel by Peter Driscoll; Associate Producer, Stanley Sopel; Assistant Director, Ivo Nightingale; Designer, Harold Pottle; Editor, Ernest Walter; In color; Rated PG; 101 minutes; April release.

CAST

Shack Twala	Sidney Poitier
Keogh	Michael Caine
Horn	Nicol Williamson
Rina	Prunella Gee
Persis Ray	Persis Khambatta
Mukerjee	Saeed Jaffrey
Van Heerden	Ryk De Gooyer
Blane Nierkirk	Rutger Hauer
Wilby	Joseph De Graf
Judge	Brian Epsom
Headman in Masai village	Abdullah Sunado
Shepherd boy	Freddy Achiang
District Commandant	Patrick Allen
Gordon	Archie Duncan

Prunella Gee, Michael Caine, also above with Sidney Poitier Top: Poitier, Nicol Williamson

Top: Prunella Gee, Persis Khambatta, Michael Caine, Saeed Jaffrey, Sidney Poitier Below: Khambatta, Jaffrey

CHILDREN OF RAGE

(LSV PRODUCTIONS) Producer, George R. Nice; Direction and Screenplay, Arthur Allan Seidelman; Based on story by Arthur Allan Seidelman, Anan Laura; Photography, Ian Wilson; Editor, Paul Davis; Associate Producers, Barry Fortus, Eleanor Fortus, Mae Grinrod, Muriel Karl; Music, Patrick Gowers; In Todd-AO 35 and Technicolor; Rated PG; 106 minutes; May release.

CAST

David Shalmon	Helmut Griem
Leyla Saleh	Olga Georges-Picot
Omar Saleh	Richard Alfieri
Ibrahim	Simon Andreu
David's Father	Cyril Cusack
Abdullah	Robert Salvio
Yaacov	Simon Ward

**Right: Olga Georges-Picot, Helmut Griem
Below: Richard Alfieri, Gus Corrado**

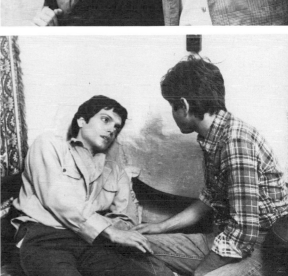

**Helmut Griem, Olga Georges-Picot, Richard Alfieri
Above: Richard Alfieri, Simon Andreu**

Richard Alfieri, Olga Georges-Picot

THE RETURN OF THE PINK PANTHER

(UNITED ARTISTS) Producer-Director, Blake Edwards; Screenplay, Frank Waldman, Blake Edwards; Music, Henry Mancini; Lyrics, Hal David; Associate Producer; Tony Adams; Photography, Geoffrey Unsworth; Art Director, Peter Mullins; Assistant Directors, Guy Sauteret, Bert Batt; Editor, Tom Priestly; In color; Rated G; 115 minutes; May release.

CAST

Inspector Jacques Clouseau	Peter Sellers
Sir Charles Litton	Christopher Plummer
Claudine Litton	Catherine Schell
Chief Inspector Dreyfus	Herbert Lom
Cato	Burt Kwouk
Colonel Sharki	Peter Arne
Chief of Police	Gregoire Aslan
General Wadafi	Peter Jeffrey
Jean Duval	David Lodge
Fat Man	Eric Pohlmann
Francois (Dreyfus Aide)	Andre Maranne
Beggar	John Bluthal
Concierge	Victor Spinetti
Bell Boy	Mike Grady
Sari Lady	Carol Cleveland
Jealous Escort	Jeremy Hawk

Left: Peter Sellers

Catherine Schell, Christopher Plummer

Peter Sellers, and above with Catherine Schell Top: Andre Maranne, Burt Kwouk, Peter Sellers

Catherine Schell, Peter Sellers Above: Sellers, Christopher Plummer, Schell Top (R): Sellers **163**

CRIME AND PUNISHMENT

(ARTKINO) Director, Lev Kulijanov; Screenplay (Russian with English subtitles), Nikolai Fisurovsky, Lev Kulijanov; Based on novel by Dostoyevsky; Photography, Vyacheslav Shumsky; A Gorky Studios Production; 200 minutes; May release.

CAST

Raskoinikov .... Georgi Taratorkin
Ins. Porfiri .... Innokenti Smoktunovsky
Sonia .... Tatyana Bedova
Dunia .... Victoria Fydorovna,
Svidrigaliov .... Yerfim Kopelyan
Marmeladov .... Maria Gulgaji
Mrs. Marmeladove, ... Maria Bulgakova
Mrs. Raskolikov .... Irian Gosheva
Luzhin .... Vladimir Basov
Razumihin .... Alexander Paplov
MRS. Ablione .... Elizaveta Evstratova
Lizaveta .... Liubov Sokolova

Left: Victoria Fydorovna

Innokenti Smoktunovsky, Georgi Taratorkin

Georgi Taratorkin, Tatyana Bedova

LANCELOT OF THE LAKE

(NEW YORKER FILMS) Director, Robert Bresson; Executive Directors, Jean-Pierre Rassam, Francois Rochas; Screenplay, Robert Bresson; Photography, Pasqualino de Santis, Editor, Germaine Lamy; Music, Philippe Sarde, Editions Yanne; Design, Pierre Charbonnier; Costumes, Gres; In color; 85 minutes; May release.

CAST

Lancelot	Luc Simon
Queen Guinevere	Laura Duke Condominas
Gawain	Humbert Balsan
King Arthur	Vladimir Antolek-Oresek
Mordred	Patrick Bernard
Lionel	Arthur de Montalembert

Left: Luc Simon

Luc Simon, Laura Duke Condominas

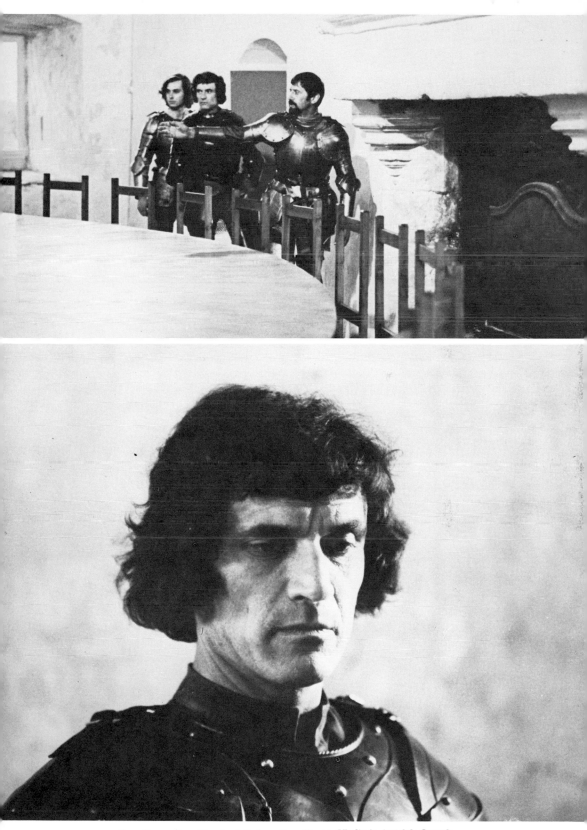

Luc Simon Top: Humbert Balsan, Luc Simon, Vladimir Antolek-Oresek

LULU THE TOOL

(NEW LINE CINEMA) Producer, Euro International Films; Director, Elio Petri, Executive Producer, Ugo Tucci; Screenplay, Ugo Pirro, Elio Petri; Art Director, Dante Ferretti; Photography, Luigi Kuveiller; Music, Ennio Morricone; 91 minutes; May release.

CAST

Lulu	Gian Maria Volonte
Ledia	Mariangela Melato
Militina	Salvo Randone
Adalgisa	Mietta Albertini

Gian Maria Volonte (also left)
Top: Mariangela Melato

LE CHAT

(JOSEPH GREEN) Executive Producer, Raymond Danon; Associate Producer, Maurice Jacquin; Director, Pierre Granier-Deferre; Screenplay, Pierre Granier-Deferre, Pascal Jardin; Based on novel by Georges Simenon; Photography, Walter Wottitz; Music, Philippe Sarde; Assistant Director, Phillippe Lefebvre; English titles, Joseph Green; In Eastmancolor; 88 minutes; June release.

CAST

Julien	Jean Gabin
Clemence	Simone Signoret
Nelly	Annie Cordy
Doctor	Jacques Rispal
Nurse	Nicole Desailly
Retired Worker	Harry Max
Delegate	Andre Rouyer
Boy on bike	Georges Mansaet
Girl on bike	Isabel del Rio
Rental Agent	Carlo Nell
Architect	Yves Barsacq
Milk Maid	Renata Birgo
Cafe Owner	Ermano Casanova
Germaine	Florence Haguenauer

Right: Simone Signoret

Simone Signoret, Jean Gabin

HENNESSY

(AMERICAN INTERNATIONAL) Producer, Peter Snell; Director, Don Sharp; Executive Producer, Samuel Z. Arkoff; Screenplay, John Gay; Story, Richard Johnson; Photography, Ernest Steward; Designer, Ray Simm; Editor, Eric Boyd-Perkins; Assistant Director, Barry Langley; Art Director, Bert Davey; Music, John Scott; In color by Movielab; Rated PG; 103 minutes; June release.

CAST

Hennessy	Rod Steiger
Kate	Lee Remick
Inspector Hollis	Richard Johnson
Commander Rice	Trevor Howard
Williams	Peter Egan
Tobin	Eric Porter
Gerry	Ian Hogg
Hawk	Stanley Lebor
Boyle	John Hallam
Tilney	Patrick Stewart
Covey	David Collings
Tipaldi	John Shrapnel
Burgess M.P	Hugh Moxey
Housekeeper	Margery Mason
Maguire	Paul Brennan
Mick	Oliver Maguire

Right: Lee Remick, Rod Steiger
Below: Ian Hogg, Richard Johnson, Stanley Lebor

Rod Steiger (c) (also above)

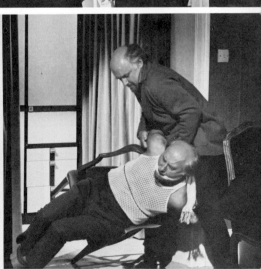

Hugh Moxey, Rod Steiger

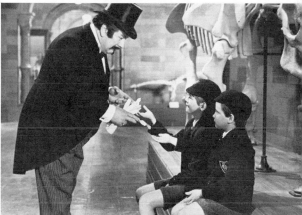

ONE OF OUR DINOSAURS IS MISSING

(BUENA VISTA) Producer, Bill Walsh; Director, Robert Stevenson; Screenplay, Bill Walsh; Based on novel "The Great Dinosaur Robbery" by David Forrest; Associate Producer, Hugh Attwooll; Photography, Paul Beeson; Music, Ron Goodwin; Art Director, Michael Stringer; Editor, Peter Boita; Assistant Directors, Terry Clegg, Dickie Bamber; Costumes, Anthony Mendleson; A Walt Disney Production; In Technicolor; Rated G; 93 minutes; July release.

CAST

Hnup Wan	Peter Ustinov
Hettie	Helen Hayes
Quon	Clive Revill
Lord Southmere	Derek Nimmo
Emily	Joan Sims
Fan Choy	Bernard Bresslaw
Susan	Natasha Pyne
Superintendent Grubbs	Roy Kinnear
B. J. Spence	Joss Ackland
Harris	Deryck Guyler
Lord Castleberry	Andrew Dove
Truscott	Max Harris

Above center: Derek Nimmo, Joan Sims, Helen Hayes, Clive Revill, Peter Ustinov

Derek Nimmo, Helen Hayes, Joan Sims Above: Peter Ustinov Top: Sims, Natasha Pyne, Hayes

KING LEAR

(ARTKINO) Direction and Screenplay, Grigory Kozintsev; Based on play by William Shakespeare; Russian translation by Boris Pasternak; Photography, Jonas Gricius; Music, Dmitry Shostakovich; A Lenfilm Production; In black and white wide screen; 136 minutes; August release.

CAST

KING LEAR	Yuri Jarvet
Goneril	Elsa Radzins
Regan	Galina Volchek
Cordelia	Valentina Shendrikova
Fool	Otar Dal
Earl of Gloster	Kiril Sebris
Edgar	Leonid Merzin
Edmund	Regimantas Adomaitis
Earl of Kent	Victor Emelyanov
Duke of Cornwall	Anton Vokach
Duke of Albany	Donatas Banianis
Oswald	Alexei Petrenko
King of France	Igor Badaitis

JUST BEFORE NIGHTFALL

(LIBRA) Producer, Andre Genoves; Director, Claude Chabrol; Screenplay, Claude Chabrol; Based on novel "The Thin Line" by Edouard Atiyah; Photography, Jean Rabier; Editor, Jacques Gaillard; Music, Pierre Jansen; Assistant Director, Patrick Saglio; Art Director, Guy Littaye; Rated PG; 100 minutes; August release.

CAST

Helene	Stephane Audran
Charles	Michel Bouquet
Francois	Francois Perier
Jeannot	Jean Carmet
Prince	Dominique Zardi
Cavanna	Henri Attal
Bardin	Paul Temps
Ginette	Marina Ninchi
Mme. Masson	Clelia Matavia
Laura	Anna Douking
Dorfmann	Daniel Lecourtois
Jacqueline	Celia
Auguste	Pascal Gillot
Josephine	Brigitte Perin
Barman	Marcel Gassouk

Michel Bouquet, Stephane Audran
Top: Michel Bouquet, Francois Perier

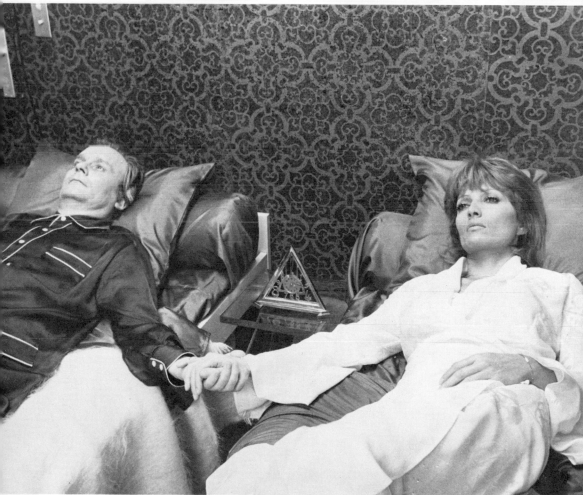

Michel Bouquet, Stephane Audran Top: Michel Bouquet, Anna Douking

DIAMONDS

(AVCO EMBASSY) Producer-Director, Menahem Golan; Co-Producer, Yoram Globus; Executive Producer, Harry N. Blum; Screenplay, David Paulsen, Menahem Golan; Story, Manahem Golan; Assistant Directors, Zion Chen, Shmuel Firstenberg, Roger Richman; A Noah Films Israel-Diamonds Production; Orta Films Switzerland Presentation; In color; Rated PG; 108 minutes; October release.

CAST

Charles/Earl Hodgson	Robert Shaw
Archie	Richard Roundtree
Sally	Barbara Seagull
Zelda Shapia	Shelley Winters
Moshe	Shai K. Ophir
Gaby	Gadi Yageel
Mustafa	Joseph Shiloah
Zippi	Jona Elian
Salzburg	Yehuda Efroni
Rabinowitz	Joseph Graber
Momo	Bomba Zur
Avram	Arie Moscona
Policewoman	Tali Goldberg
Arik	Arik Dichner
Danny Rabinowitz	Chen Plotkin
Ruth Rabinowitz	Naomi Greenbaum

Top: Richard Roundtree, Robert Shaw

Barbara Seagull, Robert Shaw
Top: Richard Roundtree

DISTANT THUNDER

(CINEMA 5) Direction and Screenplay, Satyajit Ray; Based on novel by Bibhuti Bhusan Bannerji; Photography, Soumendu Roy; Music, Satyajit Ray; Editor, Dulai Dutta; Executive Producer, Mrs. Sarbani Bhattacharvi; 100 minutes; October release.

Gangacharan .... Soumitra Chatterji
Ananga .... Babita
Chhutki .... Sandhya Roy
Dinabandhu .... Gobinda Chakravarty
Biswas .... Romesh Mukerji

Right: Soumitra Chatterji (R)

Babita

SWEPT AWAY ... by an unusual destiny in the blue sea of August

(CINEMA 5) Producer, Romano Cardarelli; Direction and Screenplay, Lina Wertmuller; Assistant Director, Giovanni Arduini; Photography, Giulio Battiferri, Giuseppe Fornari, Stefano Ricciotti; Music, Piero Piccioni; Sets and Costumes, Enrico Job; In color; Rated R; 116 minutes; October release.

CAST

Gennarino ....Giancarlo Giannini
Raffaella.. Mariangela Melato

Mariangela Melato, Giancarlo Giannini
(also above)

Mariangela Melato, Giancarlo Giannini
(also top)

CONDUCT UNBECOMING

(ALLIED ARTISTS) Producers, Michel Deeley, Barry Spikings; Co-Producer, Andrew Donally; Director, Michael Anderson; Screenplay, Robert Enders; Photography, Bob Huke; Assistant Director, David Anderson; Art Director, Ted Tester; Editor, John Glen; Costumes, Elizabeth Haffenden, Joan Bridge; Music, Stanley Myers; A British Lion Production in color; Rated PG; 107 minutes; October release.

CAST

Second Lieutenant Arthur Drake	Michael York
Major Lionel Roach	Richard Attenborough
Colonel Benjamin Strang	Trevor Howard
Captain Rupert Harper	Stacy Keach
Major Alastair Wimbourne	Christopher Plummer
Mrs. Marjorie Scarlett	Susannah York
Second Lt. Edward Millington	James Faulkner
Second Lt. Richard Fothergill	Michael Culver
Regimental Doctor	James Donald
Pradah Singh	Rafiq Anwar
Mem Strang	Helen Cherry
Lieutenant Frank Hart	Michael Fleming
Second Lt. Winters	David Robb
Second Lt. Boulton	David Purcell
Second Lt. Hutton	Andrew Lodge
Second Lt. Truly	David Neville
Mrs. Bandanai	Persis Khambatta
Second Lt. Toby Strang	Michael Byrne

Susannah York, Stacy Keach (C), Christopher Plummer Above: Trevor Howard, Susannah York

Top: Susannah York, James Faulkner

Susannah York, Michael York
Top: James Faulkner, Michael York

Christopher Plummer Above: Michael York,
Persis Khambatta Top: Richard Attenborough, York 181

THE MAGIC FLUTE

(SURROGATE) Produced, Directed and Written by Ingmar Bergman; Based on Wolfgang Amadeus Mozart's opera "The Magic Flute"; Photography, Sven Nykvist; Eric Ericson conducts the Swedish State Broadcasting Network Symphony; Presented by Carmen F. Zollo; In color; Rated G; 134 minutes; November release.

CAST

Sarastro	Ulrik Cold
Tamino	Josef Kostlinger
The Speaker	Erik Saeden
Queen of the Night	Birgit Nordin
Pamina	Irma Urrila
Papageno	Hakan Hagegard
Monostatos	Ragnar Ulfung
Three Ladies	Britt Marie Aruhn, Kirsten Vaupel, Birgitta Smiding
Three Youths	Urban Malmberg, Erland von Heijne, Ansgar Krook
Two Priests	Gosta Pruzelius, Ulf Johansson

Left: Josef Kostlinger, Irma Urrila

LIES MY FATHER TOLD ME

(COLUMBIA) Producers, Anthony Bedrich, Harry Gulkin; Executive Producers, Michael Harrison, Arnold Issenman, Arnold Schniffer; Director, Jan Kadar; Story and Screenplay, Ted Allan; Photography, Paul Van Der Linden; Editors, Edward Beyer, Richard Marks; Designer, Francois Barbeau; Music, Sol Kaplan; In color; Rated PG; 103 minutes; November release.

CAST

Zaida	Yossi Yadin
Harry Herman	Len Birman
Annie Herman	Marilyn Lightstone
David	Jeffrey Lynas
Baumgarten	Ted Allan
Mrs. Tannenbaum	Barbara Chilcott
Mrs. Bondy	Mignon Elkins
Uncle Benny	Henry Gamer
Edna	Carole Lazare
Cleo	Cleo Paskal

Left: Jeffrey Lynas

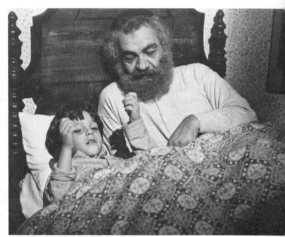

Len Birman, Marilyn Lightstone

Yossi Yadin, and above with
Jeffrey Lynas

Jeffrey Lynas, Cleo Paskal Above: Lynas,
Marilyn Lighstone

Henry Gamer, Len Birman
Above and Top: Yassi Yadin, Jeffrey Lynas

MR. QUILP

(AVCO EMBASSY) Producer, Helen M. Strauss; Director, Michael Tuchner; Music and Lyrics, Anthony Newley; Choreographer, Gillian Lynne; Costumes, Anthony Mendleson; Screenplay, Louis and Irene Kamp; Based on Charles Dickens' novel "The Old Curiosity Shop"; Photography, Christopher Challis; Associate Producer, Douglas Twiddy; Editor, John Jympson; Designer, Elliot Scott; Art Director, Norman Reynolds; Assistant Director, Kip Gowans; Presented by Reader's Digest Films; In Panavision and Technicolor; Rated G; 120 minutes; November release.

CAST

Daniel Quilp	Anthony Newley
Richard Swiveller	David Hemmings
Sampson Brass	David Warner
Grandfather/Edward Trent	Michael Hordern
Single Gent/Henry Trent	Paul Rogers
Sally Brass	Jill Bennett
Mrs. Jarley	Mona Washbourne
Kit Nubbles	Peter Duncan
Betsy Quilp	Yvonne Antrobus
Nell	Sarah Jane Varley
Duchess	Sarah Webb
George	Windsor Davies
Tom Scott	Philip Davis
Codlin	David Battley
Harris	Ronald Lacey
Mrs. Jiniwin	Margaret Whiting
Isaac List	Maxwell Shaw
Joe Jowl	Tony Caunter
Mr. Garland	Bryan Pringle
Mrs. George	Rosalind Knight
Mrs. Simmons	Jenny Tomasin

and Fred Evans (Jerry), Eddie Davies (Mr. Grinder), Norman Warwick (Vuffin), Graham Weston, Bernard Taylor (Policemen), Brian Glover (Furnaceman), Desmond Cullum-Jones (Jailer), Harry Markham (Sexton), Johnny and Suma Lamonte (Jugglers), The Barbours (Stiltwalkers), Sadie Corre (Midget), Christopher Greener (Giant), Malcolm Weaver (Acrobat)

Right: Anthony Newley (L), David Warner, Jill Bennett Top: Michael Hordern, Paul Rogers, Peter Duncan, Sarah Jane Varley

Sarah Jane Varley, Peter Duncan

Anthony Newley

THE ROMANTIC ENGLISHWOMAN

(NEW WORLD) Producer, Daniel M. Angel; Director, Joseph Losey; Screenplay, Tom Stoppard, Thomas Wiseman; Based on novel by Thomas Wiseman; Music, Richard Hartley; Associate Producer, Richard F. Dalton; Assistant Director, Anthony Wade; Photography, Gerry Fisher; Designer, Richard MacDonald; Editor, Reginald Beck; Costumes, Ruth Myers; Presented by Roger Corman; In color; Rated R; 115 minutes; November release.

CAST

Elizabeth Fielding	Glenda Jackson
Lewis Fielding	Michael Caine
Thomas	Helmut Berger
David Fielding	Marcus Richardson
Isabel	Kate Nelligan
Herman	Rene Kolldehof
Swan	Michel Lonsdale
Catherine	Beatrice Romand
Annie	Anna Steele
Miranda	Nathalie Delon
Hendrik	Bill Wallis
New Nanny	Julie Peasgood
George	David De Keyser
Mr. Wilson	Phil Brown
Mrs. Wilson	Marcella Markham
First Meal-ticket Lady	Lillias Walker
Second Meal-ticket Lady	Doris Nolan
Headwaiter	Norman Scace
Neighbor	Tom Chatto
Supermarket Cashier	Frankie Jordan
Airport Shop Assistant	Frances Tomelty

Top: Glenda Jackson, Helmut Berger, and also below with Marcus Richardson, Michael Caine

Helmut Berger, Glenda Jackson Above: Nathalie Delon, Michael Caine Top: Beatrice Romand, Berger

THE ADVENTURE OF SHERLOCK HOLMES' SMARTER BROTHER

(20th CENTURY-FOX) Producer, Richard A. Roth; Direction and Screenplay, Gene Wilder; Music, John Morris, Photography, Gerry Fisher; Choreographer, Alan Johnson, Designer, Terry Marsh; Costumes, Ruth Myers; Editor, Jim Clark; Assistant Director, David Tomblin; In DeLuxe Color; Rated PG; 91 minutes; December release.

CAST

Sigerson Holmes	Gene Wilder
Jenny	Madeline Kahn
Orville Sacker	Marty Feldman
Gambetti	Dom DeLuise
Moriarty	Leon McKern
Moriarty's Aide	Roy Kinnear
Lord Redcliff	John LeMesurier
Sherlock Holmes	Douglas Wilmer
Dr. Watson	Thorley Walters
Bruner	George Silver
Queen Victoria	Susan Field

Left: Gene Wilder

Madeline Kahn

Marty Feldman

Marty Feldman Above: Thorley Walters, Douglas Wilmer
Top: Gene Wilder, Marty Feldman

Madeline Kahn Above: Gene Wilder
Top: Dom DeLuise

BARRY LYNDON

(WARNER BROS.) Produced, Directed and Written by Stanley Kubrick; Based on novel by William Makepeace Thackeray; Executive Producer, Jan Harlan; Associate Producer, Bernard Williams; Designer, Ken Adam; Costumes, Ulla-Britt Soderlund, Milena Canonero; Photography, John Alcott; Editor, Tony Lawson; Art Director, Roy Walker; Assistant Director, Brian Cook; Music adapted by Leonard Rosenman; Choreographer, Geraldine Stephenson; A Peregrine Film; In color; Rated PG; 185 minutes; December release.

CAST

Barry Lyndon	Ryan O'Neal
Lady Lyndon	Marisa Berenson
The Chevalier	Patrick Magee
Capt. Potzdorf	Hardy Kruger
Lord Ludd	Steven Berkoff
Nora	Gay Hamilton
Barry's Mother	Marie Kean
German Girl	Diana Koerner
Rev. Runt	Murray Melvin
Sir Charles Lyndon	Frank Middlemass
Lord Wendover	Andre Morell
Highwayman	Arthur O'Sullivan
Capt. Grogan	Godfrey Quigley
Capt. Quin	Leonard Rossiter
Graham	Philip Stone
Lord Bullingdon	Leon Vitali
Narrator	Michael Hordern

with John Bindon, Roger Booth, Billy Boyle, Jonathan Cecil, Peter Cellier, Geoffrey Chater, Anthony Dawes, Patrick Dawson, Bernard Hepton, Anthony Herrick, Barry Jackson, Wolf Kahler, Patrick Laffan, Hans Meyer, Ferdy Mayne, David Morley, Liam Redmond, Pat Roach, Dominic Savage, Frederick Schiller, George Sewell, Anthony Sharp, John Sharp, Roy Spencer, John Sullivan, Harry Towb

Left and Top (R): Ryan O'Neal

Ryan O'Neal, Marisa Berenson

Ryan O'Neal, Marisa Berenson
(also top)

Marisa Berenson, Ryan O'Neal
Above: David Morley, Ryan O'Neal

THE STORY OF ADELE H.

(NEW WORLD) Executive Producers, Marcel Berbert, Claude Miller; Director, Francois Truffaut; Screenplay, Francois Truffaut, Jean Gruault, Suzanne Schiffman, Frances V. Guille; English Adaptation, Jan Dawson; Music, Maurice Jaubert; Photography, Nestor Almendros; Assistant Director, Suzanne Schiffman; Editors, Yann Didet, Martine Barraque, Jean Gargonne, Michele Nerry, Muriel Zeleny; Art Director, Jean-Pierre Kohut; Costumes, Jacqueline Guyot; Translation, Helen G. Scott; Presented by Roger Corman; In Metrocolor; Rated PG; 97 minutes; December release.

CAST

Adele .... Isabelle Adjani
Lt. Pinson .... Bruce Robinson
Mrs. Saunders .... Sylvia Marriott
Mr. Saunders .... Reubin Dorey
Mr. Whistler .... Joseph Blatchley
Colonel White .... M. White
Lt. Pinson's Batman .... Carl Hathwell
Magnetizer .... Ivry Gitlis
Mr. Lenoir .... Sir Cecil de Sausmarez
Judge Johnstone .... Sir Raymond Falla
Dr. Murdock .... Roger Martin
Mrs. Baa .... Madame Louise
Copyist .... Jean-Pierre Leursse

Left: Isabelle Adjani

Bruce Robinson, Isabelle Adjani

**Isabelle Adjani, also top with
François Truffaut**

Isabelle Adjani, Bruce Robinson

MAN FRIDAY

(AVCO EMBASSY) Producer, David Korda; Director, Jack Gold; Executive Producers, Jules Buck, Gerald Green; Screenplay, Adrian Mitchell; Based on Daniel Defoe's "Robinson Crusoe"; Designer, Peter Murton; Photography, Alex Phillips; Music and Songs, Carl Davis; Editor, Anne Coates; Art Director, Augustin Ytuarte; Choreography, Tino Rodriguez; Presented by I.T.C. and Keep Films in association with ABC Entertainment; In Panavision and color; Rated PG; 115 minutes; December release.

CAST

Crusoe	Peter O'Toole
Friday	Richard Roundtree
Carey	Peter Cellier
McBain	Christopher Cabot
Doctor	Joel Fluellen
Young Girl	Sam Seabrook
Young Boy	Stanley Clay

Peter O'Toole, Richard Roundtree
(also above)

Top: Peter O'Toole, and below
with Richard Roundtree

UNDERCOVERS HERO

(UNITED ARTISTS) Producer, John Boulting; Director, Roy Boulting; Screenplay, Leo Marks, Roy Boulting; Associate Producer, John Palmer; Music, Neil Rhoden; Musical Theme, Roy Boulting; Editor, Martin Charles; Photography, Gil Taylor; A Charter Films Production; In color; 95 minutes; Rated R; December release.

CAST

General Latour/Major Robinson/Schroeder/Hitler/ Prince Kyoto/President of France	Peter Sellers
Madame Grenier	Lila Kedrova
General von Grotjahn	Curt Jurgens
Marie-Claude	Beatrice Romand

Right: Peter Sellers in his different characterizations Below: with Lila Kedrova Left Center: with Helli-Louise

Angela Winkler

THE LOST HONOR OF KATHARINA BLUM

(NEW WORLD) Executive Producer, Eberhard Junkersdorf; Direction and Screenplay, Volker Schlondorff, Margarethe von Trotta; Based on novel of Heinrich Boll; Photography, Jost Vacano; Editor, Peter Przygodda; Music, Hans Werner Henze; In color; 102 minutes; Rated R; December release.

CAST

Katharina Blum	Angela Winkler
Belzmenne	Mario Adorf
Werner Totges	Dieter Laser
Dr. Blorna	Heinz Bennent
Trude Blorna	Hannelore Hoger
Moeding	Harald Kuhlmann
Alois Straubleder	Karl Heinz Vosgerau
Ludwig Gotten	Jurgen Prochnow

THE MAN WHO WOULD BE KING

(ALLIED ARTISTS) Producer, John Foreman; Director, John Huston; Associate Producer, James Arnett; Screenplay, John Huston, Gladys Hill; Photography, Oswald Morris; Designer, Alexander Trauner; Wardrobe, Edith Head; Art Director, Tony Inglis; Editor, Russell Lloyd; Assistant Director, Bert Batt; Music, Maurice Jarre; A Persky-Bright/Devon Picture; An Allied Artists/Columbia Pictures Production; In Panavision and Technicolor; Presented by Emanuel L. Wolf; Rated PG; 129 minutes; December release.

CAST

Daniel Dravot	Sean Connery
Peachy Carnehan	Michael Caine
Rudyard Kipling	Christopher Plummer
Billy Fish	Saeed Jaffrey
Kafu-Selim	Karroum Ben Bouih
District Commissioner	Jack May
Ootah	Doghmi Larbi
Roxanne	Shakira Caine
Babu	Mohammed Shamsi
Mulvaney	Paul Antrim
Ghulam	Albert Moses
Sikh Soldiers	Kimat Singh, Gurmuks Singh
Dancers	Yvonne Ocampo, Nadia Atbib

Left: Christopher Plummer, Michael Caine

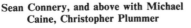
Sean Connery, and above with Michael
Caine, Christopher Plummer

Michael Caine, Sean Connery

Sean Connery, Shakira Caine
Above: Saeed Jaffrey, Michael Caine,
Sean Connery (also top)

Sean Connery, also above and
top with Michael Caine

SPECIAL SECTION

(UNIVERSAL) Producers, Jacques Perrin, Giorgio Silvagni; Director, Costa-Gavras; Screenplay, Jorge Semprun, Costa-Gavras; From the work of Herve Villere; Dialogue, Jorge Semprun; Associate Producer, Claude Heyman; Photography, Andreas Wilding; Editor, Francoise Bonnot; Music, Eric Demarsan; A French-Italian-German Co-production; In color; Rated PG; 112 minutes; December release.

CAST

Minister of Justice	Louis Seigner
Minister of the Interior	Michel Lonsdale
Admiral	Ivo Garrani
Deputy General	Francois Maistre
Attorney General	Pierre Dux
State Prosecutor	Jacques Francois
President of Special Section	Claude Pieplu
Counsellor Linais	Jean Bouise
President Cournet	Michel Galabru
Major Beumelburg	Heinz Bennent
Brechet	Guy Retore
Bastard	Yves Robert
Trzebrucki	Jacques Rispal
Samplaix	Bruno Cremer
Lawyer Lafarge	Jacques Perrin
Fredo	Jacques Spiesser
Prefect of Police Legrand	Henri Serre
Attorney General for the State	Jacques Francois
The First President	Claudio Gora
Judge Cottin	Hubert Gignoux
Counselor Larricq	Alain Nobis
Solicitor-General Guyenor	Jean Champion
Solicitor-General	Julien Bertheau
Deputy Tetaud	Julien Guiomar
Deputy Guillec	Maurice Teynac

and Roland Bertin, Hans Richter, Jacques Ouvrier, Eric Rouleau, Guy Mairesse

Left: Heinz Bennent

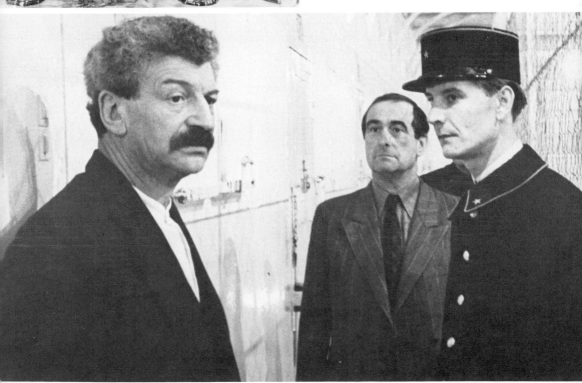

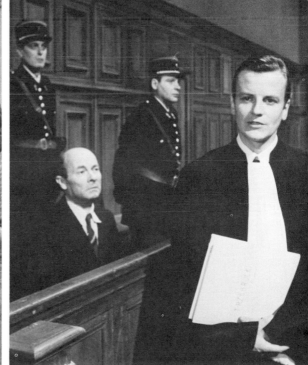

HEDDA

(BRUT) Producer, Robert Enders; Executive Producer, George Barrie; Direction and Screenplay, Trevor Nunn; Based on play "Hedda Gabler" by Henrik Ibsen; Photography, Douglas Slocombe; A Royal Shakespeare Company production; Associate Producer, Gordon L. T. Scott; Art Director, Ted Tester; Editor, Peter Tanner; Music, Laurie Johnson; Assistant Director, Kenneth Baker; In Technicolor; Rated PG; 104 minutes; December release.

CAST

Hedda Gabler	Glenda Jackson
Tesman	Timothy West
Brach	Peter Eyre
Mrs. Elvsted	Jennie Linden
Lovborg	Patrick Stewart
Julie	Constance Chapman
Bertha	Pam St. Clement

Left: Glenda Jackson, Peter Eyre
Below: Glenda Jackson, Jennie Linden

Jennie Linden, Glenda Jackson, Patrick Stewart

Pam St. Clement, Peter Eyre
Above: Glenda Jackson, Timothy West

**Vanessa Redgrave, Franco Nero
in "Dropout!"**

**Keir Dullea, Elizabeth Ashley
in "Paperback Hero"**

DROPOUT! (Scotia American) Director, Tinto Brass; In Eastmancolor; Rated R; 91 minutes; January release. CAST: Vanessa Redgrave (Mary), Franco Nero (Bruno), Frank Winsor

TENDER DRACULA (Scotia American) Presented by Victor Malle; 98 minutes; January release. CAST: Peter Cushing, Alida Valli

EVIL FINGERS (Scotia American) Producer, Manolo Bolognini; Director, Luigi Bazzoni; January release. CAST: Franco Nero, Ira Furstenberg, Edmund Purdom, Pamela Tiffin

CALLAN (Cinema National) Producer, Derek Horne; Director, Don Sharpe; Screenplay, James Mitchell from his novel "A Red File for Callan"; Associate Producer, Harry Benn; A Magnum Production; In Eastmancolor; Presented by Barney Bernhard; A Syn-Frank Enterprise Presentation; Rated PG; 91 minutes; January release. CAST: Edward Woodward, Eric Porter, Carl Mohner, Catherine Schell, Peter Egan, Russell Hunter

PAPERBACK HERO (Rumson) Producers, James Margellos, John F. Bassett; Director, Peter Pearson; Screenplay, Les Rose, Barry Pearson; Photography, Don Wilder; Editor, Kirk Jones; Music, Ron Collier; Song written and performed by Gordon Lightfoot; In Eastmancolor; Rated R; 87 minutes; January release. CAST: Keir Dullea (Rick), Elizabeth Ashley (Loretta), John Beck (Pov), Dayle Haddon (Joanna), Franz Russell (Big Ed), George R. Robertson (Burdock), Margot Lamarre (Julie), Ted Follows (Cagey), Linda Sorenson (Mona), Les Ruby (Jock), Jacquie Presly (Marlene), Chet Robertson (Father), Winnie Rowles (Mother), Gerry Cooke (Noogie), John Ottenberg (Heavy), Linda Findlay (Friend), Mike Shabaga (Referee), Pat Scott (Hippie), John Leffler (Bus Driver), Jim Arnsten, Dave Steingard (Policemen), Max Bentley (Max)

A PAGE OF MADNESS (New Line) Produced and Directed by Teinosuke Kinugasa: 60 minutes; January release. CAST: Masao Inoue, Yoshie Nakagawa, Ayako Iijima, Hiroshi Nemoto, Misao Seki

THE APPLE WAR (Svenska) Director, Tage Danielsson; Screenplay, Hans Alfredson, Tage Danielsson; Photography, Lars Swanberg; Music, Evert Taube; In color; 103 minutes; January release. CAST: Hans Alfredson (Severin), Monica Zetterlund (Anna), Hakan Serner (Eberhard), Birgitta Andersson (Huft-Hanna), Martin Ljung (Ake), Max von Sydow (Roy), Tage Danielsson (Bernhard), Gosta Ekman (Sten), Per Grunden (Jean)

THE SENSUOUS ASSASSIN (New Line) Producer, Raymond Danon; Director, Leonard Kiegel; In Eastmancolor; January release. CAST: Romy Schneider, Maurice Ronet, Simone Bach

BLUE MONEY (Crown International) Producer-Director, Alain-Patrick Chappuis; Rated R; 93 minutes; January release. CAST: Alain-Patrick Chappuis (Jim), Barbara Caron (Lisa), Inga Maria (Ingrid), Jeff Gall (Mike), Oliver Aubrey (Fatman), Steve Roberson (Freddie), Alan Bouveeat (Lawyer), John Parker (Bernie), Maria Arnold, Sandy Dempsey (Models)

CHALLENGE OF THE DRAGON (Cannon) In Technicolor; Rated R; January release. CAST: Joe Lee, Yung Ching, Robert Chin Ho

FRANKENSTEIN'S CASTLE OF FREAKS (Aquarius) Producer, Richard Randall; Director, Robert Oliver; Executive Producer, G. Robert Straub; In color; Rated PG; January release. CAST: Rossano Brazzi, Michael Dunn, Edmund Purdom, Christiane Royce

THE CASTLE OF FU MANCHU (International Cinema) Producer, Harry Alan Towers; Director, Jess Franco; Screenplay, Peter Welbeck; In color; Rated PG; January release. CAST: Christopher Lee, Richard Greene, Tsai Chin, Maria Perschy, Gunther Stoll, Howard Marion Crawford

THE ALGERIAN WAR (Reggane) Produced and Directed by Yves Courriere, Phillipe Monnier; Music, Francois de Roubaix; Screenplay, Yves Courriere; French with English titles; 155 minutes; January release. A documentary about France's long struggle in Algeria.

**Carl Mohner, Edward Woodward
in "Callan"**

**Keir Dullea (L), Franz Russell (C)
in "Paperback Hero"**

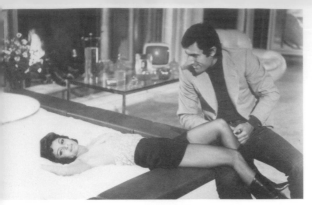

Rossana Podesta, Lando Buzzanca
in "Homo Eroticus"

THE DRAGON DIES HARD (Allied Artists) Producer, Shaw Po Wah; Director, Kong Kung; A Hallmark Presentation; In color; Rated PG; 82 minutes; January release. CAST: Cheung Nick, Nam Kung Fen

THREE BULLETS FOR A LONG GUN (Maron) Director, Peter Henkel; Producer, Ramsey Henkel; Story and Screenplay, Beau Brummell, Keith van der Wat; In color; Rated PG; January release. CAST: Beau Brummell (Major), Keith van der Wat (Lucky), Tulio Moneta (Moses)

FURY OF THE BLACK BELT (Lana) In Techniscope and Technicolor; Rated R; No other credits available; January release.

I, A WOMAN PART II (Chevron) Produced and Written by Peer Guldbrandsen; Directed and Photographed by Mac Ahlberg; Music, Sven Glydmark; In Movielab Color; Rated R; February release. CAST: Gio Petre (Siv), Lars Lunde (Hans), Hjordis Petterson (Mrs. Holm), Bertel Lauring (Svendsen), Klaus Pagh (Leo)

I, A WOMAN PART III (Orrin) Produced and Written by Peer Guldbrandsen; Director, Mac Ahlberg; In color; Rated R; February release. CAST: Inger Sundh, Tom Scott, Ellen Faison

HUMAIN, TROP HUMAIN (New Yorker) Produced and Directed by Louis Malle; Photography, Etienne Becker; Editors, Suzanne Baron, Reine Wekstein, Jocelyne Riviere; In color; 77 minutes; February release. A documentary about an automobile assembly line at a factory in Rennes, France.

MAHLER (Mayfair) Executive Producers, David Puttnam, Sanford Lieberson; Direction and Screenplay, Ken Russell; Producer, Roy Baird; Photography, Dick Bush; Editor, Michael Bradsell; Music, Bernard Haitink; In color; 115 minutes; Rated PG; February release. CAST: Robert Powell, Georgina Hale, Richard Morant, Lee Montagne, Rosalie Crutchley, Benny Lee, Miriam Karlin, Angela Down, David Collings, Ronald Pickup, Antonia Ellis, Dana Gillespie, Elaine Delmar, Michael Southgate, Gary Rich

Shai Ophir, Yossef Shiloah
in "Daughters, Daughters"

ZIG-ZAG (Peppercorn/Wormser) Direction and Screenplay, Laszlo Szabo; Photography, Jean-Pierre Baux; Editor, Jacques Witta; Music, Carl Hans Sachafer; In Eastmancolor; Rated R; 90 minutes; February release. CAST: Catherine Deneuve (Marie), Bernadette Lafont (Pauline), Hubert Deschamps (Jean), Walter Chiari (Tramp), Stephane Shandor (Bruyere), Jean-Pierre Kalfon (Guitarist), Georgette Anys (Singer)

MY PLEASURE IS MY BUSINESS (Brian) Producer, Jesse Vogel; Director, Albert S. Waxman; Screenplay, Alvin Boretz; A Tontigo Film in Panavision and Eastmancolor; Rated R; February release. CAST: Xaviera Hollander

ALIEN THUNDER (Cinerama) Title changed to "Dan Candy's Law"; Director, Claude Fournier; Associate Producer, Marie-Jose Raymond; In color; Rated PG; February release. CAST: Donald Sutherland, Chief Dan George, Kevin McCarthy, Jean Duceppe, Francine Racette

BAD MAN'S RIVER (Scotia International) Director, Eugenio Martin; In Eastmancolor; Rated PG; February release. CAST: Lee Van Cleef, Gina Lollobrigida, James Mason

VENGEANCE OF THE ZOMBIES (International Amusements) Director, Leon Klimovsky; In Technicolor; Rated R; February release. CAST: Paul Naschy, Romy, Vic Winner

SECRETS OF SWEET SIXTEEN (International Producers) Director, Ernst Hofbauer; Producer, Lisa Films; In color; Rated X; 90 minutes; February release

SUPER STOOGES VS. THE WONDER WOMEN (Shaw Brothers) Director, Al Bradley (Alfonso Brescia); Screenplay, Aldo Crudo, Alfonso Brescia; Photography, Fausto Rossi; Editor, Liliana Serra; In color; 105 minutes; February release. CAST: Yueh Hua, Karen Yeh, Nick Jordan, Mark Hannibal, Malisa Longo, Genie Woods, Riccardo Pizzuti, Kirsten Gilles

THE LEGEND OF SPIDER FOREST (New Line) Director, Peter Sykes; In Technicolor; Rated PG; 88 minutes; February release. CAST: Neda Arneric, Simon Brent

HELL HOUSE GIRLS (American International) Producer, Peter Newbrook; Director, Robert Hartford-Davis; In color; Rated R; 95 minutes; February release. CAST: Madeline Hinde, Renee Asherson, Dennis Waterman, Patrick Mower

SCHOOL GIRL BRIDE (American International) A United Producers presentation; In Eastmancolor; Rated R; February release. CAST: Barbara Klingered, Ava Christian, Katherine Conte, Ula Kopa

THE VIOLENT PROFESSIONALS (Scotia American) Director, Fernando DeLeo; Presented by Carlo Ponti; In color; Rated R; February release. CAST: Richard Conte, Luke Merenda, Delia Boccardo

THE SPECIALIST Director, Frank Agrama; Music, Fred Bongusto; In color; Rated R; February release. CAST: Richard Harrison, Erika Blanc, Ian Flynn

THE YOUNG PLAYTHINGS (Associated Films) Producer-Director, Joe Sarno; Rated R; 105 minutes; In color; February release. CAST: Christina Lindberg, Eva Portnoff, Margaretta Hellstrom

THE SAGA OF DRACULA (International Amusements) Director, Leon Klimovsky; In Technicolor; Rated R; 90 minutes; February release. CAST: Tina Sainz, Tony Isbert

PANCHO VILLA (Scotia International) Director, Eugenio Martin; In color; Rated PG; 90 minutes; February release. CAST: Telly Savalas, Clint Walker, Anne Francis, Chuck Connors

MARK OF THE DEVIL PART 2 (Hallmark) Director, Adrian Hoven; In Eastmancolor; 90 minutes; Rated R; February release. CAST: Erica Blanc, Anton Diffring, Reggie Nalder, Percy Hoven, Lukas Ammann, Jean Pierre Zola

DAUGHTERS! DAUGHTERS! (Steinmann-Baxter) Producer, Menahem Golan; Director, Moshe Mizrahi; Screenplay, Moshe Mizrahi, Shai K. Ophir; Photography, Adam Greenberg; Executive Producer, Yoram Globus; Editor, David Hoenig; Designer, Shlomo Zafrir; Music, Alex Kagan; In color; Rated PG; 88 minutes; March release. CAST: Shai K. Ophir (Sabbetay), Zaharira Harifai (Bianca), Yossef Shiloah (Joseph), Michael Bat-Adam (Esther)

HOMO EROTICUS (Universal) Producer-Director, Marco Vicario; Executive Producer, Alfonso Vicario; Story and Screenplay, Piero Chiara, Marco Vicario; Photography, Tonino Delli Colli; Designer, Flavio Mogherini; Music, Armando Trovajoli; Song sung by Nanni Svampa; Costumes, Lucia Mirisola; Atlantica Cinematografica and Earl A. Glick Presentation; In Eastmancolor; Rated R; 94 minutes; March release. CAST: Rossana Podesta (Coco), Lando Puzzanca (Michele), Luciano Salce (Achille), Adriani Asti (Marchesa), Ira Furstenberg (Signora Mezzini), Evi Marandi (Giusi), Brigitte Skay (Pina), Angela Luce (Amelia), Femi Benussi (Ersilia), Sandro Dori (Ambrogio), Bernard Blier (Dr. Mezzini), Sylva Koscina (Carla)

SHANGHAI LIL AND THE SUN LUCK KID (Bardene International) Producer, Yen Wu-Tung; Directors, Chu-Ko Chin-Yung, Yang Ching-Chen; Screenplay, Yang Ching-Chen, Chang Hsin-i; Photography, Chuang Yin-chien; Editor, Kuo Tin-hung; Music, Chou Fu-liang; In color; A Shaw Brothers Presentation; 90 minutes; March release. CAST: Sue-Sue (Chin), Chin Han (Lu), I Yuan (Nagata), Lung Fei (Lu Te-piao), Ko Hsiang-ting (Lu Ta-yeh), Chang Feng (Headman), Han So (Shop Proprietor), Chin Tu (Faithful servant), Shih Chung-Tien (Katsumasa), Li Hui (Chieko)

WOMEN FOR SALE (Independent International) Producer, Wolf C. Hartwig; Director, Ernest Farmer; In Eastmancolor; Rated R; 86 minutes; March release. CAST: Robert Woods, Veronique Vendell, Barbara Cappell, Joe Busse, Werner Puchath

THE KUNG FU MASSACRE (Aquarius) A Terry Levene presentation; Rated R; In Techniscope and Technicolor; March release.

BETWEEN THE COVERS (International Producers) No credits available; Rated X; In color; March release. CAST: Marina Blumel, Michael Buttner, Angelika Duvier, Carmen Van De Poel, Vera Schmidt

CALL HIM MR. SHATTER (AVCO Embassy) A Hammer Films production; Producers, Michael Carreras, Vee King Shaw; Director, Michael Carreras; Screenplay, Don Houghton; Photography, Brian Probyn, John Wilcox, Roy Ford; Editor, Eric Boyd-Perkins; Music, David Lindup; Assistant Director, Geoffrey Ho; Rated R; 90 minutes; March release. CAST: Stuart Whitman, Ti Lung, Lily Li, Peter Cushing, Anton Diffring, Yemi Adjibade, Liu Ka Yong

CALL OF THE WILD (Constantin) Producer, Arthur Brauner; Director, Ken Annakin; Screenplay, Hubert Frank, Tibor Reves; Based on novel by Jack London; Photography, John Cabrera, Music, Carlo Rustinelli; In color; Rated PG; 100 minutes; March release. CAST: Charlton Heston, Raimund Harmsdorf, Michele Mercier, George Eastman, Sancho Garcia, Rik Battaglia

THE CONTRACT (International Producers) Director, Claude Mulot; Screenplay, Albert Kantoff, Edgar Oppenheimer, Claude Mulot; Photography, Roger Fellous; Editor, V. Mercanton; Music, Eddy Vartan; In Eastmancolor; Rated R; 85 minutes; March release. CAST: Bruno Pradal, Eva Swann, Gabriele Tinti, Francoise Prevost, Charles Southwood, Sidney Chaplin, Patricia D'Arbanville

OIL LAMPS (Filmaco) Director, Juraj Herz; Screenplay, Vaclav Sasek, Lubor Dohanl, Juraj Herz; From novel by Jaroslav Havlicek; Photography, Dodo Simoncici; Music, Lobos Fiser; In Eastmancolor; Rated PG; 97 minutes; March release. CAST: Iva Janzurova, Peter Cepek, Marie Rosulkova, Ota Sklencka, Vladimir Jedenactik, Karel Cernoch

REDNECK (International Amusements) Director, Silvio Narizzano; Screenplay, Win Wells; In color; 89 minutes; March release. CAST: Telly Savalas, Franco Nero, Mark Lester

THE HOUSE OF WHIPCORD (American International) Producer-Director, Pete Walker; Screenplay, David McGillivray; In Movielab Color; Rated R; 94 minutes; March release. CAST: Barbara Markham, Patrick Barr, Ray Brooks, Ann Michelle, Penny Irving, Sheila Keith, Robert Tayman, Dorothy Walker

THE SWINGIN' MODELS (Hemisphere) Produced by Dity Films; Director, Ilja von Anutroff; in Eastmancolor; Rated R; March release. CAST: Angel Wehbeck, Ingrid Steeger

FAMILY KILLER (Cannon) Direction and Screenplay by Vittorio Schiraldi; Rated R; In color; 95 minutes; March release. CAST: John Saxon, Arthur Kennedy, Agostina Belli

Pierre Richard, Daniele Minazzoli in "Lucky Pierre"

LUCKY PIERRE (Seaberg) Producers, Les Films Christian Fechner, Renn Productions; Executive Producer, Bernard Artigues; Director, Claude Ziti, Photography, Henri Decae, Editor, Robert Isnardon, In Panavision and Eastmancolor; Rated PG, March release. CAST: Pierre Richard (Pierre), Jane Birkin (Jackie), Daniele Minazzoli (Daniele), Claude Pieplu (Hubert), Henri Guybet (Patrick), Jean Martin (LeProviseur), Isabelle Ceauz, Catherine De Keuchel, Isabelle Gautier (Les Nenettes), Julien Guiomar (Albert), Vittorio Caprioli (Verone), Bruno Balp (Gregoire), Jean-Marie Proslier (Le Conducteur), Clement Harari (Harry)

YOUNG CASANOVA (Seaberg) Producer, Griffon Films; Director, Max Pecas; Screenplay, Max Pecas, Michel Vocoret; In color; Rated X; March release. CAST: Yan Brian, Valerie Boisgel, Sabine Rivollier

MIDDLE OF THE WORLD (New Yorker) Executive Producers, Yves Gasser, Yves Peyrot; Director, Alain Tanner; Screenplay, John Berger, Alain Tanner; Photography, Renato Berta; Editor, Brigitte Sousseler; Music, Patrick Moray; 115 minutes; March release. CAST: Olimpia Carlisi (Adriana), Philippe Leotard (Paul), Juliet Berto (Juliet)

ALL CREATURES GREAT AND SMALL (EMI) Producers, David Susskind, Duane Bogie, Director, Claude Whatham, Screenplay, Hugh Whittmore; From the book by James Herriot; In color; 90 minutes; March release. CAST: Simon Ward, Anthony Hopkins, Lisa Harrow, Brian Sirner, Freddie Jones, T. P. McKenna, Brenda Bruce, John Collin, Daphne Oxenford, Christine Buckley, Jane Collins

THE LAND THAT TIME FORGOT (American International) Executive Producer, Robert E. Greenberg; Director, Kevin Connor; Screenplay, James Cawthorn, Michael Moorcock; Based on novel by Edgar Rice Burroughs; Photography, Alan Hume; Music, Douglas Gamley; In color; Rated PG; 90 minutes; March release. CAST: Doug McClure, John McEnery, Susan Penhaligan, Keith Barron, Anthony Ainley, Godfrey James, Bobby Farr, Declan Mulholland, Colin Farrell, Ben Howard, Roy Holder, Andrew McCulloch, Ron Pember, Grahame Mallard, Andrew Lodge

"Shanghai Lil and the Sun Luck Kid"

Ines des Longchamps, Larry Hagman, David Essex in "Stardust"

STARDUST (Columbia) Producers, David Puttnam, Sandy Lieberson; Director, Michael Apted; Screenplay, Ray Connolly; Photography, Tony Richmond; Editor, Mike Bradsell; Executive Producer, Roy Baird; In Color; Rated R; 97 minutes; March release. CAST: David Essex, Adam Faith, Larry Hagman, Keith Moon, Marty Wilde, Paul Nicholas, Dave Edmunds, Ines Des Longchamps, Karl Howman, Peter Duncan, Edd Byrnes, John Normington, Rick Le Parmentier, Rosalind Ayres, James Hazeldine, Michael Elphick, Claire Russell, Bobby Sparrow

SUNDAY IN THE COUNTRY (American International) Producer, David Perlmutter; Director, John Trent; Screenplay, Robert Maxwell, John Trent; Story, David Main; Photography, Marc Champion; Music, Paul Hoffert; Art Director, James Milton Parcher; Editor, Tony Lower; Assistant Director, Tony Thatcher; in color; Rated R; March release. CAST: Ernest Borgnine, Michael J. Pollard, Hollis McLaren, Louis Zorich, Cec Linder, Vladimir Valenta, Al Waxman, Tim Henry, Murray Westgate, Ralph Endersby, Sue Petrie, Ratch Wallace, Mark Walker, Gary Reineke, Eric Clavering, David Hughes, Carl Banas, Frank Russell, Ruth Springford, Alan King, Laddie Dennis, Joan Hurley, Winnifred Springetti, Jonathan White, Jim Barron

DIARY OF A CLOISTERED NUN (Cineglobe) Producer, Tonino Cervi; Director, Domenico Paolella; Screenplay, Tonino Cervi, Domenico Paolella; Photography, Armando Nannuzzi; Art Director, Pietro Filippone; Editor, Amadeo Giomini; Music, Piero Piccioni; In Technicolor; Rated R; March release. CAST: Catherine Spaak, Suzy Kendall, Eleanora Giorgi, Umberto Irsini

MISS LESLIE'S DOLLS (World Wide) Producer, Ralph J. Remy; Director, Joseph G. Prieto; Photography, Gregory Sandor; In color; Rated R; 85 minutes; March release. CAST: Salvador Ugarte, Terry Juston, Marcelle Bichette, Kitty Lewis, Charles W. Pitts

DANISH PASTRIES (Mature) Director, Finn Karlsson; Screenplay, Peter Hallmark; A Con Amore production; In color; Rated X; 89 minutes; March release. CAST: Ole Soltoft, Sigrid Horne Rasmussen, Lone Helmer, Bent Warburg, Benny Hansen

Jean-Louis Trintignant, Marlene Jobert in "Le Secret"

THE LEGEND OF BLOOD CASTLE (Film Ventures International) Presented by Edward L. Montoro; Director, Jorge Grau; In color; Rated R; 85 minutes; March release. CAST: Ewa Aulin, Lucia Bose

HEARTS AND MINDS (Warner Bros.-Columbia) A Touchstone Production; Conceived and Directed by Peter Davis; Photography, Richard Pearce; Editor, Lynzee Klingman, Susan Martin; Executive Producer, Bert Schneider; In color; 110 minutes; March release. A documentary on the Vietnam War. Winner of a 1974 Academy Award.

LE SECRET (Cinema National) Producer, Jacques-Eric Strauss; Director, Robert Enrico; Screenplay, Pascal Jardin; From the novel "Le Compagnon Indesirable" by Francis Ryck; Adapted by Robert Enrico, Pascal Jardin; Music, Ennio Morricone; Photography, Etienne Becker; A President Films Production; 100 minutes; April release. CAST: Jean-Louis Trintignant (David), Marlene Jobert (Julia), Philippe Noiret (Thomas), Jean-Francis Adam (Claude), Solange Pradal (Greta)

DON'T CRY WITH YOUR MOUTH FULL (New Yorker) Executive Producer, Claude Berri; Director, Pascal Thomas; Screenplay, Pascal Thomas, Roland Duval, Suzanne Schiffman; Photography, Christian Bachmann; Editor, Helene Plemianikov; Music, Michel Choquet; In color; 116 minutes; April release. CAST: Annie Cole (Annie), Jean Carmel (Father), Christiane Chamaret (Mother), Helene Dieudonne (Grandmother), Daniel Ceccaldi (Uncle), Claudine Paringaux (Aunt), Friquette (Sister), Bernard Menez (Alexander), Frederic Duru (Frederic)

THE TERRORISTS (20th Century-Fox) Producer, Peter Rawley; Director, Casper Wrede; Screenplay, Paul Wheeler; Photography, Sven Nykvist; Editor, Thelma Connell; Music, Jerry Goldsmith; Art Director, Sven Wickman; Assistant Director, Bernard Hanson; In color; 97 minutes; April release. CAST: Sean Connery (Nils), Ian McShane (Petrie), Norman Bristow (Denver), John Cording (Bert), Isabel Dean (Mrs. Palmer), William Fox (Ferris), Richard Hampton (Joe), Robert Harris (Palmer), Harry Landis (Lookout Pilot), Preston Lockwood (Hislop), James Maxwell (Bernhard), John Quentin (Shepherd), Jeffry Wickham (Barnes)

DRAGON SQUAD (In-Frame Films) Producer, C. H. Wong; Director, Wang Yu; Screenplay, Yi Kwan; In color; Rated R; 100 minutes; April release. CAST: Wang Yu (Hsiao Pao), Chen Sing (Hu Tien-tao), Chang Yu (Hung), Kam Kang (Cheng), Shikamura Yasuyoshi (Chingmu)

MAD MEMORIES OF A LIFEGUARD (Globe) Director, Sergio Casstner; Story, Heinrich von Treptow; In color; 82 minutes; April release. CAST: Gerhard Wolf, Margret Cizek, Karin Wieland, Natascha Verell, Gunther Notthoff, Gerhard Wiehura

FLATFOOT (S. J. International) Director, Steno; Screenplay, Lucio DeCaro; In color; Rated PG; April release. CAST: Bud Spencer, Adalberto Maria Merli, Juliette Mayniel, Raymond Pellegrin, Mario Pilar, Angelo Infanti

TO LOVE, PERHAPS TO DIE (Finest) Producer, Shelley Shermer; In color; Rated R; 88 minutes; April release. CAST: Sue Lyon, Chris Mitchum, Jean Sorel, Ramon Pons, Charly Bravo, Alfredo Alba, David Carpenter

HORROR HOSPITAL (Hallmark) Title changed to "Computer Killers"; Producer, Richard Gordon; Director, Anthony Balch; Screenplay, Anthony Balch, Alan Watson; In Movielab Color; Rated PG; April release. CAST: Michael Gough, Robin Askwith, Vanessa Shaw, Ellen Pollock, Skip Martin, Dennis Price

NOT NOW DARLING (Dimension) Producer, Peter J. Thompson; Directors, Ray Cooney, David Croft; An LMG-Sedgemoor Production; In color; Rated R; 93 minutes; April release. CAST: Leslie Phillips, Julie Ege, Ray Cooney, Moira Lister, Jackie Pollo, Trudi Van Doren

FOUR TIMES THAT NIGHT (Cinevision) Producer, Alfred Leone; Director, Mario Bava; In Eastmancolor; 90 minutes; April release. CAST: Brett Halsey, Daniela Giordano, Pascale Petit, Brigitte Skay

BEHIND LOCKED DOORS (Boxoffice International) Director, Charles Romine; Screenplay, Charles Romine, Stanley H. Brasloff; In color; Rated R; 90 minutes; April release. CAST: Eve Reeves, Joyce Denner, Daniel Garth

WAR GODDESS (American International) Producer, Nino Krisman; Director, Terence Young; Story, Robert Graves, Richard Aubrey; Music, Riz Ortolani; Screenplay, Richard Aubrey; In Technicolor; Rated R; 89 minutes; April release. CAST: Alena Johnston, Sabine Sun, Luciana Paluzzi, Angelo Infanti, Malisa Longo, Fausto Tozzi, Natasha Veleff

Nanette Newman, Kenneth Haigh
in "Man at the Top"

Michael York, Marlene Jobert, Michel Piccoli
in "Touch and Go"

TEN LITTLE INDIANS (AVCO Embassy) Producer, Harry Alan Towers; Director, Peter Collinson; Screenplay, Peter Welbeck; Based on novel by Agatha Christie; Photography, Fernando Arribas; Editor, John Trumper; Music, Bruno Nicolai; In color; Rated PG; 105 minutes; April release. CAST: Oliver Reed (Hugh), Elke Sommer (Vera), Stephane Audran (Ilona), Charles Aznavour (Raven), Richard Attenborough (Judge), Gert Froebe (Blore), Herbert Lom (Dr. Armstrong), Maria Rohm (Elsa), Adolfo Celi (General), Alberto de Mendoza (Martino)

THE DELUGE (Polski) Director, Jerzy Hoffman; Screenplay, Wojciech Zukrowski, Adam Kerseten, Jerzy Hoffman; Based on novel by Henryk Sienkiewicz; Photography, Jerzy Wojcik; Music, Kazimierz Serocki; In color; 300 minutes; In two parts; April release. CAST: Daniel Oldbrychski (Kmicic), Malgorzata Braunek (Olenka), Tadeusz Lomnicki (Wolodyjowski), Kazimierz Wichniarz (Zagloba), Leszek Teleszynski (Boguslaw), Leszek Herdegen (Sakowicz), Wladyslaw Hancza (Janusz), Piotr Pawlowski (King), Hugo Krzyski (Chancellor), Eugeniusz Luberadzki (Primate), Aleksander Gassowski (Senator)

SHADOWMAN (New Line Cinema) Producers, Raymond Froment, Terra Films; Director, Georges Franju; Photography, Guildo Renzo Bertoni; Screenplay, Jacques Champreux; Music, Georges Franju, Berlioz; In Eastmancolor; Rated PG; 90 minutes; May release. CAST: Gayle Hunnicutt (The Woman), Gert Froebe (Sorbier), Josephine Chaplin (Martine), Jacques Champreux (The Man), Ugo Pagliai (Paul), Patrick Prejean (Seraphin), Clement Harari (Dr. Dutreuil), Henry Lincoln (Prof. Petri)

IN SEARCH OF DRACULA (Independent International) Producer-Director, Calvin Floyd; Executive Producer, Alvar Domey; Screenplay, Yvonne Floyd; Music, Calvin Floyd; Photography, Tony Forsberg, Anders Bodin, Gunnar Larsson; In color; Rated PG; 86 minutes; May release. A documentary featuring Christopher Lee.

BRUCE LEE AND I (Pacific Grove) Producer, Shyr C. Chin; Directed and Choreographed by Bruce Lee; In color; Rated R; May release. CAST: Sheau Chyi Lin, Tsang T. B. Jau, Jin Fei

TOUCH AND GO (Libra Films) Producers, Alexandre Mnouchkine, George Dancigers; Director, Philippe De Broca; Adaptation and Dialogue, Jean-Loup Dabadie; Photography, Rene Mathelin; Music, Michel Legrand; Designer, Francois De Lamothe; In Eastmancolor; Rated PG; 110; May release. CAST: Marlene Jobert (Lorene), Michel Piccoli (Valentin), Michael York (Basil), Louis Velle (Paul-Emile), Didi Perego (Woman), Hans Verner (Officer), Amidou (Mate)

MAN AT THE TOP (Anglo EMI) Producers, Peter Charlesworth, Jock Jacobsen; Director, Mike Vardy; Screenplay, Hugh Whitemore; Additional Material, John Junkin; Based on characters created by John Braine; Music, Roy Budd; Photography, Brian Probyn; Art Director, Don Picton; Editor, Chris Barnes; Assistant Director, Ken Baker; A Hammer Production; In Technicolor; Rated R; 92 minutes; May release. CAST: Kenneth Haigh (Joe Lampton), Nanette Newman (Alex), Harry Andrews (Lord Ackerman), John Quentin (Digby), Mary Maude (Robin), Danny Sewell (Weston), Paul Williamson (Tarrant), Margaret Heald (Eileen), Angela Bruce (Joyce), Charlie Williams (George), Anne Cunningham (Mrs. Harvey), William Lucas (Marshall), John Collin (Wisbech), Norma West (Sarah), Jaron Yaltan (Harish), John Conteh (Black Boxer), Nell Brennan (Waitress), Patrick McCann (White Boxer)

TIDAL WAVE (New World) Executive Producer, Tomoyuki Tanaka; Associate Producer, Osamu Tanaka; Director, Shiro Moritani; Story, Sakyo Komatsu; Screenplay, Shinobu Hashimoto; American Dialogue, Andrew Meyer; Photography, Hiroshi Murai, Daisaka Kimura, Eric Saarinen; Music, Masaru Sato; Art Director, Yoshiro Muraki; Assistant Director, Koji Hashimoto; A Toho Company Production; In Panavision and Metrocolor; Presented by Roger Corman and Max E. Youngstein; Rated PG; 90 minutes; May release. CAST: Lorne Greene (Warren Richards), Keiju Kobayashi (Tanaka), Rhonda Leigh Hopkins (Fran), Hiroshi Fujioka (Onoda), Tetsuro Tanba (Prime Minister), Ayumi Ishida (Reiko), Shogo Shimada (Prince Watari), John Fujioka (Narita), with Tadao Nakamura, Yusuke Takita, Isao Natsuyagi, Hideaki Nitani, Nobuo Nakamura, and the talents of Marvin Miller, Susan Sennett, Ralph James, Phil Roth, Cliff Pellow, Joseph J. Dante

"Shadowman"

Lorne Greene
in "Tidal Wave"

"Nurith"

TOPELE (Risto) Producer, Menachem Golan; Director, Leo Filler; Based on story by Sholem Aleichem; Music, Yohanan Zarai; Choreography, Avraham Tzuri; A Robert S. Storch-Risto Film; In color; Rated G; 80 minutes; May release. CAST: Yaakov Nitzan, Gedi Yagil, Dassi Hadari, Rachel Atas, Shlomo Bar Shevat, Jacob Bodo

CRY OF THE PENGUINS (British Lion-EMI) Producer, Henry Trettin; Director, Al Viola; Screenplay, Anthony Shaffer; From novel by Graham Billing; Photography, Edward Scaife, Harry Waxman; Music, John Addison; Editor, Bernard Gribble; Art Director, Tony Masters; Costumes, John Furniss; Assistant Directors, Derek Cracknell, David Tringham; In Technicolor; 101 minutes; May release. CAST: John Hurt (Forbush), Hayley Mills (Tara), Dudley Sutton (Starshot), Tony Britton (George), Thorley Walters (Forbush, Sr.), Judy Campbell (Mrs. Forbush), Joss Ackland (Head of Board), Nicholas Pennell (Julian), Avril Angers, Cyril Luckham, Sally Geeson, Brian Oulton, Salmann Peer, Hugh Moxey, Norman Claridge, John Comer, Geraldine Sherman, Jumoke Debayo, Lew Luton, Burnell Tucker, Richard Bond, Margaret Lacey, Marianne Stone, Andy Robins, Amanda Steer

TERROR IN THE WOODS (American International) Director, Massimo Dallamano; Music, Ennio Morricone; In Eastmancolor; Rated R; May release. CAST: Fabio Testi, Karin Baal, Joachim Fuchsberger, Christine Galbo, Gunther W. Stoll, Clauda Butenuth

SUPER MANCHU (Capital) Producer, Raymond Chow; Director, Wu Min Msiung; In color; Rated R; 90 minutes; May release. CAST: Chang Yi, Pai Ying, Tien Mi

VOODOO BLACK EXORCIST (Horizon) Director, Manuel Cano; In Techniscope and Eastmancolor; Rated R; 90 minutes; May release. CAST: Aldo Sambrel, Eva Leon

THIS TIME I'LL MAKE YOU RICH (AVCO Embassy) Director, Frank Kramer; In Technicolor; Rated PG; 103 minutes; May release. CAST: Brad Harris, Antonio Sabato, Karin Schubert, Li Hsiu Hsien, Robin MacDavid

Matthieu Carriere, Sirpa Lane
in "Charlotte"

THE SECOND COMING OF EVE (Liberty) Director, Mac Ahlberg; In color; Rated X; May release. Featuring Brigitte Maier

WIDE OPEN MARRIAGE (Cambist) Producer, Bernd Bergemann; Director, Quirin Steiner; Rated X; 87 minutes; May release; CAST: Elizabeth Volkman, Gernot Mohner, Rose Mayre, Rinaldo Talmonti

THE MARRIED PRIEST (Matterhorn) title changed to "The Swinging Confessors"; Produced, Directed and Written by Marco Vicario; Photography, Dino DiSalvo; Art Director, Flavio Mogherini; Editor, Nino Baragli; Music, Armando Trovajoli; In Eastmancolor; Rated R; 93 minutes; May release. CAST: Rossana Podesta, Lando Buzzanca, Salvo Randone, Magali Noel, Luciano Salce, Barbara Bouchet, Enrico Maria Salerno

NURITH (Cinemagic) Director, George Ovadia; Screenplay, Ada Ben Nachum; Photography, Yechiel Ne'eman; Music, Boaz Sharabi, Shaike Paikov; Editor, Avi Lifshitz; An Arie Films Production; Rated PG; 90 minutes; June release. CAST: Sassi Keshet (Moshe), Yona Elian (Shoshana), Tova Katzav (Nurith), Jack Cohen (Father), Tova Pardo (Mother), Adi Kaplan (Stepmother), Rachel Furman (Ilana), Arie Elias, Yaacov Ben-Sira, Ezra Dagan (Troubadours)

CHARLOTTE (Gamma III) Director, Roger Vadim; Assistant Director, Jean-Michel Lacor; Photography, Pierre William Glenn; Music, Mike Oldfield; Editor, Victoria Spiri Mercanton; In Movielab Color; Rated X; 100 minutes; June release. CAST: Sirpa Lane (Charlotte), Roger Vadim (Georges), Mathieu Carriere (Eric), Michel Duchaussoy (Serge), Elisabeth Wiener (Elisabeth), Alexandre Astruc (Guy), Anne-Marie Deschodt (Elaine), Sabine Glaser (Agnes), Igor Lafaurie (Philippe), Louis Arbessier (Le Pere), Josette Harmina (La Mere), Annie Noel (Lise), Therese Liotard (Louise), Liliane Grumbach (Anne-Marie), Marie-Christine Carliez (Marie-Josephe)

THE DESTRUCTORS (American International) Produced and Written by Judd Bernard; Director, Robert Parrish; Photography, Douglas Slocombe; Editor, Willy Kemplen; Music, Roy Budd; A Kettledrum Film; 89 minutes; Rated PG; June release. CAST: Michael Caine (Deray), Anthony Quinn (Steve), James Mason (Brizard), Maureen Kerwin (Lucianne), Marcel Bozzuffi (Calmet), Catherine Rouvel (Brizard's Mistress), Maurice Ronet (Briac), Andre Oumansky (Marsac), Alexandra Stewart (Rita)

REFLECTIONS (DRY SUMMER) (Hittite) Producer, Ulvi Dogan; Directors, Ulvi Dogan, Ismail Metin; Screenplay, Necati Cumali, Jim Lehner; Photography, Ali Ugar, Peter Pallan; Editors, Ulvi Dogan, Stuart Gillman; Music, Manos Hadjidakis; In black and white; 90 minutes; June release. CAST: Ulvi Dogan (Hassman), Errol Tash (Ossman), Hulya Kotch (Bahar)

CHINESE BLUE (Melody) Producer-Director, John Chang; Photography, P. Lee, Kung Fu Men; In color; Rated X; 83 minutes; June release; No other credits available. CAST: George Ling, Penny Yang, Jeun Mei Ling, Lelen Po, Greta Mayberry, Tina Chang-hsu

A BIGGER SPLASH (Buzzy Enterprises) Director, Jack Hazan; Screenplay, Jack Hazan, David Mingay; Photography, Jack Hazan; Editor, David Mingay; Music, Patrick Gowers; In Eastmancolor; 105 minutes; June release. CAST: David Hockney, Peter Schlesinger, Celia Birtwell, Mo McDermott, Henry Geldzahler, Ossie Clark, Mike Sida

THE WICKER MAN (Warner Bros.) A Brut presentation of a British Lion production; Producer, Peter Snell; Director, Robin Hardy; Screenplay, Anthony Shaffer; Photography, Harry Waxman; Art Director, Seamus Flannery; Music, Paul Giovanni; Editor, Eric Boyd-Perkins; Assistant Director, Jake Wright; In color; Rated R; June release. CAST: Edward Woodward (Sgt. Howie), Britt Ekland (Willow), Diane Cilento (Miss Rose), Ingrid Pitt (Librarian), Christopher Lee (Lord Summerisle), Roy Boyd, Walter Carr, Lindsay Kemp, Kevin Collins, Russell Waters, Leslie Mackie, Irene Sunter, Ian Campbell, Aubrey Morris, Donald Eccles, Geraldine Cowper

DREAM LIFE (New Line) Director, Mireille Dansereau; In color; Rated R; 90 minutes; June release. CAST: Liliane Lemaitre-Auger, Jean-Francois Guite

SCHOOL FOR SWINGERS (New Line) Director, John Weeram; In color; 89 minutes; Rated X; June release. CAST: Marlies Petersen, Sandro Castell

NOTHING BUT THE NIGHT (Cinema Systems) Director, Peter Sasdy; A Charlemagne Production; Based on novel by John Blackburn; In color; Rated PG; June release. CAST: Christopher Lee, Peter Cushing, Georgia Brown, Diana Dors, Keith Barron

THE TASTE OF THE SAVAGE (World Wide) Director, Alberto Mariscal; In Panavision and Eastmancolor; Rated R; June release. CAST: Cameron Mitchell, Isela Vega, Jorge Luke, Helena Rojo, Nick Georgiade, Arthur Hansel, Roger Cudney

KILLER SNAKES (Howard Mahler) Producer, Run Me Shaw; In Eastmancolor; Rated R; June release. CAST: Maggie Lee, Kurt Lang, Kan Kuo Liang, Li Lin Lin

TEENAGE TRAMP (NMD) Producer, Anthony Parella; Director, Anton Holden; In Eastmancolor; Rated R; 80 minutes; June release. CAST: Alisha Fontaine, Tony Massina, Robin Lane, David Sawn

THE WORLD'S YOUNG BALLET (Artkino) Director, Arkadi Tsineman; Written by Pyotr Abolimov, Boris Starshov, Arkadi Tsineman; Narration in English, Boris Lvov-Anokhin; Photography, Anatoil Kaznin, Mahmud Rafikov, Gleh Chumakov; In black and white; 70 minutes; July release. A documentary of the 1969 ballet competition in Moscow's Bolshoi Theatre with Nadezhda Pavlova, Mikhail Barishnikov, Francesca Zumbo, Patrice Bart, Helgi Tomasson, Araujo Loipa, Peter Schaufus, M. Duddal-Nielson, Fugagawa, Nina Sorokina, Yuri Vladimirov, Ekaterina Maximova, Vladimir Vasiliev

KAMOURASKA (New Line Cinema) Director, Claude Jutra; Photography, Michel Brault, Francois Protat, Jean-Charles Tremblay; Editors, Renee Lichtig, Francois London, Madeleine Guerin, Suzan Kay; Assistant Directors, Yves Gelinas, Lise Abastado; French with English subtitles; Based on novel by Anne Hebert; Screenplay, Claude Jutra, Anne Hebert; Music, Maurice LeRoux, A Cinepix Production; In color; Rated R; 119 minutes; July release. CAST: Genevieve Bujold (Elisabeth), Richard Jordan (Georges), Phillipe Leotard (Antoine), Marcel Cuvelier (Jerome), Suzie Baillargeon (Aurelie), Huguette Oligny (Mme. d'Aulinicres), Janine Sutto (Aunt Adelaide), Olivette Thibault (Aunt Gertrude), Marie Fresnieres (Aunt Angelique), Camille Bernard (Mme. Rassy), Colette Courtois (Florida), Gigi Duckett (Anne-Marie), Len Watt (Governor), Andre Cailloux (Ernest)

COUNSELOR AT CRIME (Joseph Green) Executive Producer, Maurizio Amati; Director, Alberto De Martino; Screenplay, Alberto De Martino, Vincenzo Mannino, Adriano Bolzoni; Photography, Aristide Massaccesi; Editor, Otello Colanzeli; Art Director, Emilio Ruiz; Music, Riz Ortolani; Costumes, Carlo Leva; In Eastmancolor and Technioscope; Rated R; 99 minutes; July release. CAST: Martin Balsam (Don Antonio), Thomas Milian (The Consigliere), Dagmar Lassander (Laura), Francisco Rabal (Vincent), Carlo Tamberlani, Manuel Zarzo, John Anderson

BEYOND THE DOOR (Film Ventures International) Director, Oliver Hellman; Screenplay, Richard Barrett; Music, Ortolani; In DeLuxe Color; Rated R; 100 minutes; July release. CAST: Juliet Mills (Jessica), Richard Johnson (Dimitri), David Colin, Jr. (Robert), Elizabeth Turner, Gabriele Lavia

THE SLASHER (William Mishkin) Producer, Eugene Florimont; Director, Robert Montero; Screenplay, Lou Angelli, Robert Montero, I. Fasant; Photography, George Gaslini, F. Rossi; In Eastmancolor; Rated R; 88 minutes; July release. CAST: Farley Granger, Sylva Koscina, Susan Scott, Chris Avram, Paul Oxon, Krista Nell

A PAGE OF MADNESS (New Line) Director, Teinosuke Kinugasa; Screenplay, Yasunari Kawabata; Photography, Kohei Sugiyama; In color; 60 minutes; July release. CAST: Masao Ionue, Yoshie Nakagawa, Ayao Iijima, Hiroshi Nemoto

THE GREAT McGONAGALL (Scotia American) Producer, David Grant; Director, Joseph McGrath; Screenplay, Joseph McGrath, Spike Milligan; Photography, John Mackey; Music, John Shakespeare, Derek Warne; A Darlton Production; In Eastmancolor; 95 minutes; August release. CAST: Peter Sellers (Queen Victoria), Spike Milligan (William McGonagall), and Julia Foster, John Bluthal, Valentine Dyall, Clifton Jones, Julian Chagrin, Victor Spinetti, Charlie Atom

FRIGHTMARE (Ellman Enterprises) Producer-Director, Pete Walker; Screenplay, David McGillivray; Music, Stanley Meyers; Photography, Peter Jessop; In color; Rated R; 88 minutes; August release. CAST: Rupert Davies (Edmund), Sheila Keith (Dorothy), Kim Butcher (Debbie), Deborah Fairfax (Jackie), Paul Greenwood (Graham), Leo Geen (Lytell), Gerald Flood (Matthew), Jon Yule (Robin), Fiona Curzon (Merle), Tricia Mortimer (Lillian)

**Richard Jordan, Genevieve Bujold
in "Kamouraska"**

THE RETURN OF THE STREETFIGHTER (New Line) Producer, Toei Co., Ltd.; Director, Shigehiro Ozawa; Screenplay, Koji Takada, Steve Autrey; Photography, Teiji Yoshida; Music, Toshiaki Tsushima; In color; Rated R; 75 minutes; August release. CAST: Sonny Chiba, Yoko Ichiji, Masafumi Suzuki, Donald Nakajima, Milton Ishibashi, Zulu Yachi, Claud Gannyon

RUN, RABBIT, RUN (Horizon) Director, Roger Fritz; A Maris Film production; In color; Rated R; 90 minutes; Rated R; August release. CAST: Anthony Steel, Helga Anders, Francoise Prevost, Raymond Lovelock

PIPPI GOES ON BOARD (G. G. Communications) Director, Olle Hellblom; Based on book by Astrid Lindgren; In Movielab Color; Rated G; 84 minutes; August release. CAST: Inger Nilsson, Par Sundberg, Maria Persson, Margot Trooger, Hans Clarin, Paul Esser

MADE (International C-Productions) A Nat Cohen presentation of a Joseph Janni production; Director, John Mackenzie; Screenplay, Howard Barker; Based on his play "No One Was Saved"; Photography, Ernest Day; Songs composed and performed by Roy Harper; Designer, Philip Harrison; Editor, David Campling; Assistant Director, Scott Wodehouse; In Technicolor; 104 minutes; August release. CAST: Carol White (Valerie), John Castle (Father Dyson), Roy Harper (Mike), Margery Mason (Mrs Marshall), Doremy Vernon (June), Sam Dastor (Mahdav), Richard Vanstone (Ray), Michael Cashman (Joe), Brian Croucher (Arthur), Ray Smith, Carl Rigg, Bob Harris, Sean Hewitt, Michael Standing

ANITA, SWEDISH NYMPHET (Cambist) A Lee Hessel presentation; Direction and Screenplay, Torgny Wickman; Photography, Hasse Dittmer; Editor, Lasse Lundberg; In color; Rated X; 87 minutes; August release. CAST: Christina Lindberg, Stellan Skarsgard

LINDA LOVELACE MEETS MISS JONES (LMMJ) Producer-Director, Angelo Spaveni; In color; Rated X; August release. CAST: Linda Lovelace, Georgina Spelvin, Harry Reems, Darby Lloyd Rains, Ellen Smith, Eric Edwards, Cindy West, Dolly Sharp

**Martin Balsam
in "Counselor at Crime"**

**Jose Ferrer, Helmut Berger
in "Order to Kill"**

**Lee Sheung
in "Kung Fu-ry"**

ORDER TO KILL (Joseph Green) Producer-Director, Jose Maesso; Story and Screenplay, Santiago Moncada, Eugenio Martin, Massimo de Rita, Jose Maesso; Photography, Aiace Parolin; Music, Adolfo Waiztman; Co-Produced by Creative Entertainment Corp., Eduardo Palmer; Assistant Director, Felix Fernandez; Editor, Angel Serrano; Costumes, Lidia Soprani; In Eastmancolor; Rated R; 94 minutes; August release. CAST: Helmut Berger (Clyde Hart), Sydne Rome (Anne), Jose Ferrer (Inspector Reed), Kevin McCarthy (McLean), Juan Luis Galiardo (Richard), and Howard Ross, Manuel Zarzo, Avaro de Luna, Frank Brana, Romano Puppo, Jose Marie Cafferel, Elena Berrido, Claudio Chea

A PAIN IN THE A . . . (Corwin-Mahler) Producers, Georges and Alexandre Mnouchkine; Director, Edouard Molinaro; Screenplay, Francis Veber; Photography, Raoul Coutard; Music, Jacques Brel, Francois Gauber; Editors, Robert and Monique Isnardon; In color; Rated PG; 90 minutes; August release. CAST: Lino Ventura (Ralph), Jacques Brel (Pignon), Caroline Cellier (Louise), Nino Castelnuovo (Bellhop), Jean Pierre Darras (Fuchs)

POWER KILL (Aquarius) Director, Michele Lupo; A Dino De Laurentiis production; A Terry Levene presentation; In Technicolor; Rated R: August release. CAST: Lee Van Cleef, Tony LoBianco, Edwige Fenech

THE DRAGON FLIES (20th Century-Fox) Producers, Raymond Chow, John Fraser; Direction and Screenplay, Brian Trenchard Smith; Music, Noel Quinlan; Photography, Russell Boyd; Editor, Ron Williams; In Color; Rated R; 102 minutes; August release. CAST: Jimmy Wang Yu (Fang), George Lazenby (Wilton), Hugh Keays-Byrne (Morrie), Roger Ward (Bob), Ros Spiers (Caroline), Grant Page (Assassin), Rebecca Gilling (Angelica), Frank Thring (Willard)

THE HUNCHBACK OF THE MORGUE (Janus) Director, Javier Aguirre; Photography, Raul Perez Cubero; Editor, Petra de Nieva; Music, Carmelo Bernaola; In Eastmancolor; Rated R; 88 minutes; September release. CAST: Paul Naschy, Rossana Yanni, Vic Winner, Alberto Dalves, Maria Perschy

THE CORRUPTION OF CHRIS MILLER (Lanir) Producer, Xavier Armet; Director, Juan Antonio Bardem; Screenplay, Santiago Moncada; Photography, Juan Gelpi; Music, Waldo de los Rios; Editor, Emilio Rodriguez; In Eastmancolor; Rated R; 107 minutes; September release. CAST: Jean Seberg, Marisol, Barry Stokes, Perla Cristal, Gerard Tichy

THE EMPRESS DOWAGER (Shaw Bros.) Director, Li Han-Hsiang; Supervised by Runme Shaw; In color; 165 minutes; September release. CAST: Lisa Lu (Empress Dowager), Ivy Ling Po (Empress), Ti Lung (Emperor), Hsiao Yao (Concubine), Tanny (Li Chieh), Miao Tine (Li Lien), David Chiang (Kou)

KUNG FU-RY (Joseph Green) Producer, K. S. Cheung; Director, Shaw Fung James; Photography, Wong Tai; Music, J. Koo; Editor, William Leung; Fights Staged By S. P. Chan, S. L. Lieung; In Scope and Technicolor; Rated R; September release. CAST: Lee Sheung, Paul Chiang, Wong Nin Gan

ONCE UPON A TIME IN THE EAST (SNC) Director, Andre Brassard; Screenplay, Andre Brassard, Michel Tremblay; Photography, Paul Van Der Linden; Editor, Andre Corriveau; Music, Jacques Perron; In Eastmancolor; 100 minutes; September release. CAST: Denise Filiatrault (Helene), Michelle Rossignol (Pierette), Frederique Collin (Lise), Sophie Clement (Carmen), Andre Montmorency (Sandra), Amulette Garneau (Bec-Lievre)

KUNG FU GOLD (Cinema Shares International) In Technicolor; Rated R; September release. CAST: Tze Lan, Wang Kuan-Hsiung, Huang Fi-Lung

THE GAMES GIRLS PLAY (General Film) Producer, Peer J. Oppenheimer; Director, Jack Arnold; Screenplay, Jameson Brewer, Peer J. Oppenheimer; In color; Rated R; 90 minutes; September release. CAST: Christina Hart (Bunny), Jane Anthony (Jackie), Drina Pavlovic (Sal), Jill Damas (Chris), Erin Geraghty (Ducky), Gordon Sterne (O'Hara), Eunice Black (Miss Grimm)

FLOSSIE (Sunshine Unlimited) Director, Bert Torn; In color; Rated X; September release. CAST: Maria Lynn (Flossie), Jack Frank (Jack), Anita Andersson (Girl)

**Jimmy Wang Yu, George Lazenby
in "The Dragon Flies"**

**Alan Bates, Malcolm McDowell, Oliver Reed
in "Royal Flash"**

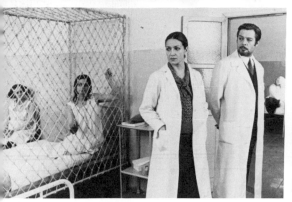

**Francoise Fabian, Marcello Mastroianni
in "Down the Ancient Stairs"**

**Malcolm McDowell, Britt Ekland
in "Royal Flash"**

HARRY AND THE HOOKERS (Joseph Brenner) Director, Lindsey Shonteff; Music, Paul Ferris; In color; Rated R; 89 minutes; September release. CAST: Gilbert Wynne, Norman Claridge, Gilly Grant, Noel Davis, Gary Hope, Margery Mason, Michael Nightingale, Ronald Lee Hunt, Valerie Shelton, Jenny Robbins, Heather Downham

THE SENSUOUS SICILIAN (Medusa) Producer, Alfonso Vicario; Direction and Screenplay, Marco Vicario; From novel by Vitaliano Brancati; Photography, Tonino Delli Colli; Designer, Flavio Mogherini; Editor, Nino Baragli; Music, Armando Trovaioli; In Eastmancolor; Rated R; 120 minutes; September release. CAST: Giancarlo Giannini (Paolo), Rossana Podesta (Lilia), Gastone Moschia (Uncle), Riccardo Cucciolla (Father), Lionel Stander (Baron), Adriana Asti (Beatrice), Vittorio Caprioli (Pharmacist), Marianne Contell (Mother), Ornella Muti (Giovanna), Femi Benussi (Whore), Neda Arneric (Caterina)

DOWN THE ANCIENT STAIRS (20th Century-Fox) Director, Mauro Bolognini; Screenplay, Raffaele Andreassi, Mario Arosio, Tullio Pinelli, Bernardino Zapponi; Based on novel by Mario Tobino; A Co-Production of Italian International Film, Les Productions Fox Europa; Costumes, Piero Tosi; Producer, Fulvic Lucisano; Photography, Ennio Guarnieri; In Technospes Color; 110 minutes; October release. CAST: Marcello Mastroianni (Prof. Bonaccorsi), Francoise Fabian (Dr. Anna Bersani), Marthe Keller (Bianca), Barbara Bouchet (Carla), Pierre Blaise (Tonio), Lucia Bose (Francesca), Adriana Asti (Gianna), Silvano Tranquilli (Prof. Rospigliosi), Charles Fawcett (Dr. Sfameni)

THE NIGHT OF COUNTING THE YEARS (New Yorker) Direction and Screenplay, Shadi Abdelsalam; Photography, Abdel Aziz Fahmy; Music, Mario Nascimbene; Editor, Kamal Abou-El-Ella; Presented by Merchant Ivory Productions; Designer, Salah Marei; In color; 100 minutes; October release. CAST: Ahmed Marei (Wanniss), Ahmad Hegazi (Brother), Zouzou El Hakim (Mother), Nadia Loutfy (Zeena), Abdelmonen Aboulfoutouh, Abdelazim Abdelhack (Uncles), Gaby Karraz (Maspero), Mohamed Khairi (Kamal), Ahmad Anan (Badawi), Mohamed Nabih (Murad), Shafik Noureddin (Ayoub), Mohamed Morshed (Stranger)

ROYAL FLASH (20th Century-Fox) Producers, David V. Picker, Denis O'Dell; Director, Richard Lester; Screenplay, George MacDonald Fraser based on his novel; Photography, Geoffrey Unsworth; In color; Rated PG; 99 minutes; October Release. CAST: Malcolm McDowell (Harry Flashman), Alan Bates (Rudi von Starnberg), Florinda Bolkan (Lola Montez), Oliver Reed (Bismarck), Britt Ekland (Duchess Irma), Lionel Jeffries (Kraftstein), Roy Kinnear (Old Rouse), Henry Cooper (John Gully), Alastair Sim (Lawyer), Tom Bell (de Gautet), Joss Ackland, Michael Hordern, Christopher Cazenove

THE DEVIL IS A WOMAN (20th Century-Fox) Producer, Anis Nohra; Direction and Story, Damiano Damiani; Screenplay, Mr. Damiani, Fabrizio Onofri, Audrey Nohra; Music, Ennio Morricone; Photography, Mario Vulpiani; Editor, Peter Taylor; A British-Italian Co-Production in color; Rated R; 105 minutes; October release. CAST: Glenda Jackson (Sister Geraldine), Claudio Cassinelli (Rodolfo), Lisa Harrow (Emily), Adolfo Celi (Father Borelli), Arnoldo Foa (Monsignor Badinsky), Rolf Tasna (Monsignor Meitner), Duilio Del Prete (Monsignor Salvi), Gabriele Lavia (Prince Ottavio), Francisco Rabal (Bishop Marquez)

SWEET MOVIE (Biograph) Producers, Vincent Malle, Richard Helman; Executive Producer, Helene Vagar, Director, Dusan Makavejev; Music, Manos Hadjidakis; Photography, Pierre L'Homme; Editor, Yann Dedet; No screenplay credit; Dialogue in English and French with English subtitles; Co-production of V. M. Productions, Mojack Films, and Maran Films; 95 minutes; October release. CAST: Carol Laure (Miss Canada), Pierre Clementi (Sailor from Potemkin), Ann Prucani (Capt Ann), Sami Frey (El Macho), Jane Mallet (Chastity Belt Lady), Marpessa Dawn (Mama), Ray Callender (Jeremiah), John Vernon (Mr. Kapital), with Otto Muehl and members of the Therapie-Komune of Vienna.

SLAP IN THE FACE (Horizon) Producer, Herbert Maris; Director, Rolf Thiele; In color; 89 minutes; Rated R; October release. CAST: Curt Jurgens, Alexandra Stewart, Gila von Weitershausen, Nadja Tiller, Balduin Baas

**Murad-Mohamed Nabih
in "Night of Counting the Years"**

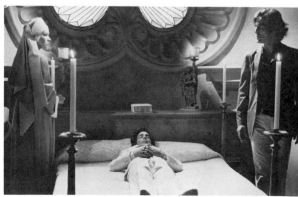

**Glenda Jackson, Gabriele Lavia, Claudio Cassinelli
in "The Devil Is a Woman"**

Louis Devos (C)
in "Moses and Aaron"

Sara Kestelman, Roger Daltrey
in "Lisztomania"

MOSES AND AARON (New Yorker) Executive Producer, Klaus Hellwig; Direction, Editing and Screenplay, Jean-Marie Straub, Daniele Huillet; Opera, Arnold Schonberg; Photography, Ugo Piccone, Saverio Diamanti, Gianni Canfarelli, Renato Berta; Music, Arnold Schonberg; Costumes, Renata Morroni, Guerrino Todero; 105 minutes; October release. CAST: Gunter Reich (Moses), Louis Devos (Aaron), Roger Lucas (Young Man), Eva Csapo (Young Woman), Richard Salter (Other Man), Werner Mann (Priest), Friedl Obrowsky (Sick Woman), Ladislav Illavsky (Ephraimite)

BLACK MOON (20th Century-Fox) Executive Producer, Director, Louis Malle; Screenplay, Louis Malle, Ghislain Uhry; Additional Dialogue, Joyce Bunuel; Photography, Sven Nykvist; Editor, Suzanne Baron; Art Director, Ghislain Uhry; Assistant Director, Fernand Moszkovicz; In color; Rated R; 100 minutes; October release. CAST: Cathryn Harrison (Lily), Therese Giehse (Old Lady), Alexandra Stewart (Sister), Joe Dallesandro (Brother)

THE MYSTERY OF KASPAR HAUSER (Cinema 5) Also released as "Every Man for Himself and God against All"; Directed and Written by Werner Herzog; Photography, Jorg Schmidt-Reitwein; Editor, Beate Mainka-Jellinghaus; Music, Pachelbel, Orlando di Lasso, Albioni, Mozart; In German with English subtitles; 110 minutes; October release. CAST: Bruno S. (Kaspar), Walter Ladengast (Daimer), Brigitte Mira (Kathe), Hans Musaus (Unknown Man), Willy Semmelrogge (Circus Director), Michael Kroecher (Lord Stanhope), Henry van Lyck (Captain)

PERSECUTION (Blueberry Hill) title changed to "The Terror of Sheba"; A Tyburn Films production; Producer, Kevin Francis; Director, Don Chaffey; Story and Screenplay, Robert B. Hutton, Rosemary Wooten; Photography, Kenneth Talbot; Art Director, Jack Shampan; Editor, Mike Campbell; In Eastmancolor; Rated PG; October release. CAST: Lana Turner (Carrie), Ralph Bates (David), Trevor Howard (Paul), Olga Georges-Picot (Monique), Suzan Farmer (Janie), Patrick Allen (Robert), Mark Weaver (David)

LISZTOMANIA (Warner Bros.) Producers, Roy Baird, David Puttnam; Direction and Screenplay, Ken Russell; Music, Rick Wakeman; Executive Producer, Sanford Lieberson; Assistant Director, Jonathan Benson; Photography, Peter Suschitzky; Art Director, Philip Harrison; Costumes, Shirley Russell; Editor, Stuart Baird; A Goodtimes Enterprises Production; In Technicolor; Rated R; 105 minutes; October release. CAST: Roger Daltry (Liszt), Sara Kestelman (Princess Carolyn), Paul Nicholas (Wagner), Fiona Lewis (Countess Marie), Veronica Quilligan (Cosima), Nell Campbell (Olga), Andrew Reilly (Hans), Ringo Starr (Pope), John Justin (Count d'Agoult), Anulka Dziubinska (Lola Montez), Imogen Claire (George Sand), Peter Brayham (Bodyguard), David English (Captain)

ILSA, SHE WOLF OF THE SS (Cambist) Director, Don Edmonds; In color; 95 minutes; October release; No other credits available. CAST: Dyann Thorne, Greg Knoph, Sandi Richman, Jo Jo DeVille, Wolfgang Roehm

VOODOO HEARTBEAT (TWI National) Direction and Screenplay, Charles Nizet; In color; Rated R; 88 minutes; October release. CAST: Ray Molina, Philip Ahn, Ern Dugo, Mary Martinez, Ebby Rhodes, Forrest Duke, Mike Zapata, Stan Mason, Ray Molina, Jr., Mike Meyers

CHALLENGE TO WHITE FANG (Premiere) Director, Lucio Fulci; Screenplay, Albert Silvestri; Based on story by Jack London; In color; Rated PG; October release. CAST: Franco Nero (Jason), Virna Lisi (Evangeline), Renato Cestie (Bill), Harry Carey, Jr., Raymond Harmsdorf, John Steiner, Werner Puchath, Yanti Somer, Hannelore Elsner

NIGHT CALLER (Columbia) Producer-Director, Henri Verneuil; Adaptation, Henri Verneuil, Jean Laborde, Francois Veber; Dialogue, Francois Veber; English language version, Paulette Rubinstein; Photography, Jean Penzer; Editors, Pierre Gillette Lanoe, Henri Lanoe; Music, Ennio Morricone; In color; Rated R; 91 minutes; November release. CAST: Jean-Paul Belmondo (Ins. Le Tellier), Charles Denner (Moissac), Adalberto-Maria Merli (Minos), Lea Massari (Norah), Rosy Varte (Germaine), Roland Dubillard (Dr. Lipstein), Jean Martin (Sabin), Catherine Morin, Germana Carnacina

Cathryn Harrison, Joe Dallesandro
in "Black Moon"

Jean-Paul Belmondo
in "Night Caller"

PERMISSION TO KILL (AVCO Embassy) Producer, Paul Mills; Executive Producers, Feinz Lazek, Robert Jungbluth; Director, Cyril Frankel; Screenplay, Robin Estridge from his novel; Photography, Freddie Young; Music, Richard Rodney Bennett; Editor, Ernest Walter; Designer, Elliot Scott; Art Director, Theo Harisch; In Technicolor; Rated PG; 93 minutes; November release. CAST: Dirk Borgarde (Alan), Ava Gardner (Katin), Bekim Fehmiu (Alexander), Timothy Dalton (Charles), Nicole Calfan (Melissa), Frederic Forrest (Scott), Alf Joint (MacNeil), Peggy Sinclair (Lily), Anthony Dutton (Jennings)

FROM BEYOND THE GRAVE (Howard Mahler) Producers, Max J. Rosenberg, Milton Subotsky; Director, Kevin Connor; Screenplay, Raymond Christodoulou, Robin Clarke; Based on stories by R. Chetwynd-Hayes; Music, Douglas Gamley; Associate Producer, John Dark; In Technicolor; Rated PG; 98 minutes; November release. CAST: Ian Bannen (Christopher), Ian Carmichael (Reginald), Peter Cushing (Shopkeeper), Diana Dors (Mabel), Margaret Leighton (Mme. Orloff), Donald Pleasence (Peddler), Nyree Dawn Porter (Susan), David Warner (Edward), Ian Ogilvy (William), Lesley-Ann Down (Rosemary), Angela Pleasence (Emily), Jack Watson (Ghost), Wendy Allnut, Rosalind Ayres, Ben Howard

THE EARTH IS A SINFUL SONG (Seaberg) Producer-Director, Rauni Mollberg; Screenplay, Rauni Mollberg, Pirjo Honkasalo, Panu Rajala; From the novel by Timo K. Mukka; Assistant Director, Pirjo Honkasalo; Photography, Kari Sohlberg, Hannu Peltomaa; Editor, Marjatta Leporinne; In Eastmancolor; 105 minutes; November release. CAST: Maritta Viitamaki, Pauli Jauhojarvi, Aimo Saukko, Milja Hiltunen, Sirkku Saarnio

"JOCK" PETERSEN (AVCO Embassy) Producer-Director, Tim Burstall; Screenplay, David Williamson; Photography, Robin Copping; Art Director, Bill Hutchinson; Editor, David Bilcock; Music, Peter Best; Presented by Hexagon; In color; Rated R; 97 minutes; November release. CAST: Jack Thompson (Tony), Jacki Weaver (Susie), Jocy Hohenfels (Debbie), Amanda Hunt (Carol), George Mallaby (Executive), Arthur Dignam (Charles), David Phillips (Heinz), Helen Morse (Jane), Christine Amor (Annie), Wendy Hughes (Trish), Ann Pendlebury (Peggy), Dina Mann (Robin), Belinda Giblin (Moira), Karen Petersen (Teresa), Syd Conabere (Annie's Father), Charmain Jacka (Annie's Mother), John Orcsik (Walter), Robert Hewitt, Lindsay Smith, Tim Robertson, Graham Mathrick (Hippies), Moira Farrow (Mrs. Blunden), Cliff Ellen, Bill Bennett (Bushmen), David Ravenswood (Dr. Fredericks), Tom Lake (Library Attendant), Lynne Flanagan (Customer), Charles Tingwell (Tony's Father), Sheila Florence (Tony's Mother), Warwick Randall (Hotel Manager), Barry Barkla (Police Sgt.), Alan Lee (Constable), Sandy Gore (Housewife)

SENSATIONS (Pic American) Produced, Directed and Written by Alberto Ferro (Lasse Braun); Editor and Additional Dialogue, Ian L. Rakoff; Score, Richard Moore; Lyrics, Falcon Stuart; In color; Rated X; November release. CAST: Brigitte Maier, Veronique Monet, Tuppy Owens, Bent Rohweder

PUSSY TALK (Catalyst) Producer, Francis Leroi; Director, Frederic Lansac; Photography, Roger Fellous; Editor, Gerard Kikoline; Music, Mike Steitheson; In color; Rated X; November release. CAST: Penelope Lamour (Joan), Beatrice Harnois (Young Joan), Sylvia Bourdon (Aunt Barbara), Ellen Earl (Martine), Nils Hortzs (Eric), Vick Messica (Richard)

THE HEROES (United Artists) Producer, Alfredo Bini; Director, Duccio Tessari; Screenplay, Luciano Vincenzoni, Sergio Donati; Music, Riz Ortolani; Executive Producer, Michael Stern; In color; Rated PG; November release. CAST: Rod Steiger, Rod Taylor, Rosanna Schiaffino, Claude Brasseur, Gianni Garko, Aldo Giuffre, Terry-Thomas

BLOOD IN THE STREETS (Independent International) Producer, Ugo Santalucia; Director, Sergio Sollima; Screenplay, Arduino Maiuri, Massimo DeRita, Sergio Sollima; Photography, Aldo Scavarda; Art Director, Carlo Simi; Editor, Sergio Montanara; Music, Ennio Morricone; In DeLuxe color; Rated R; 111 minutes; November release. CAST: Oliver Reed (Vito), Agostina Belli (Maria), Fabio Testi (Milo), Paola Pitagora, Frederic De Pasquale, Marc Mazza, Rene Koldehoff, Peter Berlin, Gunnar Warner, Daniel Baretta

THOU SHALT NOT KILL ... BUT ONCE (In-Frame Films) First Films release of a Wong Cheuk Hon production; Director, Au Yeung Chuen; In color; Rated R; 87 minutes; November release. CAST: Chen Sing, Bruce Chen, Kam Kong

Jack Thompson, Jacki Weaver
in "Jock Petersen"

BAMBINA (Buckley Brothers) Director, Alberto Lattuada; Screenplay, Ottavio Jemma, Bruno di Geronimo; Rated R; November release. CAST: Luigi Proietti, Teresa Ann Savoy, Irene Papas

THE BLONDE CONNECTION (Hampton International) In Eastmancolor; Rated R; 84 minutes; November release. CAST: Judy Winter, Werner Peters

THE SENATOR LIKES WOMEN (Horizon) Director, Lucio Fulci; Presented by Edmondo Amati; In Eastmancolor; Rated R; 96 minutes; November release. CAST: Lando Buzzanca, Lionel Stander, Laura Antonelli, Corrado Gaipa, Anita Strindberg

PAPER TIGER (Joseph E. Levine) Producer, Euan Lloyd; Director, Ken Annakin; Screenplay, Jack Davies; Photography, John Cabrera; Editor, Alan Pattillo; Music, Roy Budd; Song, Sammy Cahn; Sung by Ray Conniff Singers; Designer, Herbert Smith; Art Directors, Tony Reading, Peter Scharff; Assistant Directors, Ian Goddard, John Copeland; In Technicolor; Rated PG; 101 minutes; November release. CAST: David Niven (Walter), Toshiro Mifune (Ambassador), Hardy Kruger (Muller), Ando (Koichi), Ivan Desny (Foreign Minister), Irene Tsu (Talah), Ronald Fraser (Forster), Miiko Taka (Mme. Kagoyama), Jeff Corey (King)

DEATH KNOCKS TWICE (Horizon) Director, Harold Philipp; A PAC Rome-Maris Film Co-Production; In Eastmancolor; Rated R; 90 minutes; November release. CAST: Dean Reed, Fabio Testi, Nadja Tiller, Anita Ekberg, Adolfo Celi, Helen Chanel, Leon Askin, Ini Assmann

TOWER OF LOVE (Boxoffice International) Producer-Director, George Drazich; Screenplay, Harriet Foster; In color; 80 minutes; November release. CAST: Jean Pascal, Kitty Lombard, Tammy Smith, Tommy Walker, Joseph Peters

SEX AND THE FRENCH SCHOOLGIRL (Aquarius) Executive Producer, Lionel Wallman; Director, Pierre Unia; In Eastmancolor; Rated X; November release. CAST: Carine Francois, Marie-Christine Carliez, Yves Colignon

Lea Massari, Jean-Paul Belmondo
in "Night Caller"

Udo Kier, Corinne Clery
in "The Story of O"

Tim Curry
in "The Rocky Horror Picture Show"

THE STORY OF O (Allied Artists) Producer, Roger Fleytoux; Director, Just Jaeckin; Executive Producers, Eric Rochat, Gerard Lorin; Photography, Robert Fraisse; Screenplay, Sebastien Japrisot; Based on novel by Pauline Reage; Costumes, Cerruti 1881; Tan Guidicelli; Editor, Francine Pierre; Music, Pierre Bachelet; Presented by Emanuel L. Wolf; In Eastmancolor; Rated X; 97 minutes; November release. CAST: Corrine Clery (O), Udo Kier (Rene), Anthony Steel (Sir Stephen), Jean Gaven (Pierre), Christiane Minazzoli (Anne-Marie), Martin Kelly (Therese), Jean Pierre Andreani (Maitre II), Gabriel Cartand (Commandant), Li Sellgren (Jacqueline), Albane Navizet (Andree), Henri Piegay (Maitre I), Alain Noury (Yvan)

NO WAY OUT (Cinema Shares International) Director, Duccia Tessari; In color; Rated R; 91 minutes; November release. CAST: Alain Delon, Richard Conte (No other details available)

DELUSIONS OF GRANDEUR (Joseph Green) Director, Gerard Oury; Screenplay, Gerard Oury, Marcel Julian, Daniele Thompson; Photography, Henri Decae; A Co-production of Gaumont International, Mars Films, Coreal Produzione, and Orion Films; 85 minutes; November release. CAST: Louis De Funes (Sallustre), Yves Montand (Blaze), Alberto De Mendoza (King), Karin Schubert (Queen), Gabriele Tinti (Cesar), Alice Sapritch (Dona Juan)

THE GIRL IN THE TRUNK (Gaumont Goldstone) Director, Georges Lautner; Screenplay, Francis Veber; Photography, Maurice Fellous; Editor, Noelle Boisson; Music, Philippe Sarde; In Eastmancolor; 100 minutes; November release. CAST: Michel Constantin (Augier), Mireille Darc (Francoise), Jean-Pierre Marielle (Bloch), Amidou (Abdul), Michel Galabru (Baby), Robert Dalban (Mercier), Jean Lefebre (Porter)

OUT OF SEASON (Athenaeum) An EMI release of a Nat Cohen presentation of a Lorimar production; Produced and Written by Eric Bercovici, Reuben Bercovitch; Executive Producer, Robert Enders; Director, Alan Bridges; Photography, Arthur Ibbetson; Music, John Cameron; Art Director, Robert Jones; Assistant Director, Dominic Fulford; Editor, Peter Weatherley; In Technicolor; Rated R; 90 minutes; November release. CAST: Vanessa Redgrave (Ann), Cliff Robertson (Joe), Susan George (Joanna)

THE CATAMOUNT KILLING (Hallmark) Producer, Manfred Durniok; Executive Producer, Nat Rudich; Director, Krzysztof Zanussi; Screenplay, Julian and Sheila More; Based on "I'd Rather Stay Poor" by James Hadley Chase; Photography, Witold Sobocinski; Editor, Ilona Wasgint; Designer, Ruffin Barron Bennett; In color; 93 minutes; November release. CAST: Horst Buchholz (Mark), Ann Wedgeworth (Kit), Chip Taylor (Ken), Louise Clark (Iris), Patricia Joyce (Alice), Polly Holliday (Miss Pearson), Stuart Germain (Hardy), Rod Browning (Easton), Peter Brandon (Marthy), Lotti Krekel (Helga), Alexander Bardini (Attendant), Ernest Martin (Rudy), Leon Carter (Trooper)

THE BLACK DRAGON'S REVENGE (Howard Mahler) Director, Tommy Foo Ching; Screenplay, Norbert Albertson; In color; Rated R; November release. CAST: Ron Van Clief, Charles Bonet, Jason Pai Pow, Thomson Kao Kan, Meng Fu, Mayble, Linda Ho, Tony Pa San

THE NAUGHTY ROOMMATES (Hemisphere) Producer, Carl Szokoll; Director, Franz Antel; Screenplay, Kurt Nachman; In Eastmancolor; Rated R; November release. CAST: Terri Torday, Jaques Herlin, Andrea Rau, Elsie Pertramer, Heidi Bohlen, Ivan Nesbitt, Paul Loewinger, Herbert Heisel, Fritz Muliar, Ralph Wolzer, Rudolph Schundler

PERMISSIVE (Variety) Producer, Jack Shulton; Director, Lindsey Shonteff; Screenplay, Jeremy Craig Dryden; Music, Forever More, Titus Groan & Comus; In Eastmancolor; Rated X; November release. CAST: Maggie Stride, Gilbert Wynne, Gay Singleton, Forever More

THE KIDNAP OF MARY LOU (Joseph Brenner) Producer, Luciano Martino; Director, Umberto Lenzi; A Dania Production; In Eastmancolor; Rated R; November release. CAST: Henry Silva, Tomas Milian, Anita Strindberg, Laura Belli, Ray Lovelock

SUDDEN FURY (SCOTIA AMERICAN) Producer, Lawrence J. Caza; Directed and Written by D. Brian Damude; In color; Rated PG; 95 minutes; December release. CAST: Dominic Hogan, Gay Rowan, Dan Hennessey, Hollis McClaren, David Yorston, Eric Clavering, Sean McCann, Steve Weston, Robin Ward, Gerry Huckstep

Alain Delon
in "No Way Out"

Peter Hinwood, Tim Curry, Susan Sarandon,
Barry Bostwick in "The Rocky Horror Picture Show"

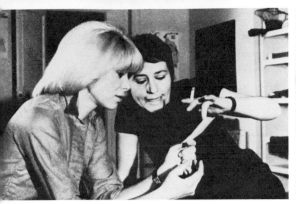

Mireille Darc, Annie Girardot
in "Where There's Smoke"

Catherine Deneuve, Jean-Louis Trintignant
in "Act of Aggression"

THE DAYDREAMER Produced, Directed, Co-Written by Pierre Richard; December release. CAST: Pierre Richard, Maria-Christine Barrault, Bernard Blier. (No other details available)

THE BULL BUSTER (Cinemagic) In color; Rated PG; 82 minutes; December release. CAST: Paul Smith, Uri Zohar (No other details available)

WHERE THERE'S SMOKE (Libra) Producer, Lucien Masse; Direction and Screenplay, Andre Cayatte; Adaption and Dialogue, Andre Cayatte, Pierre Dumayet, Photography, Maurice Fellous; Executive Producer, Jacques Bourdon; In Technicolor; 112 minutes; December release. CAST: Annie Girardot (Sylvie), Mireille Darc (Olga), Bernard Fresson (Michel), Michel Bouquet (Morlaix), Mathieu Carriere (Ulrich), Andre Falcon (Boussard), Marc Michel (J. P. Leroy), Frederic Simon (Alain), Micheline Boudet (Corinne), Paul Amiot (Georges), Pascale De Boysson (Veronique), Christine Simon (Nun), Georges Riquier (Judge), Isabelle Duly (Salesgirl)

THE ROCKY HORROR SHOW (20th Century-Fox) Executive Producer, Lou Adler; Producer, Michael White; Director, Jim Sharman; Associate Producer, John Goldstone; Screenplay, Jim Sharman, Richard O'Brien; Music and Lyrics, Richard O'Brien; Photography, Peter Suschitzky; Editor, Graeme Clifford; Design, Brian Thomson; Costumes, Sue Blane; In DeLuxe Color; December release. CAST: Tim Curry (Dr. Frank-N-Furter), Susan Sarandon (Janet), Barry Bostwick (Brad), Richard O'Brien (Riff Raff), Patricia Quinn (Magenta), Little Nell (Columbia), Jonathan Adams (Dr. Scott), Peter Hinwood (Rocky Horror), Meatloaf (Eddie), Charles Gray (Criminologist)

THE LOVES OF LISZT (Ellman) Director, Marton Keleti; Photography, Istvan Hildebrand; Music Arranged and partly composed by Ferenc Farkas; Presented by Jerry Winters; In DeLuxe Color; 130 minutes; December release. CAST: Imre Sinkovits (Liszt), Klara Luchko (Marie), Igor Dmitriev (Prince Wittgenstein), Irina Gubanova (Olga), Ariadna Shengelaya (Carolyne), Sandor Pecsi (Belloni), Larissa Trembovelskaya (Lola Montez), with singers Josef Simandy, Andras Farago, Robert Ilosfalvy, Jozsef Reti, pianists Sviatoslav Richter, Gyorgy Cziffra, the Kirov Ballet, Leningrad Opera

PLEASURE PARTY Producer-Director, Claude Chabrol; Screenplay, Paul Gegauff; No other credits submitted; December release. CAST: Paul Gegauff, Danielle Gegauff

ACT OF AGGRESSION (Joseph Green) Producers, Alain Poire, Pierre Braunberger; Director, Gerard Pires; Screenplay, Gerard Pires, Jean-Patric Manchette; Based on novel "The Shrewsdale Exit" by John Buell; Photography, Silvano Ippoliti; Music, Robert Charlebois; In color; Rated R; 94 minutes; December release. CAST: Jean-Louis Trintignant (Paul), Catherine Deneuve (Sara), Claude Brasseur (Andre), Philippe Brigaud (Escudero), Michelle Grellier (Helene), Delphine Boffy (Patty), Franco Fabrizi, Robert Charlebois, Milena Vukotic, Leonora Fani, Jacques Rispal

ICY BREASTS (Joseph Green) Direction and Screenplay, Georges Lautner; From novel by Richard Matheson; Photography, Maurice Fellous; Music, Phillipe Sarde; 105 minutes; December release. CAST: Alain Delon (Marc), Mireille Darc (Peggy), Claude Brasseur (Francois), Nicoletta Machiavelli (Jacqueline), Flora Altoviti (Denis), Andre Falcon (Garnier), Emilio Messina (Steig), Michael Peyreion (Albert)

THE MAN IN THE TRUNK (Gaumont International) Director, Georges Lautner; Screenplay, Francis Veber; Photography, Maurice Fellous; Music, Philippe Sarde; Rated PG; 100 minutes; December release. CAST: Mireille Darc (Francoise), Michel Constantin (Capt. Augier), Jean-Pierre Marielle (Maj. Bloch), Jean Lefebvre (Baggage Man), Amidou (Abdul), Robert Dalban (Mercier), Raoul Saint-Ives (Ambassador), Arch Taylor (American)

MARIKEN (Joseph Green) Producers; Rob Du Mee, Jos Stelling; Screenplay and Direction, Jos Stelling; Photography, Ernest Bresser; Executive Producer, Ton De Koff; Editor, Jan Bosdriesz; Additional Dialogue, Mies Bouhuys; Music, Ruud Bos; In color; 90 minutes; December release. CAST: Ronnie Montagne (Mariken), Sandra Bais (Moenen), Alida Sonnega (Aunt), William Van De Kooy (Uncle), Diet Van De Hulst (Berthe), Leo Koenen, Wil Hildebrand, Menno Jetten, Jan Harms (Young Men)

Mireille Darc, Claude Brasseur, Alain Delon
in "Icy Breasts"

Ronnie Montagne
in "Mariken"

"Le Lit . . . Ze Bawdy Bed"

LE LIT . . . ZE BAWDY BED (Joseph Green) Producer, Paul Laffargue; Direction and Screenplay, Jacques Lem; Adaptation and Dialogue, Jacques Lem, Rita Krauss, Robert Thomas; Photography, Raymond Le Moigne; Music, Charles Dumont; In Eastmancolor; 82 minutes; December release. CAST: Alice Sapritch (Older Woman), Michel Galabru (Charles), Jacques Preboist, Paul Preboist (Moving Men), Jean Lefebvre (Adrien), Anna Gael (Sylvianne), Robert Castel (Albert), Christian Duvaleix (First Thug), Henri Tisot (Husband), Claude Gensac (Adrienne), Patrick Topaloff (M.C.), Denise Filiatrault (Fabienne), Claude Michaud (Bell Hop), Willie Lamothe (Second Thug).

SIX PACK ANNIE (American International) Producer, John C. Broderick; Director, Graydon F. David; Screenplay, Norman Winksi, David Kidd, Wil David; Photography, Daniel Lacambre; Editor, J. H. Arrufat; Music, Raoul Kraushaar; In color; Rated R; 88 minutes; December release. CAST: Lindsay Bloom (Annie), Jana Bellan (Mary Lou), Joe Higgins (Sheriff), Larry Mahan (Bustis), Raymond Danton (O'Meyer), Richard Kennedy (Jack), Danna Hansen (Aunt Tess), Pedro Gonzales-Gonzales (Carmello), Bruce Bosleittner (Bobby Joe), Sid Melton (Angelo), Louisa Mortz (Flora), Doodles Weaver (Hank), Stubby Kaye (Bates)

KILLER FORCE (American International) Producers, Nat and Patrick Wachsberger; Director, Val Guest; Screenplay, Michael Winder; Photography, David Millin; Music, Georges Garvarentz; Art Director, Peter Church; Assistant Director, David Anderson; In Movielab Color; Rated R; 100 minutes; December release. CAST: Telly Savalas (Webb), Peter Fonda (Bradley), Hugh O'Brian (Lewis), Christopher Lee (Chilton), O. J. Simpson (Bopper), Maud Adams (Clare), Ian Yule, Michael Mayer, Victor Melleney, Richard Loring, Stuart Brown, Marina Christelis

GIFTS OF AN EAGLE (C. B. Bartell) Producer, Kent Durden; Executive Producer, C. B. Bartell; Director, Rex Fleming; Screenplay, Dale Myers; From book by Kent Durden; Photography, Ed Durden, Kent Durden, Robert Sissman; Editor, Steve Bradfield; Music, Clark Gassman; Songs, Randy Sparks, Paul Bergen, Clark Gassman; In Foro-Kem Color; Rated G; 104 minutes; December release. A documentary on the training of an eagle.

OLD DRACULA (American International) Producer, Jack H. Wiener; Director, Clive Donner; Screenplay, Jeremy Lloyd; Music, David Whitaker; Theme Song "Vampira," Anthony Newley; Art Directors Philip Harrison; Photography, Tony Richmond; Costumes, Vangie Harrison; Editor, Bill Butler; Assistant Director, Bert Batt; In Movielab Color; Rated PG; 89 minutes; December release. CAST: David Niven (Dracula), Teresa Graves (Vampira), Peter Bayliss (Maltravers), Jennie Linden (Angela), Nicky Henson (Marc), Linda Hayden (Helga), Bernard Bresslaw (Pottinger), Cathy Shirriff (Nancy), Andrea Allan (Eve), Veronica Carlson (Ritva), Minah Bird (Rose), Christopher Sandford (Milton), Freddie Jones (Gilmore), Frank Thornton (King), Aimi MacDonald, Patrick Newell (Couple in hotel), Hoima McDonald, Nicola Austine, Penny Irving (Playboy Bunnies)

BLOOD, SWEAT AND FEAR (Cinema Shares) No credits available; In color; 90 minutes; December release. CAST: Lee J. Cobb, Franco Gasparri

CRYSTAL VOYAGER (Hemdale) Producer, David Elfick; Photography, Albert Falzon, George Greenough; Music, G. Wayne Thoms, Pink Floyd; December release. No other credits available.

SEVENTEEN AND ANXIOUS (Martin) Director, Zybnek Brynych; Music, Peter Thomas; Rated R; In Eastmancolor; Rated R; December release. CAST: Anne M. Kuster, Nadja Tiller, Karl Vogler, Amadeus August

THE DRIVER'S SEAT (AVCO Embassy) Producer, Franco Rossellini; Director, Giuseppe Patroni Griffi; Screenplay, Giuseppe Patroni Griffi, Raffaele La Capria; Based on novel by Muriel Spark; Music, Franco Mannino; In Technicolor; Rated R; 101 minutes; December release. CAST: Elizabeth Taylor, Ian Bannen, Mona Washbourne, Guido Mannari, Maxence Malifort, Andy Warhol

COME HOME AND MEET MY WIFE (S. J. International) Producer, Edmondo Amati; Director, Mario Monticelli; Photography, Luigi Kuweiller; Art Director, Lorenzo Baraldi; Editor, Ruggero Mastroianni; Music, Enzo Jannacci; In Eastmancolor; Rated R; 105 minutes; December release. CAST: Ugo Tognazzi (Giulio), Ornella Muti (Vincenzina), Michele Placido (Giovanni)

VERDICT (AVCO Embassy) title changed to "Jury of One"; Director, Andre Cayatte; Screenplay, Andre Cayatte, Henri Coupon, Pierre Dumayet, Paul Andreota; Photography, Jean Badal; Editor, Paul Cayatte; Music, Louiguy; In Eastmancolor; Rated R; 95 minutes; December release. CAST: Sophia Loren (Teresa), Jean Gabin (Leguen), Henri Garcia (Lannelongue), Julien Berthau (Verlac), Michel Albertini (Andre), Muriel Catala (Annie)

THAT LUCKY TOUCH (Allied Artists) Producer, Dimitri de Grunwald; Director, Christopher Miles; Screenplay, John Briley; Based on idea by Moss Hart; Photography, Douglas Slocombe; Music, John Scott; Designer, Tony Masters; Associate Producer, Timothy Burrill; In color; Rated PG; 93 minutes; December release. CAST: Roger Moore (Roger), Susannah York (Julia), Shelley Winters (Diana), Lee J. Cobb (Gen. Steedeman), Jean-Pierre Cassel (Leo), Raf Vallone (Gen. Peruzzi), Sydne Rome (Sophie), Donald Sinden (Gen. Armstrong), Michael Shannon, Alfred Hoffman, Aubrey Woods, Timothy Carlton, Fabian Cevellos, Vincent Hall, Julie Dawn Cole, Merelina Kendall, Taki Emmanuel, Michael Green, Sultan Lalani, Jamila Massey, Marianne Stone, Linda Gray, Leonard Kavanaugh, Mercia Mansfield, Bonnie Hurren, David Enders, Franco Derossa, Donna Todd

Hugh O'Brian, Peter Fonda
in "Killer Force"

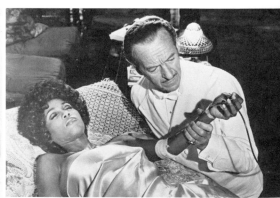

Teresa Graves, David Niven
in "Old Dracula"

Maud Adams

Eddie Albert

Eve Arden

Richard Attenborough

Ina Balin

BIOGRAPHICAL DATA
(Name, real name, place and date of birth, school attended)

ABBOTT, JOHN: London, June 5, 1905.

ABEL, WALTER: St. Paul, Minn., June 6, 1898, AADA.

ADAMS, EDIE: (Elizabeth Edith Enke) Kingston, Pa., Apr. 16, 1931. Juilliard, Columbia.

ADAMS, JULIE: (Betty May) Waterloo, Iowa, Oct. 17, 1928. Little Rock Jr. College.

ADAMS, MAUD: (Maud Wikstrom) Lulea, Sweden.

ADDAMS, DAWN: Felixstowe, Suffolk, Eng., Sept. 21, 1930. RADA.

ADJANI, ISABELLE: Paris, 1955.

ADRIAN, IRIS: (Iris Adrian Hostetter) Los Angeles, May 29, 1913.

AGAR, JOHN: Chicago, Jan. 31, 1921.

AHERNE, BRIAN: Worcestershire, Eng., May 2, 1902. Malvern College, U. of London.

AHN, PHILIP: Los Angeles, Mar. 29, 1911. U. of Calif.

AIMEE, ANOUK: Paris, Apr. 27, 1934. Bauer-Therond.

ALBERGHETTI, ANNA MARIA: Pesaro, Italy, May 15, 1936.

ALBERT, EDDIE: (Eddie Albert Heimberger) Rock Island, Ill, Apr. 22, 1908. U. of Minn.

ALBERT, EDWARD: Los Angeles, Feb. 20, 1951.

ALBRIGHT, LOLA: Akron, Ohio, July 20, 1925.

ALDA, ALAN: NYC, Jan. 28, 1936, Fordham.

ALDA, ROBERT: (Alphonso D'Abruzzo) NYC, Feb. 26, 1914. NYU.

ALEJANDRO, MIGUEL: NYC, 1958.

ALEXANDER, JANE: Boston, Mass., Oct. 28, 1939, Sarah Lawrence.

ALLBRITTON, LOUISE: Oklahoma City, July 3, 1920. U. of Okla.

ALLEN, STEVE: New York City, Dec. 26, 1921.

ALLEN, WOODY: Brooklyn, Dec. 1, 1935.

ALLENTUCK, KATHERINE: NYC, Oct. 16, 1954: Calhoun.

ALLYSON, JUNE: (Ella Geisman) Westchester, N.Y., Oct. 7, 1923.

AMECHE, DON: (Dominic Amichi) Kenosha, Wisc., May 31, 1908.

AMES, ED: Boston, July 9, 1929.

AMES, LEON: (Leon Wycoff) Portland, Ind., Jan. 20, 1903.

AMOS, JOHN: Newark, NJ., Dec. 27, Bronx Com. Col.

ANDERSON, JUDITH: Adelaide, Australia, Feb. 10, 1898.

ANDERSON, MICHAEL, JR.: London, Eng., 1943.

ANDERSSON, BIBI: Stockholm, Nov. 11, 1935, Royal Dramatic Sch.

ANDES, KEITH: Ocean City, N.J., July 12, 1920. Temple U., Oxford.

ANDRESS, URSULA: Switz., Mar. 19, 1936.

ANDREWS, DANA: Collins, Miss., Jan. 1, 1912. Sam Houston Col.

ANDREWS, EDWARD: Griffin, Ga., Oct. 9, 1914. U. VA.

ANDREWS, HARRY: Tonbridge, Kent, Eng., Nov. 10, 1911.

ANDREWS, JULIE: (Julia Elizabeth Wells) Surrey, Eng. Oct. 1, 1935.

ANGEL, HEATHER: Oxford, Eng., Feb. 9, 1909. Wycombe Abbey.

ANN-MARGRET: (Olsson) Valsjobyn, Sweden, Apr. 28, 1941. Northwestern U.

ANSARA, MICHAEL: Lowell, Mass., Apr. 15, 1922. Pasadena Playhouse.

ANTHONY, TONY: Clarksburg, W. Va., Oct 16, 1937. Carnegie Tech.

ARCHER, JOHN: (Ralph Bowman) Osceola, Neb., May 8, 1915. U. of S. Calif.

ARDEN, EVE: (Eunice Quedens) Mill Valley, Calif., Apr. 30, 1912.

ARKIN, ALAN: NYC, Mar. 26, 1934. LACC.

ARLEN, RICHARD: Charlottesville, VA., Sept. 1, 1900. St. Thomas College.

ARNAZ, DESI: Santiago, Cuba, Mar. 2, 1917, Colegio de Dolores.

ARNAZ, DESI, JR.: Los Angeles, 1953.

ARNESS, JAMES: (Aurness) Minneapolis, Minn., May 26, 1923. Beloit College.

ARTHUR, BEATRICE: NYC, May 13, 1926, New School.

ARTHUR, JEAN: NYC, Oct. 17, 1908.

ARTHUR, ROBERT: (Robert Arthaud) Aberdeen, Wash., June 18. U. of Wash.

ASHLEY, ELIZABETH: Ocala, Fla., Aug. 30, 1939.

ASTAIRE, FRED: (Fred Austerlitz) Omaha, Neb., May 10, 1899.

ASTIN, JOHN: Baltimore, Md., Mar. 30, 1930, UMinn.

ASTOR, MARY: (Lucile V. Langhanke) Quincy, Ill., May 3, 1906. Kenwood-Loring School.

ATHERTON, WILLIAM: New Haven, Conn., July 30, 1947, Carnegie Tech.

ATTENBOROUGH, RICHARD: Cambridge, Eng., Aug. 29, 1923. RADA.

AUBERJONOIS, RENE: NYC, June 1, 1940, Carnegie Tech.

AUGER, CLAUDINE: Paris, Apr. 26, Dramatic Cons.

AULIN, EWA: Stockholm, Sweden, Feb. 14, 1950.

AUMONT, JEAN PIERRE: Paris, Jan. 5, 1913. French Nat'l School of Drama.

AUTRY, GENE: Tioga, Texas, Sept. 29, 1907.

AVALON, FRANKIE: (Francis Thomas Avallone) Philadelphia, Sept. 18, 1940.

AYLMER, FELIX: Corsham, Eng., Feb. 21, 1889. Oxford.

AYRES, LEW: Minneapolis, Minn., Dec. 28, 1908.

AZNAVOUR, CHARLES: (Varenagh Aznourian) Paris, May 22, 1924.

BACALL, LAUREN: (Betty Perske) NYC, Sept. 16, 1924. AADA.

BACKUS, JIM: Cleveland, Ohio, Feb. 25, 1913. AADA.

BADDELEY, HERMIONE: Shropshire, Eng., Nov. 13, 1908. Margaret Morris School.

BAILEY, PEARL: Newport News, Va., March 29, 1918.

BAIN, BARBARA: Chicago, Sept. 13, 1934. U. Ill.

BAKER, CARROLL: Johnstown, Pa., May 28, 1931. St. Petersburg Jr. College.

BAKER, DIANE: Hollywood, Calif, Feb. 25, USC

BAKER, STANLEY: Glamorgan, Wales, Feb. 28, 1928.

BALABAN, ROBERT: Chicago, Aug. 16, 1945, Colgate.

BALIN, INA: Brooklyn, Nov. 12, 1937. NYU.

BALL, LUCILLE: Celaron, N.Y., Aug. 6, 1911. Chatauqua Musical Inst.

Martin Balsam **Brigitte Bardot** **Tom Bell** **Jacqueline Bisset** **Jean-Paul Belmondo**

BALSAM, MARTIN: NYC Nov. 4, 1919. Actors Studio.

BANCROFT, ANNE: (Anna Maria Italiano) Bronx, N.Y., Sept. 17, 1931. AADA.

BANNEN, IAN: Airdrie, Scot., June 29, 1928.

BARDOT, BRIGITTE: Paris, Sept. 28, 1934.

BARRIE, WENDY: London, May 8, 1919.

BARRON, KEITH: Mexborough, Eng., Aug. 8, 1936. Sheffield Playhouse.

BARRY, DONALD: (Donald Barry de Acosta) Houston, Tex. Texas School of Mines.

BARRY, GENE: (Eugene Klass) NYC, June 14, 1921.

BARRYMORE, JOHN BLYTH: Beverly Hills, Calif., June 4, 1932. St. John's Military Academy.

BARTHOLOMEW, FREDDIE: London, Mar. 28, 1924.

BASEHART, RICHARD: Zanesville, Ohio, Aug. 31, 1914.

BATES, ALAN: Allestree, Derbyshire, Eng., Feb. 17, 1934. RADA.

BAXTER, ALAN: East Cleveland, Ohio, Nov. 19, 1911. Williams U.

BAXTER, ANNE: Michigan City, Ind., May 7, 1923, Ervine School of Drama.

BAXTER, KEITH: South Wales, Apr. 29, 1933, RADA.

BEAL, JOHN: (J. Alexander Bliedung) Joplin, Mo., Aug. 13, 1909. Pa. U.

BEATTY, ROBERT: Hamilton, Ont., Can., Oct. 19, 1909. U. of Toronto.

BEATTY, WARREN: Richmond, Virginia, March 30, 1937.

BEERY, NOAH, JR.: NYC, Aug. 10, 1916. Harvard Military Academy.

BELAFONTE, HARRY: NYC, Mar. 1, 1927.

BELASCO, LEON: Odessa, Russia, Oct. 11, 1902.

BEL GEDDES, BARBARA: NYC, Oct. 31, 1922.

BELL, TOM: Liverpool, Eng., 1932.

BELLAMY, RALPH: Chicago, June 17, 1905.

BELMONDO, JEAN-PAUL: Paris, Apr. 9, 1933.

BENEDICT, DIRK: Montana, 1945, Whitman Col.

BENJAMIN, RICHARD: NYC, May 22, 1938, Northwestern U.

BENNETT, BRUCE: (Herman Brix) Tacoma, Wash., U. of Wash.

BENNETT, JILL: Penang, Malay, Dec. 24, 1931.

BENNETT, JOAN: Palisades, N.J., Feb. 27, 1910. St. Margaret's School.

BENSON, ROBBY: Dallas, Tex., Jan. 21, 1956.

BERENSON, MARISA: NYC, Feb. 15, 1948.

BERGEN, CANDICE: Los Angeles, May. 8, 1946.

BERGEN, EDGAR: Chicago, Feb. 16, 1903. Northwestern U.

BERGEN, POLLY: Knoxville, Tenn., July 14, 1930. Compton Jr. College.

BERGER, HELMUT: Salzburg, Aus., 1945.

BERGER, WILLIAM: Austria, Jan. 20, 1928, Columbia.

BERGERAC, JACQUES: Biarritz, France, May 26, 1927. Paris U.

BERGMAN, INGRID: Stockholm, Sweden, Aug. 29, 1915. Royal Dramatic Theatre School.

BERLE, MILTON: (Milton Berlinger) NYC, July 12, 1908. Professional Children's School.

BERLIN, JEANNIE: Los Angeles, Nov. 1, 1949.

BERLINGER, WARREN: Brooklyn, Aug. 31, 1937. Columbia.

BEST, JAMES: Corydon, Ind., July 26, 1926.

BETTGER, LYLE: Philadelphia, Feb. 13, 1915. AADA.

BETZ, CARL: Pittsburgh, Mar. 9. Duquesne, Carnegie Tech.

BEYMER, RICHARD: Avoca, Iowa, Feb. 21, 1939.

BIKEL, THEODORE: Vienna, May 2, 1924. RADA.

BISHOP, JOEY: (Joseph Abraham Gottlieb) Bronx, N.Y., Feb. 3, 1918.

BISHOP, JULIE: (formerly Jacqueline Wells) Denver, Colo., Aug. 30, 1917. Westlake School.

BISSET, JACQUELINE: Waybridge, Eng., Sept. 13, 1944.

BIXBY, BILL: San Francisco, Jan. 22, 1934. U. Cal.

BLACK, KAREN: (Ziegler) Park Ridge, Ill., July 1, 1942. Northwestern.

BLAINE, VIVIAN: (Vivian Stapleton) Newark, N.J., Nov. 21, 1924.

BLAIR, BETSY: (Betsy Boger) NYC, Dec. 11.

BLAIR, JANET: (Martha Jane Lafferty) Blair, Pa., Apr. 23, 1921.

BLAIR, LINDA: Westport, Ct., 1959.

BLAKE, AMANDA: (Beverly Louise Neill) Buffalo, N.Y., Feb. 20.

BLAKE, ROBERT: (Michael Gubitosi) Nutley, N.J., Sept. 18, 1933.

BLAKELY, SUSAN: Frankfurt, Germany 1950. U. Tex.

BLAKLEY, RONEE: Stanley, Id., 1946. Stanford U.

BLONDELL, JOAN: NYC, Aug. 30, 1909.

BLOOM, CLAIRE: London, Feb. 15, 1931. Badminton School.

BLYTHE, ANN: Mt. Kisco, N.Y., Aug. 16, 1928. New Wayburn Dramatic School.

BOGARDE, DIRK: London, Mar. 28, 1921. Glasgow & Univ. College.

BOLGER, RAY: Dorchester, Mass., Jan. 10, 1906.

BOND, DEREK: Glasgow, Scot., Jan. 26, 1920. Askes School.

BONDI, BEULAH: Chicago, May 3, 1892.

BOONE, PAT: Jacksonville, Fla., June 1, 1934. Columbia U.

BOONE, RICHARD: Los Angeles. June 18, 1917, Stanford U.

BOOTH, SHIRLEY: (Thelma Ford) NYC, Aug. 30, 1907.

BORGNINE, ERNEST: (Borgnino) Hamden, Conn., Jan. 24, 1918. Randall School.

BOTTOMS, TIMOTHY: Santa Barbara, Ca., Aug. 30, 1951.

BOWKER, JUDI: Shawford, Eng., Apr. 6, 1954.

BOWMAN, LEE: Cincinnati, Dec. 28, 1914. AADA.

BOYD, STEPHEN: (William Miller) Belfast, Ire., July 4, 1928.

BOYER, CHARLES: Figeac, France, Aug. 28, 1899. Sorbonne.

BOYLE, PETER: Philadelphia, Pa., 1937, LaSalle Col.

BRACKEN, EDDIE: NYC, Feb. 7, 1920. Professional Children's School.

BRADY, SCOTT: (Jerry Tierney) Brooklyn, Sept. 13, 1924. Bliss-Hayden Dramatic School.

BRAND, NEVILLE: Kewanee, Ill., Aug. 13, 1921.

BRANDO, JOCELYN: San Francisco, Nov. 18, 1919. Lake Forest College. AADA.

BRANDO, MARLON: Omaha, Neb., Apr. 3, 1924. New School.

BRASSELLE, KEEFE: Elyria, Ohio, Feb. 7.

BRAZZI, ROSSANO: Bologna, Italy, 1916. U. of Florence.

BRENT, GEORGE: Dublin, Ire., Mar. 15, 1904. Dublin U.

BRENT, ROMNEY: (Romulo Larralde) Saltillo, Mex., Jan. 26, 1902.

Geraldine Brooks

Barry Brown

Leslie Caron

Richard Castellano

Rosalind Cash

BRIAN, DAVID: NYC, Aug. 5, 1914. CCNY.

BRIDGES, BEAU: Los Angeles, Dec. 9, 1941. UCLA.

BRIDGES, JEFF: Los Angeles, Dec. 4, 1949.

BRIDGES, LLOYD: San Leandro, Calif., Jan. 15, 1913.

BRITT, MAY: (Maybritt Wilkins) Sweden, March 22, 1936.

BRODIE, STEVE: (Johnny Stevens) Eldorado, Kan., Nov. 25, 1919.

BROLIN, JAMES: Los Angeles, July 18, 1940. UCLA.

BROMFIELD, JOHN: (Farron Bromfield) South Bend, Ind., June 11, 1922. St. Mary's College.

BRONSON, CHARLES: (Buchinsky) Ehrenfield, Pa., Nov. 3, 1922.

BROOKS, GERALDINE: (Geraldine Stroock) NYC, Oct. 29, 1925. AADA.

BROWN, BARRY: San Jose, Cal., Apr. 19, 1951. LACC.

BROWN, JAMES: Desdemona, Tex., Mar. 22, 1920. Baylor U.

BROWN, JIM: Manhasset, L.I., N.Y., Feb. 17, 1935 Syracuse U.

BROWN, TOM: NYC, Jan. 6, 1913. Professional Children's School.

BROWNE, CORAL: Melbourne, Aust., July 23, 1913.

BRUCE, VIRGINIA: Minneapolis, Sept. 29, 1910.

BRYNNER, YUL: Sakhalin Island, Japan, July 11, 1913.

BUCHHOLZ, HORST: Berlin, Ger., Dec. 4, 1933. Ludwig Dramatic School.

BUETEL, JACK: Dallas, Tex., Sept. 5, 1917.

BUJOLD, GENEVIEVE: Montreal, Can., July 1, 1942.

BURKE, PAUL: New Orleans, July 21, 1926. Pasadena Playhouse.

BURNETT, CAROL: San Antonio, Tex., Apr. 26, 1933. UCLA.

BURNS, CATHERINE: NYC, Sept. 25, 1945, AADA.

BURNS, GEORGE: (Nathan Birnbaum) NYC, Jan. 20, 1896.

BURR, RAYMOND: New Westminster, B.C., Can., May 21, 1917. Stanford, U. of Cal., Columbia.

BURSTYN, ELLEN: (Edna Rae Gillooly) Detroit, Mich., Dec. 7, 1932.

BURTON, RICHARD (Richard Jenkins) Pontrhydyfen, S. Wales, Nov. 10, 1925. Oxford.

BUTTONS, RED: (Aaron Chwatt) NYC, Feb. 5, 1919.

BUZZI, RUTH: Wequetequock, R.I., July 24, 1936. Pasadena Playhouse.

BYGRAVES, MAX: London, Oct. 16, 1922. St. Joseph's School.

BYRNES, EDD: NYC, July 30, 1933. Haaren High.

CAAN, JAMES: Bronx, NY, Mar. 26, 1939.

CABOT, SUSAN: Boston, July 6, 1927.

CAESAR, SID: Yonkers, N.Y., Sept. 8, 1922.

CAGNEY, JAMES: NYC, July 1, 1904. Columbia.

CAGNEY, JEANNE: NYC, Mar. 25, 1919. Hunter.

CAINE, MICHAEL: (Maurice Michelwhite) London, Mar. 14, 1933.

CAINE, SHAKIRA: (Baksh) Guyana, Feb. 23, 1947. Indian Trust Col.

CALHOUN, RORY: (Francis Timothy Durgin) Los Angeles, Aug. 8, 1923.

CALLAN, MICHAEL: (Martin Calinieff) Philadelphia, Nov. 22, 1935.

CALVERT, PHYLLIS: London, Feb. 18, 1917. Margaret Morris School.

CALVET, CORRINE: (Corrine Dibos) Paris, Apr. 30. UParis.

CAMBRIDGE, GODFREY: NYC, Feb. 26, 1933. CCNY.

CAMERON, ROD: (Rod Cox) Calgary, Alberta, Can., Dec. 7, 1912.

CAMPBELL, GLEN: Delight, Ark. Apr. 22, 1935.

CANALE, GIANNA MARIA: Reggio Calabria, Italy, Sept. 12.

CANNON, DYAN: (Samille Diane Friesen) Jan. 4, 1929, Tacoma, Wash.

CANOVA, JUDY: Jacksonville, Fla., Nov. 20, 1916.

CAPERS, VIRGINIA: Sumter, SC, 1925, Juilliard.

CAPUCINE: (Germaine Lefebvre) Toulon, France, Jan. 6, 1935.

CARDINALE, CLAUDIA: Tunis, N. Africa, Apr. 15, 1939; College Paul Cambon.

CAREY, HARRY, JR.: Saugus, Calif., May 16, Black Fox Military Academy.

CAREY, MACDONALD: Sioux City, Iowa, Mar. 15, 1913. U. of Wisc., U. of Iowa.

CAREY, PHILIP: Hackensack, N.J., July 15, 1925. U. of Miami.

CARMICHAEL, HOAGY: Bloomington, Ind., Nov. 22, 1899. Ind. U.

CARMICHAEL, IAN: Hull, Eng., June 18, 1920. Scarborough Col.

CARNE, JUDY: (Joyce Botterill) Northampton, Eng., 1939. Bush-Davis Theatre School.

CARNEY, ART: Mt. Vernon, N.Y., Nov. 4, 1918.

CARON, LESLIE: Paris, July 1, 1931. Nat'l Conservatory, Paris.

CARR, VIKKI: (Florence Cardona) July 19, 1942. San Fernardo Col.

CARRADINE, DAVID: Hollywood, Dec. 8, 1936. San Francisco State.

CARRADINE, JOHN: NYC, Feb. 5, 1906.

CARREL, DANY: Tourane, Indochina, Sept. 20, 1936. Marseilles Cons.

CARROLL, DIAHANN: (Johnson) NYC, July 17, 1935. NYU.

CARROLL, MADELEINE: West Bromwich, Eng., Feb. 26, 1906. Birmingham U.

CARROLL, PAT: Shreveport, La., May 5, 1927. Catholic U.

CARSON, JOHN DAVID: 1951, Calif. Valley Col.

CARSON, JOHNNY: Corning, Iowa, Oct. 23, 1925. U. of Neb.

CARSTEN, PETER: (Ransenthaler) Weissenberg, Bavaria, Apr. 30, 1929; Munich Akademie.

CASH, ROSALIND: Atlantic City, NJ, Dec. 31, 1938, CCNY.

CASON, BARBARA: Memphis, Tenn., Nov. 15, 1933, UIowa

CASS, PEGGY: (Mary Margaret) Boston, May 21, 1925.

CASSAVETES, JOHN: NYC, Dec. 9, 1929. Colgate College, AADA.

CASSEL, JEAN-PIERRE: Paris, 1932.

CASSIDY, DAVID: NYC, Apr. 12, 1950.

CASSIDY, JOANNA: Camden, NJ, 1944, Syracuse U.

CASTELLANO, RICHARD: Bronx, NY, Sept. 3, 1934.

CAULFIELD, JOAN: Orange, N.J., June 1. Columbia U.

CAVANI, LILIANA: Bologna, Italy, Jan. 12, 1937; UBologna.

CELI, ADOLFO: Sicily, July 27, 1922, Rome Academy.

CHAKIRIS, GEORGE: Norwood, O., Sept. 16, 1933.

CHAMBERLAIN, RICHARD: Beverly Hills, Cal., March 31, 1935. Pomona.

CHAMPION, GOWER: Geneva, Ill., June 22, 1921.

CHAMPION, MARGE: Los Angeles, Sept. 2, 1926.

Carol
Channing

Bill
Cosby

Anjanette
Comer

Tim
Conway

Kim
Darby

CHANNING, CAROL: Seattle, Jan. 31, 1921. Bennington.

CHANNING, STOCKARD: (Susan Stockard) NYC, 1944. Radcliffe

CHAPLIN, CHARLES: London, Apr. 16, 1889.

CHAPLIN, GERALDINE: Santa Monica, Cal. July 31, 1944. Royal Ballet.

CHAPLIN, SYDNEY: Los Angeles, Mar. 31, 1926. Lawrenceville.

CHARISSE, CYD: (Tula Ellice Finklea) Amarillo, Tex., Mar. 3, 1923. Hollywood Professional School.

CHASE, ILKA: NYC, Apr. 8, 1905.

CHER: (Cheryl La Piere) 1946.

CHIARI, WALTER: Verona, Italy, 1930.

CHRISTIAN, LINDA: (Blanca Rosa Welter) Tampico, Mex., Nov. 13, 1923.

CHRISTIE, JULIE: Chukua, Assam, India, Apr. 14, 1941.

CHRISTOPHER, JORDAN: Youngstown, O., Oct. 23, 1940. Kent State.

CHURCHILL, SARAH: London, Oct. 7, 1916.

CILENTO, DIANE: Queensland, Australia, Oct. 5, 1933. AADA.

CLARK, DANA: NYC, Feb. 18, 1915. Cornell, Johns Hopkins U.

CLARK, DICK: Mt. Vernon, N.Y., Nov. 30, 1929, Syracuse U.

CLARK, MAE: Philadelphia, Aug. 16, 1910.

CLARK, PETULA: Epsom England, Nov. 15, 1932.

CLARK, SUSAN: Sarnid, Ont., Can., Mar. 8. RADA

CLAYBURGH, JILL: NYC, Apr. 30, 1944; Sarah Lawrence.

CLEMENTS, STANLEY: Long Island, N.Y., July 16, 1926.

CLERY, CORINNE: Italy, 1950.

CLOONEY, ROSEMARY: Maysville Ky., May 23, 1928.

COBB, LEE J.: NYC, Dec. 8, 1911. CCNY.

COBURN, JAMES: Laurel, Neb., Aug. 31, 1928. LACC.

COCA, IMOGENE: Philadelphia, Nov. 18, 1908.

COCO, JAMES: NYC, Mar. 21, 1929.

CODY, KATHLEEN: Bronx, NY, Oct. 30, 1953.

COLBERT, CLAUDETTE: (Claudette Chauchoin) Paris, Sept. 13, 1907. Art Students League.

COLE, GEORGE: London, Apr. 22, 1925.

COLLINS, JOAN: London, May 23, 1933. Francis Holland School.

COMER, ANJANETTE: Dawson, Tex., Aug. 7, 1942. Baylor, Tex. U.

CONANT, OLIVER: NYC, Nov. 15, 1955; Dalton.

CONNERY, SEAN: Edinburgh, Scot. Aug. 25, 1930.

CONNORS, CHUCK: (Kevin Joseph Connors) Brooklyn, Apr. 10, 1924. Seton Hall College.

CONRAD, WILLIAM: Louisville, Ky., Sept. 27, 1920.

CONWAY, TIM: (Thomas Daniel) Willoughby, Oh., Dec. 15, 1933. Bowling Green State.

COOGAN, JACKIE: Los Angeles, Oct. 25, 1914. Villanova College.

COOK, ELISHA, JR.: San Francisco, Dec. 26, 1907. St. Albans.

COOPER, BEN: Hartford, Conn., Sept. 30. Columbia U,

COOPER, JACKIE: Los Angeles, Sept. 15, 1921.

COOTE, ROBERT: London, Feb. 4, 1909. Hurstpierpont College.

CORBY, ELLEN: (Hansen) Racine, Wisc., June 13, 1914.

CORCORAN, DONNA: Quincy, Mass., Sept. 29.

CORD, ALEX: (Viespi) Floral Park, N.Y., Aug. 3, 1931. NYU, Actors Studio.

CORDAY, MARA: (Marilyn Watts) Santa Monica, Calif., Jan. 3, 1932.

COREY, JEFF: NYC, Aug. 10, 1914. Fagin School.

CORRI, ADRIENNE: Glasgow, Scot., Nov. 13, 1933. RADA.

CORTESA, VALENTINA: Milan, Italy, Jan. 1, 1925.

COSBY, BILL: Philadelphia, 1937. Temple U.

COTTEN, JOSEPH: Petersburg, Va., May 13, 1905.

COURTENAY, TOM: Hull, Eng., Feb. 25, 1937. RADA.

CORLAN, ANTHONY: Cork City, Ire., May 9, 1947; Birmingham School of Dramatic Arts.

COURTLAND, JEROME: Knoxville, Tenn., Dec. 27, 1926.

CRABBE, BUSTER (LARRY): (Clarence Linden) Oakland, Calif., U. of S. Cal.

CRAIG, JAMES: (James H. Meador) Nashville, Tenn., Feb. 4, 1912. Rice Inst.

CRAIG, MICHAEL: India in 1929.

CRAIN, JEANNE: Barstow, Cal., May 25, 1925.

CRANE, BOB: Waterbury, Conn., July 13.

CRAWFORD, BRODERICK: Philadelphia, Dec. 9, 1911.

CRAWFORD, JOAN: (Billie Cassin) San Antonio, Tex., Mar. 23, 1908.

CRENNA, RICHARD: Los Angeles, Nov. 30, 1927. USC.

CRISTAL, LINDA: (Victoria Moya) Buenos Aires, 1935.

CROSBY, BING: (Harry Lillith Crosby) Tacoma, Wash., May 2, 1904. Gonzaga College.

CROWLEY, PAT: Olyphant, Pa., Sept. 17, 1933.

CULLUM, JOHN: Knoxville, Tenn., Mar. 2, 1930, UTenn.

CULP, ROBERT: Oakland, Calif., Aug. 16, 1930. U. Wash.

CULVER, CALVIN: Canandaigua, NY, 1943.

CUMMINGS, CONSTANCE: Seattle, Wash., May 15, 1910.

CUMMINGS, ROBERT: Joplin, Mo., June 9, 1910. Carnegie Tech.

CUMMINS, PEGGY: Prestatyn, N. Wales, Dec. 18, 1926. Alexandra School.

CURTIS, KEENE: Salt Lake City, U., Feb. 15, 1925, U. Utah.

CURTIS, TONY: (Bernard Schwartz) NYC, June 3, 1925.

CUSHING, PETER: Kenley, Surrey, Eng., May 26, 1913.

DAHL, ARLENE: Minneapolis, Aug. 11, 1927. U. Minn.

DALLESANDRO, JOE: Pensacola, Fla., Dec. 31, 1948.

DALTON, TIMOTHY: Wales, 1945; RADA.

DAMONE, VIC: (Vito Farinola) Brooklyn, June 12, 1928.

DANIELS, WILLIAM: Bklyn, Mar. 31, 1927. Northwestern.

DANNER, BLYTHE: Philadelphia, Pa., Bard Col.

DANO, ROYAL: NYC, Nov. 16, 1922, NYU.

DANTE, MICHAEL: (Ralph Vitti) Stamford, Conn., 1935. U Miami.

DANTINE, HELMUT: Vienna, Oct. 7, 1918. U. Calif.

DANTON, RAY: NYC, Sept. 19, 1931. Carnegie Tech.

DARBY, KIM: (Deborah Zerby) North Hollywood, Cal., July 8, 1948.

DARCEL, DENISE: (Denise Billecard) Paris, Sept. 8, 1925. U. Dijon.

DARREN, JAMES: Philadelphia, June 8, 1936. Stella Adler School.

DARRIEUX, DANIELLE: Bordeaux, France, May 1, 1917. Lycee LaTour.

DA SILVA, HOWARD: Cleveland, Ohio, May 4, 1909. Carnegie Tech.

Claude Dauphin	Tamara Dobson	Keir Dullea	Samantha Eggar	Leif Erickson

DAUPHIN, CLAUDE: Crobeil, France, Aug. 19, 1903. Beaux Arts.

DAVIDSON, JOHN: Pittsburgh, Dec. 13, 1941. Denison U.

DAVIES, RUPERT: Liverpool, Eng., 1916.

DAVIS, BETTE: Lowell, Mass., Apr. 5, 1908. John Murray Anderson Dramatic School.

DAVIS, OSSIE: Cogdell, Ga., Dec. 18, 1917. Howard U.

DAVIS, SAMMY, JR.: NYC, Dec. 8, 1925.

DAY, DENNIS: (Eugene Dennis McNulty) NYC, May 21, 1917. Manhattan College.

DAY, DORIS: (Doris Kappelhoff) Cincinnati, Apr. 3, 1924.

DAY, LARAINE: (Johnson) Roosevelt, Utah, Oct. 13, 1920.

DAYAN, ASSEF: Israel, 1945. U. Jerusalem.

DEAN, JIMMY: Plainview, Tex., Aug. 10, 1928.

DE CARLO, YVONNE: (Peggy Yvonne Middleton) Vancouver, B.C., Can., Sept. 1, 1924. Vancouver School of Drama.

DEE, FRANCES: Los Angeles, Nov. 26, 1907. Chicago U.

DEE, JOEY: (Joseph Di Nicola) Passaic, N.J., June 11, 1940. Patterson State College.

DEE, RUBY: Cleveland, O., Oct. 27, Hunter Col.

DEE, SANDRA: (Alexandra Zuck) Bayonne, N.J., Apr. 23, 1942.

DE FORE, DON: Cedar Rapids, Iowa, Aug. 25, 1917. U. Iowa.

DE HAVEN, GLORIA: Los Angeles, July 23, 1925.

DE HAVILLAND, OLIVIA: Tokyo, Japan, July 1, 1916. Notre Dame Convent School.

DELL, GABRIEL: Barbados, BWI, Oct. 7, 1930.

DELON, ALAIN: Sceaux, Fr., Nov. 8, 1935.

DEL RIO, DOLORES: (Dolores Ansunsolo) Durango, Mex., Aug. 3, 1905. St. Joseph's Convent.

DE NIRO, ROBERT: NYC, Aug. 17, 1943, Stella Adler.

DENISON, MICHAEL: Doncaster, York, Eng., Nov. 1, 1915. Oxford.

DENEUVE, CATHERINE: Paris, Oct. 22, 1943.

DENNER, CHARLES: Tarnow, Poland, May 29, 1926.

DENNIS, SANDY: Hastings, Neb., Apr. 27, 1937. Actors Studio.

DEREK, JOHN: Hollywood, Aug. 12, 1926.

DERN, BRUCE: Chicago, June 4, 1936, UPa.

DEVINE, ANDY: Flagstaff, Ariz., Oct. 7, 1905. Ariz. State College.

DEWHURST, COLLEEN: Montreal, June 3, 1926, Lawrence U.

DEXTER, ANTHONY: (Walter Reinhold Alfred Fleischmann) Talmadge, Neb., Jan. 19, 1919. U. Iowa.

DHIEGH, KHIGH: New Jersey 1910.

DICKINSON, ANGIE: Kulm, N. Dak., Sept. 30, 1932. Glendale College.

DIETRICH, MARLENE: (Maria Magdalene von Losch) Berlin, Ger., Dec. 27, 1904. Berlin Music Academy.

DILLER, PHYLLIS: Lima, O., July 17, 1917. Bluffton College.

DILLMAN, BRADFORD: San Francisco, Apr. 14, 1930.

DOBSON, TAMARA: Baltimore, Md., 1947, Md. Inst. of Art.

DOMERGUE, FAITH: New Orleans, June 16, 1925.

DONAHUE, TROY: (Merle Johnson) NYC, Jan. 27, 1937. Columbia U.

DONNELL, JEFF: (Jean Donnell) South Windham, Me., July 10, 1921. Yale Drama School.

DONNELLY, RUTH: Trenton, N.J., May 17, 1896.

DORS, DIANA: Swindon, Wilshire, Eng., Oct. 23, 1931. London Academy of Music.

D'ORSAY, FIFI: Montreal, Can., Apr. 16, 1904.

DOUGLAS, KIRK: Amsterdam, N.Y., Dec. 9, 1916. St. Lawrence U.

DOUGLAS, MELVYN: (Melvyn Hesselberg) Macon, Ga., Apr. 5, 1901.

DOUGLAS, MICHAEL: Hollywood, Sept. 25, 1944, U. Cal.

DOURIF, BRAD: Huntington, W.Va., Mar. 18, 1950. Marshall U.

DOWN, LESLEY ANN: London, Mar. 17, 1954.

DRAKE, BETSY: Paris, Sept. 11, 1923.

DRAKE, CHARLES: (Charles Rupert) NYC, Oct. 2, 1914. Nichols College.

DREW, ELLEN: (formerly Terry Ray) Kansas City, Mo., Nov. 23, 1915.

DREYFUSS, RICHARD: Brooklyn, NY, 1948.

DRIVAS, ROBERT: Chicago, Oct. 7, 1938. U. Chi.

DRU, JOANNE: (Joanne LaCock) Logan, W. Va., Jan. 31, 1923. John Robert Powers School.

DUFF, HOWARD: Bremerton, Wash., Nov. 24, 1917.

DUKE, PATTY: NYC, Dec. 14, 1946.

DULLEA, KEIR: Cleveland, N.J., May 30, 1936. Neighborhood Playhouse, SF State Col.

DUNAWAY, FAYE: Bascom, Fla., Jan, 14, 1941. Fla. U.

DUNCAN, SANDY: Henderson, Tex., Feb. 20, 1946; Len Morris Col.

DUNNE, IRENE: Louisville, Ky., Dec. 20, 1904. Chicago College of Music.

DUNNOCK, MILDRED: Baltimore, Jan. 25, 1906. Johns Hopkins and Columbia U.

DURANTE, JIMMY: NYC, Feb. 10, 1893.

DURNING, CHARLES: Highland Falls, NY, Feb. 28, 1933, NYU.

DUSSOLLIER, ANDRE: Annecy, France, Feb. 17, 1946.

DUVALL, ROBERT: San Diego, Cal., 1930, Principia Col.

DVORAK, ANN: (Ann McKim) NYC, Aug. 2, 1912.

EASTON, ROBERT: Milwaukee, Nov. 23, 1930. U. of Texas.

EASTWOOD, CLINT: San Francisco, May 31, 1930 LACC.

EATON, SHIRLEY: London, 1937. Aida Foster School.

EBSEN, BUDDY: (Christian, Jr.) Belleville, Ill. Apr. 2, 1910. UFla.

ECKEMYR, AGNETA: Karlsborg, Swed., July 2. Actors Studio.

EDEN, BARBARA: (Moorhead) Tucson, Ariz., 1934.

EDWARDS, VINCE: NYC, July 9, 1928. AADA.

EGAN, RICHARD: San Francisco, July 29, 1923. Stanford U.

EGGAR, SAMANTHA: London, Mar. 5, 1939.

EKBERG, ANITA: Malmo, Sweden, Sept. 29, 1931.

ELLIOTT, DENHOLM: London, May 31, 1922. Malvern College.

ELSOM, ISOBEL: Cambridge, Eng., Mar. 15, 1894.

ELY, RON: (Ronald Pierce) Hereford, Tex. June 21, 1938.

EMERSON, FAYE: Elizabeth, La., July 8, 1917. San Diego State Col.

ENSERRO, MICHAEL: Soldier, Pa., Oct. 5, 1918. Allegheny Col.

ERDMAN, RICHARD: Enid, Okla., June 1, 1925.

ERICKSON, LEIF: Alameda, Calif., Oct. 27, 1911. U. of Calif.

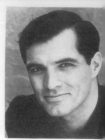

Douglas Fairbanks, Jr.   **Barbara Feldon**   **Mel Ferrer**   **Judy Geeson**   **John Gavin**

ERICSON, JOHN: Dusseldorf, Ger., Sept. 25, 1926. AADA.

ESMOND, CARL: Vienna, June 14, 1906. U. of Vienna.

EVANS, DALE: (Francis Smith) Uvalde, Texas, Oct. 31, 1912.

EVANS, EDITH: London, Feb. 8, 1888.

EVANS, GENE: Holbrook, Ariz., July 11, 1922.

EVANS, MAURICE: Dorchester, Eng., June 3, 1901.

EVERETT, CHAD: (Ray Cramton) South Bend, Ind., June 11, 1936.

EWELL, TOM: (Yewell Tompkins) Owensboro, Ky., Apr. 29, 1909. U. of Wisc.

FABARES SHELLEY: Los Angeles, Jan. 19, 1944.

FABIAN: (Fabian Forte) Philadelphia, Feb. 6, 1940.

FABRAY, NANETTE: (Ruby Nanette Fabares) San Diego, Oct. 27, 1920.

FAIRBANKS, DOUGLAS JR.: NYC, Dec. 9, 1909, Collegiate School.

FALK, PETER: NYC, Sept. 16, 1927, New School.

FARENTINO, JAMES: Brooklyn, Feb. 24, 1938.

FARR, FELICIA: Westchester, N.Y., Oct. 4, 1932. Penn State Col.

FARRELL, CHARLES: Onset Bay, Mass., Aug. 9, 1901. Boston U.

FARROW, MIA: Los Angeles, Feb. 9, 1945.

FAULKNER, GRAHAM: London, Sept. 26, 1947, Webber-Douglas.

FAYE, ALICE: (Ann Leppert) NYC, May 5, 1915.

FELDON, BARBARA: (Hall) Pittsburgh, Mar. 12, 1941. Carnegie Tech.

FELLOWS, EDITH: Boston, May 20, 1923.

FERRER, JOSE: Santurce, P.R., Jan. 8, 1912. Princeton U.

FERRER, MEL: Elberon, N.J., Aug. 25, 1917. Princeton U.

FERRIS, BARBARA: London 1943.

FERZETTI, GABRIELE: Italy 1927; Rome Acad. of Drama.

FIELD, SALLY: Pasadena, Cal., Nov. 6, 1946.

FIGUEROA, RUBEN: NYC 1958.

FINCH, PETER: London, Sept. 28, 1916.

FINNEY, ALBERT: Salford, Lancashire, Eng., May 9, 1936. RADA.

FISHER, EDDIE: Philadelphia, Aug. 10, 1928.

FITZGERALD, GERALDINE: Dublin, Ire., Nov. 28, 1914. Dublin Art School.

FLANNERY, SUSAN: Jersey City, N.J. July 31, 1943.

FLEMING, RHONDA: (Marilyn Louis) Los Angeles, Aug. 10, 1922.

FLEMYNG, ROBERT: Liverpool, Eng., Jan. 3, 1912. Haileybury Col.

FLETCHER, LOUISE: Birmingham, Al., July 1934.

FOCH, NINA: Leyden, Holland, Apr. 20, 1924.

FONDA, HENRY: Grand Island, Neb., May 16, 1905. Minn. U.

FONDA, JANE: NYC, Dec. 21, 1937. Vassar.

FONDA, PETER: NYC, Feb. 23, 1939. U. of Omaha.

FONTAINE, JOAN: Tokyo, Japan, Oct. 22, 1917.

FORD, GLENN: (Gwyllyn Samuel Newton Ford) Quebec, Can., May 1, 1916.

FORD, PAUL: Baltimore, Nov. 2, 1901. Dartmouth.

FOREST, MARK: (Lou Degni) Brooklyn, Jan. 1933.

FORREST, STEVE: Huntsville, Tex., Sept. 29. UCLA.

FORSTER, ROBERT: (Foster, Jr.) Rochester, N.Y., July 13, 1941. Rochester U.

FORSYTHE, JOHN: Penn's Grove, N.J., Jan. 29, 1918.

FOSTER, JODIE: Bronx, NY, 1963.

FOX, EDWARD: London, 1937, RADA.

FOX, JAMES: London, 1939.

FRANCIOSA, ANTHONY: NYC, Oct. 25, 1928.

FRANCIS, ANNE: Ossining, N.Y., Sept. 16.

FRANCIS, ARLENE: (Arlene Kazanjian) Boston, Oct. 20, 1908. Finch School.

FRANCIS, CONNIE: (Constance Franconero) Newark, N.J., Dec. 12, 1938.

FRANCISCUS, JAMES: Clayton, Mo., Jan. 31, 1934, Yale.

FRANCKS, DON: Vancouver, Can., Feb. 28, 1932.

FRANZ, ARTHUR: Perth Amboy, N.J., Feb. 29, 1920. Blue Ridge College.

FRANZ, EDUARD: Milwaukee, Wisc., Oct. 31, 1902.

FRAZIER, SHEILA: NYC, 1949.

FREEMAN, AL, JR.: San Antonio, Texas, 1934. CCLA.

FREEMAN, MONA: Baltimore, Md., June 9, 1926.

FREY, LEONARD: Brooklyn, Sept. 4, 1938, Neighborhood Playhouse.

FURNEAUX, YVONNE: Lille, France, 1928. Oxford U.

GABEL, MARTIN: Philadelphia, June 19, 1912. AADA.

GABIN, JEAN: Villette, France, May 17, 1904.

GABOR, EVA: Budapest, Hungary, Feb. 11, 1925.

GABOR, ZSA ZSA: (Sari Gabor) Budapest, Hungary, Feb. 6, 1923.

GAM, RITA: Pittsburgh, Pa., Apr. 2, 1928.

GARBER, VICTOR: Montreal, Can., Mar. 16, 1949.

GARBO, GRETA: (Greta Gustafson) Stockholm, Sweden, Sept. 18, 1906.

GARDENIA, VINCENT: Naples, Italy, Jan. 7, 1922.

GARDINER, REGINALD: Wimbledon, Eng., Feb. 1903. RADA.

GARDNER, AVA: Smithfield, N.C., Dec. 24, 1922. Atlantic Christian College.

GARFIELD, ALLEN: Newark, N.J., Nov. 22, 1939. Actors Studio.

GARNER, JAMES: (James Baumgarner) Norman, Okla., Apr. 7, 1928. Okla. U.

GARNER, PEGGY ANN: Canton, Ohio, Feb. 3, 1932.

GARR, TERI: Lakewood, Ohio, 1952.

GARRETT, BETTY: St. Joseph, Mo., May 23, 1919. Annie Wright Seminary.

GARRISON, SEAN: NYC, Oct. 19, 1937.

GARSON, GREER: Ireland, Sept. 29, 1908.

GASSMAN, VITTORIO: Genoa, Italy, Sept. 1, 1922. Rome Academy of Dramatic Art.

GAVIN, JOHN: Los Angeles, Apr. 8, 1935. Stanford U.

GAYNOR, JANET: Philadelphia, Oct. 6, 1906.

GAYNOR, MITZI: (Francesca Marlene Von Gerber) Chicago, Sept. 4, 1930.

GAZZARA, BEN: NYC, Aug. 28, 1930.

GEER, WILL: Frankfort, Ind., Mar. 9, 1902, Columbia.

GEESON, JUDY: Arundel, Eng., Sept. 10, 1948, Corona.

GENN, LEO: London, Aug. 9, 1905. Cambridge.

GEORGE, CHIEF DAN: (Geswanouth Slaholt) North Vancouver, Can., June 24, 1899.

GHOLSON, JULIE: Birmingham, Ala., June 4, 1958.

Lee Grant   **Harry Guardino**   **Joan Hackett**   **Richard Harris**   **Eileen Heckart**

GIANNINI, GIANCARLO: Spezia, Italy, Aug. 1, 1942; Rome Acad. of Drama.

GIELGUD, JOHN: London, Apr. 14, 1904. RADA.

GILLMORE, MARGALO: London, May 31, 1897. AADA.

GILMORE, VIRGINIA: (Sherman Poole) Del Monte, Calif., July 26, 1919. U. of Calif.

GINGOLD, HERMIONE: London, Dec. 9, 1897.

GISH, LILLIAN: Springfield, Ohio, Oct. 14, 1896.

GLEASON, JACKIE: Brooklyn, Feb. 26, 1916.

GODDARD, PAULETTE: (Levy) Great Neck, N.Y., June 3, 1911.

GONZALES-GONZALEZ, PEDRO: Aguilares, Tex., Dec. 21, 1926.

GORDON, GALE: (Aldrich) NYC, Feb. 2, 1906.

GORDON, RUTH: (Jones) Wollaston, Mass., Oct. 30, 1896. AADA.

GORING, MARIUS: Newport, Isle of Wright; 1912; Cambridge; Old Vic.

GORMAN, CLIFF: Jamaica, NY, Oct. 13, 1936, NYU.

GOULD, ELLIOTT: (Goldstein); Bklyn, Aug. 29, 1938. Columbia U.

GOULET, ROBERT: Lawrence, Mass., Nov. 26, 1933. Edmonton.

GRAHAME, GLORIA: (Gloria Grahame Hallward) Los Angeles, Nov. 28, 1929.

GRANGER, FARLEY: San Jose, Calif., July 1, 1925.

GRANGER, STEWART: (James Stewart) London, May 6, 1913. Webber-Douglas School of Acting.

GRANT, CARY: (Archibald Alexander Leach) Bristol, Eng., Jan. 18, 1904.

GRANT, KATHRYN: (Olive Grandstaff) Houston, Tex., Nov. 25, 1933. UCLA.

GRANT, LEE: NYC, Oct. 31, 1929, Juilliard.

GRANVILLE, BONITA: NYC, Feb. 2, 1923.

GRAVES, PETER: (Aurness) Minneapolis, Mar. 18, 1926. U. of Minn.

GRAY, COLEEN: (Doris Jensen) Staplehurst, Neb., Oct. 23, 1922. Hamline U.

GRAYSON, KATHRYN: (Zelma Hedrick) Winston-Salem, N.C., Feb. 9, 1923.

GREENE, LORNE: Ottawa, Can., Feb. 12, 1915.

GREENE, RICHARD: Plymouth, Eng., Aug. 25, 1918. Cardinal Vaughn School.

GREENWOOD, JOAN: London, 1919. RADA.

GREER, JANE: Washington, D.C., Sept. 9, 1924.

GREER, MICHAEL: Galesburg, Ill., Apr. 20, 1943.

GREY, JOEL: (Katz) Cleveland, O., Apr. 11, 1932.

GREY, VIRGINIA: Los Angeles, Mar. 22, 1923.

GRIEM, HELMUT: Hamburg, Ger. UHamburg.

GRIFFITH, ANDY: Mt. Airy, N.C., June 1, 1926. U.N.C.

GRIFFITH, HUGH: Marian Glas, Anglesey, N. Wales, May 30, 1912.

GRIFFITH, MELANIE: NYC, Aug. 9, 1957. Pierce Col.

GRIMES, GARY: San Francisco, June 2, 1955.

GRIMES, TAMMY: Lynn, Mass., Jan. 30, 1934, Stephens Col.

GRIZZARD, GEORGE: Roanoke Rapids, N.C., Apr. 1, 1928. U.N.C.

GRODIN, CHARLES: Pittsburgh, Pa., Apr. 21, 1935.

GUARDINO, HARRY: Brooklyn, Dec. 23, 1925, Haaren High.

GUINNESS, ALEC: London, Apr. 2, 1914. Pembroke Lodge School.

GWILLIM, DAVID: Plymouth, Eng., Dec. 15, 1948, RADA.

HACKETT, BUDDY: (Leonard Hacker) Brooklyn, Aug. 31, 1924.

HACKETT, JOAN: NYC, May 1, Actors Studio.

HACKMAN, GENE: San Bernardino, Jan. 30, 1931.

HADDON, DALE: Montreal, Can., May 26, 1949, Neighborhood Playhouse.

HALE, BARBARA: DeKalb, Ill., Apr. 18, 1922. Chicago Academy of Fine Arts.

HAMILTON, GEORGE: Memphis, Tenn., Aug. 12, 1939. Hackley.

HAMILTON, MARGARET: Cleveland, Ohio, Dec. 9, 1902. Hathaway-Brown School.

HAMILTON, NEIL: Lynn, Mass., Sept. 9, 1899.

HAMPSHIRE, SUSAN: London, May 12, 1941.

HARDIN, TY: (Orison Whipple Hungerford II) NYC, 1930.

HARDING, ANN: (Dorothy Walton Gatley) Fort Sam Houston, Texas, Aug. 17, 1904.

HARRINGTON, PAT: NYC, Aug. 13, 1929, Fordham U.

HARRIS, BARBARA: (Sandra Markowitz) Evanston, Ill., 1937.

HARRIS, JULIE: Grosse Pointe, Mich., Dec. 2, 1925. Yale Drama School.

HARRIS, RICHARD: Limerick, Ire., Oct. 1, 1930. London Acad.

HARRIS, ROSEMARY: Ashby, Eng., Sept. 19, 1930. RADA

HARRISON, NOEL: London, Jan. 29, 1936.

HARRISON, REX: Huyton, Cheshire, Eng., Mar. 5, 1908.

HARTMAN, DAVID: Pawtucket, RI., May 19. Duke U.

HARTMAN, ELIZABETH: Youngstown, O., Dec. 23, 1941. Carnegie Tech.

HAVER, JUNE: Rock Island, Ill., June 10, 1926.

HAVOC, JUNE: (June Hovick) Seattle, Wash., Nov. 8, 1916.

HAWN, GOLDIE: Washington, DC, Nov. 21, 1945.

HAYDEN, LINDA: Stanmore, Eng., Aida Foster School.

HAYDEN, STERLING: (John Hamilton) Montclair, N.J., March 26, 1916.

HAYES, HELEN: (Helen Brown) Washington, D.C., Oct. 10, 1900. Sacred Heart Convent.

HAYES, MARGARET: (Maggie) Baltimore, Dec. 5, 1925.

HAYWORTH, RITA: (Margarita Cansino) NYC, Oct. 17, 1919.

HEATHERTON, JOEY: NYC, Sept. 14, 1944.

HECKART, EILEEN: Columbus, Ohio, Mar. 29, 1919. Ohio State U.

HEDISON, DAVID: Providence, R.I., May 20, 1929. Brown U.

HEMMINGS, DAVID: Guilford, Eng.; Nov. 18, 1938.

HENDERSON, MARCIA: Andover, Mass., July 22, 1932. AADA.

HENDRIX, WANDA: Jacksonville, Fla., Nov. 3, 1928.

HENDRY, GLORIA: Jacksonville, Fla., 1949.

HENREID, PAUL: Trieste, Jan. 10, 1908.

HENRY, BUCK: (Zuckerman) NYC, 1931; Dartmouth.

HEPBURN, AUDREY: Brussels, Belgium, May 4, 1929.

HEPBURN, KATHARINE: Hartford, Conn., Nov. 8, 1909. Bryn Mawr.

HESTON, CHARLTON: Evanston, Ill., Oct. 4, 1924. Northwestern U.

HEYWOOD, ANNE: (Violet Pretty) Birmingham, Eng., Dec. 11, 1933.

Hal Holbrook	Celeste Holm	Page Johnson	Katy Jurado	Richard Jordan

HICKMAN, DARRYL: Hollywood, Cal., July 28, 1931. Loyola U.

HICKMAN, DWAYNE: Los Angeles, May 18, 1934. Loyola.

HILL, STEVEN: Seattle, Wash., Feb. 24, 1922. U. Wash.

HILL, TERENCE: (Mario Giotti) Venice, Italy, 1941, URome)

HILLER, WENDY: Bramhall, Cheshire, Eng., Aug. 15, 1912. Winceby House School.

HOFFMAN, DUSTIN: Los Angeles, Aug. 8, 1937. Pasadena Playhouse.

HOLBROOK, HAL: (Harold) Cleveland, O., Feb. 17, 1925. Denison.

HOLDEN, WILLIAM: O'Fallon, Ill., Apr. 17, 1918. Pasadena Jr. Coll.

HOLLIMAN, EARL: Tennesas Swamp, Delhi, La., Sept. 11, UCLA.

HOLLOWAY, STANLEY: London, Oct. 1, 1890.

HOLM, CELESTE: NYC, Apr. 29, 1919.

HOMEIER, SKIP: (George Vincent Homeier) Chicago, Oct. 5, 1930. UCLA.

HOMOLKA, OSCAR: Vienna, Aug. 12, 1898. Vienna Dramatic Academy.

HOOKS, ROBERT: Washington, D.C., Apr. 18, 1937. Temple.

HOPE, BOB: London, May 26, 1904.

HOPPER, DENNIS: Dodge City, Kan., May 17, 1936.

HORNE, LENA: Brooklyn, June 30, 1917.

HORTON, ROBERT: Los Angeles, July 29, 1924. UCLA.

HOUGHTON, KATHARINE: Hartford, Conn., Mar. 10, 1945. Sarah Lawrence.

HOUSER, JERRY: Los Angeles, July 14, 1952; Valley Jr. Col.

HOUSEMAN, JOHN: Bucharest, Sept. 22, 1902.

HOWARD, KEN: El Centro, Cal., Mar. 28, 1944, Yale.

HOWARD, RON: Duncan, Okla., Mar. 1, 1954.

HOWARD, RONALD: Norwood, Eng., Apr. 7, 1918. Jesus College.

HOWARD, TREVOR: Kent, Eng., Sept. 29, 1916. RADA.

HOWES, SALLY ANN: London, July 20, 1934.

HUDSON, ROCK: (Roy Scherer Fitzgerald) Winnetka, Ill., Nov. 17, 1925.

HUGHES, BARNARD: Bedford Hills, NY, July 16, 1915, Manhattan Col.

HUNNICUTT, ARTHUR: Gravelly, Ark., Feb. 17, 1911. Ark. State.

HUNNICUTT, GAYLE: Ft. Worth, Tex., Feb. 6, 1943, UCLA.

HUNT, MARSHA: Chicago, Oct. 17, 1917.

HUNTER, IAN: Cape Town, S.A., June 13, 1900. St. Andrew's Col.

HUNTER, KIM: (Janet Cole) Detroit, Nov. 12, 1922.

HUNTER, TAB: (Arthur Galien) NYC, July 11, 1931.

HUSSEY, RUTH: Providence , R.I., Oct. 30, 1917. U. of Mich.

HUSTON, JOHN: Nevada, Mo., Aug. 5, 1906.

HUTTON, BETTY: (Betty Thornberg) Battle Creek, Mich., Feb. 26, 1921.

HUTTON, LAUREN: (Mary): Charleston, S.C., Nov. 17, 1943. Newcomb Col.

HUTTON, ROBERT: (Winne) Kingston, N.Y., June 11, 1920. Blair Academy.

HYDE-WHITE, WILFRID: Gloucestershire, Eng., May 13, 1903. RADA.

HYER, MARTHA: Fort Worth, Tex., Aug. 10, 1930. Northwestern U.

IRELAND, JOHN: Vancouver, B.C., Can., Jan. 30, 1915.

IVES, BURL: Hunt Township, Ill., June 14, 1909. Charleston Ill. Teachers College.

JACKSON, ANNE: Alleghany, Pa., Sept. 3, 1926. Neighborhood Playhouse.

JACKSON, GLENDA: Hoylake, Cheshire, Eng., May 9, 1936. RADA.

JACOBI, LOU: Toronto, Can., Dec. 28, 1913.

JACOBY, SCOTT: Chicago, Nov. 19, 1956.

JAECKEL, RICHARD: Long Beach, N.Y., Oct. 10, 1926.

JAFFE, SAM: NYC, Mar. 8, 1898.

JAGGER, DEAN: Lima, Ohio, Nov. 7, 1903. Wabash College.

JANSSEN, DAVID: (David Meyer) Naponee, Neb., Mar. 27, 1930.

JARMAN, CLAUDE, JR.: Nashville, Tenn., Sept. 27, 1934.

JASON, RICK: NYC, May 21, 1926. AADA.

JEAN, GLORIA: (Gloria Jean Schoonover) Buffalo, N.Y. Apr. 14, 1928.

JEFFREYS, ANNE: (Carmichael) Goldsboro, N.C., Jan. 26, 1923. Anderson College.

JEFFRIES, LIONEL: London, 1927, RADA.

JERGENS, ADELE: Brooklyn, Nov. 26, 1922.

JESSEL, GEORGE: NYC, Apr. 3, 1898.

JOHNS, GLYNIS: Durban, S. Africa, Oct. 5, 1923.

JOHNSON, CELIA: Richmond, Surrey, Eng., Dec. 18, 1908. RADA.

JOHNSON, PAGE: Welch, W. Va., Aug. 25, 1930. Ithaca.

JOHNSON, RAFER: Hillsboro, Tex., Aug. 18, 1935. UCLA.

JOHNSON, RICHARD: Essex, Eng., 1927. RADA.

JOHNSON, VAN: Newport, R.I., Aug. 28, 1916.

JONES, CAROLYN: Amarillo, Tex., Apr. 28, 1933.

JONES, CHRISTOPHER: Jackson, Tenn., Aug. 18, 1941, Actors Studio.

JONES, DEAN: Morgan County, Ala., Jan. 25, 1936. Ashburn College.

JONES, JACK: Bel-Air, Calif., Jan. 14, 1938.

JONES, JAMES EARL: Arkabutla, Miss., Jan 17, 1931. U. Mich.

JONES, JENNIFER: (Phyllis Isley) Tulsa, Okla., Mar. 2, 1919. AADA.

JONES, SHIRLEY: Smithton, Pa., March 31, 1934.

JONES, TOM: (Thomas Jones Woodward) Pontypridd, Wales, June 7, 1940.

JORDAN, RICHARD: NYC, July 19, 1938, Harvard.

JORY, VICTOR: Dawson City, Can., Nov. 28, 1902. CalU.

JOURDAN, LOUIS: Marseilles, France, June 18, 1921.

JURADO, KATY: (Maria Christina Jurado Garcia) Guadalajara, Mex., 1927.

KAHN, MADELINE: Boston, Mass., Sept. 29, 1942, Hofstra U.

KANE, CAROL: Cleveland, O., 1952.

KASZNAR, KURT: Vienna, Aug. 12, 1913. Gymnasium, Vienna.

KAUFMANN, CHRISTINE: Lansdorf, Graz, Austria, Jan. 11, 1945.

KAYE, DANNY: (David Daniel Kominski) Brooklyn, Jan. 18, 1913.

KAYE, STUBBY: NYC, Nov. 11, 1918.

KEACH, STACY: Savannah, Ga., June 2, 1941; UCal., Yale.

| Sally Kellerman | Aron Kincaid | Margot Kidder | Peter Lawford | Janet Leigh |

KEATON, DIANE: (Hall) Los Angeles, Ca., Jan. 5, 1946. Neighborhood Playhouse.

KEDROVA, LILA: Greece, 1918.

KEEL, HOWARD: (Harold Keel) Gillespie, Ill., Apr. 13, 1919.

KEELER, RUBY: (Ethel) Halifax, N.S. Aug. 25, 1909.

KEITH, BRIAN: Bayonne, N.J., Nov. 14, 1921.

KELLERMAN, SALLY: Long Beach, Cal., June 2, 1938; Actors Studio West.

KELLY, GENE: Pittsburgh, Aug. 23, 1912. U. of Pittsburgh.

KELLY, GRACE: Philadelphia, Nov. 12, 1929. AADA.

KELLY, JACK: Astoria, N.Y., Sept. 16, 1927. UCLA.

KELLY, NANCY: Lowell, Mass., Mar. 25, 1921. Bentley School.

KEMP, JEREMY: Chesterfield, Eng., 1935, Central Sch.

KENNEDY, ARTHUR: Worcester, Mass., Feb. 17, 1914. Carnegie Tech.

KENNEDY, GEORGE: NYC, Feb. 18, 1925.

KERR, DEBORAH: Helensburgh, Scot., Sept. 30, 1921. Smale Ballet School.

KERR, JOHN: NYC, Nov. 15, 1931. Harvard, Columbia.

KHAMBATTA, PERSIS: Bombay, 1950.

KIDDER, MARGOT: Yellow Knife, Can., Oct. 17, 1948; UBC.

KIER, UDO: Germany, Oct. 14, 1944.

KILEY, RICHARD: Chicago, Mar. 31, 1922. Loyola.

KINCAID, ARON: (Norman Neale Williams III) Los Angeles, June 15, 1943. UCLA.

KING, ALAN: (Irwin Kniberg) Brooklyn, Dec. 26, 1927.

KITT, EARTHA: North, S.C., Jan. 26, 1928.

KLEMPERER, WERNER: Cologne, Mar. 22, 1920.

KNIGHT, ESMOND: East Sheen, Eng., May 4, 1906.

KNIGHT, SHIRLEY: Goessel, Kan., July 5. Wichita U.

KNOWLES, PATRIC: (Reginald Lawrence Knowles) Horsforth, Eng., Nov. 11, 1911.

KNOX, ALEXANDER: Strathroy, Ont., Can., Jan. 16, 1907.

KNOX, ELYSE: Hartford, Conn., Dec. 14, 1917. Traphagen School.

KOHNER, SUSAN: Los Angeles, Nov. 11, 1936. U. of Calif.

KORVIN, CHARLES: (Geza Korvin Darpathi) Czechoslovakia, Nov. 21. Sorbonne.

KOSLECK, MARTIN: Barkotzen, Ger., Mar. 24, 1914. Max Reinhardt School.

KOTTO, YAPHET: NYC, Nov. 15, 1937.

KREUGER, KURT: St. Moritz, Switz., July 23, 1917. U. of London.

KRISTOFFERSON, KRIS: 1936, Brownsville, Tx., Pomona Col.

KRUGER, HARDY: Berlin, Ger., April. 12, 1928.

KUNTSMANN, DORIS: Hamburg, 1944.

KWAN, NANCY: Hong Kong, May 19, 1939. Royal Ballet.

LACY, JERRY: Sioux City, I., Mar. 27, 1936, LACC.

LADD, DIANE: (Ladnier) France, Nov. 29, 1932.

LAMARR, HEDY: (Hedwig Kiesler) Vienna, Sept. 11, 1915.

LAMAS, FERNANDO: Buenos Aires, Jan. 9, 1920.

LAMB, GIL: Minneapolis, June 14, 1906. U. of Minn.

LAMOUR, DOROTHY: Dec. 10, 1914. Spence School.

LANCASTER, BURT: NYC, Nov. 2, 1913. NYU.

LANCHESTER, ELSA: (Elsa Sullivan) London, Oct. 28, 1902.

LANDON, MICHAEL: (Eugene Orowitz) Collingswood, N.J., 1936.

LANE, ABBE: Brooklyn, Dec. 14, 1935.

LANGAN, GLENN: Denver, Colo., July 8, 1917.

LANGE, HOPE: Redding Ridge, Conn., Nov. 28, 1933. Reed Col.

LANGTON, PAUL: Salt Lake City, Apr. 17, 1913. Travers School of Theatre.

LANSBURY, ANGELA: London, Oct. 16, 1925. London Academy of Music.

LANSING, ROBERT: (Brown) San Diego, Cal., June 5.

LAURIE, PIPER: (Rosetta Jacobs) Detroit, Jan. 22, 1932.

LAW, JOHN PHILLIP: Hollywood, Sept. 7, 1937. Neighborhood Playhouse, UHawaii.

LAWFORD, PETER: London, Sept. 7, 1923.

LAWRENCE, BARBARA: Carnegie, Okla., Feb. 24, 1930. UCLA.

LAWRENCE, CAROL: (Laraia) Melrose Park, Ill., Sept. 5, 1935.

LAWSON, LEIGH: Atherston, Eng., July 21, 1945, RADA.

LEACHMAN, CLORIS: Des Moines, Iowa, Apr. 30, 1930. Northwestern U.

LEDERER, FRANCIS: Karlin, Prague, Czech., Nov. 6, 1906.

LEE, CHRISTOPHER: London, May 27, 1922. Wellington College.

LEE, MICHELE: (Dusiak) Los Angeles, June 24, 1942. LACC.

LEIBMAN, RON: NYC, Oct. 11, 1937, Ohio Wesleyan.

LEIGH, JANET: (Jeanette Helen Morrison) Merced, Calif., July 6, 1927. College of Pacific.

LEIGHTON, MARGARET: Barnt Green, Worcestershire, Eng., Feb. 26, 1922. Church of England Col.

LEMBECK, HARVEY: Brooklyn, Apr. 15, 1923. U. of Ala.

LEMMON, JACK: Boston, Feb. 8, 1925. Harvard.

LENZ, RICK: Springfield, Ill., Nov. 21, 1939. U. Mich.

LEONARD, SHELDON: (Bershad) NYC, Feb. 22, 1907, Syracuse U.

LEROY, PHILIPPE: Paris, Oct. 15, 1930; UParis.

LESLIE, BETHEL: NYC, Aug. 3, 1929. Breaney School.

LESLIE, JOAN: (Joan Brodell) Detroit, Jan. 26, 1925. St. Benedict's.

LESTER, MARK: Oxford, Eng., July 11, 1958.

LEVENE, SAM: NYC, 1907.

LEWIS, JERRY: Newark, N.J., Mar. 16, 1926.

LIGON, TOM: New Orleans, La., Sept. 10, 1945.

LILLIE, BEATRICE: Toronto, Can., May 29, 1898.

LINCOLN, ABBEY: (Anna Marie Woolridge) Chicago, Aug. 6, 1930.

LINDFORS, VIVECA: Uppsala, Sweden, Dec. 29, 1920. Stockholm Royal Dramatic School.

LISI, VIRNA: Rome, 1938.

LITTLE, CLEAVON: Chickasha, Okla., June 1, 1939, San Diego State.

LIVESEY, ROGER: Barry, Wales, June 25, 1906. Westminster School.

LOCKE, SONDRA: Shelbyville, Tenn., 1947.

LOCKHART, JUNE: NYC, June 15, 1925. Westlake School.

LOCKWOOD, GARY: Van Nuys, Cal., 1937.

LOCKWOOD, MARGARET: Karachi, Pakistan, Sept. 15, 1916. RADA.

LOLLOBRIGIDA, GINA: Subiaco, Italy, 1928. Rome Academy of Fine Arts.

Carol Lynley   George Maharis   Barbara McNair   Steve McQueen   Marisa Mell

LOM, HERBERT: Prague, Czechoslovakia, 1917. Prague U.

LONDON, JULIE: (Julie Peck) Santa Rosa, Calif., Sept. 26, 1926.

LOPEZ, PERRY: NYC, July 22, 1931. NYU.

LORD, JACK: (John Joseph Ryan) NYC, Dec. 30, 1928. NYU.

LOREN, SOPHIA: (Sofia Scicolone) Rome, Italy, Sept. 20, 1934.

LOUISE, TINA: (Blacker) NYC, Feb. 11, 1934. Miami U.

LOVELACE, LINDA: Bryan, Tex., 1952.

LOY, MYRNA: (Myrna Williams) Helena, Mont., Aug. 2, 1905. Westlake School.

LUND, JOHN: Rochester, N.Y., Feb. 6, 1913.

LUPINO, IDA: London, Feb. 4, 1918. RADA.

LYNDE, PAUL: Mt. Vernon, Ohio, June 13, 1926. Northwestern U.

LYNLEY, CAROL: (Jones) NYC, Feb. 13, 1942.

LYNN, JEFFREY: Auburn, Mass., 1910. Bates College.

LYON, SUE: Davenport, Iowa, July 10, 1946.

LYONS, ROBERT F.: Albany, N.Y.; AADA.

MacARTHUR, JAMES: Los Angeles, Dec. 8, 1937. Harvard.

MacGINNIS, NIALL: Dublin, Ire., Mar. 29, 1913. Dublin U.

MacGRAW, ALI: NYC, Apr. 1, 1939, Wellesley.

MacLAINE, SHIRLEY: (Beatty) Richmond, Va., Apr. 24, 1934.

MacMAHON, ALINE: McKeesport, Pa., May 3, 1899. Barnard College.

MacMURRAY, FRED: Kankakee, Ill., Aug. 30, 1908. Carroll Col.

MACNEE, PATRICK: London, Feb. 1922.

MacRAE, GORDON: East Orange, N.J., Mar. 12, 1921.

MADISON, GUY: (Robert Moseley) Bakersfield, Calif., Jan. 19, 1922. Bakersfield Jr. College.

MAHARIS, GEORGE: Astoria, N.Y., Sept. 1, 1928. Actors Studio.

MAHONEY, JOCK: (Jacques O'-Mahoney) Chicago, Feb. 7, 1919. U. of Iowa.

MALDEN, KARL: (Mladen Sekulovich) Gary, Ind., Mar. 22, 1914.

MALONE, DOROTHY: Chicago, Jan. 30, 1925. S. Methodist U.

MARAIS, JEAN: Cherbourg, France, Dec. 11, 1913. St. Germain.

MARGO: (Maria Marguerita Guadalupe Boldoay Castilla) Mexico City, May 10, 1918.

MARGOLIN, JANET: NYC, July 25, 1943. Walden School.

MARIN, JACQUES: Paris, Sept. 9, 1919. Conservatoire National.

MARLOWE, HUGH: (Hugh Hipple) Philadelphia, Jan. 30, 1914.

MARSHALL, BRENDA: (Ardis Anderson Gaines) Isle of Negros, P.I., Sept. 29, 1915. Texas State College.

MARSHALL, E. G.: Owatonna, Minn., June 18, 1910. U. of Minn.

MARSHALL, WILLIAM: Gary, Ind., Aug. 19, 1924, NYU.

MARTIN, DEAN: (Dino Crocetti) Steubenville, Ohio, June 17, 1917.

MARTIN, MARY: Weatherford, Tex., Dec. 1, 1914. Ward-Belmont School.

MARTIN, STROTHER: Kokomo, Ind., 1919, UMich.

MARTIN, TONY: (Alfred Norris) Oakland, Cal., Dec. 25, 1913. St. Mary's College.

MARVIN, LEE: NYC, Feb. 19, 1924.

MARX, GROUCHO: (Julius Marx) NYC, Oct. 2, 1895.

MASON, JAMES: Huddersfield, Yorkshire, Eng., May 15, 1909. Cambridge.

MASON, MARSHA: St. Louis, Mo., Apr. 3, 1942, Webster Col.

MASON, PAMELA: (Pamela Kellino) Westgate, Eng., Mar. 10, 1918.

MASSEN, OSA: Copenhagen, Den., Jan. 13, 1916.

MASSEY, DANIEL: London, Oct. 10, 1933. Eaton and King's Col.

MASSEY, RAYMOND: Toronto, Can., Aug. 30, 1896. Oxford.

MASTERSON, PETER: Angleton, Tex., June 1, 1934; Rice U.

MASTROIANNI, MARCELLO: Fontana Liri, Italy, Sept. 28, 1924.

MATTHAU, WALTER: (Matuschanskayasky) NYC, Oct. 1, 1920.

MATURE, VICTOR: Louisville, Ky., Jan. 29, 1916.

MAY, ELAINE: (Berlin) Philadelphia, Apr. 21, 1932.

MAYEHOFF, EDDIE: Baltimore, July 7, Yale.

McCALLUM, DAVID: Scotland, Sept. 19, 1933. Chapman Coll.

McCAMBRIDGE, MERCEDES: Jolliet, Ill., March 17, 1918, Mundelein College.

McCARTHY, KEVIN: Seattle, Wash., Feb. 15, 1914. Minn. U.

McCLORY, SEAN: Dublin, Ire., March 8, 1924. U. of Galway.

McCLURE, DOUG: Glendale, Calif., May 11, 1938. UCLA.

McCOWEN, ALEC: Tunbridge Wells, Eng., May 26, 1925, RADA.

McCREA, JOEL: Los Angeles, Nov. 5, 1905. Pomona College.

McDERMOTT, HUGH: Edinburgh, Scot., Mar. 20, 1908.

McDEVITT, RUTH: Coldwater, Mich., Sept. 13, 1895; AADA.

McDOWALL, RODDY: London, Sept. 17, 1928. St. Joseph's.

McDOWELL, MALCOLM: (Taylor) Leeds, Eng., June 13, 1943.

McENERY, PETER: Walsall, Eng., Feb. 21, 1940.

McGAVIN, DARREN: Spokane, Wash., May 7, 1922. College of Pacific.

McGUIRE, BIFF: New Haven, Conn., Oct. 25, 1926, Mass. State Col.

McGUIRE, DOROTHY: Omaha, Neb., June 14, 1919.

McKAY, GARDNER: NYC, June 10, 1932. Cornell.

McKENNA, VIRGINIA: London, June 7, 1931.

McKUEN, ROD: Oakland, Cal., Apr. 29, 1933.

McLERIE, ALLYN ANN: Grand Mere, Can., Dec. 1, 1926.

McNAIR, BARBARA: Chicago, March 4, 1939. UCLA.

McNALLY, STEPHEN: (Horace McNally) NYC, July 29, Fordham U.

McNAMARA, MAGGIE: NYC, June 18. St. Catherine.

McQUEEN, BUTTERFLY: Tampa, Fla., Jan. 8, 1911. UCLA.

McQUEEN, STEVE: Slater, Mo., Mar. 24, 1932.

MEADOWS, AUDREY: Wuchang, China, 1924. St. Margaret's.

MEADOWS, JAYNE: (formerly, Jayne Cotter) Wuchang, China, Sept. 27, 1923. St. Margaret's.

MEDFORD, KAY: (Maggie O'Regin) NYC, Sept. 14, 1920.

MEDWIN, MICHAEL: London, 1925. Instut Fischer.

MEEKER, RALPH: (Ralph Rathgeber) Minneapolis, Nov. 21, 1920. Northwestern U.

MELL, MARISA: Vienna, Austria, 1942.

MERCOURI, MELINA: Athens, Greece, Oct. 18, 1915.

MEREDITH, BURGESS: Cleveland, Ohio, Nov. 16, 1909. Amherst.

MEREDITH, LEE: (Judi Lee Sauls) Oct. 1947. AADA.

MERKEL, UNA: Covington, Ky., Dec. 10, 1903.

| Jason Miller | Dina Merrill | Greg Morris | Merle Oberon | Don Nute |

MERMAN, ETHEL: (Ethel Zimmerman) Astoria, N.Y., Jan. 16, 1909.

MERRILL, DINA: (Nedinia Hutton) NYC, Dec. 9, 1925. AADA.

MERRILL, GARY: Hartford, Conn., Aug. 2, 1915. Bowdoin, Trinity.

MICHELL, KEITH: Adelaide, Aus., Dec. 1, 1926.

MIFUNE, TOSHIRO: Tsingtao, China, Apr. 1, 1920.

MILES, SARAH: Ingatestone, Eng., Dec. 31, 1943. RADA.

MILES, SYLVIA: NYC, Sept. 9, 1932.

MILES, VERA: (Ralston) Boise City, Okla., Aug. 23, 1929. UCLA.

MILLAND, RAY: (Reginald Trustcott-Jones) Neath, Wales, Jan. 3, 1908. King's College.

MILLER, ANN: (Lucille Ann Collier) Chireno, Tex., Apr. 12, 1919. Lawler Professional School.

MILLER, JASON: Long Island City, NY, Apr. 22, 1939, Catholic U.

MILLER, MARVIN: St. Louis, July 18, 1913. Washington U.

MILLS, HAYLEY: London, Apr. 18, 1946. Elmhurst School.

MILLS, JOHN: Suffolk, Eng., Feb. 22, 1908.

MILNER, MARTIN: Detroit, Mich., 1933.

MIMIEUX, YVETTE: Los Angeles, Jan. 8, 1941. Hollywood High.

MINNELLI, LIZA: Los Angeles, Mar. 12, 1946.

MIRANDA, ISA: (Isabella Sampietro) Milan, Italy, July 5, 1917.

MITCHELL, CAMERON: Dalastown, Pa., Nov. 1918. N.Y. Theatre School.

MITCHELL, JAMES: Sacramento, Calif., Feb. 29, 1920. LACC.

MITCHUM, JAMES: Los Angeles, Cal., May 8, 1941.

MITCHUM, ROBERT: Bridgeport, Conn., Aug. 6, 1917.

MONTALBAN, RICARDO: Mexico City, Nov. 25, 1920.

MONTAND, YVES: (Yves Montand Livi) Mansummano, Tuscany, Oct. 13, 1921.

MONTGOMERY, BELINDA: Winnipeg, Can., July 23, 1950.

MONTGOMERY, ELIZABETH: Los Angeles, Apr. 15, 1933. AADA.

MONTGOMERY, GEORGE: (George Letz) Brady, Mont., Aug. 29, 1916. U. of Mont.

MONTGOMERY, ROBERT: (Henry, Jr.) Beacon, N.Y., May 21, 1904.

MOOR, BILL: Toledo, O., July 13, 1931, Northwestern.

MOORE, CONSTANCE: Sioux City, Iowa, Jan. 18, 1922.

MOORE, DICK: Los Angeles, Sept. 12, 1925.

MOORE, KIERON: County Cork, Ire., 1925. St. Mary's College.

MOORE, MARY TYLER: Brooklyn, Dec. 29, 1937.

MOORE, ROGER: London, Oct. 14, 1927. RADA.

MOORE, TERRY: (Helen Koford) Los Angeles, Jan. 7, 1929.

MOORE, KENNETH: Gerrards Cross, Eng., Sept. 20, 1914. Victoria College.

MOREAU, JEANNE: Paris, Jan. 3, 1928.

MORENO, RITA: (Rosita Alverio) Humacao, P.R., Dec. 11, 1931.

MORGAN, DENNIS: (Stanley Morner) Prentice, Wisc., Dec. 10, 1920. Carroll College.

MORGAN, HARRY (HENRY): (Harry Bratsburg) Detroit, Apr. 10, 1915. U. of Chicago.

MORGAN, MICHELE: (Simone Roussel) Paris, Feb. 29, 1920. Paris Dramatic School.

MORIARTY, MICHAEL: Detroit, Mich., Apr. 5, 1941. Dartmouth.

MORISON, PATRICIA: NYC, 1919.

MORLEY, ROBERT: Wiltshire, Eng., May 26, 1908. RADA.

MORRIS, GREG: CLeveland, O., 1934. Ohio State.

MORRIS, HOWARD: NYC, Sept. 4, 1919, NYU.

MORROW, VIC: Bronx, N.Y., Feb. 14, 1932. Fla. Southern College.

MORSE, ROBERT: Newton, Mass., May 18, 1931.

MOSTEL, ZERO: Brooklyn, Feb. 28, 1915. CCNY.

MULLIGAN, RICHARD: NYC, Nov. 13, 1932.

MURPHY, GEORGE: New Haven, Conn., July 4, 1902. Yale.

MURRAY, DON: Hollywood, July 31, 1929. AADA.

MURRAY, KEN: (Don Court) NYC, July 14, 1903.

NADER, GEORGE: Pasadena, Calif., Oct. 19, 1921. Occidental College.

NAPIER, ALAN: Birmingham, Eng., Jan. 7, 1903. Birmingham University.

NATWICK, MILDRED: Baltimore, June 19, 1908. Bryn Mawr.

NAUGHTON, JAMES: Middletown, Conn., Dec. 6, 1945. Yale.

NEAL, PATRICIA: Packard, Ky., Jan. 20, 1926. Northwestern U.

NEFF, HILDEGARDE: (Hildegard Knef) Ulm, Ger., Dec. 28, 1925. Berlin Art Academy.

NELSON, BARRY: (Robert Nielsen) Oakland, Cal., 1925.

NELSON, DAVID: NYC, Oct. 24, 1936. USC.

NELSON, GENE: (Gene Berg) Seattle, Wash., Mar. 24, 1920.

NELSON, HARRIET HILLIARD: (Peggy Lou Snyder) Des Moines, Iowa, July 18.

NELSON, LORI: (Dixie Kay Nelson) Santa Fe, N.M., Aug. 15, 1933.

NELSON, RICK: (Eric Hilliard Nelson) Teaneck, N.J., May 8, 1940.

NESBITT, CATHLEEN: Cheshire, Eng., Nov. 24, 1889. Victoria College.

NEWLEY, ANTHONY: Hackney, London, Sept. 21, 1931.

NEWMAN, BARRY: Boston, Ma., Mar. 26, 1938. Brandeis U.

NEWMAN, PAUL: Cleveland, Ohio, Jan. 26, 1925. Yale.

NEWMAN, SCOTT: NYC 1954; Washington Col.

NEWMAR, JULIE: (Newmeyer) Los Angeles, Aug. 16, 1935.

NICHOLS, MIKE: (Michael Igor Peschkowsky) Berlin, Nov. 1931. U. Chicago.

NICHOLSON, JACK: Neptune, N.J., Apr. 22, 1937.

NICOL, ALEX: Ossining, N.Y., Jan. 20, 1919. Actors Studio.

NIELSEN, LESLIE: Regina, Saskatchewan, Can., Feb. 11, 1926. Neighborhood Playhouse.

NIVEN, DAVID: Kirriemuir, Scot., Mar. 1, 1910. Sandhurst College.

NOLAN, LLOYD: San Francisco, Aug. 11, 1902. Stanford U.

NORRIS, CHRISTOPHER: NYC, Oct. 7, 1943; Lincoln Square Acad.

NORTH, HEATHER: Pasadena, Cal., Dec. 13, 1950; Actors Workshop.

NORTH, SHEREE: (Dawn Bethel) Los Angeles, Jan. 17, 1933. Hollywood High.

NOVAK, KIM: (Marilyn Novak) Chicago, Feb. 18, 1933. LACC.

NUGENT, ELLIOTT: Dover, Ohio, Sept. 20, 1900. Ohio State U.

NUTE, DON: Connellsville, Pa., Mar. 13, Denver U.

NUYEN, FRANCE: (Vannga) Marseilles, France, July 31, 1939. Beaux Arts School.

OATES, WARREN: Depoy, Ky., July 5, 1928.

OBERON, MERLE: (Estelle Merle O'Brien Thompson) Tasmania, Feb. 19, 1911.

| Hugh O'Brian | Valerie Perrine | Brock Peters | Rossana Podesta | Vincent Price |

O'BRIAN, HUGH: (Hugh J. Krampe) Rochester, N.Y., Apr. 19, 1928. Cincinnati U.

O'BRIEN, CLAY: Ray, Ariz., May 6, 1961.

O'BRIEN, EDMOND: NYC, Sept. 10, 1915. Fordham, Neighborhood Playhouse.

O'BRIEN, MARGARET: (Angela Maxine O'Brien) Los Angeles, Jan. 15, 1937.

O'BRIEN, PAT: Milwaukee, Nov. 11, 1899. Marquette U.

O'CONNELL, ARTHUR: NYC, Mar. 29, 1908. St. John's.

O'CONNOR, CARROLL: Bronx, N.Y., Aug. 2, 1925; Dublin National Univ.

O'CONNOR, DONALD: Chicago, Aug. 28, 1925.

O'CONNOR, GLYNNIS: NYC, Nov. 19, 1956, NYSU.

O'HARA, MAUREEN: (Maureen FitzSimons) Dublin, Ire., Aug. 17, 1921. Abbey School.

O'HERLIHY, DAN: Wexford, Ire., May 1, 1919. National U.

OLIVIER, LAURENCE: Dorking, Eng., May 22, 1907. Oxford.

OLSON, NANCY: Milwaukee, Wisc., July 14, UCLA.

O'NEAL, PATRICK: Ocala, Fla., Sept. 26, 1927. U. of Fla.

O'NEAL, RON: Utica, NY, Sept. 1, 1937, Ohio State.

O'NEAL, RYAN: Los Angeles, Apr. 20, 1941.

O'NEAL, TATUM: Los Angeles, Nov. 5, 1963.

O'NEIL, TRICIA: Shreveport, La., Mar. 11, 1945, Baylor U.

O'NEILL, JENNIFER: Rio de Janeiro, Feb. 20, 1949; Neighborhood Playhouse.

O'SULLIVAN, MAUREEN: Byle, Ire., May 17, 1911. Sacred Heart Convent.

O'TOOLE, PETER: Connemara, Ireland, Aug. 2, 1932. RADA.

OWEN, REGINALD: Wheathampstead, Eng., Aug. 5, 1887. Tree's Academy.

PACINO, AL: NYC, Apr. 25, 1940.

PAGE, GERALDINE: Kirksville, Mo., Nov. 22, 1924. Goodman School.

PAGET, DEBRA: (Debralee Griffin) Denver, Aug. 19, 1933.

PAIGE, JANIS: (Donna Mae Jaden) Tacoma, Wash., Sept. 16, 1922.

PALANCE, JACK: (Walter Palanuik) Lattimer, Pa., Feb. 18, 1920. U. N.C.

PALMER, BETSY: East Chicago, Ind., Nov. 1, 1929. DePaul U.

PALMER, GREGG: (Palmer Lee) San Francisco, Jan. 25, 1927. U. Utah.

PALMER, LILLI: Posen, Austria, May 24, 1914. Ilka Gruning School.

PALMER, MARIA: Vienna, Sept. 5, 1924. College de Bouffement.

PAPAS, IRENE: Chiliomodion, Greece, 1929.

PARKER, ELEANOR: Cedarville, Ohio, June 26, 1922. Pasadena Playhouse.

PARKER, FESS: Fort Worth, Tex., Aug. 16, 1927. USC.

PARKER, JEAN: (Mae Green) Deer Lodge, Mont., Aug. 11, 1918.

PARKER, SUZY: (Cecelia Parker) San Antonio, Tex. Oct. 28, 1933.

PARKER, WILLARD: (Worster Van Eps) NYC, Feb. 5, 1912.

PARKINS, BARBARA: Vancouver, Can., May 22, 1945.

PARSONS, ESTELLE: Lynn, Mass. Nov. 20, 1927. Boston U.

PATRICK, DENNIS: Philadelphia, Mar. 14, 1918.

PATRICK, NIGEL: London, May 2, 1913.

PATTERSON, LEE: Vancouver, Can., 1929. Ontario College.

PAVAN, MARISA: (Marisa Pierangeli) Cagliari, Sardinia, June 19, 1932. Torquado Tasso College.

PEACH, MARY: Durban, S. Africa, 1934.

PEARSON, BEATRICE: Denison, Tex., July 27, 1920.

PECK, GREGORY: La Jolla, Calif., Apr. 5, 1916. U. of Calif.

PEPPARD, GEORGE: Detroit, Oct. 1, 1933. Carnegie Tech.

PERKINS, ANTHONY: NYC, Apr. 14, 1932. Rollins College.

PERREAU, GIGI: (Ghislaine) Los Angeles, Feb. 6, 1941.

PERRINE, VALERIE: Galveston, Tx., Sept. 3, 1946. UAriz.

PETERS, BERNADETTE: Jamaica, NY, Feb. 28, 1948.

PETERS, BROCK: NYC, July 2, 1927, CCNY.

PETERS, JEAN: (Elizabeth) Canton, Ohio, Oct. 15, 1926. Ohio State U.

PETTET, JOANNA: London, Nov. 16, 1944; Neighborhood Playhouse.

PHILLIPS, MacKENZIE: Hollywood, Ca. 1960.

PHILLIPS, MICHELLE: (Holly Gilliam) NJ, June 4, 1944.

PICERNI, PAUL: NYC, Dec. 1, 1922. Loyola U.

PICKENS, SLIM: (Louis Bert Lindley, Jr.) Kingsberg, Calif., June 29, 1919.

PICKFORD, MARY: (Gladys Mary Smith) Toronto, Can., Apr. 8, 1893.

PIDGEON, WALTER: East St. John, N.B., Can., Sept. 23, 1898.

PINE, PHILLIP: Hanford, Calif., July 16, 1925. Actors' Lab.

PLAYTEN, ALICE: NYC, Aug. 28, 1947, NYU.

PLEASENCE, DONALD: Workshop, Eng, Oct. 5, 1919. Sheffield School.

PLESHETTE, SUZANNE: NYC, Jan. 31, 1937. Syracuse U.

PLUMMER, CHRISTOPHER: Toronto, Can., Dec. 13, 1927.

PODESTA, ROSSANA: Tripoli, June 20, 1934.

POITIER, SIDNEY: Miami, Fla., Feb. 27, 1927.

POLITO, LINA: Naples, Italy, Aug. 11, 1954.

POLLARD, MICHAEL J.: Pacific, N.J., May 30, 1939.

PORTER, ERIC: London, Apr. 8, 1928, Wimbledon Col.

POWELL, ELEANOR: Springfield, Mass., Nov. 21, 1913.

POWELL, JANE: (Suzanne Burce) Portland, Ore., Apr. 1, 1929.

POWELL, WILLIAM: Pittsburgh, July 29, 1892. AADA.

POWERS, MALA: (Mary Ellen) San Francisco, Dec. 29, 1921. UCLA.

PRENTISS, PAULA: (Paula Ragusa) San Antonio, Tex., Mar. 4, 1939. Northwestern U.

PRESLE, MICHELINE: (Micheline Chassagne) Paris, Aug. 22, 1922. Rouleau Drama School.

PRESLEY, ELVIS: Tupelo, Miss., Jan. 8, 1935.

PRESNELL, HARVE: Modesto, Calif., Sept. 14, 1933. USC.

PRESTON, ROBERT: (Robert Preston Meservey) Newton Highlands, Mass., June 8, 1913. Pasadena Playhouse.

PRICE, VINCENT: St. Louis, May 27, 1911. Yale.

PRINCE, WILLIAM: Nicholas, N.Y., Jan. 26, 1913. Cornell U.

PRINCIPAL, VICTORIA: Tokyo, Jan. 3, 1945, Dade Jr. Col.

PRINZE, FREDDIE: NYC, 1954.

PROVINE, DOROTHY: Deadwood, S.D., Jan. 20, 1937. U. of Wash.

PROWSE, JULIET: Bombay, India, Sept. 25, 1936.

PRYOR, RICHARD: Peoria, Ill., Dec. 1, 1940.

PURCELL, LEE: Cherry Point, N.C., 1947; Stephens.

| Deborah Raffin | Jason Robards | Lee Remick | Cesar Romero | Susan Sarandon |

PURCELL, NOEL: Dublin, Ire., Dec. 23, 1900. Irish Christian Brothers.

PURDOM, EDMUND: Welwyn Garden City, Eng., Dec. 19, St. Ignatius College.

QUAYLE, ANTHONY: Lancashire, Eng., Sept. 7, 1913. Old Vic School.

QUINN, ANTHONY: Chihuahua, Mex., Apr. 21, 1915.

RAFFERTY, FRANCES: Sioux City, Iowa, June 16, 1922. UCLA.

RAFFIN, DEBORAH: Los Angeles, Mar. 13, 1953.

RAFT, GEORGE: NYC, 1903.

RAINES, ELLA: (Ella Wallace) Snoqualmic Falls, Wash., Aug. 6, 1921. U. of Wash.

RAMPLING, CHARLOTTE: Surmer, Eng., Feb. 5, 1946; UMadrid.

RAMSEY, LOGAN: Long Beach, Cal., Mar. 21, 1921; St. Joseph.

RANDALL, TONY: Tulsa, Okla., Feb. 26, 1920. Northwestern U.

RANDELL, RON: Sydney, Australia, Oct. 8, 1920. St. Mary's Col.

RASULALA, THALMUS: (Jack Crowder) Miami, Fla., Nov. 15, 1939. U. Redlands.

RAY, ALDO: (Aldo DeRe) Pen Argyl, Pa. Sept. 25, 1926. UCLA.

RAYE, MARTHA: (Margie Yvonne Reed) Butte, Mont., Aug. 27, 1916.

RAYMOND, GENE: (Raymond Guion) NYC, Aug. 13, 1908.

REAGAN, RONALD: Tampico, Ill., Feb. 6, 1911. Eureka College.

REASON, REX: Berlin, Ger., Nov. 30, 1928. Pasadena Playhouse.

REDFORD, ROBERT: Santa Monica, Calif., Aug. 18, 1937. AADA.

REDGRAVE, CORIN: London, July 16, 1939.

REDGRAVE, LYNN: London, Mar. 8, 1943.

REDGRAVE, MICHAEL: Bristol, Eng., Mar. 20, 1908. Cambridge.

REDGRAVE, VANESSA: London, Jan. 30, 1937.

REDMAN, JOYCE: County Mayo, Ire., 1919. RADA.

REED, DONNA: (Donna Mullenger) Denison, Iowa, Jan. 27, 1921. LACC.

REED, OLIVER: Wimbledon, Eng., Feb. 13, 1938.

REED, REX: Ft. Worth, Tex., Oct. 2, 1939, LSU.

REEMS, HARRY: Bronx, NY, 1947. UPittsburgh.

REEVES, STEVE: Glasgow, Mont., Jan. 21, 1926.

REID, ELLIOTT: NYC, Jan. 16, 1920.

REINER, CARL: NYC, Mar. 20, 1922. Georgetown.

REINER, ROBERT: NYC, 1945, UCLA.

REMICK, LEE: Quincy, Mass., Dec. 14, 1935. Barnard College.

RETTIG, TOMMY: Jackson Heights, N.Y., Dec. 10, 1941.

REVILL, CLIVE: Wellington, NZ, Apr. 18, 1930.

REYNOLDS, BURT: West Palm Beach, Fla. Feb. 11, 1936. Fla. State U.

REYNOLDS, DEBBIE: (Mary Frances Reynolds) El Paso, Tex., Apr. 1, 1932.

REYNOLDS, MARJORIE: Buhl, Idaho, Aug. 12, 1921.

RHOADES, BARBARA: Poughkeepsie, N.Y., 1947.

RICH, IRENE: Buffalo, N.Y., Oct. 13, 1897. St. Margaret's School.

RICHARDS, JEFF: (Richard Mansfield Taylor) Portland, Ore., Nov. 1. USC.

RICHARDSON, RALPH: Cheltenham, Eng., Dec. 19, 1902.

RICKLES, DON: NYC, May 8, 1926. AADA.

RIGG, DIANA: Doncaster, Eng., July 20, 1938. RADA.

ROBARDS, JASON: Chicago, July 26, 1922. AADA.

ROBERTS, TONY: NYC, Oct. 22, 1939. Northwestern U.

ROBERTS, RACHEL: Llanelly, Wales, Sept. 20, 1927. RADA.

ROBERTS, RALPH: Salisbury, NC, Aug. 17, 1922. UNC.

ROBERTSON, CLIFF: La Jolla, Calif., Sept. 9, 1925. Antioch Col.

ROBINSON, CHRIS: 1938, West Palm Beach, Fla., LACC.

ROBINSON, ROGER: Seattle, Wash., May 2, 1941; USCal.

ROBSON, FLORA: South Shields, Eng., Mar. 28, 1902. RADA.

ROCHESTER: (Eddie Anderson) Oakland, Calif., Sept. 18, 1905.

ROGERS, CHARLES "BUDDY": Olathe, Kan., Aug. 13, 1904. U. of Kan.

ROGERS, GINGER: (Virginia Katherine McMath) Independence, Mo., July 16, 1911.

ROGERS, ROY: (Leonard Slye) Cincinnati, Nov. 5, 1912.

ROGERS, WAYNE: Birmingham, Ala., Apr. 7, 1933. Princeton.

ROLAND, GILBERT: (Luis Antonio Damaso De Alonso) Juarez, Mex., Dec. 11, 1905.

ROMAN, RUTH: Boston, Dec. 23. Bishop Lee Dramatic School.

ROMERO, CESAR: NYC, Feb. 15, 1907. Collegiate School.

ROONEY, MICKEY: (Joe Yule, Jr.) Brooklyn, Sept. 23, 1920.

ROSS, DIANA: Detroit, Mich., Mar. 26, 1945.

ROSS, KATHARINE: Hollywood, Jan. 29, 1943.

ROTH, LILLIAN: Boston, Dec. 13, 1910.

ROUNDS, DAVID: Bronxville, NY, Oct. 9, 1938, Denison U.

ROUNDTREE, RICHARD: New Rochelle, N.Y., Sept. 7, 1942. Southern Ill.

ROWLANDS, GENA: Cambria, Wisc., June 19, 1936.

RULE, JANICE: Cincinnati, Aug. 15, 1931.

RUPERT, MICHAEL: Denver, Co. Oct. 23, 1951. Pasadena Playhouse.

RUSH, BARBARA: Denver, Colo., Jan. 4. U. of Calif.

RUSSELL, JANE: Bemidji, Minn., June 21, 1921. Max Reinhardt School.

RUSSELL, JOHN: Los Angeles, Jan. 3, 1921. U. of Calif.

RUSSELL, KURT: Springfield, Mass., March 17, 1951.

RUSSELL, ROSALIND: Waterbury, Conn., June 4, 1911. AADA.

RUTHERFORD, ANN: Toronto, Can., 1924.

RUYMEN, AYN: Brooklyn, July 18, 1947, HB Studio.

SAINT, EVA MARIE: Newark, N.J., July 4, 1924. Bowling Green State U.

ST. JACQUES, RAYMOND: (James Arthur Johnson) Conn.

ST. JOHN, BETTA: Hawthorne, Calif., Nov. 26, 1929.

ST. JOHN, JILL: (Jill Oppenheim) Los Angeles, Aug. 19, 1940.

SALT, JENNIFER: Los Angeles, Sept. 4, 1944. Sarah Lawrence Col.

SANDS, TOMMY: Chicago, Aug. 27, 1937.

SAN JUAN, OLGA: NYC, Mar. 16, 1927.

SARANDON, CHRIS: Beckley, W.Va., July 24, 1942. UWVa. Catholic U.

SARANDON, SUSAN: (Tomaling) NYC, Oct. 4, 1946. Catholic U.

SARGENT, RICHARD: (Richard Cox) Carmel, Cal., 1933. Stanford.

SARRAZIN, MICHAEL: Quebec City, Can., May 22, 1940.

SAVALAS, TELLY: (Aristotle) Garden City, N.Y., Jan. 21, 1925. Columbia.

SAXON, JOHN: (Carmen Orrico) Brooklyn, Aug. 5, 1935.

Maria Schneider	Martin Sheen	Jean Seberg	Gary Springer	Sylvia Sidney

SCHEIDER, ROY: Orange, N.J., Nov. 10, 1935, Franklin-Marshall.

SCHELL, MARIA: Vienna, Jan. 15, 1926.

SCHELL, MAXIMILIAN: Vienna, Dec. 8, 1930.

SCHNEIDER, MARIA: Paris, Mar. 27, 1952.

SCHNEIDER, ROMY: Vienna, Sept. 23, 1938.

SCOFIELD, PAUL: Hurstpierpoint, Eng., Jan. 21, 1922. London Mask Theatre School.

SCOTT, GEORGE C.: Wise, Va., Oct. 18, 1927. U. of Mo.

SCOTT, GORDON: (Gordon M. Werschkul) Portland, Ore., Aug. 3, 1927. Oregon U.

SCOTT, MARTHA: Jamesport, Mo., Sept. 22, 1914. U. of Mich.

SCOTT, RANDOLPH: Orange County, Va., Jan. 23, 1903. U. of N.C.

SEAGULL, BARBARA HERSHEY: (Herzstein) Hollywood, Feb. 5, 1948.

SEARS, HEATHER: London, 1935.

SEBERG, JEAN: Marshalltown, Iowa, Nov. 13, 1938. Iowa U.

SECOMBE, HARRY: Swansea, Wales, Sept. 8, 1921.

SEGAL, GEORGE: NYC, Feb. 13, 1934, Columbia.

SELLERS, PETER: Southsea, Eng., Sept. 8, 1925. Aloysius College.

SELWART, TONIO: Watenberg, Ger., June 9, 1906. Munich U.

SERNAS, JACQUES: Lithuania, July 30, 1925.

SEYLER, ATHENE: (Athene Hannen) London, May 31, 1889.

SEYMOUR, ANNE: NYC, Sept. 11, 1909. American Laboratory Theatre.

SEYMOUR, JANE: Hillingdon, Eng., Feb. 15, 1951.

SHARIF, OMAR: (Michel Shalboub) Alexandria, Egypt, Apr. 10, 1933. Victoria Col.

SHATNER, WILLIAM: Montreal, Can., Mar. 22, 1931. McGill U.

SHAW, ROBERT: Orkney Isles, Scot., Aug. 9, 1925, RADA.

SHAW, SEBASTIAN: Holt, Eng., May 29, 1905. Gresham School.

SHAWLEE, JOAN: Forest Hills, N.Y., Mar. 5, 1929.

SHAWN, DICK: (Richard Shulefand) Buffalo, N.Y., Dec. 1. U. of Miami.

SHEARER, MOIRA: Dunfermline, Scot., Jan. 17, 1926. London Theatre School.

SHEARER, NORMA: Montreal, Can., Aug. 19, 1904.

SHEEN, MARTIN: (Ramon Estevez) Dayton, O., Aug. 3, 1940.

SHEFFIELD, JOHN: Pasadena, Calif., Apr. 11, 1931. UCLA.

SHEPHERD, CYBILL: Memphis, Tenn., 1950. Hunter, NYU.

SHORE, DINAH: (Frances Rose Shore) Winchester, Tenn., Mar. 1, 1917. Vanderbilt U.

SHOWALTER, MAX: (formerly Casey Adams) Caldwell, Kan., June 2, 1917. Pasadena Playhouse.

SIDNEY, SYLVIA: NYC, Aug. 8, 1910. Theatre Guild School.

SIGNORET, SIMONE: (Simone Kaminker) Wiesbaden, Ger., Mar. 25, 1921. Solange Sicard School.

SILVERS, PHIL: (Philip Silversmith) Brooklyn, May 11, 1912.

SIM, ALASTAIR: Edinburgh, Scot., 1900.

SIMMONS, JEAN: London, Jan. 31, 1929. Aida Foster School.

SIMON, SIMONE: Marseilles, France, Apr. 23, 1914.

SINATRA, FRANK: Hoboken, N.J., Dec. 12, 1917.

SINDEN, DONALD: Plymouth, Eng., Oct. 9, 1923. Webber-Douglas.

SKELTON, RED: (Richard) Vincennes, Ind., July 18, 1913.

SLEZAK, WALTER: Vienna, Austria, May 3, 1902.

SMITH, ALEXIS: Penticton, Can., June 8, 1921. LACC.

SMITH, JOHN: (Robert E. Van Orden) Los Angeles, Mar. 6, 1931. UCLA.

SMITH, KATE: (Kathryn Elizabeth) Greenville, Va., May 1, 1909.

SMITH, KENT: NYC, Mar. 19, 1907. Harvard U.

SMITH, MAGGIE: Ilford, Eng., Dec. 28, 1934.

SMITH, ROGER: South Gate, Calif., Dec. 18, 1932. U. of Ariz.

SNODGRESS, CARRIE: Chicago, Oct. 27, 1946. UNI.

SOMMER, ELKE: Berlin, Nov. 5, 1941.

SONNY: (Salvatore Bono) 1935.

SORDI, ALBERTO: Rome, Italy, 1925.

SORVINO, PAUL: NYC, 1939, AMDA.

SOTHERN, ANN: (Harriet Lake) Valley City, N.D., Jan. 22, 1909. Washington U.

SPRINGER, GARY: NYC, July 29, 1954. Hunter Col.

STACK, ROBERT: Los Angeles, Jan. 13, 1919. USC.

STADLEN, LEWIS J.: Brooklyn, Mar. 7, 1947, Neighborhood Playhouse.

STAMP, TERENCE: London, 1940.

STANDER, LIONEL: NYC, Jan. 11, 1908. UNC.

STANG, ARNOLD: Chelsea, Mass., Sept. 28, 1925.

STANLEY, KIM: (Patricia Reid) Tularosa, N.M., Feb. 11, 1921. U. of Tex.

STANWYCK, BARBARA: (Ruby Stevens) Brooklyn, July 16, 1907.

STAPLETON, MAUREEN: Troy, N.Y., June 21, 1925.

STEEL, ANTHONY: London, May 21, 1920. Cambridge.

STEELE, TOMMY: London, Dec. 17, 1936.

STEIGER, ROD: Westhampton, N.Y., Apr. 14, 1925.

STERLING, JAN: (Jane Sterling Adriance) NYC, Apr. 3, 1923. Fay Compton School.

STERLING, ROBERT: (William Sterling Hart) Newcastle, Pa., Nov. 13, 1917. U. of Pittsburgh.

STEVENS, CONNIE: (Concetta Ann Ingolia) Brooklyn, Aug. 8, 1938. Hollywood Professional School.

STEVENS, KAYE: (Catherine) Pittsburgh, July 21, 1933.

STEVENS, MARK: (Richard) Cleveland, Ohio, Dec. 13, 1922.

STEVENS, STELLA: (Estelle Eggleston) Hot Coffee, Miss., Oct. 1, 1936.

STEWART, ALEXANDRA: Montreal, Can., June 10. Louvre.

STEWART, ELAINE: Montclair, N.J., May 31, 1929.

STEWART, JAMES: Indiana, Pa., May 20, 1908. Princeton.

STEWART, MARTHA: (Martha Haworth) Bardwell, Ky., Oct. 7, 1922.

STOCKWELL, DEAN: Hollywood, March 5.

STORM, GALE: (Josephine Cottle) Bloomington, Tex., Apr. 5, 1922.

STRASBERG, SUSAN: NYC, May 22, 1938.

STRAUD, DON: Hawaii, 1943.

STREISAND, BARBRA: Brooklyn, Apr. 24, 1942.

STRODE, WOODY: Los Angeles, 1914.

STRUDWICK, SHEPPERD: Hillsboro, N.C., Sept. 22, 1907. U. of N.C.

STRUTHERS, SALLY: Portland, Ore., July 28, 1948, Pasadena Playhouse.

| Barry Sullivan | Loretta Swit | Philip Thomas | Liv Ullmann | Jon Voight |

SULLIVAN, BARRY: (Patrick Barry) NYC, Aug. 29, 1912. NYU.

SULLY, FRANK: (Frank Sullivan) St. Louis, 1910. St. Teresa's Col.

SUTHERLAND, DONALD: St. John, New Brunswick, July 17, 1934. U. Toronto.

SWANSON, GLORIA: (Josephine May Swenson) Chicago, Mar. 27, 1898. Chicago Art Inst.

SWINBURNE, NORA: Bath, Eng., July 24, 1902. RADA.

SWIT, LORETTA: Passaic, NJ, Nov. 4, AADA.

SYLVESTER, WILLIAM: Oakland, Calif., Jan. 31, 1922. RADA.

SYMS, SYLVIA: London, 1934. Convent School.

TABORI, KRISTOFFER: Los Angeles, Aug. 4, 1952.

TALBOT, LYLE: (Lysle Hollywood) Pittsburgh, Feb. 8, 1904.

TALBOT, NITA: NYC, Aug. 8, 1930. Irvine Studio School.

TAMBLYN, RUSS: Los Angeles, Dec. 30.

TANDY, JESSICA: London, June 7, 1909. Dame Owens' School.

TAYLOR, DON: Freeport, Pa., Dec. 13, 1920. Penn State U.

TAYLOR, ELIZABETH: London, Feb. 27, 1932. Byron House School.

TAYLOR, KENT: (Louis Weiss) Nashua, Iowa, May 11, 1907.

TAYLOR, ROD: (Robert) Sydney, Aust., Jan. 11, 1930.

TAYLOR-YOUNG, LEIGH: Wash., D.C., Jan. 25, 1945. Northwestern.

TEAGUE, ANTHONY SKOOTER: Jacksboro, Tex., Jan. 4, 1940.

TEAL, RAY: Grand Rapids, Mich., Jan. 12, 1902. Pasadena Playhouse.

TEMPLE, SHIRLEY: Santa Monica, Calif., Apr. 23, 1928.

TERRY-THOMAS: (Thomas Terry Hoar Stevens) Finchley, London, July 14, 1911. Ardingly College.

TERZIEFF, LAURENT: Paris, 1935.

THACKER, RUSS: Washington, DC, June 23, 1946, Montgomery Col.

THATCHER, TORIN: Bombay, India, Jan. 15, 1905. RADA.

THAXTER, PHYLLIS: Portland, Me., Nov. 20, 1921. St. Genevieve.

THOMAS, DANNY: (Amos Jacobs) Deerfield, Mich., Jan. 6, 1914.

THOMAS, MARLO: (Margaret) Detroit, Nov. 21, 1938. USC.

THOMAS, PHILIP: Columbus, O., May 26, 1949. Oakwood Col.

THOMAS, RICHARD: NYC, June 13, 1951. Columbia.

THOMPSON, JACK: (John Payne) Sydney, Aus., 1940. UBrisbane.

THOMPSON, MARSHALL: Peoria, Ill., Nov. 27, 1925. Occidental.

THOMPSON, REX: NYC, Dec. 14, 1942.

THOMPSON, SADA: Des Moines, Io., Sept. 27, 1929, Carnegie Tech.

THORNDIKE, SYBIL: Gainsborough, Eng., Oct. 24, 1882. Guild Hall School of Music.

THULIN, INGRID: Solleftea, Sweden, Jan. 27, 1929, Royal Drama Theatre.

TIERNEY, GENE: Brooklyn, Nov. 20, 1920. Miss Farmer's School.

TIERNEY, LAWRENCE: Brooklyn, Mar. 15, 1919. Manhattan College.

TIFFIN, PAMELA: (Wonso) Oklahoma City, Oct. 13, 1942.

TODD, RICHARD: Dublin, Ire., June 11, 1919. Shrewsbury School.

TOLO, MARILU': Rome, Italy, 1948.

TOPOL: (Chaim Topol) Tel-Aviv, Israel, Sept. 9, 1935.

TORN, RIP: Temple, Tex., Feb. 6, 1931. U. Tex.

TORRES, LIZ: NYC, 1947, NYU.

TOTTER, AUDREY: Joliet, Ill., Dec. 20.

TRAVERS, BILL: Newcastle-on-Tyne, Eng., Jan. 3, 1922.

TRAVIS, RICHARD: (William Justice) Carlsbad, N.M., Apr. 17, 1913.

TREMAYNE, LES: London, Apr. 16, 1913. Northwestern Columbia, UCLA.

TRINTIGNANT, JEAN-LOUIS: Pont-St. Esprit, France, Dec. 11, 1930. Dullin-Balachova Drama School.

TRYON, TOM: Hartford, Conn., Jan. 14, 1926. Yale.

TSOPEI, CORINNA: Athens, Greece, June 21, 1944.

TUCKER, FORREST: Plainfield, Ind., Feb. 12, 1919. George Washington U.

TURNER, LANA: (Julia Jean Mildred Frances Turner) Wallace, Idaho, Feb. 8, 1920.

TUSHINGHAM, RITA: Liverpool, Eng., 1942.

TUTTLE, LURENE: Pleasant Lake, Ind., Aug. 20, 1906, USC.

TWIGGY: (Lesley Hornby) London, Sept. 19, 1949.

TYLER, BEVERLY: (Beverly Jean Saul) Scranton, Pa., July 5, 1928.

TYSON, CICELY: NYC, Dec. 19.

UGGAMS, LESLIE: NYC, May 25, 1943.

ULLMANN, LIV: Tokyo, Dec. 16, 1939, Webber-Douglas Acad.

USTINOV, PETER: London, Apr. 16, 1921. Westminster School.

VACCARO, BRENDA: Brooklyn, Nov. 18, 1939. Neighborhood Playhouse.

VALLEE, RUDY: (Hubert) Island Pond, Vt., July 28, 1901. Yale.

VALLI, ALIDA: Pola, Italy, May 31, 1921. Rome Academy of Drama.

VAN, BOBBY: (Stein) NYC, Dec. 6, 1930.

VAN CLEEF, LEE: Somerville, N.J., Jan. 9, 1925.

VAN DEVERE, TRISH: (Patricia Dressel) Englewood Cliffs, NJ, Mar. 9, 1945, Ohio Wesleyan.

VAN DOREN, MAMIE: (Joan Lucile Olander) Rowena, S.D., Feb. 6, 1933.

VAN DYKE, DICK: West Plains, Mo., Dec. 13, 1925.

VAN FLEET, JO: Oakland, Cal., 1922.

VAN PATTEN, DICK: NYC, Dec. 9, 1928.

VAN PATTEN, JOYCE: NYC, Mar. 9, 1934.

VAUGHN, ROBERT: NYC, Nov. 22, 1932. USC.

VEGA, ISELA: Mexico 1940.

VENUTA, VENAY: San Francisco, Jan. 27, 1911.

VERA-ELLEN (Rohe): Cincinnati, Feb. 16, 1926.

VERDON, GWEN: Culver City, Calif., Jan. 13, 1925.

VINCENT, JAN-MICHAEL: Denver, Col., July 15, 1944. Ventura Col.

VIOLET, ULTRA: (Isabelle Collin-Dufresne) Grenoble, France.

VITALE, MILLY: Rome, Italy, July 16, 1938. Lycee Chateaubriand.

VOIGHT, JON: Yonkers, N.Y., Dec. 29, 1938. Catholic U.

VOLONTE, GIAN MARIA: Milan, Italy, Apr. 9, 1933.

VON SYDOW, MAX: Lund, Swed., July 10, 1929, Royal Drama Theatre.

VYE, MURVYN: Quincy, Mass., July 15, 1913. Yale.

WAGNER, LINDSAY: Los Angeles, 1949.

WAGNER, ROBERT: Detroit, Feb. 10, 1930.

Patrick Wayne	Gwen Welles	Stuart Whitman	Estelle Winwood	Billy Dee Williams

WAITE, GENEVIEVE: South Africa 1949.

WALKEN, CHRISTOPHER: Astoria, NY, Mar. 31, 1943. Hofstra.

WALKER, CLINT: Hartfold, Ill., May 30, 1927. USC.

WALKER, NANCY: (Ann Myrtle Swoyer) Philadelphia, May 10, 1921.

WALLACH, ELI: Brooklyn, Dec. 7, 1915. CCNY, U. of Tex.

WALLIS, SHANI: London, Apr. 5, 1941.

WALSTON, RAY: New Orleans, Nov. 22, 1918. Cleveland Playhouse.

WALTER, JESSICA: Brooklyn, NY, Jan. 31, 1940. Neighborhood Playhouse.

WANAMAKER, SAM: Chicago, 1919. Drake.

WARD, BURT: (Gervis) Los Angeles, July 6, 1945.

WARDEN, JACK: Newark, N.J., Sept. 18, 1920.

WARREN, LESLEY ANN: NYC, Aug. 16, 1946.

WARRICK, RUTH: St. Joseph, Mo., June 29, UMo.

WASHBOURNE, MONA: Birmingham, Eng., Nov. 27, 1903.

WATERS, ETHEL: Chester, Pa., Oct. 31, 1900.

WATERSTON, SAM: Cambridge, Mass., Nov. 15, 1940. Yale.

WATLING, JACK: London, Jan. 13, 1923. Italia Conti School.

WATSON, DOUGLASS: Jackson, Ga., Feb. 24, 1921, UNC.

WAYNE, DAVID: (Wayne McKeehan) Travers City, Mich., Jan. 30, 1914. Western Michigan State U.

WAYNE, JOHN: (Marion Michael Morrison) Winterset, Iowa, May 26, 1907. USC.

WAYNE, PATRICK: Los Angeles, July 15, 1939. Loyola.

WEAVER, DENNIS: Joplin, Mo., June 4, 1925. U. Okla.

WEAVER, MARJORIE: Crossville, Tenn., Mar. 2, 1913. Indiana U.

WEBB, ALAN: York, Eng., July 2, 1906. Dartmouth.

WEBB, JACK: Santa Monica, Calif. Apr. 2, 1920.

WEBBER, ROBERT: Santa Ana, Cal., Oct. 14, Compton Jr. Col.

WELCH, RAQUEL: (Tejada) Chicago, Sept. 5, 1940.

WELD, TUESDAY: (Susan) NYC, Aug. 27, 1943. Hollywood Professional School.

WELDON, JOAN: San Francisco, Aug. 5, 1933. San Francisco Conservatory.

WELLES, GWEN: NYC, Mar. 4.

WELLES, ORSON: Kenosha, Wisc., May 6, 1915. Todd School.

WERNER, OSKAR: Vienna, Nov. 13, 1922.

WEST, MAE: Brooklyn, Aug. 17, 1892.

WHITAKER, JOHNNY: Van Nuys, Cal., Dec. 13. 1959.

WHITE, CAROL: London, Apr. 1, 1944.

WHITE, CHARLES: Perth Amboy, NJ, Aug. 29, 1920, Rutgers U.

WHITE, JESSE: Buffalo, N.Y., Jan. 3, 1919.

WHITMAN, STUART: San Francisco, Feb. 1, 1929. CCLA.

WHITMORE, JAMES: White Plains, NY, Oct. 1, 1922. Yale.

WIDDOES, KATHLEEN: Wilmington, Del., Mar. 21, 1939.

WIDMARK, RICHARD: Sunrise, Minn., Dec. 26, 1914. Lake Forest.

WILCOX-HORNE, COLIN: Highlands N.C., Feb. 4, 1937. U. Tenn.

WILCOXON, HENRY: British West Indies, Sept. 8, 1905.

WILDE, CORNEL: NYC, Oct. 13, 1915. CCNY, Columbia.

WILDER, GENE: Milwaukee, Wis., June 11, 1936. U Iowa.

WILDING, MICHAEL: Westcliff, Eng., July 23, 1912. Christ's Hospital.

WILLIAMS, BILLY DEE: NYC, Apr. 6, 1937.

WILLIAMS, CINDY: Van Nuys, Ca., 1948, LACC.

WILLIAMS, EMLYN: Mostyn, Wales, Nov. 26, 1905. Oxford.

WILLIAMS, ESTHER: Los Angeles, Aug. 8, 1923.

WILLIAMS, GRANT: NYC, Aug. 18, 1930. Queens College.

WILLIAMS, JOHN: Chalfont, Eng., Apr. 15, 1903. Lancing College.

WILLIAMSON, FRED: Gary, Ind., 1938, Northwestern.

WILSON, DEMOND: NYC, Oct. 13, 1946, Hunter Col.

WILSON, FLIP: (Clerow Wilson) Jersey City, N.J., Dec. 8, 1933.

WILSON, NANCY: Chillicothe, O., Feb. 20, 1937.

WILSON, SCOTT: Atlanta, Ga., 1942.

WINDOM, WILLIAM: NYC, Sept. 28, 1923, Williams Col.

WINDSOR, MARIE: (Emily Marie Bertelson) Marysvale, Utah, Dec. 11, 1924. Brigham Young U.

WINFIELD, PAUL: Los Angeles, 1940, UCLA.

WINKLER, HENRY: NYC, Oct. 30, 1945. Yale.

WINN, KITTY: Wash., D.C., 1944. Boston U.

WINTERS, JONATHAN: Dayton Ohio, Nov. 11, 1925. Kenyon Col.

WINTERS, ROLAND: Boston, Nov. 22, 1904.

WINTERS, SHELLEY: (Shirley Schrift) St. Louis, Aug. 18, 1922. Wayne U.

WINWOOD, ESTELLE: Kent, Eng., Jan. 24, 1883. Lyric Stage Academy.

WITHERS, GOOGIE: Karachi, India, Mar. 12, 1917. Italia Conti.

WOOD, NATALIE: (Natasha Gurdin) San Francisco, July 20, 1938.

WOOD, PEGGY: Brooklyn, Feb. 9, 1894.

WOODLAWN, HOLLY: (Harold Ajzenberg) Juana Diaz, PR, 1947.

WOODS, JAMES: Vernal, U., Apr. 18, 1947, MIT.

WOODWARD, JOANNE: Thomasville, Ga., Feb. 27, 1931. Neighborhood Playhouse.

WOOLAND, NORMAN: Dusseldorf, Ger., Mar. 16, 1910. Edward VI School.

WRAY, FAY: Alberta, Can., Sept. 15, 1907.

WRIGHT, TERESA: NYC, Oct. 27, 1918.

WYATT, JANE: Campgaw, N.J., Aug. 10, 1912. Barnard College.

WYMAN, JANE: (Sarah Jane Fulks) St. Joseph, Mo., Jan. 4, 1914.

WYMORE, PATRICE: Miltonvale, Kan., Dec. 17, 1927.

WYNN, KEENAN: NYC, July 27, 1916. St. John's.

WYNN, MAY: (Donna Lee Hickey) NYC, Jan. 8, 1930.

WYNTER, DANA: London, June 8, Rhodes U.

YORK, DICK: Fort Wayne, Ind., Sept. 4, 1928. De Paul U.

YORK, MICHAEL: Fulmer, Eng., Mar. 27, 1942. Oxford.

YORK, SUSANNAH: London, Jan. 9, 1941. RADA.

YOUNG, ALAN: (Angus) North Shield, Eng., Nov. 19, 1919.

YOUNG, GIG: (Byron Barr) St. Cloud, Minn., Nov. 4, 1913. Pasadena Playhouse.

YOUNG, LORETTA: (Gretchen) Salt Lake City, Jan. 6, 1913. Immaculate Heart College.

YOUNG, ROBERT: Chicago, Feb. 22, 1907.

ZETTERLING, MAI: Sweden, May 27, 1925. Ordtuery Theatre School.

ZIMBALIST, EFREM, JR.: NYC, Nov. 30, 1923. Yale.

Hardie Albright
(1932)

Ben Blue
(1950)

Evelyn Brent
(1935)

Pamela Brown
(1967)

Richard Conte
(1966)

OBITUARIES

HARDIE ALBRIGHT, 71, film, stage, tv actor, teacher and author, died of congestive heart failure and pneumonia in Mission Viejo, CA., Dec. 7, 1975. After appearing with Eva Le Gallienne's Civic Repertory Theatre in NY, he went to Hollywood in 1928. He appeared in such films as "Young Sinners," "Hush Money," "Skyline," "Heartbreak," "So Big," "The Purchase Price," "Jewel Robbery," "The Crash," "A Successful Calamity," "Cabin in the Cotton," "This Sporting Age," "The Match King," "The Working Man," "Song of Songs," "Three-Cornered Moon," "House on 56th St.," "Ninth Guest," "White Heat," "Crimson Romance," "Silver Streak," "Sing Sing Nights," "Red Salute," "Ski Patrol," "Flight from Destiny," "Marry the Boss's Daughter," "Pride of the Yankees," "Loves of Edgar Allan Poe," "Angel on My Shoulder," and "Mom and Dad." He appeared in tv's "Gunsmoke" and "Twilight Zone" series. Surviving are his second wife, and a daughter.

SIG ARNO, 79, German-born film and stage character actor, died from complications of Parkinson's disease Aug. 17, 1975 in Woodland Hills, CA. He came to the U.S. in the late 1930's and made his Hollywood film debut in 1941 in "This Thing Called Love." Subsequently he appeared in "New Wine," "Two Yanks in Trinidad," "Juke Box Jenny," "Tales of Manhattan," "The Devil with Hitler," "Palm Beach Story," "The Crystal Ball," "Mister Taxi," "His Butler's Sister," "Up in Arms," "Song of the Open Road," "A Song to Remember," "Bring on the Girls," "One More Tomorrow," "Holiday in Havana," "The Great Lover," "Duchess of Idaho," "Toast of New Orleans," and "Diplomatic Courier." He is survived by his widow, and a son.

JOHN BARAGREY, 57, Alabama-born stage, film and tv actor, died Aug. 4, 1975 in his NYC home. His film credits include "Loves of Carmen," "Four Days Leave," "Pardners," "The Fugitive Kind," "The Saxon Charm," and "Shockproof." He appeared in many tv shows, including "Blacklist" and "The Last Tycoon." He is survived by his widow, actress Louise Larabee.

SAM BISCHOFF, 84, one of Hollywood's most prolific producers, died May 21,1975 in Hollywood of general debilitation. He produced many two-reel comedies and serials before turning to full-length features for major studios, and for himself. Among the more than 400 films he produced are "War Paint," "The Last Mile," "Hollywood Hotel," "Boy Meets Girl," "Angels with Dirty Faces," "Charge of the Light Brigade," "20,000 Years in Sing Sing," "Three Men on a Horse," "A Night to Remember," "Intrigue," "Pitfall," "A Bullet for Joey," "Phenix City Story," "Operation Eichmann," "King of the Roaring Twenties" and "The Strangler." A sister survives.

PIERRE BLAISE, 24, French star of "Lacombe, Lucien," was killed Aug. 31, 1975 in a car crash near Montauban, France. "Lacombe, Lucien" was his first film. No survivors were reported.

BEN BLUE, 73, Canadian-born sad-faced comedian, died in Hollywood March 7, 1975. From the time he entered show business as a 15-year-old chorus boy, he was more of a mime than a speaking comedian. He appeared for more than 50 years in music halls, vaudeville, films, nightclubs, radio and tv. His film credits include "College Holiday," "Top of the Town," "High, Wide and Handsome," "Artists and Models," "Big Broadcast of 1938," "Panama Hattie," "For Me and My Gal," "Broadway Rhythm," "One Sunday Afternoon," "It's a Mad, Mad, Mad, Mad World," "The Russians Are Coming, The Russians Are Coming, and "Where Were You When the Lights Went Out?" He leaves his second wife, former show girl Axie Dunlap, and two sons.

LARRY BLYDEN, 49, a versatile performer who produced, directed, and acted on stage, in movies and television for over 25 years, died June 6, 1975 in Agadir, Morocco, where he was on vacation. His death was a result of injuries suffered in an auto accident. His film appearances were in "Bachelor Party" and "Kiss Them for Me." A son and daughter survive.

BERNARD B. BOSSICK, 37, producer-director, and former actor, died Nov. 10, 1975 of a heart attack in his Hollywood home. He had also written for such teleseries as "Kung-Fu." Surviving are his widow, a son, and a daughter.

EVELYN BRENT, 74, Florida-born film star of the 1920's and '30's, died of a heart attack June 4, 1975 in her Los Angeles home. Among her more memorable pictures are "Pagan Lady," "The Silver Horde," "Broadway," "The Showdown," "Tiger Lady," "Framed," "Madonna of the Streets," and "Dangerous Lady." Her third husband, vaudevillian Harry Fox, died in 1959.

CHARLES BROKAW, 77, screen and stage actor, died Oct. 23, 1975 in a NYC hospital. His films include "Fascinating Youth," "I Cover the War," "The Outer Gate," "Idol of the Crowd," and "Murder in the Air." Survivors include a brother and a stepson.

PAMELA BROWN, 58, British film and stage actress, died in London Sept. 18, 1975. Her screen credits include "One of Our Aircraft Is Missing," "I Know Where I'm Going," "Tales of Hoffman," "Alice in Wonderland," "Personal Affair," "Richard III," "Lust for Life," "The Scapegoat," "Cleopatra," "Becket," "Secret Ceremony," "Wuthering Heights," "On a Clear Day" and "Lady Caroline Lamb." She received an "Emmy" for her performance in "Victoria Regina." She was divorced from Peter Copley.

SIDNEY BUCHMAN, 73, scenarist and film producer, died Aug. 23, 1975 in Cannes, France, where he had lived for the last ten years. He began his career as a Broadway playwright, moving to Hollywood in 1930. His credits include "Sign of the Cross," "I'll Love You Always," "Theodora Goes Wild," "Holiday," "Mr. Smith Goes to Washington," "Howards of Virginia," "Here Comes Mr. Jordan," "Talk of the Town," "A Song to Remember," "Over 21," "Cleopatra," "Saturday's Hero," and "Jolson Sings Again." Survivors include his widow, and a daughter by a former marriage.

HENRY CALVIN, nee Wimberly Calvin Goodman, Jr., 57, screen, tv and stage actor, died Oct. 6, 1975 in Dallas, Tx. Among his film credits are "Toby Tyler," "Babes in Toyland," and "The Sign of Zorro." He was best known for his portrayal of Sgt. Garcia on the "Zorro" tv series. No reported survivors.

RICHARD CONTE, 65, film, tv and stage actor, died from a massive heart attack in Los Angeles on Apr. 15, 1975. He appeared in over 75 U.S. films and 23 foreign pictures, including "Guadalcanal Diary," "Call Northside 777," "Cry of the City," "Purple Heart," "Slaves of Babylon," "Hollywood Story," "NY Confidential," "I'll Cry Tomorrow," "Brothers Rico," "They Came to Cordura," "Assault on a Queen," "The Greatest Story Ever Told," "Hotel," "Synanon," "A Walk in the Sun," "A Bell for Adano," "Oceans 11," and "The Godfather." He was a guest on numerous tv programs. Surviving is his second wife, actress Shirlee Garner, an adopted son, and two stepsons.

CLANCY COOPER, 68, movie and stage actor, died in Hollywood June 14, 1975 of a heart attack while driving his car. He appeared in 35 Broadway plays before going to Hollywood where he made 60 films and 200 tv episodes. Screen credits include "Native Land," "Flight Lieutenant," "The Whistler," "The Enchanted Forest," "Lulu Belle," "Sainted Sisters," "Mr. Belvedere Goes to College," "Distant Drums," "The Wild North," and "All the Brothers Were Valiant." He leaves his widow, authoress Elizabeth Cooper, and a son.

| Cyril Delevanti (1965) | Jean Del Val (1966) | Philip Dorn (1941) | Larry Fine | Mark Frechette (1970) |

INEZ COURTNEY, 67, stage and screen actress, died Apr. 5, 1975 in Neptune, NJ. Among her many films are "Song of the Flame," "Not Damaged," "Sunny," "Bright Lights," "Break of Hearts," "The Raven," "The Girl Friend," "Magnificent Obsession," "Suzy," "Hit Parade," "Hurricane," "Having Wonderful Time," "Shop around the Corner," "Blondie Meets the Boss," "The Farmer's Daughter," and "Turnabout." No reported survivors.

WADE CROSBY, 70, character actor, died Oct. 2, 1975 aboard a yacht at Newport Beach, Ca. During his 50 year career, his many credits include "Ride a Crooked Mile," "Arizona," "The Paleface," "The Black Book," "Invasion U.S.A.," "Westworld," and "Airport '75." No reported survivors.

CASS DALEY, 59, slim, bucktoothed singer-comedienne of film, radio, and stage, bled to death Mar. 22, 1975 after a freak accident when she fell on a goblet that shattered and cut her throat in her Hollywood apartment. Philadelphia-born, she began her career as a singer in local nightclubs. Screen credits include "The Fleet's In," "Star Spangled Rhythm," "Crazy House," "Riding High," "Out of This World," "Duffy's Tavern," "Here Comes the Groom," "Ladies Man," and "Red Garters." She was a regular on the radio series "The Fitch Bandwagon" for which she was voted radio's most popular comedienne. She is survived by her second husband, Robert Williamson, and a son.

CYRIL DELEVANTI, 86, British-born stage and screen actor, died of lung cancer in Hollywood Dec. 13, 1975. Among his film credits are "Black Eye," "Soylent Green," and the grandfather in "Night of the Iguana." A son and daughter survive.

JEAN DEL VAL, 83, French-born character actor, nee Jean Gautier, died of a heart attack Mar. 13, 1975 in his Pacific Palisades, Ca., home. He had lived in Hollywood since the 1920's, and had appeared in such films as "Sainted Devil," "Sea Legs," "Magnificent Lie," "For Whom the Bell Tolls," "Paris after Dark," "Molly and Me," "Return of Monte Cristo," "The Hitch-Hiker," "Little Boy Lost," "Funny Face," and "Fantastic Voyage." He leaves his widow.

JOHN A. DeMOTT, 63, former child actor and tv pioneer, died of heart failure Mar. 19, 1975 in San Diego, Ca. One of the original members of "Our Gang" comedies, he turned to production in 1947. Surviving are his widow, and two sons, John and Michael.

JOHN DIERKES, 69, veteran character actor of screen and tv, died Jan. 8, 1975 of emphysema in Hollywood. Among his many screen credits are "Macbeth," "Red Badge of Courage," "Shane," "The Moonlighter," "Naked Jungle," "Prince Valiant," "Jubal," "The Buccaneer," "The Alamo," "Comancheros," "Haunted Palace," and "Oklahoma Crude." He also appeared in several segments of tv's "Gunsmoke." His widow survives, as do two sons, and two daughters.

PHILIP DORN, 75, Netherlands-born film and stage actor, died May 9, 1975 of a heart attack in Woodland Hills, Ca. He began his career at 14 and came to the U.S. in 1939. He appeared in such films as "Enemy Agent," "Ski Patrol," "Escape," "Ziegfeld Girl," "Underground," "Tarzan's Secret Treasure," "Calling Dr. Gillespie," "Random Harvest," "Passage to Marseille," "I Remember Mama," "The Fighting Kentuckian," "Spy Hunt," "Blond Fever," and "Sealed Cargo." He had been incapacitated for 10 years after a head injury on stage in Europe. Surviving are his widow and a daughter.

PATRICIA DOYLE, 60, former film actress and dancer, died Sept. 22, 1975 of cancer in Los Angeles. Her most important role was in "Grapes of Wrath." She is survived by her husband, producer-director Robert Wise, and a son.

MINTA DURFEE, 85, pioneer film actress, died of a heart ailment Sept. 9, 1975 in Woodland Hills, Ca. She was Fatty Arbuckle's first wife, Charlie Chaplin's first leading lady in "Making a Living," and a member of Mack Sennett's original company. She had appeared in character roles on tv until after she was 80. Her films include "How Green Was My Valley," "Naughty Marietta," "Rose Marie," "The Unsinkable Molly Brown" and "It's a Mad, Mad, Mad World." A brother survives.

ERIC EMERSON, 30, film and stage actor, was killed May 28, 1975 by a hit-and-run driver. He had appeared in "The Chelsea Girls," "Lonesome Cowboys," and "Heat." No reported survivors.

BRENDAN FAY, 54, stage and film actor, died Feb. 7, 1975 of a heart attack while rehearsing a play in Brooklyn. Among his film credits are "The Hustler," and "Juke Box Racket." His mother and two sisters survive.

LARRY FINE, 73, the frizzy-haired member of the comedy team, The Three Stooges, died Jan. 24, 1975 after a stroke in Woodland Hills, Ca. The Stooges appeared in 218 movie shorts, and subsequently appeared in such films as "Stop, Look and Laugh," "Snow White and the Three Stooges," "The Three Stooges Meet Hercules," "The Outlaw Is Coming," "Start Cheering," "Time out for Rhythm," "The Three Stooges Go around the World in a Daze," "It's a Mad, Mad, Mad World," "Meet the Baron," "Dancing Lady," and "The Three Stooges in Orbit." He is survived by a daughter.

LILIAN FONTAINE, 88, film and stage actress, and teacher, died Feb. 20, 1975 in Santa Barbara, Ca. Her film credits include "Lost Weekend," "Time Out of Mind," "Suddenly It's Spring," "The Locket," "Ivy," and "The Bigamist." She was the mother of actresses Joan Fontaine and Olivia DeHavilland who survive.

MARK FRECHETTE, 27, star of "Zabriskie Point," died Sept. 27, 1975 from a freak prison accident. He was killed when he was lying on a bench and the bar of a 160 pound weight he was lifting fell on his throat. He was in the Norfolk, Ma. prison where he was serving time for an armed bank robbery in Boston in 1973. No reported survivors.

PIERRE FRESNAY, 77, French star of stage and film, died Jan. 9, 1975 in a hospital near Paris where he had been confined for a respiratory ailment. He had appeared in over 70 movies, but is probably best known for "La Grande Illusion," Pagnol's trilogy, "Marius," "Fanny" and "Cesar." Other film credits include "La Dame aux Camelias," "The Man Who Knew Too Much," "Three Waltzes," "Carnival of Sinners," "The Raven," "Monsieur Vincent," "Tainted," "The Perfectionist," "Amazing Monsieur Fabre," and "Voyage to America." He was married to actress Yvonne Printemps.

URS B. FURRER, 41, a leading cinematographer, died Aug. 30, 1975 in Detroit of a heart attack while shooting an industrial film. Born of Swiss parents in Indonesia, he began his photography career as a youth before coming to the U.S. in the 1950's. In addition to many documentary and industrial films, his credits include such films as "Desperate Characters," "Where the Lilies Bloom," "Shaft," and "Seven-Ups." Surviving are his widow and four children.

DAGMAR GODOWSKY, 78, "vamp" of the silent screen, died Feb. 13, 1975 in a NYC hospital. She was the daughter of pianist-composer Leopold Godowsky. Her film credits include "A Sainted Devil" with Valentino, "Story without a Name," "Red Lights," "Common Law," "Virtuous Liars," and "The Price of a Party." She was married twice. Surviving is a brother, Leopold.

| Dagmar Godowsky (1924) | Susan Hayward (1967) | Moe Howard | James Robertson Justice (1968) | Annette Kellermann (1956) |

BERNARD GREEN, 66, nee Greenwald, composer, conductor, and arranger died Aug. 8, 1975 in his Westport, Ct. home. His career of more than 40 years embraced radio, tv and films. His film background scores include "All the Way Home" and "30 Years of Fun." He composed for several radio and tv series. He leaves his widow, three sons, and a daughter.

JOHN GREGSON, 55, British actor, died Jan. 8, 1975 while vacationing in Porlock Weir, Eng. His films include "Tight Little Island," "Treasure Island," "Lavendar Hill Mob," "Submarine Command," "The Brave Don't Cry," "The Assassin," "The Holly and the Ivy," "Genevieve," "Cash on Delivery," "Pursuit of the Graf Spee," "Captain's Table," "The Longest Day," "Night of the Generals." More recently he had been on the British tv series "Gideon's Way." No survivors reported.

ETHEL GRIFFIES, 97, the oldest working actress in the English-speaking theatre, died Sept. 9, 1975 in London after a stroke. Her career began as a baby in 1881 when she was carried onstage by her acting parents. She had appeared in over 100 films, many of them made in Hollywood. Her movies include "Old English," "Changes," "Stepdaughters," "Waterloo Bridge," "Manhattan Parade," "Of Human Bondage," "Love Me Tonight," "Alice in Wonderland," "Bulldog Drummond Strikes Back," "Anna Karenina," "Return of Peter Grimm," "Irene," "A Yank in the R.A.F.," "How Green Was My Valley," "Holy Matrimony," "Jane Eyre," "The Horn Blows at Midnight," "Molly and Me," "Uncle Harry," "Saratoga Trunk," and "Billy Liar." She was twice married, to actors Walter Beaumont who died in 1910, and Edward Cooper who died in 1956.

WILLIAM HANSEN, 64, screen and stage actor, died June 23, 1975 in Woodland Hills, Ca. After appearing in many Broadway plays, he went to Hollywood where his film credits include "Pinky," "Member of the Wedding," "Bramble Bush," "Birdman of Alcatraz," "Fail Safe," "Save the Tiger," and "Homebodies." No survivors were reported.

WILLIAM HARTNELL, 67, British character actor of stage, film and tv, died Apr. 24, 1975 in London. He had appeared in "The Way Ahead," "Murder in Reverse," "Odd Man Out," "Escape," "The Agitator," "Young Scarface," "The Holly and the Ivy," "Pickwick Papers," "The Mouse That Roared," "Carry on Sergeant," "Heavens Above!," and "This Sporting Life." Surviving are his widow, playwright and former actress, Heather McIntyre, and a daughter.

SUSAN HAYWARD, 55, Brooklyn-born, auburn-haired, Academy-Award-winning actress, died Mar. 14, 1975 in her Beverly Hills, Ca., home after a seizure and two years of suffering from an inoperable brain tumor. Born Edythe Marrener, she began her career as a model, and had her name changed when she went to Hollywood for films. She ultimately became one of the world's most popular screen stars, and appeared in over 50 features, for five of which she was nominated for an Academy Award. In 1958 she received an "Oscar" for her performance in "I Want to Live." Among her other screen credits are "Girls on Probation," "Beau Geste," "Adam Had Four Sons," "Reap the Wild Wind," "I Married a Witch," "Hit Parade of 1943," "The Hairy Ape," "Deadline at Dawn," "Smash-Up," "The Saxon Charm," "Tulsa," "House of Strangers," "I Can Get It for You Wholesale," "With a Song in My Heart," "Snows of Kilimanjaro," "The President's Lady," "Garden of Evil," "Untamed," "I'll Cry Tomorrow," "Woman Obsessed," "Back Street," "Stolen Hours," "The Honey Pot," "Where Love Has Gone," "Valley of the Dolls," and "The Revengers." Surviving are her twin sons by her first marriage to actor Jess Barker. Her second husband, lawyer Floyd Eaton Chalkley, died in 1966. Interment was in Carrollton, Ga., where she and Mr. Chalkley had lived since 1957.

BERNARD HERRMANN, 64, Academy-Aware-winning composer, died Dec. 24, 1975 in his sleep in Los Angeles, apparently of a heart attack. He lived in London but was in Los Angeles to complete the score for the film "Taxi Driver." In addition to "All That Money Can Buy" for which he won his "Oscar," he scored such films as "Citizen Kane," "Psycho," "The Man Who Knew Too Much," "The Devil and Daniel Webster," "The Magnificent Ambersons," "Snows of Kilimanjaro," and "King of the Khyber Rifles." He is survived by his widow and two daughters.

MOE HOWARD, 78, the last member of the comedy team The Three Stooges, died May 4, 1975 of lung cancer in Los Angeles. He was the mop-haired leader of the slapstick trio that appeared in such films as "Soup to Nuts," "Dancing Lady," "Time out for Rhythm," "Rockin' in the Rockies," "Snow White and the Three Stooges," "The Three Stooges Meet Hercules," "The Three Stooges Go Around the World in a Daze," "It's a Mad, Mad, Mad World," "The Three Stooges in Orbit," and 218 movie shorts. Surviving are his widow, a son and a daughter.

MURIEL HUTCHISON, 60, stage and film actress, died of cancer Mar. 24, 1975 in NYC. Her screen credits include "One Third of a Nation," "The Women," and "Another Thin Man." She retired in 1953 when she married art dealer John Nicholson who died in 1962.

HOWARD JOSLIN, 67, an actor and assistant director, died Aug. 1, 1975 of a heart attack in Woodland Hills, Ca. His credits include "Mr. Quebec," and "Detective Story." Surviving are his widow, a daughter, and three sons.

JAMES ROBERTSON JUSTICE, 70, Scottish-born stage and screen actor, was found dead in bed in his home in King's Somborne, Eng. He had never fully recovered from a stroke suffered three years previously. In the 1950's he made several films in Hollywood. Among his screen credits are "Against the Wind," "Christopher Columbus," "Tight Little Island," "Black Rose," "David and Bathsheba," "Capt. Horatio Hornblower," "The Lady Says No," "Story of Robin Hood," "Les Miserables," "Murder Will Out," "The Sword and the Rose," "Doctor in the House," "Land of the Pharaohs," "Doctor at Sea," "Moby Dick," "Iron Petticoat," "The Living Idol," "Upstairs and Downstairs," "Operation X," "Guns of Navarone," "Doctor in Love," "Doctor in Distress," "Dr. Crippen," "Chitty Chitty Bang Bang." He was divorced from his wife in 1968.

ANNETTE KELLERMANN, 87, Australian-born actress and world-famous swimmer, died Nov. 5, 1975 in Southport, Aust. After winning several aquatic contests, and appearing in vaudeville as "Australia's Million Dollar Mermaid," she made several films, including "A Daughter of the Gods," "The Honor System," "Queen of the Sea," and "The Art of Diving." She retired from performing in the 1930's. The story of her life, called "Million Dollar Mermaid," was filmed in 1951 with Esther Williams playing Miss Kellerman. She was arrested in Boston in 1907 for wearing her famous one-piece bathing suit. She was married to her manager, James R. Sullivan. Her sister survives.

HARRY LACHMAN, 88, film director and painter, died Mar. 19, 1975 of a heart attack in his Beverly Hills home. He abandoned his post-impressionistic painting at 39 to begin his successful 30-year career as a film director. His credits include "Compulsory Husband," "The Outsider," "Face in the Sky," "Baby, Take a Bow," "Dante's Inferno," "Charlie Chan at the Circus," "One Night of Love," "Paddy the Next Best Thing," "Dead Men Tell," and "The Loves of Edgar Allan Poe." His widow survives.

| Cullen Landis (1922) | Francine Larrimore (1930) | Al Lettieri (1972) | Tilly Losch (1936) | William Lundigan (1951) |

CULLEN LANDIS, 79, one of the first stars of the silent screen, died Aug. 26, 1975 in Bloomfield Hills, MI. He starred in the first all-talking picture "Lights of New York." Other films of his over 100, include "The Girl from Outside," "It's a Great Life," "Bunty Pulls the String," "Remembrance," "The Famous Mrs. Fair," "Soul of the Beast," "Pampered Youth," "Sweet Rosie O'Grady," and "We're All Gamblers." In 1930 he moved to Detroit as a director-producer of industrial films. He had been in retirement for several years.

FRANCINE LARRIMORE, 77, noted French-born stage and screen actress, died Mar. 7, 1975 of pneumonia in her NYC home. She was brought to the U.S. as a child by her parents, members of the distinguished Adler acting family, and made her debut as a child actress. Among her film credits are "Devil's Darling," "The Princess from the Poorhouse," "Max Wants a Divorce," and "John Meade's Woman." She was divorced from her first husband, songwriter Con Conrad, and her second husband, Alfred T. Mannon, died in 1972.

ROWLAND LEE, 84, director, died Dec. 21, 1975 of a heart attack in his home in Palm Desert, Ca. His film credits include "Barbed Wire," "Three Sinners," "Wolf of Wall Street," "The Mysterious Dr. Fu Manchu," "Doomsday," "Count of Monte Cristo," "The Three Musketeers," "Bridge of San Luis Rey," and "The Big Fisherman" which was nominated for an Academy Award. He directed and produced over 60 films, and collaborated on several screenplays. His widow survives.

RUTH LEE, 79, film actress, died Aug. 3, 1975 in Woodland Hills, Ca., after a long illness. Among her many films are "Sensations of 1945" and "Whirlpool."

AL LETTIERI, 47, stage and screen actor, died Oct. 18, 1975 in NYC. He had appeared in several films, including "The Bobo," "The Godfather," "The Getaway," "Mr. Majestyk," "The Don Is Dead," "McQ," "Deadly Trackers," and "Bordella." Surviving are his widow, and a son.

MARIE LOHR, 84, Australian-born stage and film actress, died Jan. 21, 1975 in London. Her list of credits includes such pictures as "My Heart Is Calling," "Pygmalion," "Mozart," "Major Barbara," "Notorious Gentleman," "Anna Karenina," "The Winslow Boy," "Escapade," and "Man in a Cocked Hat." A daughter survives.

TILLY LOSCH, Austrian-born exotic dancer and actress in her 70's, died Dec. 24, 1975 of cancer in a NYC hospital. Her film credits include "The Garden of Allah," "The Good Earth," and "Duel in the Sun." She had no immediate survivors.

WILLIAM LUNDIGAN, 61, screen actor for 38 years, died Dec. 21, 1975 in Duarte, Ca., after a long illness. His career began as a radio announcer in Syracuse, NY., and his impressive voice got him a screen test and Hollywood contract. He appeared in over 125 films, including "Armored Car," "Three Smart Girls Grow Up," "Dodge City," "The Old Maid," "Fighting 69th," "Three Cheers for the Irish," "The Sea Hawk," "Courtship of Andy Hardy," "Dishonored Lady," "The Fabulous Dorseys," "Pinky," "I'll Get By," "House on Telegraph Hill," "Inferno," "I'd Climb the Highest Mountain," and "Riders to the Stars." He was host for the tv series "Climax" and "Shower of Stars." Surviving are his widow and a daughter.

JACKIE "MOMS" MABLEY, 78, comedienne of screen, stage, radio, vaudeville, and tv, died May 23, 1975 in White Plains, NY. She was born Loretta Mary Aiken in Brevard, N.C. Her screen credits include "Boarding House Blues," "Emperor Jones," and her last in which she starred, "Amazing Grace." Surviving are three daughters.

NOEL MADISON, 77, actor, producer and director, died Jan. 6, 1975 in Ft. Lauderdale, FL. In the 30's and 40's he appeared in many Hollywood and British films, including "Doorway to Hell," "Hatchet Man," "Man about Town," "The Last Mile," "Me and My Gal," "House of Rothschild," "G Men," "Manhattan Melodrama," "Missing Girls," "Man with 100 Faces," "Great Plane Robbery," "Footsteps in the Dark," Bombs over Burma," and "Jitterbugs." His widow and a son survive.

MARJORIE MAIN, 85, Indiana-born stage and film character actress, died of cancer Apr. 10, 1975 in Los Angeles. After a successful Broadway career, she went to Hollywood where she appeared in over 100 films which include "Music in the Air," "Stella Dallas," "Dead End," "Test Pilot," "They Shall Have Music," "The Women," "Another Thin Man," "Susan and God," "Trial of Mary Dugan," "A Woman's Face," "Shepherd of the Hills," "We Were Dancing," "Heaven Can Wait," "Johnny Come Lately," "Meet Me in St. Louis," "The Harvey Girls," "Undercurrent," "The Show-Off," "Summer Stock," "The Belle of New York," and "Friendly Persuasion." For her performance in "The Egg and I" in 1947, she was nominated for an Academy Award, and the film became the first of a successful series in which she and Percy Kilbride played Ma and Pa Kettle. Her last film was "The Kettles on Old MacDonald's Farm" in 1957. She was the widow of Dr. Stanley Krebs, a Chatauqua lecturer.

FREDRIC MARCH, 77, popular and versatile stage and screen actor for 50 years, died of cancer Apr. 14, 1975 in Los Angeles. He was born Frederick McIntyre Bickel in Racine, Wisc. After preparing for a banking career, he switched to acting and became a Broadway matinee idol. His movie career began in 1929 with "The Dummy," and ended with his 69th film in 1973, "The Iceman Cometh." He received "Oscars" for "Dr. Jekyll and Mr. Hyde" in 1932, and for "The Best Years of Our Lives" in 1946. His other film credits include "Jealousy," "Paris Bound," "Sarah and Son," "True to the Navy," "Manslaughter," "Royal Family of Broadway," "Smilin' Through," "Sign of the Cross," "Tonight Is Ours," "Design for Living," "Death Takes a Holiday," "Barretts of Wimpole Street," "Les Miserables," "Anna Karenina," "Mary of Scotland," "Anthony Adverse," "A Star Is Born," "Nothing Sacred," "Susan and God," "So Ends Our Night," "Tomorrow the World," "Another Part of the Forest," "Death of a Salesman," "Man on a Tightrope," "Executive Suite," "Bridges at Toko-Ri," "The Desperate Hours," "Alexander the Great," "Inherit the Wind," "Seven Days in May," and "Hombre." He leaves his widow, actress Florence Eldridge, and two adopted children, a son and a daughter.

CHARLES "RED" MARSHALL, 76, film actor, and former burlesque and vaudeville comedian, died of pneumonia Apr. 15, 1975 in Jersey City, NJ. His movie appearances include "A Wave, a Wac and a Marine," and "Spectre of the Rose." No survivors reported.

GEORGE E. MARSHALL, 84, director of more than 400 films, died of pneumonia Feb. 17, 1975 in Los Angeles. In 1912 he became involved in the birth of the film industry, and spent most of his working 62 years for Samuel Goldwyn productions. He began as an extra and stunt man, subsequently appearing occasionally as an actor, most recently in "Crazy World of Julius Vrooder." Among his directorial credits are "Ever Since Eve," "Life Begins at 40," "In Old Kentucky," "A Message to Garcia," "Goldwyn Follies," "Destry Rides Again," "Star Spangled Rhythm," "Riding High," "Monsieur Beaucaire," "The Perils of Pauline" (1947), "My Friend Irma," "Fancy Pants," "Houdini," "Scared Stiff," "Sad Sack," "Mating Game," "The Gazebo," "How the West Was Won," and "The Wicked Dreams of Paula Schultz." Three days before his death he was inducted into the Academy of Motion Picture Arts and Sciences Hall of Fame. No reported survivors.

MUIR MATHIESON, 64, Scotish-born British film conductor, died Aug. 2, 1975 in Oxford, Eng. He had arranged and conducted music for more than 600 films, including "Brief Encounter," "Hamlet," and "Oliver Twist." No survivors reported.

Marjorie Main
(1945)

Fredric March
(1955)

John McGiver
(1966)

Doro Merande
(1968)

Ozzie Nelson
(1955)

MOYNA McGILL, 80, Irish-born stage and screen actress, died Nov. 25, 1975 in Santa Monica, Ca. She was a successful actress on the London stage before moving to Hollywood where her film credits include "Gaslight," "Frenchman's Creek," "Picture of Dorian Gray," "Uncle Harry," "Black Beauty," "Green Dolphin Street," "Three Daring Daughters," and "Kind Lady." She was the widow of Edgar Lansbury, a British timber man and politician. Surviving are her actress daughter, Angela Lansbury, two sons, producers Edgar and Bruce Lansbury, and a daughter by her first marriage to actor-director-writer Reginald Denham.

JOHN McGIVER, 62, character actor on stage, tv, and films, died of a heart attack Sept. 9, 1975 in West Fulton, NY. In 1955 he gave up a teaching job in a NYC public school, and devoted his time to acting. His film assignments include "Love in the Afternoon," "Man in the Raincoat," "The Gazebo," "Love in a Goldfish Bowl," "Breakfast at Tiffany's," "Bachelor in Paradise," "Mr. Hobbs Takes a Vacation," "Manchurian Candidate," "Who's Got the Action?," "My Six Lovers," "Take Her, She's Mine," "Made in Paris," "Glass Bottom Boat," "Period of Adjustment," "Fitzwilly," "The Apple Dumpling Gang." He leaves his widow, scenic designer Ruth Schmigelsky, and ten children.

DORO MERANDE, tv, stage and screen character actress who was in her 70's, died Nov. 1, 1975 in Miami, FL., where she was performing in a Jackie Gleason "Honeymooners" special for tv. Among her film credits are "The Silver Whistle," "Our Town," "Mr. Belvedere Rings the Bell," "The Whistle at Eaton Falls," "Seven Year Itch," "Man with the Golden Arm," "The Gazebo," "The Cardinal," "Kiss Me, Stupid," "Skidoo," and "Hurry Sundown." No reported survivors.

TORBEN MEYER, 90, Danish-born character actor, died of bronchial pneumonia May 22, 1975 in Hollywood Among the many films in which he was featured are "The Way of All Flesh," "The Viking," "Roberta," "The King and the Chorus Girl," "Prisoner of Zenda," "Four Sons," "Christmas in July," "Sunny," "Berlin Correspondent," "Edge of Darkness," "Miracle of Morgan's Creek," "Purple Heart," "Tovarich," "Mad Wednesday," and "The Matchmaker." He had been in retirement for several years.

BARBOURA MORRIS, 43, film and stage actress, died Oct. 23, 1975 in Santa Monica, Ca., of a stroke and complications from cancer. Her film credits include "Teenage Doll," "Rock All Night," "Sorority Girl," "The Wild and the Innocent," "Wasp Woman," "Machine Gun Kelly," "A Bucket of Blood," "Atlas," "Haunted Palace," and "The Dunwich Horror." She also used the name of Barboura O'Neal. Surviving are her husband and a son.

CLIVE MORTON, 71, British stage and screen character actor, died Sept. 24, 1975 in London. He had appeared in over 60 films, including "Dead Men Tell No Tales," "A Run for Your Money," "Kind Hearts and Coronets," "While the Sun Shines," "Lavendar Hill Mob," "Night without Stars," "Court Martial," "Richard III," "Lucky Jim," and "The Alphabet Murders." He leaves his widow, actress Fanny Rowe, and a daughter by a previous marriage.

JOHN MYLONG, 82, Austrian-born character actor, died Sept. 8, 1975 after a long illness in his Beverly Hills, Ca. home. He was a veteran of many films in Austria and Germany before going to Hollywood in 1939. He was also known as Jack Mylong-Muenz. Among his more than 100 film credits are "Overture to Glory," "Crossroads," "For Whom the Bell Tolls," "Strange Death of Adolf Hitler," "Hostages," "The Falcon in San Francisco," "Crooked Web," and "The Eddy Duchin Story." His widow survives.

OZZIE NELSON, 68, bandleader who became producer, director and co-star of "The Adventures of Ozzie and Harriet" on radio and television, died of cancer June 3, 1975 in his home in San Fernando Valley, Ca. His film credits include "People Are Funny" and "The Impossible Years." Although he had a popular band, he and his wife, singer Harriet Hilliard, attained their greatest popularity with their tv series that ran for 14 years. They were joined in the series by their two sons, David and Rick, who survive.

GERTRUDE NIESEN, 62, Broadway and Hollywood singer-actress, and nightclub vocalist, died Mar. 27, 1975 in Glendale, Ca., after a long illness. She had trained for an operatic career but found herself becoming a popular musical comedy star. Her films include "Top of the Town," "Start Cheering," "Rookies on Parade," "He's My Guy," "This Is the Army," and "The Babe Ruth Story." She leaves her husband, Albert Greenfield, a former nightclub owner.

GERTRUDE OLMSTED, 70, silent film star, died Jan. 18, 1975 in her home in Beverly Hills, Ca. After winning a Chicago beauty contest, she signed a contract to go to Hollywood in 1920. She first appeared as Hoot Gibson's leading lady in 5 westerns, subsequently in such films as "Ben-Hur" (the original), "Cameo Kirby," "Babbitt," "Cobra," "Puppets," "The Cheerful Fraud," "Mr. Wu," "The Callahans and the Murphys," "Sporting Goods," "Bringing Up Father," "The Lone Wolf's Daughter," "Sonny Boy," "The Time, the Place and the Girl," and "Show of Shows." She retired in 1927. She was the widow of director Robert Leonard who died in 1968.

LYUBOV ORLOVA, 72, popular comedienne in Soviet films, died Jan. 26, 1975 after a long illness in Moscow. Among her films shown in the U.S. are "Petersburg Nights," "Moscow Laughs," "Volga-Volga," "Tanya," "Spring," "Mussorgsky," and "Man of Music." No reported survivors.

LARRY PARKS, 60, stage and screen actor, died Apr. 13, 1975 of a heart attack in his home in Studio City, Ca. After several parts with the Group Theatre, he went to Hollywood in 1941, subsequently appearing in over 30 films. His career was virtually destroyed in 1951 when he was the first actor to admit that he had belonged to a Communist cell from 1941 to 1945. He found occasional work but in recent years had been a real estate agent. His credits include "Mystery Ship," "Harmon of Michigan," "Canal Zone," "Flight Lieutenant," "You Were Never Lovelier," "Counter-Attack," "Down to Earth," "The Swordsman," "Love Is Better than Ever," "Freud," and his best known "The Jolson Story" and "Jolson Sings Again." Surviving are his widow, actress Betty Garrett, and two sons.

PIER PAOLO PASOLINI, 53, Italian film director, poet, and novelist, died near Rome on Nov. 2, 1975 after his thorax was crushed by the wheels of his own car that was being stolen by a teenage delinquent. His films include "The Gospel According to St. Matthew," "The Hawks and the Sparrows," "Accatone," "The Canterbury Tales," "The Decameron," "Oedipus Rex," "Medea," "A Thousand and One Nights," and he had just completed "The 120 Days of Sodoma." His mother survives.

DOROTHY PATTEN, 70, stage, screen, and tv actress, died Apr. 11, 1975 at her home in Westhampton, NY. Her most important film role was in "Botany Bay." No reported survivors.

MARY PHILIPS, 74, former stage and film actress, died Apr. 22, 1975 in Santa Monica, Ca., after a long illness. Among her film credits are "Life Begins," "Farewell to Arms," "Wings over Honolulu," "That Certain Woman," "The Bride Wore Red," "Lady in the Dark," "Incendiary Blond," "Kiss and Tell," "Leave Her to Heaven," "Dear Ruth," "Dear Wife," "I Can Get It for You Wholesale," and "Prince Valiant." Her first marriage to the late Humphrey Bogart ended in divorce. She was the widow of actor and story editor, Kenneth MacKenna, who died in 1964.

| Gertrude Niesen (1941) | Gertrude Olmsted (1926) | Larry Parks (1950) | Mary Phillips (1937) |

ARTHUR PIERSON, 73, Norwegian-born actor-writer-director, died Jan. 1, 1975 in Santa Monica, Ca. His long career included Broadway, films, and tv. He had appeared in such films as "Tomorrow and Tomorrow," "The Strange Case of Clara Deane," "Bachelor's Affairs," "Hat Check Girl," "Air Hostess," "The Way to Love," "You Belong to Me," and "Murder in the Clouds." His widow and a son survive.

FRANK PUGLIA, 83, Sicilian-born actor, died Oct. 25, 1975 in South Pasadena, Ca. His career spanned 65 years, and his film credits include "Orphans of the Storm," "Romola," "Viva Villa," "Men in White," "The Devil Is a Sissy," "The Bride Wore Red," "Bulldog Drummond's Revenge," "Dramatic School," "Maisie," "Mark of Zorro," "Jungle Book," "Flight Lieutenant," "Now, Voyager," "Casablanca," "Mission to Moscow," "For Whom the Bell Tolls," "Phantom of the Opera," "Brazil," "A Song to Remember," "Blood on the Sun," "My Favorite Brunette," "Brute Force," "Escape Me Never," "Road to Rio," "Dream Girl," "Casanova's Big Night," "Serenade," "Black Orchid," "Cry Tough," and "Mr. Ricco." A brother survives.

JACK RAY, 58, who appeared as Freckles in "Our Gang" comedies, died Nov. 1, 1975 in Montclair, Ca. He later appeared in vaudeville. No reported survivors.

THOMAS REICHMAN, 30, cameraman and documentary film maker, was found dead, an apparent suicide, in his NYC apartment Jan. 26, 1975. In 1972 he was a co-recipient of an Academy Award for the film "Marjoe." His other credits include "Mingus," "World of Sports Illustrated," "Our Latin Thing," and "Khrushchev Remembers." His parents survive.

ROY ROBERTS, 69, stage, film and tv character actor, died May 28, 1975 in Los Angeles. In his 40 year career, he had appeared in over 900 films, including "Guadalcanal Diary," "A Bell for Adano," "The Sullivans," "My Darling Clementine," "The Shocking Miss Pilgrim," "Foxes of Harrow," "Gentleman's Agreement," "Daisy Kenyon," "Captain from Castile," "Force of Evil," "Chicken Every Sunday," "He Walked by Night," "Chain Lightning," "Santa Fe," "The Tanks Are Coming," "House of Wax," "The Chapman Report," "Hotel," "The Outfit," and "Chinatown." Surviving is his widow.

SHIRLEY ROSS, 62, singer-actress, died Mar. 9, 1975 in Menlo Park, Ca., after a long illness. She sang with the Gus Arnheim band and on radio. Her film credits include "Age of Indiscretion," "Devil's Squadron," "San Francisco," "Big Broadcast of 1937," "Blossoms on Broadway," "Waikiki Wedding," "Thanks for the Memory," "Paris Honeymoon," "Cafe Society," "Some Like It Hot," and "Unexpected Father." Two sons and a daughter survive.

SHEILA RYAN, 54, actress, died of a lung ailment Nov. 4, 1975 in Los Angeles, Ca. She had appeared in over 60 films, including "Gay Caballero," "Dead Men Tell," "Dressed to Kill," "Great Guns," "A-Haunting We Will Go," "The Gang's All Here," "Something for the Boys," "Caribbean Mystery," "Getting Gertie's Garter," "Deadline for Murder," "The Big Fix," and "Ringside." She is survived by her husband, actor Pat Buttram, and a daughter.

HARRY SEGALL, 78, Academy-Award winning screenwriter, died Nov. 25, 1975 in Woodland Hills, Ca. Prior to entering films he was a newspaperman and playwright. His screenplays include "Don't Turn 'Em Loose," "Outcasts of Poker Flats," "She's Got Everything," "Blind Alibi," "The Bride Wore Boots," "Angel on My Shoulder," "Monkey Business," "Two Yanks in Trinidad," "The Powers Girl," and his Oscar-winning "Here Comes Mr. Jordan." Surviving are his widow and a son.

ROD SERLING, 50, writer and producer for films and television, died June 28, 1975 in Rochester, NY, after suffering complications during open-heart surgery. His screen credits include "The Rack," "Incident in an Alley," "Requiem for a Heavyweight," "Saddle in the Wind," "Seven Days in May," "Assault on a Queen," and "Planet of the Apes." He won 5 Emmy awards for his tv scripts, and was host for the long-running series "The Twilight Zone" and "Night Gallery." His widow and two children survive.

MICHEL SIMON, 80, Swiss-born French film and stage actor, died May 30, 1975 in a hospital near Paris. He had appeared in 145 movies and 40 plays. Among his screen credits are "The Passion of Joan of Arc," "Boudu Saved from Drowning," "L'Atalante," "Port of Shadows," "Beauty and the Devil," "Panic," "Fabiola," "Anatomy of Love," "Candide," "The Train," "The Marriage Came Tumbling Down," and his best known "The Two of Us." Surviving is his actor son, Francois Simon.

JOHN SLATER, 58, British stage and screen actor, died Jan. 9, 1975 in London of a heart attack. His movie credits include "48 Hours," "Murder in Reverse," "Passport to Pimlico," "Prelude to Fame," "Man with a Million," "Star of India," and "Three on a Spree." He was probably best known for his role in the popular tv series "Z Cars." His widow survives.

NICHOLAS SOUSSANIN, Russian-born character actor, died Apr. 27, 1975 in a NYC hospital. He came to the U.S. in 1923 and subsequently appeared in such films as "The Swan," "The Midnight Sun," "Hotel Imperial," "The Spotlight," "A Gentleman of Paris," "The Last Command," "Night Watch," "The Squall," "Criminal Code," "White Shoulders," "Daughter of the Dragon," "The Yellow Lily," and "Under Two Flags." He leaves two sons and two daughters.

CHARLES SPAAK, 71, Belgian-born screenwriter, died Mar. 4, 1975 after an arterial operation in Nice, France. Among his best known scripts are "Carnival in Flanders," "Grand Illusion," "The Idiot," "The Eternal Husband," "Crime and Punishment" (1958), "Justice Is Done," and "The Adulteress." Surviving are his widow and two daughters.

GEORGE STEVENS, 70, producer-director, died Mar. 8, 1975 of a heart attack in Lancaster, Ca. He began his career at 5, acting with his parents. At 17 he arrived in Hollywood and began working behind the camera on two-reel comedies, many starring Laurel and Hardy. Subsequently he directed "The Cohens and Kellys in Trouble," "Kentucky Kernels," "Laddie," "Alice Adams," "Annie Oakley," "Quality Street," "A Damsel in Distress," "Gunga Din," "Penny Serenade," "Woman of the Year," "Talk of the Town," "The More the Merrier," "I Remember Mama," "Shane," "Diary of Anne Frank," "The Greatest Story Ever Told," and his last, "The Only Game in Town." He received Academy Awards for "A Place in the Sun," and "Giant." He leaves his widow, and a son.

ROBERT STOLZ, 95, Austrian-born conductor and Academy-Award winning composer, died June 27, 1975 in West Berlin, Ger. He began his professional career at 7, and subsequently wrote over 2000 songs, 50 operettas, and scores for over 100 films. His "Oscars" were for the song "Two Hearts in Three-Quarter Time" from "Spring Parade," and for the score of "It Happened Tomorrow." He is survived by his fifth wife.

ROBERT STRAUSS, 61, film, stage and tv character actor, died in NYC Feb. 20, 1975 of complications resulting from a stroke. He scored a hit in Broadway's "Stalag 17" and repeated the role in the film for which he received an Academy Award nomination. Other screen credits include "Native Land," "Sailor Beware," "Here Come the Girls," "Atomic Kid," "The Bridges at Toko-Ri," "The Seven Year Itch," "Man with the Golden Arm," "Li'l Abner," "Wheeler Dealers," "Frankie and Johnny," and "Fort Utah." He leaves his widow, and three children by his first wife.

**Shirley Ross
(1941)**

**Michel Simon
(1967)**

**Arthur Treacher
(1949)**

**Mary Ure
(1968)**

FRANK SULLY, 67, character actor who appeared in over 1200 films, died Dec. 17, 1975 in Woodland Hills, Ca. After vaudeville and Broadway, he went to Hollywood in 1935 and subsequently appeared in such movies as "Mary Burns, Fugitive," "Some Like It Hot," "Grapes of Wrath," "The Doctor Takes a Wife," "A Girl, A Guy and a Gob," "Private Nurse," "The Boogie Man Will Get You," "My Sister Eileen," "Two Senoritas from Chicago," "Thousands Cheer," "Along Came Jones," "Renegades," "The Last Hurrah," and "Funny Girl." A daughter survives.

WALTER TETLEY, 60, stage, radio, film and tv actor, died Sept. 4, 1975 in Calif. NY-born, he began his career on stage at 6. He was probably best known to radio audiences as the nephew of "The Great Gildersleeve." His screen credits include "Lord Jeff," "Boy Slaves," "They Shall Have Music," "Military Academy," "Thunder Birds," "Who Done It," "Gorilla Man," "Tower of London," "Molly and Me," and "The Lodger." No reported survivors.

WILLIAM J. THIELE, 85, Vienna-born film director, died Sept. 7, 1975 in Woodland Hills, Ca. He directed in Germany and France before going to Hollywood. His credits include "His Late Excellency," "Hurrah I'm Alive," "Le Bal," "Waltz Time," "Jungle Princess," "Beg, Borrow or Steal," "Bridal Suite," and "Tarzan's Desert Mystery." Surviving are his widow, two sons, and a daughter.

ARTHUR TREACHER, 81, English-born character actor of stage, film and tv, died Dec. 14, 1975 in Manhasset, NY, from a heart ailment. He was the "perfect butler" in scores of movies after he came to the U.S. in 1926. For several years he was a regular on the Merv Griffin tv show. His more than 60 film credits include "Gambling Lady," "Madame Du Barry," "Forsaking All Others," "No More Ladies," "A Midsummer Night's Dream," "Magnificent Obsession," "Anything Goes," "Thank You, Jeeves," "You Can't Have Everything," "Heidi," "My Lucky Star," "Little Princess," "Irene," "Star Spangled Rhythm," "The Amazing Mrs. Holiday," "National Velvet," "That Midnight Kiss," "Love That Brute," "Mary Poppins." More recently he had been involved with Call Arthur Treacher Service System, and Arthur Treacher's Fish and Chips fast-food chain. His widow survives.

MARY URE, 42, prominent British actress of stage and screen, died in London Apr. 3, 1975 a few hours after opening in a new play. Cause of death was an accidental mixture of alcohol and barbiturates. Born in Scotland, she made her London stage debut in 1954 and success came rapidly. Her film credits include "Storm over the Nile," "Windom's Way," "Look Back in Anger," "Sons and Lovers," "The Mind Benders," "The Luck of Ginger Coffey," "Custer of the West," and "Where Eagles Dare." She was divorced from her first husband, playwright John Osborne. Surviving are her second husband, actor Robert Shaw, and nine children.

LILLIAN WALKER, 88, popular star of silent films, died Oct. 10, 1975 in Trinidad. As Dimples Walker, she appeared in early Vitagraph comedies, such as "Love, Luck and Gasoline." She later was in more serious roles, in such films as "The Blue Envelope Mystery," "Troublesome Stepdaughters," "Kitty MacKay," "The New Secretary," "The Grain of Dust," and "The Embarrassment of Riches." She was the widow of Dr. Eugene W. Senior.

BILL WALSH, 61, writer and producer for Disney studios, died Jan. 27, 1975 in Los Angeles of a heart attack. He had produced 18 Disney films, including "Bedknobs and Broomsticks," "The Love Bug," "That Darned Cat," "The Absent-Minded Professor," "Son of Flubber," and "Mary Poppins." No reported survivors.

ANTHONY WARDE, 66, former screen actor, died Jan. 8, 1975 in Hollywood where he had a men's clothing store. His film credits include "Buck Rogers," "Law of the Underworld," "Affairs of Annabel," "Mr. Moto Takes a Vacation," "Chip of the Flying U," "So You Won't Talk," "Where Are Your Children?," "Allotment Wives," "Are These Our Parents?," "Black Market Babies," "High Tide," and "Atomic City." Surviving are his widow and a son.

RICHARD WATTIS, 62, British character actor, died Feb. 1, 1975 in London of a heart attack while dining at a restaurant. He first appeared in pictures in 1937, and subsequently made over 100 films including "Happiest Days of Your Life," "Importance of Being Earnest," "Hobson's Choice," "Man Who Knew Too Much," "Prince and the Showgirl," "Blue Murder at St. Trinian's," "The Captain's Table," "Come Fly with Me," "The V.I.P.'s," and "Operation Crossbow." No survivors reported.

LELAND T. WEED, 74, a singing cowboy, died of a stroke Aug. 29, 1975 in Prescott, Az. He had appeared in 22 movies with Hoot Gibson and Hopalong Cassidy. When he retired he became a policeman in Flagstaff, Az. No reported survivors.

LAWRENCE WEINGARTEN, 77, producer, died Feb. 6, 1975 in Hollywood of leukemia. Early in his career he produced Buster Keaton comedies and Marie Dressler-Polly Moran movies. From 1927 he was with MGM and produced 75 of their pictures, including "A Day at the Races," "The Last of Mrs. Cheyney," "Too Hot to Handle," "Without Love," "Adam's Rib," "Pat and Mike," "The Actress," "Tender Trap," "I'll Cry Tomorrow," "Cat on a Hot Tin Roof," "Gazebo," "Period of Adjustment," "Signpost to Murder," "The Unsinkable Molly Brown," and his last "The Impossible Years" in 1968. His widow survives.

WILLIAM A. WELLMAN, 79, a pioneer director, died of leukemia Dec. 9, 1975 in his Los Angeles home. After a brief acting career, he began directing in 1923. His impressive list of credits, for 82 films, includes "Young Eagles," "Woman Trap," "Public Enemy," "Hatchet Man," "So Big," "Call of the Wild," "A Star Is Born," "Nothing Sacred," "Beau Geste," "The Light That Failed," "Roxie Hart," "The Ox-Bow Incident," "Lady of Burlesque," "Story of G. I. Joe," "The High and Mighty," "Gallant Journey," "Lafayette Escadrille," "Battleground," and "Wings," the first film to win an Academy Award. He was married five times and had seven children.

HOWARD WENDELL, 67, stage, film and tv character actor, died Aug. 11, 1975 at his home in Oregon City, OR. He went to Hollywood in 1950 and subsequently appeared in such films as "Affair in Trinidad," "You for Me," "By the Light of the Silvery Moon," "The Big Heat," "The Black Dakotas," "Athena," "Stranger in My Arms," "Capt. Scarface," "The View from Pompey's Head," and "Day of Fury." Surviving are his widow, three sons, and a daughter.

BILLY WEST, 82, silent film comedian, died of a heart attack July 21, 1975 in Hollywood. He wrote, directed, and starred in his own series, Billy West Comedies. His widow, and son survive.

LEIGH WHIPPER, 98, the first black member of Actors Equity Assoc., died July 26, 1975 in NYC. He was also a founder of the Negro Actors Guild. He appeared in 21 Broadway plays, and his film credits include "Of Mice and Men," "Virginia," "Bahama Passage," "The Vanishing Virginian," "White Cargo," "Mission to Moscow," "The Ox-Bow Incident," "Undercurrent," "Untamed Fury," "Lost Boundaries," "The Shrike," "The Young Don't Cry," "The Harder They Fall," "Marjorie Morningstar." Surviving are a son and a daughter.

BOB WILLS, 70, singer-actor, and originator of Western swing country music, died of bronchial pneumonia May 13, 1975 in Ft. Worth, Tx. He starred in 26 movies, including "Go West, Young Lady." In 1968 he was named to the Country Music Hall of Fame. Surviving are his widow, 3 daughters, and a son.

INDEX

239

243